CLOTHED IN ROBES OF SOVEREIGNTY

CLOTHED IN ROBES OF SOVEREIGNTY

The Continental Congress and the People Out of Doors

BENJAMIN H. IRVIN

OXFORD
UNIVERSITY PRESS

Oxford University Press, Inc., publishes works that further
Oxford University's objective of excellence
in research, scholarship, and education.

Oxford   New York

Auckland   Cape Town   Dar es Salaam   Hong Kong   Karachi
Kuala Lumpur   Madrid   Melbourne   Mexico City   Nairobi
New Delhi   Shanghai   Taipei   Toronto

With offices in

Argentina   Austria   Brazil   Chile   Czech Republic   France   Greece
Guatemala   Hungary   Italy   Japan   Poland   Portugal   Singapore
South Korea   Switzerland   Thailand   Turkey   Ukraine   Vietnam

Copyright © 2011 by Oxford University Press, Inc.

Published by Oxford University Press, Inc.
198 Madison Avenue, New York, NY 10016

www.oup.com

Oxford is a registered trademark of Oxford University Press

Library of Congress Cataloging-in-Publication Data
Irvin, Benjamin H.
Clothed in robes of sovereignty: the Continental Congress
and the people out of doors / Benjamin H. Irvin.
p.   cm.
Includes index.
ISBN 978-0-19-973199-2
1. United States. Continental Congress.
2. United States—History—Revolution, 1775-1783—Social aspects.
3. Political culture—United States—History—18th century.
4. Sovereignty—Social aspects—United States—History—18th century.
5. National characteristics, American.
6. United States—Politics and government—1775-1783. I. Title.
E303.I79   2011
973.3—dc22
2010025255

1 3 5 7 9 8 6 4 2

Printed in the United States of America
on acid-free paper

For Alison,
and in memory of Lynda and Lelia

Contents

ACKNOWLEDGMENTS   ix

Introduction: To "Stamp the Character of the People"   *1*

Part I

A "STEADY, MANLY, UNIFORM, AND PERSEVERING OPPOSITION"

1 *The Republicans' New Clothes*   *23*
2 *The Continental Congress Unmanned*   *52*

Part II

THE OUTCOME IS IN DOUBT

3 *"[A]n Impression upon the Mind"*   *75*
4 *The Pride and Pomp of War*   *97*

Part III

E PLURIBUS UNUM

5 *"The spirits of the whigs must be kept up"*   *133*
6 *"[U]ncommon and Extraordinary Movements"*   *165*

Part IV

"THE SYMBOL OF SUPREME POWER & AUTHORITY"

7 *"[T]he most amiable Garbs of publick Virtue"*   *207*
8 *Naked and Unadorned*   *239*

Conclusion: "[T]he Sign of the Thirteen
Starrs"   *274*

ABBREVIATIONS   285

NOTES   287

INDEX   366

Acknowledgments

Looking back over the long life of this project, I see now that the colleagues and friends who aided me most were not those who shared their expertise or knowledge—though such persons helped me tremendously—but rather those who expressed confidence in my work and encouraged me to carry on. For their humbling generosity I offer immense and heartfelt gratitude.

At Brandeis University, my doctoral advisor Jane Kamensky challenged me to think creatively about the writing of history. More valuably still, she shared with me her own professional development so that I might learn from her excellent example. Like so many Austen fans, I often find myself asking, What would Jane do? David Hackett Fischer and Peter Onuf, who joined Jane on my dissertation committee, rigorously reviewed my work and held it to the highest standards of historical scholarship. Jacqueline Jones, Morton Keller, and James Kloppenberg offered wise counsel at a formative stage of research. My Brandeis classmates, the Crown Fellows, comprised a warm and supportive cohort. I thank Darra Mulderry, a considerate housemate and late-night conversationalist; Jenny Hale Pulsipher, whose "Massacre at Hurtleberry Hill" I read across the long drive to Boston and whose careful scholarship I have emulated ever since; and Matthew Rainbow Hale, whose concern for political culture and national identity has helped to sustain my own. While in Boston, I also learned much from thoughtful discussions with Karen N. Barzilay, who shared my interest in the social and cultural history of the Continental Congress.

My manuscript began to take its present form during a generous Mellon Postdoctoral Fellowship at the McNeil Center for Early American Studies.

Robert Blair St. George and Alison Olson brought me to the McNeil Center and received me with unfailing kindness. Dan Richter and Michael Zuckerman read the dissertation with alacrity, offering incisive criticism and challenging me to boldness. Cathy Matson honed my chapter on the continental currency before returning to that summer's tour of the Dave Matthews Band. T. H. Breen took a cold call from me, graciously agreed to read my book prospectus, and responded with keen insight on national identity in the Revolutionary period. John Murrin heartened me with his enthusiasm for my study and caused me to reflect on the debts historians owe to documentary editors, in my case especially Worthington C. Ford and Paul H. Smith. Carla Mulford urged me to pay greater attention to the history of Revolutionary New Jersey; toward that end she cordially presented me the poems of Annis Boudinot Stockton. Bruce Mann befriended me and offered cheerful advice at every opportunity. Amy Baxter-Bellamy provided diligent assistance and good humor. The McNeil Center fellows, as well as the many participants in our brown bags and Friday seminars, taught me a great deal about early American history and literature. That these individuals are too numerous to mention attests to the vitality of the McNeil Center, to the hard work of its directors, and to the beneficence of its donors. I particularly wish to thank the audience of my seminar at Independence Hall, a locale made possible by the gracious interposition of George Boudreau.

My research has benefited from the financial support of the American Antiquarian Society, the David Library of the American Revolution, the Robert H. Smith International Center for Jefferson Studies, the Library Company of Philadelphia, and the Historical Society of Pennsylvania. A number of archivists, associated faculty and staff members, and scholars ensured that my visits to those institutions were both productive and fun, including John Hench, Joanne Chaison, and Caroline Sloat; Richard Ryerson; Cheryl Collins, James Horn, Charlene Boyer Lewis, James Lewis, Christine Coalwell McDonald, Barbara Oberg, Peter Onuf, and Leonard Sadosky; James Green and Wendy Woloson; and many others. Karen Stevens offered much appreciated assistance in the library of Independence National Historical Park. Historical Database also provided digital copies of Paul H. Smith's *Letters of Delegates to Congress, 1774–1789*, before those volumes were readily available on the Library of Congress website.

Portions of this book appeared previously as "The Streets of Philadelphia: Crowds, Congress, and the Political Culture of Revolution, 1774–1783," *Pennsylvania Magazine of History and Biography* 129 (2005): 7–44; "Benjamin Franklin's '*Enriching Virtues*': Continental Currency and the Creation of a

Revolutionary Republic," *Common-place: The Interactive Journal of Early American Life* 6 (2006); and "Of 'Manly' and 'Monstrous' Eloquence," in *New Men*, ed. Thomas A. Foster (New York, 2010). For their insightful comments on those essays, I thank Tammy Gaskell, Bill Pencak, Judith Van Buskirk, Ed Gray, Anne Lombard, and Tom Foster. I also thank the organizers and participants of conferences where I have presented drafts, including the annual meetings of the Omohundro Institute of Early American History and Culture and the Society for Historians of the Early American Republic; the Colonial Society of Massachusetts Graduate Student Forum; the Deerfield / Wellesley Symposium on American Culture; the Maryland Early American Seminar; the McNeil Center's "Faces and Places in Early America: An Interdisciplinary Conference on Art and the World of Objects"; the University of Paris-Diderot's "From Colonies into Republics in an Atlantic World: North America and the Caribbean in a Revolutionary Age"; and Birkbeck College of the University of London's "What Is Masculinity?" At those gatherings I enjoyed vibrant exchanges with Robert Middlekauff, Sally Webster, Lester Olson, Sarah Knott, Cathy Kelly, Kenneth Miller, Martha Rojas, and numerous others.

At the University of Arizona, I have received substantial research support from the College of Social and Behavioral Sciences and from the Social and Behavioral Sciences Research Institute. My colleagues—especially Karen Anderson, Jack Marietta, Katherine Morrissey, and Roger Nichols—have championed my scholarship and cheered me along the way. Jack deserves my enduring gratitude for reading the unedited manuscript in its entirety. Martha Few invited me to share a chapter with the very capable students of her graduate seminar on gender history. Kari McBride and the Group for Early Modern Studies provided a collegial forum for me to present my work. Genoa Shepley performed exceptional research. Alison Futrell corrected my Latin; Luise Betterton looked over my French.

Here in the virtuous West, far from the decadent metropoles of Boston, Philadelphia, and Williamsburg, two uniquely lively and engaging organizations have fostered my study of early American history. The Front Range Early American Consortium is full of FREACs. I am grateful for the friendship and professional encouragement of Caroline Cox, Jim Drake, Ron Hatzenbuehler, Eric Hinderaker, Chris Hodson, Ann Little, Gloria Main, Jack Marietta, Matthew Mason, Mick Nicholls, Jenny Pulsipher, Brett Rushforth, T. J. Tomlin, Vikki Vickers, Neil York, and our ever expanding bunch. Many of those same individuals, as participants in the Rocky Mountain Seminar in Early American History, led me to the Red Iguana and introduced me to the Holy Molé. For that I am *so* grateful.

At Oxford, Susan Ferber demonstrated extraordinary commitment to my project, waited patiently as I waded through many a rising creek, and edited with a deft pencil. Rhys Isaac and an anonymous reader gave liberally of their time and acumen. Nancy Toff and Richard Bernstein have always been valued members of my Oxford community.

In closing, I wish to thank my family: my parents, siblings, inlaws, and especially my young nephews and nieces who both lift me up to heaven and bring me down to earth. I thank my colleagues and friends Martha Few and Kei Hirano, who taught me to lean back off the toe edge if I want to shred the pow pow. I thank Brian Luskey, a good friend, a great listener, and a historian on the make. Brian too read the unedited manuscript without protest. I thank J. Michael Morgan, who coached me through the long and consuming process of writing. I thank Ruby the Superdog, who bided many hours of tedium for a few paltry minutes of frisbee and who restored laughter and exercise to my life. Finally, I thank my partner, Alison, who has sacrificed a great deal—more than I know—to make this book possible. I dedicate it to her and to the memory of my aunt, Lynda, and of my grandmother, Bee, the former whom I admired for her eloquence, the latter for her spunk.

CLOTHED IN ROBES OF SOVEREIGNTY

Introduction: To "Stamp the Character of the People"

Shortly after adopting the Declaration of Independence on July 4, 1776, the Continental Congress appointed a committee "to bring in a device for a seal for the United States of America." As members of Congress understood, every political entity—be it a state or, in this instance, a union of states— needed a seal. Bearing ornate, difficult-to-forge devices, seals served the practical purpose of authenticating treaties, commissions, and other formal memoranda. As instruments of executive authority, seals further attested to the dignity and prerogative of sovereigns. The heads of European states possessed distinctive seals, and if the United States were to assume an equal station among the powers of the earth, Congress must possess one too. Writing on July 9, John Adams suggested that the Declaration would not be complete, would not even be suitable for signature, until Congress had affixed a seal: "As soon as an American Seal is prepared," Adams announced, "the Declaration will be Subscribed by all the Members."[1]

Yet, seals did not simply validate public documents or warrant princely will. Commonly bearing royal coats of arms, the likenesses of monarchs, or emblems of peoples, seals also gave potent, iconographic expression to nations. In a seal's waxy imprint materialized the official symbols of national identity. At the moment of independence, Congress perceived an opportunity to conjure for the former British colonists a vision of the infant United States, as Adams's anticipation of an *American* seal suggests.

For this essential project, Congress called on three of its most creative minds: John Adams, Benjamin Franklin, and Thomas Jefferson.[2] Each of these statesmen brought a pet design to the drafting table, a figure which to his particular way of thinking spoke an essential truth about America and its revolutionary cause. Adams drew on Greek and Roman mythology, proposing the laborious Hercules forced to choose between the "rugged Mountain" of Virtue and the "flowery paths" of Vice. Profoundly concerned with morality and civic devotion in the war-torn republic, Adams beheld in this classical allegory the alternatives Americans now faced. Franklin, by contrast, turned to the Old Testament, offering Moses and the Israelites emerging from the Red Sea while Pharaoh flailed in the waters behind. Likening political subjugation to slavery and justifying resistance as the colonists' spiritual duty, Franklin suggested the motto Rebellion to Tyrants Is Obedience to God. Jefferson, finally, borrowed from English history, volunteering the Saxon chiefs Hengist and Horsa, who held their lands in absolute dominion, and from whom, as Jefferson imagined, the "farmers" of America had descended. As heirs of Saxon liberty—or so Jefferson had argued in his *Summary View of the Rights of British America* (1774)—the colonists owed no feudal obligations to George III.

Each of these compositions offered a meaningful lesson for American patriots, yet each was deeply flawed. Adams's contribution was disagreeably unoriginal. Hercules—a darling of Renaissance painters and sculptors— lorded over palaces and plazas all over Europe. The particular illustration Adams now submitted, the Choice or Judgment of Hercules, had haunted the Whig imagination since 1714, when the moral philosopher Anthony Ashley Cooper, the third earl of Shaftsbury, made it the centerpiece of his widely read treatise on aesthetics.[3] Franklin's recommendation, meanwhile, was a hoax. The regicidal proverb, "Rebellion to Tyrants Is Obedience to God," derived not from the epitaph of John Bradshaw, condemnor of Charles I, as Franklin wanted Americans to believe, but rather from Franklin's own vibrant imagination. The genius of Silence Dogood and Poor Richard had baldly fabricated the motto, and published it in the *Pennsylvania Evening Post* months before, in order to provoke his conscientious neighbors to war.[4] Finally, Jefferson's submission was singularly obscure; worse, it predicated American rights dubiously on the allodial land tenures of folkloric Saxon warriors.[5]

More discouragingly, not one of these proposed designs captured the essence of the American people. In fairness, it was almost impossible that any of them could, for the fledgling United States possessed little in the way of a national character. Though bound no longer by the customs or traditions of the British nation, the former colonists had scarcely begun to conceptualize themselves as members of a new nation. Each of the thirteen individual states celebrated its own distinctive history. Their inhabitants, moreover, spoke a multitude of languages and claimed a diversity of racial, ethnic, and religious heritages. Only *just* declared into existence and still far from properly confederated, the United States could not be readily reduced to a single emblem or motto. Neither Hercules, nor Moses, nor Hengist and Horsa would suffice. And so, the Continental Congress continued to cast about, searching throughout the course of the Revolution for an apt symbol of American identity.

———————

Every modern nation-state boasts a unique material and ceremonial culture, an assortment of sacred objects and rituals that together give face to the nation. These include flags and insignia; pledges, anthems, and popular songs; military parades and machinery; monuments, statues, and public architecture; and calendars of official holidays. These phenomena are often created for the specific purpose of shaping or emblematizing the character of a nation. Even when built to serve prosaic, mechanical functions, an item's ornamental or symbolic content will contribute to that nation's distinctive iconography. Artifacts and ceremonies of state must thus be understood as media through which nations are imagined and expressed.[6] Careful analysis provides clues to the makers' conceptualizations of the people and governments they represent.

When a nation is created anew, as in the case of a coup or revolution, such texts offer particularly rich insight. A nascent administration will often dismantle the hallmarks and civic traditions of the old regime and either invent new ones or revive antiquated ones to take their place. These apparatuses perform or are intended to perform a variety of functions. They promote the ideologies or belief systems on which the revolution has been founded. They distinguish the sovereign regnant from the sovereign overthrown. They legitimate the ascendant government and foster obedience to its laws. They instill patriotism. In sum, they signal a break from the nation's past, a new era for a renewed people.

The French Revolution provides a wealth of examples. In 1792, the National Convention forsook the king's image and instead adopted the Goddess Liberty as an icon of the state. When the Jacobins rose to power, they discarded

Liberty in favor of the heroic masculine figure, Hercules. They organized national festivals dedicated to republican virtues such as Reason and Work. They even adopted a revolutionary calendar, renaming the days and months and dividing every hour into decimal minutes in an ambitious effort to recon-figure time.[7] Similar examples—some as fully programmatic and philoso-phized as the French, others less so—may be found in the Haitian Revolution, in Latin America's many revolutions, in the Russian Revolution, in the Chi-nese Revolution, indeed in every revolution in modern history. The American Revolution is no exception.[8] The Continental Congress labored, in far greater earnest than historians have appreciated, to create new and distinctive sym-bols, artifacts, and observances for the United States, and by those creations to inspire national allegiance in the American public.

The Continental Congress has most often been remembered for its written and spoken word, and with good reason. The delegates who gath-ered in Philadelphia to unify the colonial resistance movement ultimately predicated the United States' claims to independence on Enlightenment notions of the social contract. As conceived by a generation of American revolutionaries, the social contract depended on willful engagement by the people for the securement of their rights. Governments, the Declaration of Independence affirmed, derive their "just powers from the consent of the governed." That consent presumed volition; it necessitated a rational and deliberate weighing of evidence.[9] To obtain the consent of the American people, Congress regularly submitted its "facts" to "a candid world." Indeed, this was one of the most common ways by which Congress justified its revolutionary endeavors. In 1774, the Continental Congress circulated the Articles of Association, setting forth a scheme of economic resistance and urging patriots to participate. In 1775, Congress issued a Declaration on Taking Arms, decrying the British offensive at Lexington and Concord and warning the colonists to prepare for hostilities. In 1776, Congress published the Declaration of Independence, chronicling King George III's "long train of abuses and usurpations" and inviting all of humanity to judge whether the American colonists were not justified in casting off the yoke of British tyranny. Throughout its administration, Congress printed journals of its daily proceedings, reciting the delegates' credentials and establishing a record of their votes. So often did the Continental Congress submit its "facts," so frequently did it appeal to reason and free will, one might fairly conclude that this was the only means by which Congress ventured to sway its constituents. But such was not the case. To animate the American people, to rally them for war, to coax their faith in independence and their affection for a newborn republic, the Continental Congress fashioned an artful material and ceremonial culture for the Revolutionary United States.

This book examines the invented traditions by which Congress endeavored to fortify the resistance movement and to make meaning of American independence.[10] Patriotic and hortatory in nature, Congress's inventions consisted of a wide variety of things: behavioral codes, such as proscriptions against horseracing, cockfighting, and theatergoing; holidays, such as fast days, thanksgivings, and anniversaries of independence; iconography, such as emblems and mottoes printed on the continental currency; ceremonies of state, such as public audiences granted to foreign ministers; and commemorative artifacts, such as swords and medals awarded to distinguished army officers and monuments erected to their memory. By crafting rituals, celebrations, and objets d'art, Congress appealed not merely to reason, but to emotion, passion, faith, morality, sensibility, and aesthetics. This was not a volitional model of governance, but rather an affective one.[11]

Eighteenth-century Anglo-Americans inhabited a world abundant with national ritual and symbol. Indeed, Britons relied heavily on such phenomena to mediate their relationships with the Crown and empire. As historian Brendan McConville has demonstrated, British society legitimated the Act of Settlement—the legislative artifice that brought the Protestant House of Hanover to the throne—by producing, distributing, and consuming rich material culture and pageantry for the Georgian kings. Britain's North American colonists particularly desired to partake in the Hanoverian monarchy. Situated at the far reaches of the king's dominions, the colonists lacked many of the political mechanisms that obliged home islanders to the state: patronage, a system of land tenure, and a majestic church.[12] Still, Anglo-Americans felt a keen sense of British nationalism. Decades of war with France and Spain bound the colonists fast to the British Empire. Deep-seated repugnance at Native American "savagery" and African American "brutishness" nurtured white colonists' chauvinistic affinity for English "civilization." A nagging mindfulness of their social and political inferiority, as provincials, heightened the colonists' insistence that they were full and faithful subjects of the king. For all of these reasons and more, Americans adorned their lives with the ornaments of Britannia. By hanging portraits of the royal family above their mantles, by studying the dynastic lineages printed in their calendar almanacs, by illuminating their windows on the anniversaries of the king's coronation, British colonists affirmed their devotion to an ever more glorious empire.[13]

The Revolution shattered Anglo-Americans' perceptions of their national identity.[14] During the 1760s and early 1770s, Parliament's persistent efforts to levy taxes and to subordinate the colonial assemblies disheartened British Americans and alienated many from government. The outbreak of war in 1775 compelled even the king's most loyal subjects to reconsider their place within the empire. In August, George III declared that many colonists had forgotten the "allegiance which they owe[d]" and were engaged in "traitorous conspiracies" and "avowed rebellion." That winter, Parliament outlawed "all manner of trade and commerce" with the colonies and authorized the Royal Navy to seize American ships as if they sailed under the flag of Britain's "open enemies." In the spring of 1776, the king enlisted tens of thousands of German soldiers—mercenaries, as many saw them—to put down the American rebellion. Peeling back legal protections and casting the colonists out of his majesty's paternal care, the "home" administration rendered it increasingly difficult for Americans to imagine themselves as part of the British nation. The collaborative enterprises of resistance and war enabled some to conceptualize themselves as members of a new polity. But the character and composition of this polity—its moral, political, and racial boundaries (to say nothing of its territorial boundaries)—were not at all clear.

Several influential members of the Continental Congress believed that the very kinds of artifacts and celebrations that riveted the colonists to the British nation might just as well loose them from it. John and Samuel Adams, Benjamin Franklin, and Thomas Jefferson all shared a uniquely strong faith in the efficacy of symbols and rituals to shape persons' political beliefs and behaviors. By such mechanisms of affective communication, these congressmen endeavored to steel Americans for war, to inspire loyalty to the United States, and ultimately to mold the nation's temperament and values.

John Adams disdained the worship of graven images. Though his personal religious beliefs tended toward Unitarianism, Adams harbored a puritanical suspicion of idolatry. The trappings and liturgies of the Catholic faith—"[H]oly Water, Crossings, Bowings, Kneelings and Genuflections, Images, Paintings, Crucifixes, Velvet, Gold, but above all, the Musick"—Adams denounced as charms for the bewitchment of "the simple and ignorant."[15] But though Adams condemned rituals, icons, and relics as snares of false religion, Adams endorsed them enthusiastically as instruments of effective nationcraft.[16] Bred to the monarchical traditions of the Hanoverian dynasty, Adams sought to harness the beguiling powers of symbols and ceremonies and to put them in the service of the Revolution. As a member of the Continental Congress, Adams urged that medals be struck to commemorate the battlefield heroics of valiant officers. He called for "Painting, Sculpture, Statuary, [and] Poetry . . . to assist in publishing to the

World, and perpetuating to Posterity, the horrid deeds of our Enemies." He wished that every American "Town and Village" would burn or hang effigies of the Howe brothers, commanders of the British army and navy. And he jubilantly predicted that the anniversary of independence would be "solemnized with Pomp and Parade, with Shews, Games, Sports, Guns, Bells, Bonfires and Illuminations from one End of this Continent to the other from this Time forward forever more." Adams advocated these measures quite deliberately to excite Americans' passions. "The Passions of Men," Adams pointedly observed, "must cooperate with their Reason in the Prosecution of War. The public may be clearly convinced that a War is just, and yet, untill their Passions are excited, [they] will carry it languidly on."[17]

John Adams's cousin, Samuel, melded puritan Christianity with republican political thought. The elder Adams believed that "true Religion and good Morals"—to borrow the language of a resolution he once pressed on Congress—"are the only solid foundations of public liberty and happiness." He also worried that "Superfluity of Dress," "Vanity & Levity," and "Dissipation & Folly" would corrupt a virtuous citizenry. But Adams perceived that legislators and governors might exemplify civic virtue in their ethics and demeanor. He called on American statesmen to "stamp the Character of the People" by taking office with modesty and sobriety. To make his stamp, that is, to safeguard the American republic against vice and corruption, Adams repeatedly prevailed on Congress to prohibit debauching pastimes and to appoint days of fasting and thanksgiving.[18]

Benjamin Franklin brought to Congress both the artistic sensibility and the technical expertise he had accumulated during his long career as printer and publisher of the *Pennsylvania Gazette*. More significantly, Franklin carried into office an empiricist's faith in the malleability of human behavior. For nearly a quarter of a century, the philosopher Franklin, in the gentle but heroically didactic character of Poor Richard, had goaded readers of his almanac to hard work, temperate living, and thrift. As the congressman most responsible for the design and production of continental currency, Franklin made it his project to cultivate those same virtues. He decorated Congress's new paper bills with emblems and mottoes intended to persuade Americans that though the war would be costly, it would ultimately secure their prosperity and happiness.

Like Franklin, Thomas Jefferson labored vigorously to promote the moral economy of the American resistance. In 1774, Jefferson persuaded the Virginia House of Burgesses to proclaim a fast day—the first Virginia fast in thirty years—as an expression of solidarity with the distressed inhabitants of Boston. That same year, he helped to popularize the First Continental Congress's Articles of Association by making a showy compliance with its nonimportation provisions. Most commonly remembered as the author of the Declaration of Independence, Jefferson also worked determinedly to establish seals and medals for the United States. As an architect, he possessed an eye for ornament; as a violinist, he possessed an ear for music. For the benefit of the new nation, Jefferson created both.

Other members of Congress shared the Adamses', Franklin's, and Jefferson's faith in the utility of emblems and rituals. George Washington, veteran of the Seven Years' War and colonel in the Virginia militia, knew firsthand the allure of drumbeat and parade. Washington, who appeared at the Second Continental Congress dressed in full regimental uniform, personified the *rage militaire* that swept across the colonies after the eruption of hostilities at Lexington and Concord. Elevated to the command of the Continental Army, Washington ordered that Congress's fast days be observed, he mustered his troops to hear independence declared, and he encouraged his officers to celebrate the Franco-American alliance.[19] By resigning his commission in a dramatic congressional audience in December 1783, Washington not only reaffirmed the supremacy of the civil authority over the military, but by that same act achieved a sort of apotheosis, becoming in his own person a more potent symbol of the United States than any Congress could ever produce.[20]

Meanwhile, in the later years of the war, responsibility for the United States' seal and currency designs fell to the belletrist Francis Hopkinson. A student of the arts—especially heraldry, painting, poetry, and music— Hopkinson fabricated seals for the American Philosophical Society, for the State of New Jersey, and for Congress's Boards of Treasury and Admiralty. In 1777, he designed the United States' flag, and after Franklin departed for Paris, Hopkinson devised emblems for voluminous emissions of paper dollars. Hopkinson, who deemed these labors his "fancy work," yearned vainly for public recognition.

These persons did not bear sole responsibility either for the production, or the ideological content, of Congress's material artifacts and celebrations. The presidents of Congress, as figureheads of the American republic, featured prominently in its rituals and festivities. Secretary Charles Thomson recorded accounts of congressional ceremonies in painstaking detail for publication in U.S. newspapers. The women of Philadelphia, especially the wives of congressional delegates, entertained dignitaries, danced at balls, turned out for parades, and made shows of patriotic sentiment at memorial services and on thanksgiving days. The French ministers Conrad-Alexandre Gérard and

Anne César de La Luzerne helped to choreograph their audiences before Congress; kept tables for the delegates' feasting; and hosted grand soirees, far more extravagant than Congress's humble banquets, on occasions sacred to the House of Bourbon. A host of artists also shaped the material culture of the revolutionary capital, including the Swiss naturalist Pierre Eugène Du Simitière, who consulted with the first seal committee and later proposed a medallic history of the United States; the British officer John André, who reintroduced theater to Philadelphia and orchestrated a notoriously extravagant going-away party for General William Howe; and the radical Constitutionalist Charles Willson Peale, who crafted papier-mâché effigies and window transparencies to exhilarate and to illuminate the city. A variety of professionals and artisans likewise played important roles in celebrating and solemnizing the Revolution, most notably the clerics of Philadelphia, especially the college provost William Smith and the Anglican minister Jacob Duché; as well as the printers William and David Hall, William Sellers, and Robert Aitken.

Together, members of Congress and their many collaborators worked to produce a surprisingly rich assortment of emblems, artifacts, and formal observances for the United States. In so doing, they pursued numerous, diverse objectives. First, Congress aimed to strengthen the American resistance by cultivating civic virtue. Much in the spirit of the Herculean choice that John Adams proposed for the Great Seal, Congress invented traditions that promoted righteous living, hard work, and financial restraint. As economic resistance gave way to armed conflict, Congress attempted to hearten patriots for the escalating war. Like Franklin's fabricated motto, Rebellion to Tyrants Is Obedience to God, Congress assured Americans that it was both lawful and just to fight in defense of their liberties. On the occasions of continental victory, Congress awarded medals and swords to valorous officers, both to applaud their deeds and to prompt others to like action. In doling out merits, Congress attempted to negotiate its often contentious relationship with the Continental Army. During the war, Congress and the American officer corps clashed repeatedly over a host of contentious matters: appointments, promotions, and the politics of seniority, the commissioning of French officers, the payment of back salaries, and the establishment of pensions, to name only a few. By bestowing laurels and trophies of war, Congress distinguished an aggrieved officer corps that it otherwise struggled to provision and remunerate.

After declaring independence, Congress utilized symbol and ceremony to glorify the infant nation. The thirteen American colonies came to the

Revolution disjointedly. Regional prejudices, rancorous boundary disputes, and economic rivalries all strained the fragile union.[21] Though the shared experience of British oppression fostered solidarity among the new states, the disparate military and financial impacts of the far-flung war dampened the emergence of national sentiment. By feting the union, Congress worked to patch over states' differences and to create a facade of national cohesion. Toward this end, it devised new symbols of American liberty, and revitalized old ones, such as the freeholding Saxon chiefs of Jefferson's remembrance.

The conclusion of the Franco-American alliance in 1778, which necessitated the implementation of novel diplomatic protocols, afforded the Continental Congress additional means by which to champion the sovereignty of the new nation. In anticipation of granting an audience to the French minister plenipotentiary, Congress crafted diplomatic ceremony to promote the dignity and self-determination of the United States. Some congressmen insisted on grandeur in these proceedings. They wished to emulate, if only in some distant way, the stateliness of St. James's and Versailles. Other congressmen, particularly Samuel Adams, feared that monarchical pomp would corrode the republican foundations of the United States. Diplomatic protocol thus impelled Congress to reflect on and deliberate the political character of the American confederation.

Perhaps most significantly, Congress formulated symbols and rituals to inspire the people's love for the United States. To achieve independence, American patriots destroyed the Britannic mementos that once adorned their lives. They pulled down statues of King George III; they trampled on the British lion; they tore the Hanoverian arms from their state house walls; and they let pass uncelebrated the anniversaries of royal births and accessions.[22] The Continental Congress worked concertedly to supplant the tokens and habits of the British nation with fresh ones devoted to the United States. It implemented codes of conduct by which patriotic Americans could distinguish those who belonged to their imagined community from those who did not. It offered emblematic assurances, during the bleakest moments of the war, that the United States would persevere. It seized opportunities, slowly though they came at first, to embarrass the British enemy and to celebrate American triumph. By crafting monuments, insignia, and civic traditions, Congress aimed at nothing less than a revolution in Americans' national identity.

By these same means, the Continental Congress also endeavored to legitimate its institutional authority. Here was an assembly of dubious constitutionality; an assembly whose powers were greatly circumscribed; an assembly whose members were ridiculed by the king's friends as boorish, upstart provincials. More worrisome still, here was an assembly whose contentious scheme of resistance provoked war with the mightiest empire in the world. How could such an assembly coordinate an effective opposition? How could it prevail on eager consumers to forbear the luxury goods and comestibles they had so voluminously imported these last forty years? How could it persuade farmer-militiamen to abandon their fields and make regular war against a professional army? How could it entice merchants and shopkeepers to accept paper dollars backed only with the loose promises of a rebel government? How, ultimately, could it persuade a people, long devoted to monarchy and empire, to transfer their allegiance to a newly established republic? The submission of "facts" would not alone serve these ends. To win the people's trust, to demonstrate its fitness for government, Congress had to avail itself of every possible mode of suasion.

In designing symbol, ritual, and festivity for the United States, Congress occasionally innovated, but far more often it drew on familiar, time-honored traditions. Like Adams conjuring a neoclassical Hercules, Franklin invoking a biblical Moses, or Jefferson reinvigorating medieval Saxon chiefs, Congress endeavored to ground the Revolution in an ennobling past.[23] Even those of Congress's inventions that hinted toward the emergence of a new political order typically retained traditional elements. On the anniversaries of independence, for example, Congress jubilated the breach with Great Britain and the birth of an American republic in precisely the same manner that the British colonists had formerly celebrated the king's birthday: with banqueting, militia exercises, firework displays, the burning of bonfires, and the illumination of windows. By retaining these older modes of rejoice, Congress signaled both the reaches and limitations of the American Revolution. Members of Congress seldom if ever imagined their war as the Jacobins of France would theirs, as a rupture in the fabric of time. They saw it not as a violent or totalizing abnegation of history, but first as a battle for the restoration of American rights, and later as a struggle for independence.

In pursuit of that independence, Congress consciously patterned the United States' material and ceremonial identity after that of other nations. The Declaration of Independence announced the United States' intention to do all "Acts and Things which Independent States may of right do." Creating emblems and rituals for the nation was among those acts and things. In imitation of British practice, Congress celebrated important anniversaries of state. In the fashion of European sovereigns, it bestowed swords, monuments, and medals on distinguished military officers. In the style of European courts, but also in the manner of Native American council fires, Congress instituted diplomatic ceremonies and forms. That Congress emulated the practice of foreign nations, particularly foreign republics, should not be interpreted as a failure of creativity, but rather as a deliberate assertion that the United States now held a separate and equal station among the powers of the earth. By rejoicing the confederation's holy days, by exalting the nation's heroes, and by receiving the ministers of foreign governments, Congress labored to fulfill the expectations of an autonomous republic and in so doing to strengthen the United States' claim to independence.

Nothing here or in the pages that follow is intended to overstate the depth or intentionality of Congress's material and ceremonial endeavors. To the contrary, one of the important themes of this book is the haphazardness with which the Continental Congress created artifacts and observances for the American people. It did so at irregular intervals; without a single, clearly articulated objective; in response to shifting political imperatives; and under the moral and aesthetic direction of an evolving roll of delegates. As in all parliamentary bodies, the members of the Continental Congress debated, negotiated, clashed, and compromised over their imaginings of the American resistance and of the United States. Both the meagerness of fine arts in the young republic and the war's disruption of Atlantic economies further hindered Congress's efforts. Many of the artistic productions that Congress commissioned for the United States—its seals, swords, monuments, and medals—would not be completed until after the war, and then only in Paris. Yet, piecemeal and haltingly though it proceeded, Congress nevertheless put forward a sizable and meaningful body of emblems, rituals, and things.

A careful analysis of these phenomena illuminates the manner in which the Continental Congress gave tangible expression to the systems of belief that fueled the American resistance. The most influential members of Congress presupposed that they might actuate individuals for the common good by means of symbolic material and ceremony. These delegates conceived of icons, monuments, and processions as technologies of governance, and they utilized them as such. In Congress's inventions, the ideologies that propelled the Revolution—republicanism, liberalism, work-ethic Protestantism, and puritan covenantalism, to name only a few—all took manifest form.

A close study of congressional material and ceremonial creations also sheds bright light on the social underpinnings of political authority in late-colonial British North America and the Revolutionary United States. Members of Congress staked their legitimacy on the rights of freeborn Englishmen and on the powers vested in them by their respective provincial assemblies and conventions. But in a broader sense, members of Congress staked their legitimacy on their stature as elite white gentlemen. Throughout the war, the Continental Congress self-consciously presented itself as a respectable and august assembly, worthy of the public faith and justified in its pretense to power. To accomplish this, individual delegates made extravagant displays of their fortunes and good breeding. They brandished fine possessions—houses, equipage, clothing, and in some cases slaves—and they flaunted refined manners—oratory, polite conversation, and dance, for example. The point is not simply that the gentry possessed a disproportionate share of wealth in Revolutionary America, but rather that the gentry deployed material signifiers of that wealth to authenticate and secure their political power.[24] By predicating their authority on performative displays of white male sociability, members of Congress perpetuated a social hierarchy very much at odds with the democratizing impulses of the Revolution. That hierarchy, in turn, depended on distinctions of race, class, and gender.

How, then, did the American public react to Congress's vision of the infant republic? How did ordinary laborers, women, loyalists, and other marginalized persons receive a body of works that bore all the social and political prejudices of its elite patriot makers? For answers to these questions, this book turns to the people out of doors. Eighteenth-century Britons used the descriptive phrase "out of doors" to distinguish popular political action and discourse—that which took place in taverns, in coffeehouses, and out in the streets—from official proceedings that unfolded within the halls of government. In recent decades, social and political historians have adapted the phrase "out of doors" to signify early American mobs, or crowds, and to evoke the public spaces in which they gathered for demonstration. Such crowds performed a unique function in Anglo-American society. As Gordon S. Wood has explained,

> America had a long tradition of extra-legislative action by the people, action that more often than not had taken the form of mob violence and crowd disturbance. . . . These were not the anarchic uprisings of the poor and destitute; rather they represented a common form of political protest and political action in both England and the colonies during the eighteenth century by groups who could find no alternative institutional expression for their demands and grievances, which were more often than not political. . . . Good Whigs, particularly those in the Commonwealth tradition, recognized and appreciated the political existence

of the people "out-of-doors," that is, outside of the legal representative institutions, and under certain circumstances were even
willing to grant a measure of legitimacy to their actions.[25]

The people out of doors articulated their political will through the vernacular
of folk ritual. They hanged and burned effigies and buried them in mock
funerals; they assaulted houses and public buildings; they carted offenders
about town to the discordant rhythms of "rough music"; and they paraded
mock heroes, often persons of low social standing, in saturnine parody of
their "betters."[26] During the taxation controversies of the 1760s and 1770s,
British colonists came to depend on these sorts of folk rituals as particularly
vital modes of protest. Deprived of representation in Parliament, British
North Americans constructed effigies of Lord Bute, tore down office buildings of would-be stamp distributors, tarred and feathered customs infor-
mants, and burned vessels belonging to the royal navy. Even the Bostonians'
destruction of East India Company tea may be rightly understood within
this out-of-doors tradition.[27]

   The people out of doors did not passively acquiesce to the Continental
Congress, or to the rites, symbols, and celebrations by which it encouraged
American resistance. To the contrary, they responded in ways that Congress
did not intend or anticipate, and often in ways that Congress could not
control. As will be seen, Philadelphia crowds threatened to tear down the
opulent City Tavern if necessary to enforce Congress's Articles of Association; they smashed windows and once paraded a "strumpet" through the city
to commemorate independence; they twice burned Benedict Arnold in
effigy, in part to signal their detest of his treason but in part to register their
displeasure with Congress. When not acting collectively, in a theatrical or
violent fashion, the people out of doors found other ways to participate in the
making of, or in the critique of, revolutionary civic tradition. Gathering to
welcome members of Congress as they arrived in town, raising a glass in
concurrence with a patriotic toast, assembling in solemn order to witness the
memorial procession of a slain continental officer, cheering at the proclamation of American independence, lighting candles in windows to commemorate the union, or rushing to view the French foreign minister as he rode
through the streets: in the midst of a civil war, the doing or *not* doing of any
of these things might constitute a political act.

   By "the people out of doors," I also mean persons, regardless of class, not
represented in the Continental Congress. Delegates to Congress were most
commonly elected by provincial conventions or by colonial or state legislatures.

This mode of appointment disenfranchised substantial portions of the American population, including women, Native Americans, African Americans, and the working poor. It further disenfranchised loyalists and other "disaffected" persons who, often as a matter of conscience, refused to swear oaths of allegiance to newly formed state constitutions. Yet, in spite of their exclusion from government, these groups and classes of people poignantly articulated their approval of, or disdain for, Congress and its vision of a national polity. Women actively participated in Congress's nonimportation, nonexportation, and nonconsumption campaigns. They conspicuously assembled to mourn America's war dead. And they humiliated Congress and the patriots of Philadelphia by attending balls in the company of British officers. (Which is to say nothing of the woman who urged her congressman-husband to "Remember the Ladies.") Likewise, loyalist poets and essayists ridiculed Congress's currency designs; they derided the "barefoot and unhealthy" soldiers who mustered in honor of independence; and they mocked the pretentious ceremonies by which Congress greeted French diplomats. In 1776, a party of Six Nation Indians entertained Congress and assumed a prominent place in the martial pageantry by gathering to dance for war. Two years later, a delegation of Delaware chiefs embarrassed the United States by paying more fulsome deference to the French minister than to the president of Congress. In these and numerous other ways, large segments of the American population, much larger than those that actually voted for members of Congress, contributed to or deliberately detracted from Congress's making of a symbolic and ceremonial identity for the United States.

The people out of doors responded to Congress in diverse, unpredictable, and often disobliging ways. Almost invariably, they infused Congress's material culture and festivity with significances and practices that Congress did not expect or wish. Congress never dictated the meanings of the Revolution to an inert or uncritical public. Rather, it created objects, emblems, and rites to spur the American public to action. Unwilling to accept those phenomena at face value, the people out of doors devised uses and connotations for them all their own. Properly speaking, this book is neither a history from the top down nor a history from the bottom up, but rather a history of a place in between, a place where elite statesmen and ordinary individuals together forged and contested the values of the Revolution and the identity of the American republic.[28]

Concerned as it is with the people out of doors, this book focuses intensively on Revolutionary Philadelphia. The history of the Continental

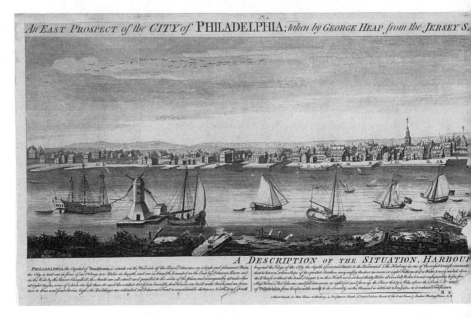

Detail of *An East Prospect of the City of Philadelphia; Taken by George Heap from the Jersey Shore, under the Direction of Nicholas Scull, Surveyor General of the Province of Pennsylvania* (London, 1768). Library of Congress, Prints and Photographs Division, LC-DIG-pga-01698.

Congress, and of the pains it took to invent an identity for the United States, is an assuredly national one. For in its quest to devise symbols and rituals for the confederation, Congress aimed chiefly to unify the former colonists and to situate the United States among other sovereign nations. Print media—especially newspapers, but also pamphlets, broadsides, and magazines—aided Congress in this effort, as did the private and public correspondence of congressional delegates and other eyewitnesses to its inaugural ceremonies of state. By relaying minutely detailed accounts of the revolutionary spectacle throughout the United States, print and letters invited the most distant plowman to participate in the making of a nation.[29]

But the history of the Continental Congress is also a decidedly local one. As the primary seat of government from 1774 to 1783, the city of Philadelphia determined how congressmen would work and live. The Carpenters' Company of Philadelphia offered the First Continental Congress a suitable meeting hall. The Library Company of Philadelphia kept Congress well stocked with political tracts and treatises on international law. Members of

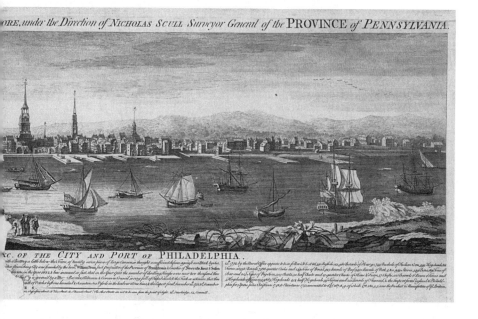

Philadelphia's extensive medical community inoculated the delegates against smallpox and cared for them in times of illness. Ministers from all the city's congregations tended to the congressmen's spiritual needs. The city's private homes, taverns, and boarding houses quartered these statesmen, while working Philadelphians kept them fed, clothed, shod, shaved, and transported about town.

The American Revolution both kindled and was enkindled by a separate and distinct revolution in Pennsylvania. The Townshend Revenue Act and the Tea Act galvanized Philadelphia artisans and journeymen and brought them to the fore of the resistance movement. Congress's plea for the creation of local committees of safety and inspection democratized city politics, elevating new ranks of men to the public service. The outbreak of war at Lexington and Concord inspired thousands of Philadelphians—many of whom had lost work to Congress's trade boycotts—to associate in brigades of volunteers. Congress's May 1776 recommendation that royal administration be suppressed provoked a repudiation of Pennsylvania's ancient charter and gave rise to a new frame of government more radical than many persons could abide. The British occupation of 1777 drove Congress and untold numbers of patriots into exile, just as the British evacuation of 1778 forced many embittered loyalists to flee. The whole of the conflict cleaved Philadelphia's sizable

Quaker community and subjected its members, committed by conscience to pacifism and lawful authority, to partisan suspicion and outrage.[30]

As the war-torn capital of the American resistance, the city of Philadelphia provided the backdrop against which Congress's festive and ceremonial performances unfolded. In Philadelphia's churches and meeting houses, patriots worshipped on congressionally appointed days of fasting and thanksgiving. On the state house lawn, brigades of volunteer associators exercised for Congress's pleasure. Along the wharves of the Delaware River, vast concourses of spectators cheered a naval exhibition organized by Congress to celebrate the first anniversary of independence. At the City Tavern, distinguished guests dined on Congress's banquets and lifted their glasses to the cause of liberty. Through the streets of Philadelphia, a United States coach and an escort of light horse paraded the French minister plenipotentiary to his historic audience with Congress. Through those same streets, a continental officer, attended by a band of musicians and a party of light dragoons, carried the unfurled standards of Cornwallis's army and laid them at Congress's feet.

At the war's end, the Continental Congress faltered in its efforts to manufacture a material and ceremonial identity for the United States. Bereft of credit, plagued by absenteeism, enfeebled by the constitutional limitations and procedural constraints of the Articles of Confederation, and censured for its failure to clothe and feed the Continental Army, Congress declined in both stature and authority. Meanwhile, rival institutions—particularly the French embassy and the Society of the Cincinnati—rose to fill the festive and commemorative void. By that time, however, the Continental Congress and its successor, the Confederation Congress, had made enduring impressions on the material and ceremonial culture of the Revolution and on the national identity of the United States. By manufacturing new emblems and rituals, Congress provided the people out of doors with a vocabulary by which to articulate their own vision of national identity. The Continental Congress could not stabilize the meanings of its inventions. In their very mutability lay power for the people out of doors. Rather than passively adopting Congress's creations, the American people embraced, rejected, reworked, ridiculed, or simply ignored them as they saw fit.

Part I

A "Steady, Manly, Uniform, and Persevering Opposition"

This emblem, which adorned the journal of the First Continental Congress, features a column standing upon the pedestal, Magna Carta. The cap, or pileus, atop the column signifies liberty. The emblem contains a visual ambiguity: do the twelve arms support the liberty column, or do they rest upon it? The Latin motto suggests both: "We uphold this, we lean upon this." Detail of the title page of the *Journal of the Proceedings of the Congress, Held at Philadelphia, September 5, 1774* (Philadelphia, 1774), Library of Congress, Prints and Photographs Division, LC-USZ62-57840.

The delegates who gathered in Philadelphia in the early autumn of 1774 clothed themselves in robes of Anglo-British nationalism. In pleading for redress of political grievances, these delegates styled their constituents "the Inhabitants of the English Colonies." They evoked the memory of their ancestors, "free and natural-born subjects, within the realm of England." They sought the protection of the English constitution and of English common and statutory law. They professed "sentiments of duty" to King George III and declared "affection" for their "parent state." Above all else, they claimed a right to "English liberty" and based that right on the most English of all pedestals, Magna Carta, as illustrated by the emblem that adorned their journal.[1]

Yet, though this irregular assembly appealed to an ancient English heritage, it also contributed, in at least three important ways, to the emergence of an American national identity. First, the calling of a *general* congress enabled British colonists to imagine themselves as members of a larger American polity, a polity that extended beyond the boundaries of any single province or region. The congress of 1774 attracted delegates broadly from the British mainland colonies situated "between Nova Scotia & Georgia," and it pursued explicitly collective ends.[2] Endeavoring to rise above narrow political and economic interests, it aimed to unify British Americans for the restoration of their rights. In this spirit, this general congress came quickly to be known by its glorious but geographically inapt name, the Grand Continental Congress. Hoping to take advantage of such sentiment, Patrick Henry opened congressional debate by declaring, "The Distinctions between Virginians, Pennsylvanians, New Yorkers, and New Englanders, are no more. I am not a Virginian, but an American."[3]

The Continental Congress also nurtured the development of a distinctive American identity by enlisting the colonists in a comprehensive trade boycott known as the Association. An ambitious scheme of nonimportation, nonexportation, and nonconsumption, the Association bound participants in shared acts of economic restraint. It demanded collaborative effort and mutual trust. Like the antitaxation boycotts of the mid- and late 1760s, the Association fostered solidarity among British colonists, as the historian T. H. Breen has demonstrated.[4]

Finally, the Continental Congress gave character to a nascent American community by infusing the colonial resistance movement with a rigorous moral sensibility and work ethic. To strengthen the boycotts, Congress called on British colonists to abstain from expensive, frivolous, and debauching pastimes. It urged them instead to embrace an ethos of sobriety, industry, and humility. Congress thus predicated the colonists' political salvation on their individual conduct. Hinging the restoration of American rights on personal behavior and morality, Congress made austere living the duty and hallmark of all good patriots.

In these efforts, Congress met with potent opposition, not only from persons who defended the British administration, but also from a few ardent champions of American liberties. The problem was not that colonists refused to embrace the cause. To the contrary, Parliament's Coercive Acts provoked extraordinary resentment and galvanized the colonial resistance movement. The problem was not even that colonists objected to the Spartan existence Congress thrust on them. Indeed, colonial newspapers initially reported widespread adherence to Congress's boycotts and behavioral proscriptions. Rather, hostility to Congress and its Association arose out of popular concern for class, racial, and gender equity. As the imperial crisis escalated and its hardships came to be keenly felt, middling and working-rank colonists began to perceive that they alone shouldered the burdens of patriotic sacrifice. Politicized by a decade of resistance, Philadelphia's beleaguered townsfolk found ways to make their will known. In the very city that Congress called home, popular grievances threatened to unstitch the delegates' carefully knitted consensus.

In the meantime, the king's friends—particularly the Anglican clergymen of New York and New Jersey—attacked the Articles of Association by challenging the masculinity of congressional delegates. Members of Congress often goaded their supporters to "firm" and "manly" resistance. For example, the militant Suffolk Resolves, endorsed by Congress in mid-September 1774, urged colonists to adopt a "steady, manly, uniform, and persevering opposition."[5] Likewise, the emblem that adorned Congress's *Journal* depicted American liberty as a column, supporting and supported by the strength of twelve masculine arms.[6] Neatly capturing the masculinist ethos of the Articles of Association, this emblem quickly became a favorite of American patriots.[7]

In hostile response to the Association, a trio of Anglican churchmen worked furiously to unman the Continental Congress. These satirists utilized gendered rhetoric to mobilize opposition to Congress and to demolish its platform of economic resistance. They denounced members of Congress as infirm madmen and henpecked husbands, undeserving of the public trust. They ridiculed the committeemen brought to power by Congress's Association as rustic provincials, unfit to govern within the king's realm. These writers greatly embarrassed Congress and might have destroyed its political credibility had not the British offensive against Lexington and Concord outraged the American people.

1

The Republicans' New Clothes

ON THE AFTERNOON OF NOVEMBER 24, 1775, a Philadelphia committeeman named Christopher Marshall strode on an urgent but delicate errand to the Pennsylvania State House, where the Continental Congress then sat. A staunch supporter of American rights and an active participant in Philadelphia's resistance movement, Marshall had recently won election to the city's Committee of Inspection and Observation. Formed at the direction of the Continental Congress, this committee shouldered responsibility for enforcing the Articles of Association, a series of trade boycotts leveled against Great Britain. As a member of that committee, it was Marshall's duty to monitor the business affairs and personal conduct of all Philadelphians and to ensure their compliance with the Association. Marshall now approached the state house both in his official capacity and as a concerned citizen.

Arriving at three o'clock, the hour when Congress was accustomed to rise, Marshall hoped to meet President John Hancock as he exited the building. But seeing no sign of the president, and fretful for the lateness of the day, Marshall asked the congressional doorman to summon Samuel Adams instead. Marshall had befriended the Massachusetts delegate, as stout a Whig as himself, earlier that fall. They shared "free conversation" in local coffeehouses and at Adams's lodgings. On this day, however, Marshall brought awkward and distressing news. It seems that several members of Congress, perhaps even President Hancock himself, planned to attend a ball in honor of Martha Washington to be held that very evening at the elegant City Tavern. Unfortunately, as Marshall now dutifully explained to Adams, this ball appeared to violate Congress's *own* Articles of Association. Out in the streets, word of the evening's proposed entertainment had already sparked indignation and ire. Several ominous threats had been "thrown out." As Marshall had heard it, "if the ball assembled this night . . . the New Tavern would cut but a poor figure to-morrow morning."[1]

This remarkable episode raises a variety of intriguing questions. What did a night of dancing have to do with the crisis in imperial affairs? What was the relationship between boycotts and balls? More importantly, how had members of Congress fallen so afoul of their own code of conduct? And why did the people of Philadelphia feel aggrieved by this seemingly judicious bending of the rules? Did not the commander's wife merit a gesture of gratitude and admiration? Finally, what, if anything, could Marshall and Adams do to appease an angry city and salvage Congress's reputation?

The answers to these questions enable us to better understand the Continental Congress and the nature of its social and political authority. Most fundamentally, they illuminate the ways in which members of Congress, like the colonial gentry as a whole, employed material wealth and polite sociability to assert their prerogative to rule. They further demonstrate how the British North American social order stood on hierarchical notions of class, gender, and race. Such notions—or prejudices—were woven into the fabric of colonial society, stitched even into the ideological systems that emboldened American resistance. Congress's Articles of Association—a compact as socially conservative as it was politically radical—not only sanctioned these prejudices, but charged them full with patriotic significance.

And yet, as the threats "thrown out" against the City Tavern also reveal, congressional power was not absolute. Rather, it depended heavily on the acquiescence of ordinary people. Some folks balked at Congress's efforts to preserve a social system based on elite privilege. Others embraced the Articles of Association for the sake of their rights and liberties, but insisted that the boycotts be equitably enforced, even against Congress itself. Congress's efforts to shape a moral economy for the colonial resistance movement would not go uncontested. The people of Philadelphia—vigilant against class injustice and exploitation—would have their say.

On a midsummer's evening in 1774, just a few weeks before the "Grand Continental Congress" was scheduled to convene, more than a year before

Christopher Marshall came calling at the state house door, another unexpected visitor, on a very different sort of errand, presented himself at Samuel Adams's family home in Boston. Rising from its dinner, the Adams family discovered that the surprise visitor was a "well-known tailor." As Adams's daughter later remembered, this tailor politely asked to take Adams's measure, but "firmly refused" to explain who had sent him or why. Adams at last consented to the measurements, but no sooner had the tailor taken his leave, and the family resumed their meal, than they were once again interrupted by a knock on the door. Now, "the most approved hatter in Boston" presented himself, and the entire farce repeated itself. The hatter was then succeeded by a shoemaker, the shoemaker by a wigmaker, and so the evening continued, each attendant "observing a strict silence as to the persons whose orders they were obeying." Several days later, "a large trunk" appeared on the Adamses' doorstep. Addressed to Mr. Samuel Adams, it contained a complete suit of clothes. No humble homespun this, Adams's new wardrobe consisted of two pairs of shoes "of the best style," a set of silver shoe-buckles, six pairs of "the best silk hose," six pairs of "fine thread" hose, a set of gold knee-buckles, a set of gold sleeve-buttons, a gold-headed cane, a red cloak, a new wig, and an "elegant cocked hat." Though the trunk was delivered anonymously, Adams discovered a telltale Liberty Cap embossed on each new button. Boston's Sons of Liberty apparently recognized that the Continental Congress was no place for Samuel Adams's notoriously threadbare wardrobe. This maltster-statesman would have to present well, if he were to well represent the people of Massachusetts. The Sons of Liberty had determined to send Adams off in style.[2]

True to these Liberty Boys' hopes, Samuel Adams emerged as an important and influential figure in the First Continental Congress. A detailed account of the politicking and deliberations that transpired in Congress is beyond the purview of this chapter, but it is useful to note just briefly what Adams and like-minded radicals accomplished in the fall of 1774.[3] Most every member of Congress roundly opposed Parliament's efforts to tax the colonists for the purpose of raising a revenue. Nearly to a man, these delegates resented the ministry's efforts to strong-arm the colonists into political submission. Where the delegates' paths diverged was on the wisest course of resistance. The most radical members of Congress took great umbrage at the Coercive Acts. These delegates included Samuel and John Adams of Massachusetts, Richard Henry Lee and Patrick Henry of Virginia, and Thomas Lynch and Christopher Gadsden of South Carolina, as well as a handful of other representatives from New England and the Middle Colonies. Having little faith that King George III would bend his ear to the

John Singleton Copley's portrait of Samuel Adams, taken about the year 1772, captures the patriot's political vigor and determination, but also his accustomed dishevelment. The mis-buttoned waistcoat and rumpled lapels of Adams's modest wool suit help to explain why the Sons of Liberty presented Adams a new wardrobe before his departure for the Continental Congress in 1774. *Samuel Adams*, John Singleton Copley, ca. 1772. Photograph © 2011 Museum of Fine Arts, Boston.

colonists' supplications, and dreading that war might break out any day between the British army and the inhabitants of Massachusetts, these congressmen favored aggressive protest. They carried to Philadelphia, moreover, a powerful mandate. Across the long summer of 1774, popular resolve for commercial opposition had stiffened. More than sixty local meetings and provincial conventions expressly urged their congressmen to adopt a continental boycott.[4]

In modest counterpose to these radicals stood a contingent of delegates whose first political instincts tended toward rapprochement. These congressmen viewed the infringement of American rights with genuine dismay, but they believed that the surest path to redress lay in palliative measures. Joseph Galloway, speaker of the Pennsylvania assembly, most vocally advocated conciliation, but a host of other moderate and conservative congressmen lent their support, including John Alsop, James Duane, John Jay, and Isaac Low of New York; John Morton, George Ross, and the belatedly elected John Dickinson of Pennsylvania; Benjamin Harrison and Edmund Pendleton of Virginia; and the brothers John and Edward Rutledge of South Carolina. For an array of reasons, these delegates viewed the prospect of an

American embargo with grave reticence. Some felt an abiding sense of duty to the Crown and laws of Britain. Others feared that by escalating the imperial dispute, Congress risked provoking a wrathful ministry and jeopardizing the very real protections that Britain afforded the colonies. Still others sympathized with planters and merchants who wished to avoid the pecuniary losses of yet another boycott.[5]

To their credit, more radical congressmen perceived that many British colonists harbored real misgivings toward commercial resistance, especially toward the idea of nonexportation.[6] The delegates from Massachusetts further recognized that their colony's reputation for leveling principles and violent politics, as well as its supposed aspirations to independence, might prejudice the Congress against them. For these reasons, the cousins Samuel and John Adams carefully strategized their appearance in Congress. Acting on the hint of New York Son of Liberty Alexander McDougall, who warned that too much New England zeal might estrange more cautious delegates, the Adamses resolved "to avoid every Expression . . . which looked like an Allusion to the last Appeal." Determined "to keep . . . out of Sight, and to feel Pulses, and Sound the Depths," the congressmen from Massachusetts instead allowed their allies from Virginia and South Carolina to take the lead.[7] Thus it was on the motion of Thomas Lynch that Congress agreed to sit in Carpenters' Hall, whose very bricks and beams breathed a spirit of industry and civic virtue, rather than in the elegant Pennsylvania State House, proffered by the conservative Joseph Galloway. And it was at the urging of that same Carolina delegate that Congress appointed Charles Thomson, a vocal leader of the city's resistance movement, said to be "the Sam. Adams of Phyladelphia—the Life of the Cause of Liberty," to serve as its secretary.[8]

Meanwhile, the Massachusetts delegation worked to stoke congressional sentiment for the suffering townspeople of Boston. Prior to setting out for Philadelphia, Samuel Adams arranged for express riders to deliver pressing intelligence to Congress. On Tuesday, September 6, just as Congress began to deliberate preliminary questions of parliamentary procedure, one such rider brought the dire news that British soldiers had marched on Charlestown to seize its gunpowder stores and that the British navy had opened fire on the town of Boston. Ultimately, these reports proved greatly exaggerated and in many points untrue, but for nearly two days, rumors of a horrible bombardment provoked dismay and sympathy among the people of Philadelphia. "This city is in the utmost Confusion," wrote the Connecticut congressman Silas Deane to his wife. "The Bells toll muffled, & the most unfeigned marks of sorrow appear in every Countenance."[9]

Amid such scenes of distress, the congressmen of Massachusetts self-consciously presented themselves as cool, rational, even tolerant men. When Thomas Cushing proposed that Congress be opened with prayer, some delegates objected, noting the "difference of religious Tenets among the Members." But Samuel Adams rose to declare that "he was no Bigot, and could hear a Prayer from a Gentleman of Piety and Virtue, who was at the same Time a Friend to his Country."[10] Adams, a stalwart puritan and a long-time adversary of the Church of England in America, then nominated the prominent Anglican clergyman Jacob Duché, rector of St. Peter's Episcopal Church in Philadelphia, to lead Congress in worship. Against this gesture of outreach, opposition withered.[11]

In this manner, the "brace of Adamses" and their resistance-minded colleagues budged the Continental Congress, plank by plank, toward a platform of bold opposition. On September 17, members of Congress voted their unanimous endorsement of the incendiary Suffolk Resolves—yet another dispatch from Massachusetts, carried by the express rider Paul Revere—which audaciously enjoined the "brave and hardy" people of that colony "to acquaint themselves with the art of war."[12] Less than two weeks later, a slim majority prevailed on Congress to table Joseph Galloway's Plan of Union, a visionary proposal for the establishment of a Grand American Council, offered as a dilatory alternative to nonimportation and nonexportation.[13] In mid-October, Congress adopted a declaration of grievances that—in spite of its nationalistic invocation of Magna Carta and the British constitution—premised American rights on "the immutable laws of nature": laws against which Parliament possessed no power to legislate, laws that implied the right of revolution.[14]

Of all the accomplishments of this Continental Congress, none more squarely set the colonies in opposition to the British administration and none more effectively mobilized the American people than did its adoption of the Articles of Association. On and off for a decade now, the American colonists had protested parliamentary taxation by implementing trade boycotts. In response to the Sugar, Stamp, and Townshend Revenue Acts of the 1760s, various towns and localities as well as private associations of patriotic merchants had sworn off trade with Great Britain, refusing in particular to import British manufactured goods. By boycotting British merchants and manufacturers, Whig organizers intended to bring political pressure to bear on Parliament, compelling it to acknowledge Americans' liberties and privileges. But these nonimportation campaigns suffered from irregularity. Typically organized by local authorities in at best partial cooperation with other communities, they provoked heated opposition and often collapsed amid suspicions of noncompliance or abuse.[15]

To coax the participation of their multitudinous constituents, members of Congress negotiated a clear and definitive agreement known as the Articles of Association. These Articles, fourteen in all, called on merchants to refrain from importing British goods and foodstuffs and from participating in the Atlantic slave trade. They bound planters, farmers, fishermen, distillers, lumbermen, and other producers from exporting their yields to Great Britain, Ireland, and the West Indies. So as not to unduly burden farmers who had recently harvested their fields or who still had crops in the ground, the Association postponed nonexportation for one year, until September 1775. To protect consumers, the Association further prohibited vendors and merchants from raising prices on scarce goods. As a mechanism of enforcement, Congress recommended that every county, city, and town organize a committee "whose business it shall be attentively to observe the conduct of all persons touching this association." And to further ensure compliance, Congress asked all Americans to abstain from purchasing any "goods, wares, or merchandise" imported in violation thereof.[16]

Though its fundamental purpose was political in nature, Congress's Association bore tremendous implications for American society and culture. Most significantly, the Association called an abrupt halt to the phenomenon that historians now know as the "consumer revolution." Several decades earlier, beginning sometime around the 1720s and 1730s, Britain's North American colonists had begun to import and consume increasing quantities of European merchandise and commodities, including furniture, silver, fabric, and global foodstuffs such as tea and chocolate. In the five decades preceding Congress's Articles of Association, per capita consumption of British exports rose almost 50 percent.[17] This process resulted from a variety of factors: the British Empire's increasingly efficient extraction of natural resources and agricultural profits, much of which was accomplished by slave labor; the maturation of Britain's settler colonies, including the accumulation of disposable wealth by the gentry and middling ranks; the expansion and development of transatlantic trade networks and credit systems; and the invention of new modes and technologies of production that would ultimately propel the industrialization of Great Britain. The consumer revolution refashioned the material landscape of British North America, while at the same time instilling in its participants a vigorous market ethos. It provided new objects for the articulation of status. It opened novel possibilities for personal expression and identity. It heightened the significance of fashion and taste as arbiters of an individual's sophistication. It generated fresh anxieties about dangerous imposters who elided the boundaries of class and race by adorning themselves in finery. Most fundamentally, the consumer revolution accustomed certain classes of British colonists to the acquisition, possession, use, and display of imported manufactured items, as manifest for example in Samuel Adams's new suit of clothes. The Articles of Association asked American patriots to forego their habituated consumerism for however long the British ministry persisted in its arbitrary and unjust rule. This was no small demand.[18]

To promote this arduous nonconsumption campaign, Congress spurred its constituents to "frugality, economy, and industry." Specifically, Congress urged Associators to relinquish popular leisure activities and expensive social customs. The eighth article of the Association declared, "[We] will discountenance and discourage every species of extravagance and dissipation, especially all horse-racing, and all kinds of games, cock fighting, exhibitions of shews, plays, and other expensive diversions and entertainments." Reaching even unto the deeply personal realm of mourning practice, the Association mandated, "[O]n the death of any relation or friend, none of us, or any of our families will go into any further mourning-dress, than a black crepe or ribbon on the arm or hat, for gentlemen, and a black ribbon and necklace for ladies, and we will discontinue the giving of gloves and scarves at funerals."[19]

Behavioral proscriptions such as these had an incredibly rich history in Britain and colonial North America. Ideologically speaking, the origins of such proscriptions may be traced to at least two complexly interwoven and mutually invigorating systems of belief and thought: low-church pietism and republicanism. Euro-American pietists—Protestants of all denominations including puritan Congregationalists, Presbyterians, Quakers, Baptists, Lutherans, as well as a host of smaller reformed sects—denounced sinful activities such as gambling and excessive drinking. They censured idle amusements and vain fashions that distracted individuals from their spiritual obligations. And they questioned the repentance of sinners who refused to mend their ways.[20] The morality of pietism melded with and reinforced the political economy of republicanism, perhaps the most potent strain of English political thought in the seventeenth and eighteenth centuries. Both in its classical and commonwealth iterations, republicanism disparaged luxury as a canker that slowly devoured civil liberty. Only a virtuous citizenry—upright, educated, and civically engaged, a citizenry uncorrupted by vice and licentiousness—could preserve its freedom against the encroachment of arbitrary power.[21]

During the English Civil War, Parliament gave legal expression to these pietistic and republican principles, repeatedly ordering the suppression of stage plays and the tearing down of theaters. Oliver Cromwell, upon assuming the protectorate, also banned cockfighting and horseracing and condemned all pastimes that disturbed "the Publique Peace, and [were] commonly accompanied with Gaming, Drinking, Swearing, Quarrelling and other dissolute Practices, to the Dishonour of God."[22] Later, the Protestant king William III issued an edict "for Preventing and Punishing Immorality and Profaneness," in which he charged all legal and clerical authorities with the prosecution of "Immoral or Dissolute practices."[23] English migrants codified their aversions to vice and profligacy in colonial charters and laws. The 1682 Pennsylvania Charter of Liberties, for example, mandated that the governor and council severely punish "All Prizes, Stage-plays, Cards, Dice, May-games, Masques, Revels, Bull-Baitings, Cock-fightings, Bear-baitings, and the like."[24] By the mid-eighteenth century, each of Britain's thirteen mainland colonies had passed laws regulating or forbidding outright some form of gaming.[25] Meanwhile, opponents of the theater endeavored to prevent its establishment too. In the eyes of its critics, the English theater made too light of sin. By portraying vanity, lewdness, and gluttony with wicked irreverence, theatrical performances threatened to corrupt women, children, and the poor—or so charged the theater's paternalistic foes. Playhouses, they further objected, promoted idleness, licentiousness, and vice.[26] Despite the best efforts of ministers and magistrates, gambling, rowdy spectator events, and the theater flourished in many regions of British North America. Horseracing and cockfighting, for example, thrived in the eighteenth-century South, especially in the Chesapeake.[27] Theater also took root in Williamsburg and New York City.[28] Throughout the colonies, the ongoing efforts of colonial authorities to stamp out such activities suggests what popular appeal they bore.

Intriguingly, the Continental Congress's Association of 1774 was the first colonial antitaxation boycott to ban rambunctious leisure activities. Some previous nonimportation and nonexportation agreements denounced luxury and extravagance in general, but few if any placed particular strictures on theatergoing, horseracing, or cockfighting.[29] Regrettably, no evidence exists in the Congress's journals or letters to explain why the delegates prohibited "expensive diversions and entertainments." But we may productively speculate about their motivations. In purely economic terms, Article 8 strengthened the Association's nonimportation and nonconsumption provisions by encouraging Americans to reflect on their expenditures. The boycott would manifestly dampen if not debilitate the colonial economy. Should the British ministry retaliate with a blockade or should the imperial crisis escalate into war—both very real possibilities in 1774—the colonies would be thrust into a period of sustained economic hardship. By calling an end to penny-foolish amusements, Congress endeavored to brace the public for whatever calamity lay ahead.

Congress's decision to implement Article 8, however, could not have been a purely economic one, at least not for stalwart Whigs and old puritans such as Samuel Adams. For Adams, the fate of American resistance, indeed the fate of the American people, depended on public morality. By the logic of republicanism, Americans' abstention from frivolous consumer goods and wanton pastimes would fortify the colonists against tyrannical government. In debate on the floor of Congress, the Massachusetts representative Robert Treat Paine fiercely rebuked the suggestion that Americans would suffer under the Association. Paine acerbically proclaimed, "They will Suffer themselves to grow Rich by a Disuse of the fopperies & Superfluities Imported from G[reat] Brittain. . . . They will Suffer themselves to grow wise & virtuous & healthy by a disuse of the Intoxicating Poisons & needless Luxuries. . . . They will Suffer themselves to grow Ingenious & Industrious in Manufacturing their own Necessaries."[30]

Likewise, by the dictates of puritan conscience, Americans' solemn living would appease the Lord. New England's earliest migrants believed that they, as true believers and worshippers, had entered into a divine pact with God. This pact not only established the terms of their spiritual and ecclesiastical mission—their errand into the wilderness—it also shaped the boundaries of their community in exile. It distinguished them as God's chosen people. The Articles of Association drew upon this covenantal tradition. The Association itself *was* a covenant, a mutual promise that "solemnly bound" individual subscribers for the sake of their collective welfare. And though the Association made no explicit reference or appeal to divine authority, its call for chastity and humility tended to sacralize American economic resistance. Were the colonists ever to withstand a scheming administration, they would surely need to rely on the blessings of Providence. Those blessings could not be obtained so long as the people languored in sin. The historian T. H. Breen has demonstrated that pre-Revolutionary trade boycotts united Americans in reciprocal acts of consumer self-denial.[31] Likewise, Article 8 united Americans in reciprocal acts of *moral* self-denial. By binding Americans in a common and sacred cause, the Association bore the power to promote a collective, even a national, consciousness.

There were numerous other good reasons, more political than religious, for Congress to proscribe illicit behaviors. By championing morality, Congress curried the favor of the British and American public.[32] Assuming a posture of decency, order, and sobriety, Congress claimed for the American resistance a moral high ground and distanced itself from the lawless "rabble." In drafting Article 8, Congress also appealed to America's "disaffected" religious minorities, including Baptists who had recently complained to Congress about religious oppression in Massachusetts, and more particularly Quakers, many of whom opposed Congress's trade boycott, both out of pacifist ideology and mercantile interest, but who, as a denomination, ardently decried profane amusements such as gaming and the theater. Further, by banning popular leisure activities, Congress helped to democratize the American resistance movement. Not every colonist had a shop to close or purchase orders to cancel, but every American with a penny to pinch could bestow it on a distressed Bostonian, and every American with a moment to spare could deny it to idleness and devote it instead to the cause of liberty.

Notwithstanding the many good arguments in favor of Article 8, delegates to the Continental Congress understood that neither it nor any other provision of the Association would rest easily on the American people. In its nonimportation and nonconsumption campaigns, the Continental Congress boldly attempted to quash a consumer revolution nearly half a century in the making. In the very same breath, Congress called a halt to favorite pastimes that bore no immediate relation to parliamentary taxation or colonial rights. In so doing, Congress demanded prodigious restraint from the American people. Some delegates questioned whether the colonists were equal to the Association's obliging austerity. "Will, Can the People bear a total Interruption of the [We]st India Trade?" asked the New York congressman, Isaac Low. "Can [they] live without Rum, Sugar, and [Mo]lasses? Will not their Impatience, and Vexation defeat the [Me]asure?" These sorts of doubts continued to haunt Congress through the early phases of the war. John Adams recognized that the Association would succeed only if the colonists transformed their most basic manners of living. In October 1775, not long after nonexportation went into effect and scarcely a month before Christopher Marshall came calling at Congress's door, Adams cautioned, "We must change our Habits, our Prejudices, our Palates, our Taste in Dress, Furniture, Equipage, Architecture etc." Perceiving that Americans would not forever subject themselves to privation and self-discipline, Adams confided, "That they have not virtue to bear it always, I take for granted." "How long," Adams wondered, "will their Virtue last?"[33]

Instead of questioning Americans' virtue, Adams might have done well to question their sense of fairness or equity. For not only did the Articles of Association impose rigorous codes of economic and moral behavior, it also tended to harden distinctions of class, race, and gender. Congress's Association aimed chiefly at the restoration of American rights; it did *not* aspire to challenge class relations or to topple the social order. To the contrary, many of the Association's provisions, particularly those contained in Article 8, were borne of an impulse to preserve Anglo-American social hierarchy.

Congress's ban on extravagant mourning, for example, functioned to reinforce distinctions between wealthy and poor, much as did earlier colonial sumptuary laws. In British North America, opulent funerals provided occasions for common people to adopt material signifiers of wealth and prestige, that is, to dress and to give gifts as rich folks did. For decades, New England legislators strove to suppress this behavior on the grounds that it impoverished poor and middling families. "[M]any," the *Boston Gazette* warned, "must become a burthen to the community . . . through a vain ambitious humour to copy the example of their wealthy neighbors."[34] Antimourning laws aimed to save the lower classes from their own demise and thus to shield the public treasury from demands for poor relief. But their practical effect was to deny working people an opportunity to assert claims to higher social rank.[35] The campaign against expensive mourning also reaffirmed the paternalistic privilege and class responsibility of the colonial gentry. In calling for funerary modesty in the 1760s, Whig organizers appealed directly to "well disposed persons," to "the most respectable inhabitants," and to "principal Families."[36] Encouraging the well-to-do to behave with restraint in hope that the rest of society might follow their good example, colonial leaders positioned elites as the natural conservators of the public welfare. By discontinuing the giving of gloves and scarves, the Articles of Association invested American resistance in the preservation of class boundaries.

Similarly, by discountenancing and discouraging "every species of extravagance and dissipation," the Articles of Association predicated the cause of American liberty on the maintenance of racial distinctions. In British North America, spectatorial gaming, especially open-air contests such as horseracing and cockfighting, attracted all ranks of society. In 1752, the governor of Virginia moved to ban those sports because of their corrupting influence on the poor. "[Gaming]," he protested, "is now much practiced among the lower Class of our People: I mean Tradesmen and inferior Planters, who . . . follow the Examples of their Superiors."[37] As in New England, Virginia authorities perceived a danger in allowing "mean" and "inferior" persons to mimic the behavior of their genteel "betters." But gaming events, and the motley crowds they attracted, also provoked concerns about social interaction among persons of different races. Recounting a cockfight in 1787, one new-comer to Virginia described the footloose gathering: "The roads, as we approached the scene, were alive with carriages, horses, and pedestrians, black and white, hastening to the point of attraction."[38] Some colonists balked at this sort of promiscuous intermingling. Polite Philadelphians, for example, particularly among the Quaker community, had long petitioned the mayor and his council to cancel that city's biannual fairs, which took place every May and November. They alleged that fairs promoted "license, riot, races, gambling, and drunkenness." No less alarmingly, they mixed young people in company with "vicious servants and negroes." In 1775, these protesters at last persuaded local officials to cancel the fairs, perhaps because Congress's recently circulated Association gave new heft to their push against morally and racially debauching activities.[39]

Like fairs, cockfights amalgamated whites and blacks in boisterous carousal, much to the consternation of race-conscious elites. Later in the Revolution, Philadelphia's most celebrated cockfighter—the brewer, shopkeeper, disowned Quaker, and political upstart Timothy Matlack—came under fire for consort-ing with African Americans. In an effort to discredit Matlack, who had risen to prominence in Pennsylvania's revolutionary government, one of his enemies pointedly wrote,

> Altho', dear Tim, you've rose so great
> From trimming cocks to trim the State
> ....
> And yet, you know, with truth 'twas said,
> Your hapless babes oft' wanted bread;
> While you, unfeeling, idled time
> With Negroes . . .

Still another of Matlack's foes railed, "By all his former friends abandon'd quite / Game-cocks and Negroes were his sole delight."[40] This doggerel chas-tised Matlack, not simply for gaming or neglecting his children, but for wasting his days in the company of black persons. When read in tandem with Quaker protests against Philadelphia's city fairs, it suggests that racist senti-ment fueled British Americans' contempt for gaming crowds. Congress's ban on horseracing and cockfighting thus gave patriotic and quasi-legal sanction to a racially circumscribed social order.

The Articles of Association also embodied patriarchal beliefs about male superiority. Summoning Americans to engage in mutually beneficial acts of forbearance—beseeching them to surrender their livelihoods, to abstain from luxuries and necessities, and to renounce playful amusements—the Association was, above all else, an exercise in virtue. Members of Congress expressly bound their constituents under virtue's "sacred ties." But these ties were woven of gendered assumptions. In the Revolutionary Era, virtue signified male honor and action. Derived from the Latin root, *vir*, meaning "man," virtue synthesized a complex of masculine attributes, including vigor, restraint, and selflessness. Predicated on political and economic independence as secured through the ownership of land, or on valor and sacrifice as exhibited on the field of battle, virtue was neither expected of women nor readily attainable by them.[41]

Members of Congress explicitly juxtaposed masculine virtue and effeminate luxury. Both classical and Protestant tradition envisioned luxury as a female seductress whose beguiling charms softened the political will. During the 1760s and 1770s, the gendered rhetoric of virtue and luxury suffused debates over the worsening imperial crisis.[42] Shortly after the First Continental Congress adjourned, John Adams drafted an agenda for English constitutional reform. Typifying Whig chauvinism, Adams ranked effeminacy among a host of moral and structural defects: "Shorter parliaments, a more equitable representation, the abolition of taxes and the payment of the debt, the reduction of placemen and pensioners, the annihilation of bribery and corruption, *the reformation of luxury, dissipation and effeminacy*, the disbanding the army, are all necessary to restore your country to a free government, and to a safe, honourable, and happy life" (italics added).[43]

As a strategy of economic resistance, the Continental Association compounded Whig ideologies of virtue and luxury with an equally masculinist ethos about women's place in the burgeoning world of goods. Many of the wares and comestibles that flooded American ports during the mid-eighteenth century were marketed specifically for female consumption.[44] Fabrics, for example, such as silk, fine linen, and lace, largely appealed to women of fashion; likewise, the accoutrements of tea consumption—tea service, tea tables, table cloths, napkins, china, and silverware—marked the feminized space of the tea salon.[45] By tempting women to spend, the consumer revolution posed a threat to male privilege. As consumers, women exercised control over household finances; they exerted authority over property that, under the doctrine of coverture, legally belonged to their husbands. For these reasons, the consumer revolution piqued anxieties about women's frailty.[46] Cautioning against women's participation in the marketplace, ministers, editorialists, and the writers of prescriptive literature invoked ancient suppositions of female sensuousness, the classical and biblical notion that women are more vulnerable to temptation and less capable of rational self-control than men.[47]

Despite the sacrifices of countless patriotic women in pre-Revolutionary America—the Daughters of Liberty, who fomented boycotts and organized spinning meetings, for example—Whig preconceptions about female fragility persisted.[48] In his *Thoughts on Government* (1776), John Adams claimed that "vanities, levities, and fopperies" posed a grave threat "to all great, manly, and warlike virtues."[49] As an antidote to womanly vice, the Continental Congress prescribed manly virtue, and it did so in a proud, manful voice. On the day that Congress voted its support for the inflammatory Suffolk Resolves— by which the people of Boston proclaimed their stout opposition to British administration—John Adams declared, "This was one of the happiest Days of my Life. In Congress We had generous, noble Sentiments, and manly Eloquence."[50]

In the Articles of Association, then, lay a tremendous irony. For ten years, the American resistance movement had drawn strident support from the people out of doors: from artisans, mechanics, sailors, dockhands, and apprentices who willingly yielded their livelihoods to boycott; from small farmers who determined to withhold their produce from market; from mixed-race and mixed-gender crowds who gathered for street protest; and from women who committed themselves to nonconsumption.[51] Without the enthusiastic backing of ordinary people, neither the spirited remonstrances of colonial legislatures nor the carefully drawn conspiracies of the Sons of Liberty could have so rocked the British Empire. And yet, despite widespread public support for economic resistance, the Continental Congress produced a scheme of boycotts and behavioral proscriptions that tautened the ropes of class, race, and gender. The Articles of Association thus risked alienating the very members of society who most supported the cause of liberty.

Sensible of the extraordinary demands that the Association would make on the American people, some members of Congress endeavored to set examples of patriotic sacrifice in their own private lives. To induce public compliance with the Association, they along with local resistance leaders conspicuously modeled their abidance with its terms.[52] In December 1774, for instance, Thomas Jefferson, who joined Congress the following spring, penned a letter to a Virginia county committee entrusted with enforcing the nonimportation agreement. In this letter, Jefferson explained that he had ordered from London fourteen pairs of sash windows, "ready made and glazed," *before* Congress had established the Association. Unfortunately, Jefferson expected these windows to arrive in Virginia *after* nonimportation had gone into effect. And so, in accordance with the Association, Jefferson now happily surrendered those sash windows to the committee. Jefferson likely wrote this high-minded letter for the sake of a public readership. Jefferson certainly had popular opinion in mind, for, as he declared in his letter, he resolved to forfeit the windows so that his business would not give opponents "a handle for traducing our measures." No one could say that *he* had violated the American pact. Other delegates demonstrated their compliance in a variety of ways. In May 1775, the newly elected congressman Benjamin Franklin reported that "Gentlemen, who used to entertain with two or three courses, pride themselves now in treating with simple beef and pudding." Later that summer, two delegates from Georgia attended the Second Continental Congress bedecked in patriotic homespun suits, far more humble than the fancy threads Samuel Adams had donned the previous fall. In October, delegates agreed to attend the funeral of past congressional president Peyton Randolph wearing no other mourning than the black crepe armbands mandated by the Association. And in November, John Adams wrote Mercy Otis Warren to proclaim how greatly he disdained popular diversions such as "Balls, Assemblies, Concerts, Cards, Horses, [and] Dogs."[53]

During the winter of 1774–75, these congressmen and other proponents of economic resistance took heart in widespread accounts of compliance with the Association. From all quarters came approbative reports of communities having embraced its provisions, including the onerous eighth article. In Charleston, for example, the St. Caecilia Society canceled its winter concert season. In Annapolis, the Jockey Club called a halt to its races. In New York City, the managers of a puppet theater struck their show after a local committee decreed such performances "offensive" to patriotic inhabitants. Also in New York, a panel of jurors refused to hear a dispute about a horse race that had been run in violation of the Association. Meanwhile, throughout the colonies, mourners conducted their funerals in the "plainest manner."[54] None of these anecdotes should suggest that the British colonists universally embraced the boycotts. To the contrary, the proceedings of the First Continental Congress provoked bitter denunciation, particularly in the rural districts of New York. But members of Congress and Americans who supported the Association could take heart in early accounts of widespread adherence.[55]

Unfortunately, compliance with the Association did not come so easily to the Continental Congress itself. The social cachet and political authority of the Anglo-American gentry were largely predicated on conspicuous displays of affluence and sociability. In the British colonies, material wealth and etiquette functioned both to secure and to signify one's place in polite society. Lacking titles of nobility and holding few of the political or military offices by which the English bourgeoisie claimed rank, American elites articulated their status through prominent displays of extravagant houses, furniture, carriages, and clothing. As Richard Bushman and other historians have demonstrated, America's planters and prosperous merchants emulated the European beau monde as fully as their unique colonial circumstances would admit.[56]

The pursuit of refinement—that is, the exhibition of rich material possessions and the cultivation of genteel manners—gave political legitimacy to the Continental Congress and shaped the social world of its members, their families, and the people of Philadelphia and beyond. This process unfolded in three important ways, the first of which is most clearly revealed in delegates' accounts of the rich pageantry and fanfare as well as the sumptuous entertaining to which they were treated along their passage to Philadelphia. Many delegates to the First Continental Congress, especially those traveling great distances, departed their homes several days or even weeks before their business was slated to commence. Both the urgency of the imperial crisis and the novelty of the "Grand Congress" augmented the celebrity of these dignitaries, who met with rousing acclaim at every stop. When the Massachusetts delegation arrived in New Haven, Connecticut, for example, "[A]ll the Bells in Town were sett to ringing," John Adams recalled. "The People Men, Women and Children, were crouding at the Doors and Windows as if it was to see a coronation. At Nine O Clock the Cannon were fired. . . . No Governor of a Province, nor General of an Army was ever treated with so much Ceremony and Assiduity."[57] Similarly, the inhabitants of New York bade their congressmen farewell with "colours flying, music playing, loud Huzzas" and cannon fire.[58]

In these travels, members of Congress took repose and repast in genteel homes and in handsome taverns and inns. America's most prominent families opened their doors, offering lavish meals and accommodations not only to honor and impress the congressmen, but also to enhance their own reputations by the presence of their luminary guests. The inhabitants of New York, for example, received the New England delegations with an opulence that astounded John Adams. Breakfast at the home of John Morin Scott, Adams recorded: "rich Plate—a very large Silver Coffee Pott, a very large Silver Tea Pott—Napkins of the very finest materials, and toast and bread and butter in great Perfection." A sitting room at the home of Zephaniah Platt: "as elegant a Chamber as ever I saw—the furniture as rich and splendid as any of Mr. Boylstones." A meal at the Exchange Chamber, hosted by the New York committee of correspondence: "the most splendid Dinner I ever saw—a Profusion of rich dishes &c., &c."[59] More hospitality awaited. As the New England delegations approached the city of Philadelphia, a "Number of Carriages and Gentlemen" rode out to greet them. This welcoming committee escorted the New Englanders, "dirty, dusty, and fatigued" though they were, to the City Tavern and presented them a supper "as elegant as ever was laid upon a Table."[60] In the weeks that followed, the representatives dined in the homes of "the nobles in Philadelphia," as the Massachusetts delegate Thomas Cushing described his hosts, "with seldom less than Ten, Twelve or fifteen in Company."[61] Their fare comprised the "most sinfull Feast[s] . . . Every Thing which could delight the Eye, or allure the Taste, Curds and Creams, Jellies, Sweet meats of various sorts, 20 sorts of Tarts, fools, Trifles, floating Islands, whippd Sillabubs &c. &c.—Parmesan Cheese, Punch, Wine, Porter, Beer &c. &c."[62] The point is not simply that the welcome was warm, but that it was effusively courteous and patently expensive. Here, cordiality must be understood not merely as an expression of generosity but more significantly as an articulation of social status and wealth. These hosts showcased their command not only of financial resources, but of human resources too, the labor, male and female, free and enslaved, that made such hospitality possible. In short, this entertaining testified to the prestige of the hosts and of the congressmen in their midst.

A second way in which refinement and polite sociability enhanced the political authority of Congress may be seen in the delegates' performances of gentility and statesmanship. The Continental Congress was a new political assembly. Few of its members enjoyed prior parliamentary relationships with one another, and no pecking order had yet been established. Far removed from their native assembly halls, delegates wielded only so much clout as their reputations and demonstrable talents afforded.[63] Congress's early determination that every colony, regardless of its population or wealth, would share an equal voice in American affairs further leveled distinctions among its members.[64] Meanwhile, public scrutiny of Congress ran high, as many colonists believed that their fate hung in the balance of its proceedings. For all of these reasons, the performative attributes of refined masculinity—dress, demeanor, and public speaking, to name only a few—bore heightened, even exaggerated, significance.

Within Carpenters' Hall and without, members of Congress bid for the admiration and esteem of their new colleagues. For example, John Dickinson, renowned author of the *Letters from a Farmer in Pennsylvania*, visited the New England delegates not long after they had settled in their lodgings. Dickinson arrived "in his Coach" with "four beautifull Horses." He "very politely" introduced himself. He expressed how "exceedingly glad" he was to meet the "Gentlemen" and he later invited them to dine at "his Seat at Fair Hill," which Robert Treat Paine remembered as a "convenient, decent, elegant, Philosophers Rural Retreat."[65] In sum, Dickinson displayed perfect gentility and grace. (Dickinson would join the Continental Congress that October, after first winning a seat in the Pennsylvania assembly.) Courtesies such as Dickinson's had the power to oblige. Soon after the New Englanders settled in Philadelphia, they made a point "to return Visits to the Gentlemen who had visited us." As Adams recorded, "We visited a Mr. Cadwallader a Gentleman of large Fortune, a grand and elegant House And Furniture. We then visited Mr. Powell, another splendid Seat. We then visited the Gentlemen from S. Carolina. . . . We dined at Friend Collins's."[66]

Genteel women, equal participants in the pursuit of refinement, contributed vibrantly to this social milieu. Some congressmen's wives and families traveled with their husbands, and Philadelphia's elite women actively participated in the reception of these eminent visitors. John Adams recorded taking one meal for example in the company of John Dickinson, his wife Mary Norris Dickinson, and three of her sisters and cousins.[67] Like the members of Congress, these women expressed their social status through material wealth and gentility. Adams noted that when he was first introduced to Hannah Motte Lynch, the wife of the delegate Thomas Lynch of South Carolina, she "enquired kindly after Mrs. Adams's Health, and Mrs. Smith and family and Mr. Boylstone And Mrs. and Mr. Gill &c."[68] A woman's patriotism, no less than her courtesy or grace, reflected well on herself and her male family members. Silas Deane described Esther DeBerdt Reed, wife of the Pennsylvania lawyer Joseph Reed, as "a Daughter of Liberty zealously affected in a good Cause."[69] The Massachusetts congressman Thomas Cushing did not bring his wife Deborah Fletcher Cushing to Philadelphia, but he did share several of her letters with John Dickinson, who admired the author's "calm & undaunted spirit."[70] These exchanges hint at the many roles women played in the creation of a patriotic community. They also reveal the considerable extent to which wives contributed to the reputation and social standing of their congressmen-husbands.[71] Numerous delegates in fact owed great portions of their wealth to their wives' dowries or inheritances. John Dickinson's "elegant" rural retreat, Fairhill, for example, had been the family home of his wife, Mary Norris, and would later descend to her fraternal cousins.[72]

Congressmen exhibited their fortunes and good breeding in a variety of other ways. Many congressmen brought servants to Philadelphia; some brought slaves. Thomas Jefferson, for example, arrived at the Second Continental Congress attended by three bondsmen: Jesse, Richard, and Jupiter, the last of whom worked as Jefferson's manservant.[73] Possession of slaves attested to a congressman's personal wealth. It provided opportunities for him to demonstrate the command or dominion expected of a gentleman, particularly of a Southern planter.[74] Other delegates found different means to display their prosperity or to vie for stature. Edward Rutledge of South Carolina, for example, trumpeted his education and urbanity, boasting of his three years' study at London's Inns of Court. Perhaps feeling self-conscious about his age—at twenty-five, he was the youngest delegate to Congress—Rutledge opined, "Gentlemen ought to travel early, because that freedom and Ease of Behaviour, which is so necessary, cannot be acquired but in early Life."[75]

Still other congressmen endeavored to prove themselves by their oratory, perhaps the most admired of all the eighteenth-century gentleman's talents.[76] Whether manifest in debate on the floor of Congress or in toasts at the City Tavern, oratorical ability betokened the gentleman's erudition: his command of the English language; his skill at rhetoric and logic; his learning in Greek, Roman, and British history; and above all else, his mastery of both reason and emotion. The Virginians Richard Henry Lee and Patrick Henry—hailed in Williamsburg as "the Demosthenes, & Cicero of America"—quickly distinguished themselves as the finest orators in Congress. John Adams described Lee as a "masterly Man." Silas Deane lamented that he could not convey in a letter the "Music" of Henry's voice "or the highwrought, yet Natural elegance of his Stile, & Manner."[77] By showcasing their erudition and talent, no less than their patriotism, congressmen such as Lee and Henry bandied for respect and influence.

Many of the New England delegates claimed not to put much stock in the riches of this world. John Adams, who would later be celebrated for his own "gravity and plain brown hair," wrote approvingly of the New Jersey delegate William Livingston, describing him as "a plain Man, tall, black, wears his Hair [as opposed to a powdered wig]—nothing elegant or genteel about him. They say he is no public Speaker, but very sensible, and learned, and a ready Writer." Similarly, the Connecticut delegate Silas Deane praised Thomas Lynch of South Carolina in a letter to his wife: "[C]ould You see him, I need say nothing more. . . . He wears the Manufacture of this Country, is plain, Sensible, above Ceremony, and carries with him more Force in his very appearance, than most powdered Folks, in their Conversation. He wears his hair strait, his Cloaths in the plainest order, and is highly esteemed."[78]

Yet even the sober and stern congressmen of New England could at times be carried away by the pretense of their new office. Samuel Adams's new suit of clothes attests both to the perceived importance of Congress and to the potency of fashion and material wealth as signifiers of social and political authority. Though not by nature disposed toward the pursuit of refinement, the elder Adams began to grasp the implications of self-presentation after serving only a few months in the Continental Congress. Adams, for instance, had long been averse to horseback riding. But in the late summer of 1775, as he traveled back to Philadelphia during a brief adjournment, his cousin John prompted him to descend from his carriage and take mount of a horse. "Some Degree of Skill and Dexterity in Horsemanship," John opined, goading Samuel from the carriage, "was necessary to the Character of a Statesman."[79] Upon retiring from Congress to Massachusetts in 1776, Adams's colleague Robert Treat Paine likewise began to apprehend that a statesman's public character depended on genteel performance. Perhaps anticipating his upcoming bid for state office, Paine did up his formerly "short straight hair" in a "Prodigious fore top, Ear Curls, and an immense quantity of hair tyed in a Club behind . . . in the true Macharoni stile."[80] This was the same Robert Treat Paine who at the First Continental Congress had raged against "fopperies and superfluities." For Adams and Paine, as for other congressmen, the imperative to statesmanlike fashionability trumped the imperative to patriotic sacrifice. Courtesy, eloquence, attire, horsemanship, and coiffure: these were all means by which suddenly self-conscious congressmen endeavored to prove themselves on a continental stage. Consequently, by mid-September 1775, just a few short months after the Battle of Bunker Hill, the New Jersey congressman Richard Smith had cause to lament that his homespun suit was an "Adornment few other Members can boast of."[81]

The final way in which gentility and splendor augmented the delegates' authority may be seen in two "elegant Entertainment[s]" hosted in Congress's honor. Colonial governments routinely sponsored dinners and balls to celebrate monarchs' birthdays, to commemorate imperial anniversaries, and to ring in the appointment of royal governors.[82] In the fall of 1774, the Philadelphia gentry and Pennsylvania officials independently resolved to fete the Continental Congress. In mid-September, local "gentlemen" welcomed five hundred guests—notable clergy, "genteel strangers," and "respectable citizens" "from every province on the Continent"—to a dinner at the state house. The Delaware congressman Caesar Rodney recorded that this gala was "intended to be the greatest en[t]ertainment that ever was made in this City, the Expence of Which is Computed to a Thousand pounds at least." The menu featured "a plenty of everything eatable, & drinkable & no scarcity of good Humor, & diversion."[83] (This first dinner took place on the very evening before Congress deliberated the Suffolk Resolves, and though the timing was coincidental, critics of Congress grieved that the feasting, the drinking of toasts, the music, and the firing of cannonade inebriated and impassioned the delegates on the eve of their auspicious vote.)[84] In late October, before Congress's business drew to a close, the Pennsylvania assembly hosted one hundred guests to a dinner at the City Tavern.[85] Though more modest than the first celebration, this dinner nevertheless united attendees in patriotic conviviality, while at the same time enabling them to jostle for social distinction through raiment and polite conversation. Extending the sphere of celebration, provincial newspapers circulated accounts of these events throughout the continent.[86]

As these few examples suggest, opulence, grandeur, and refinement were technologies of governance in the eighteenth century. The Crown and Parliament deployed them, as did colonial executives and legislatures. The Continental Congress, a nascent political institution of questionable constitutionality and arguably rebellious intent, utilized these same mechanisms to legitimize its power. But by adopting the material signifiers of political authority, Congress placed itself at odds with the virtuous self-denial demanded by its own Articles of Association.

Congress's disregard for the Association did not provoke immediate outcry among the people out of doors. Rather, its bold scheme of economic resistance rapidly mobilized patriots in defense of their rights. Rechanneling agricultural, mercantile, and artisanal energies, nonimportation and the imminent nonexportation began to transform the economies of British North America. Throughout Congress's host city, cottage industries sprang up for the making of glass, carpets, spermaceti, "American porter," and saltpeter. In the spring of 1775, a group of prominent Whigs, including Christopher Marshall, established the United Company of Philadelphia for Promoting American Manufactures. Funded by private subscription, this organization employed more than four hundred women to process raw cotton, linen, and wool purchased from local farmers. Meanwhile, Pennsylvania's provincial convention entertained proposals for the domestic production of metal and metalwares, including plates, nails, wire, and kettles.[87]

Ironically, even as the Association's economic and moral provisions functioned to preserve social order, its enforcement provisions—that is, its call for the establishment of committees of observation—tended to democratize local politics. During the Townshend crisis of the late 1760s, Philadelphia's artisans and mechanics came to recognize their mutual interests and influence. Soon these urban laborers began to cohere as a political force.[88] In November 1774, this radicalized bloc of voters elected a large and remarkably heterogeneous committee to oversee Congress's trade boycotts. As the historian Richard Ryerson has observed, the Committee of Observation and Inspection "gave every occupational group and every class above the level of unskilled laborer," as well as most religious denominations and the city's minority German population, "a direct and significant voice in political affairs for the first time in Philadelphia's history."[89] Just a few months later, in April 1775, the outbreak of hostilities at Lexington and Concord further politicized Philadelphia's laboring classes. Roused by news of the British offensive, nearly eight thousand Philadelphians turned out to defend "their Property, Liberty, and lives." These volunteers, who came mostly from the ranks of the working poor, quickly organized themselves into companies and battalions.[90]

This initial enthusiasm did not endure: by the autumn of 1775 declining commerce and incessant preparations for war began to exact an economic and psychological toll on the British colonists. Months of aggressive nonimportation dampened colonial business. Nonexportation loomed grimly on the horizon. To make matters worse, Parliament responded to the Continental Congress and its Association by restraining trade with the American colonies.[91] In Pennsylvania, local authorities secured the Delaware River against naval attack by sinking chevaux-de-frise, whose iron-clad points jutted forth from the murk knowing no distinction between naval and merchant hulls. Between September 1775 and March 1776, Philadelphia's import tonnage fell 66 percent off its peacetime average, leaving river pilots to fish and dredge oysters for their livelihood.[92]

Amid this economic turmoil, class tension began to percolate. The city's battalions—whose ranks swelled with craftsmen, journeymen, and manual laborers, many of whom had lost their incomes to the escalating imperial trade war—became loci of political agitation. Working-rank soldiers organized to demand political rights and military reforms. They insisted that they receive pay for their training, that they be allowed to wear inexpensive hunting shirts, and that the hardships of war be distributed equitably, across class lines, through a system of compulsory military service.[93] This last point carried particular weight, for many associators believed that Pennsylvania's wealthy inhabitants, including members of the pacifist Quaker community, had unfairly ducked their fair share of military duty. Writing to the Pennsylvania assembly, the Chester County committeeman and future brigadier general Anthony Wayne lamented, "[T]he burthen of [military obligation] falls chiefly on the poor and middling sort of the inhabitants,—whilst the more opulent are, for the most part, exempt [sic]."[94] Pennsylvania's working-rank soldiers refused to bear the war's every brunt.

At the same time, Philadelphia's laboring classes, who most fully felt the weight of the war and who had voluntarily sacrificed many of life's comforts for the cause of liberty, began to lose patience with Congress's high living. Newspaper reports of the substantial sums of money that various colonial or provincial authorities set aside to defray their congressmen's expenses could have only deepened the public's dismay. South Carolina, for example, allotted £300 for each of its five representatives to the First Continental Congress. Connecticut and Rhode Island provided every delegate three dollars per day, plus expenses, as well as the use of two horses and a servant. Even Pennsylvania congressmen, who did not travel or require lodgings, received twenty shillings per day in office.[95] Hoping to capitalize on popular discontent, loyalist writers protested congressional exorbitance. Writing as a "friend to peace and good order," the Massachusetts pamphleteer Harrison Gray objected that Congress assembled "with all the pomp and grandeur of Plenipotentiaries."[96]

The fullest and most forceful critique of congressional "pomp and grandeur" appeared in The Poor Man's Advice to His Poor Neighbours, a spirited ballad published anonymously in pamphlet form by the New York newspaperman James Rivington shortly after the First Continental Congress adjourned.[97] The Poor Man's Advice cautioned would-be patriots against the social injustices inherent in the Articles of Association. Though the author of this ballad may not have actually been a poor man, he or she captured precisely the spirit of class indignation that prompted out-of-doors Philadelphians to threaten the City Tavern one year later. The Poor Man wrote for a workfolk audience, setting his "advice" to the tune of the popular English anthem "Chevy Chace" and peppering his lyrics with mild vulgarities. He or she distilled an array of arguments against Congress and its Association into simple, humorous verse. The Poor Man asserted that George III was a "just and good" sovereign aggrieved by the colonists' insubordination. He denounced Congress's scheme of economic resistance as a conspiracy of New England smugglers. He railed against "Congress spies," that is, committeemen such as Christopher Marshall, who the Poor Man feared would soon come snooping through private homes and shops without judicial authority. And he predicted that rather than winning redress for American grievances the Association would provoke a war that would prove profitable for English merchants but deadly for impoverished soldiers.[98]

As evident in the latter claim, the Poor Man's "advice" drew much of its poignancy from the author's sensitivity to class politics and resentment. Unlike most critics, who portrayed members of the Continental Congress as debtors, bankrupts, and men of *"desperate fortunes,"* the Poor Man suggested that congressional delegates were rather too *wealthy* to fairly represent the interests of ordinary people.[99] The Poor Man opened his ballad by questioning whether members of Congress truly understood Americans' needs and interests:

> AH! have you read, my neighbours dear,
> Our famous *Congress* Book?
> Alas! I grievously do fear
> They have our case mistook.[100]

More scandalously, the Poor Man alleged that disingenuous congressmen had hoarded foodstuffs and consumer goods so that they could continue to live the high life, even as working people suffered under the Association:

> They've tea in plenty for themselves,
> And other good things too,
> Be we, alas, poor wretched elves,
> Shall not know what to do.
> They've all laid in great stock of things,
> To last them many a year,
> For they're as rich as any Kings,
> But what shall poor folks wear?

The Poor Man accused congressional delegates of flaunting their wealth. He even predicted that members of Congress would continue to indulge in gay and frivolous pastimes, contrary to the eighth Article of the Association:

> They'll ride in coach and chariot fine,
> And go to ball, and play,
> When we've not wherewithal to dine,
> Though we work hard all day.[101]

Appealing not simply to the independent spirit of freeborn Englishmen, but more particularly to the pridefulness of the laboring classes, the Poor Man urged his poor neighbors not to be made the "harrant fools" of Congress, not to be bent "like pliant coil." By presuming to dictate the minutia of Americans' lives, Congress, the Poor Man suggested, had worked a greater tyranny, in the name of liberty no less, than ever the king or Parliament. With bitter sarcasm he declared,

> Rare sons of freedom, this Congress!
> So just as they think right,
> We are to eat,—drink,—frolick,—dress;
> Pray masters, may we s[hit]e.[102]

The Poor Man's Advice might be dismissed as a crude appeal to class prejudice, or even as mere cynicism, but for two countervailing considerations. First, members of Congress *did* "ride in coach and chariot fine" and "go to ball, and play." Second, within a year of the Poor Man's publication, Congress's flagrant conviviality would drive the distressed people of Philadelphia fully to the brink of riot.

Laying bare the Continental Congress's most fundamental pretense to power, the Poor Man's allegations help us to understand the threats thrown out against the City Tavern. In Philadelphia, popular frustration with Congress and its ostentatious governance came to a head at precisely the same time of year when the fall fair *would* have taken place had not the city council forbidden it. On the twenty-first of November 1775, Martha Washington arrived in town while traveling en route to visit her husband at his camp outside of Boston. Greatly acclaimed and saluted along her journey, she received a dignitary's welcome. Philadelphia's Second Battalion, commanded by Colonel Daniel Roberdeau, greeted Washington at the Schuylkill River and escorted her into the city under the arms of light infantry and horse. Meanwhile, several of her friends—including, presumably, the congressmen from Virginia—organized a ball to be held at the City Tavern in her honor.[103] John Hancock, president of Congress, and his wife, Dorothy, were rumored to be on the guest list.[104]

News that a ball had been scheduled for the evening of November 24 filtered into the streets and angered the people of Philadelphia. Perhaps the preparatory commotion at the tavern garnered attention, or perhaps the anticipatory chatter of the guests caught an indignant ear. Whatever the case, the people out of doors became agitated and rumors of an attack against the

City Tavern began to swirl about town. We do not know who threw out these threats. If Marshall had any inkling, he did not record their names. But we may imaginatively reconstruct the intentions of whoever menacingly warned, "[T]he New Tavern would cut but a poor figure to-morrow." The historian and folklorist Robert Blair St. George has illustrated that house assaults such as the one threatened here were not mere acts "of frenzied vandalism," but rather "performed different kinds of cultural work on a variety of symbolic levels." For some participants, the house assault expressed a moral judgment against inhabitants who behaved in some abominable way. For others, the house assault articulated a social impulse, the leveling of wealth and distinction, as well as a related, communitarian concern that the residents of the house had taken unfair advantage of their wealth, to the detriment of their poor neighbors.[105]

By these criteria, the City Tavern made an easy and obvious target. As the site of the proposed ball, it bore the taint of members of Congress and local elites who, though professing patriotism, appeared to thumb their noses at the Association, even as laboring people suffered without daily necessities. More generally, the City Tavern structurally embodied the social authority of Philadelphia elites. Erected in 1772–73 for the substantial sum of three thousand pounds, the tavern had been financed by the subscriptions of fifty-two of the city's leading citizens as well as by a sizable loan from John Penn. Finished and furnished to suit the most proper tastes, the tavern had been built in mimicry of the finest establishments of London. On his first arrival in Philadelphia, John Adams proclaimed it the "most genteel" tavern in America. By threatening to raze this structure, the people of Philadelphia signaled their growing disdain for the city's hierarchical social order. They insisted that the Association be equitably enforced, even against Congress.[106]

Marshall and Samuel Adams could afford neither the black mark on Congress and its Association nor the deep tear in Philadelphia's social fabric. And they had good reason to take the threats seriously. Earlier that same fall, an incensed Philadelphia crowd—said to consist of militiamen, "lads," "hearty jolly tars," and "market people"—attacked the home of John Kearsley, "a violent enemy of the cause," breaking his windows, doors, and furniture with stones and brickbats.[107] Adams, of course, also remembered the Stamp Act crowds of August 1765, which tore the Massachusetts lieutenant governor Thomas Hutchinson's house to the ground and ransacked the homes and offices of three other admiralty and customs officers.[108] These house-razing crowds meant business. And so both men worked quickly to prevent the evening's entertainment. After leaving Adams, Marshall proceeded to Philosophical

The City Tavern, site of numerous congressional banquets and celebrations, was in November 1775 an object of popular ire. Detail of "Bank of Pennsylvania, South Second Street Philadelphia," drawn, engraved, and published by William Birch and Son (1800; restrike, Philadelphia, 1860). The Library Company of Philadelphia.

Hall, where a specially convened meeting of the Committee of Inspection and Observation debated the "propriety" of the event. "After due and mature consideration," the committee determined that the ball should be canceled and no other balls organized "while these troublesome times continued." The committee then appointed several members to present their apologies to Martha Washington and beg her cooperation. Finally, Adams urged President Hancock to exert his sway against the ball. By these actions, Marshall and Adams managed to avert potential disaster. Assuaged by the ball's cancellation, the townspeople did not gather that evening, and the City Tavern lived to entertain another day.

Not all congressmen felt that justice had been served. That same evening, the Virginian Benjamin Harrison proceeded to Adams's lodgings to "rebuke" him for preventing the ball. Harrison believed that the reception and entertainment of dignitaries such as Martha Washington were important and legitimate undertakings. A friend to the Washington family, Harrison protested that the intended ball was "legal, just and laudable." Certainly the traditions and social practices of British America's ruling gentry provided ample precedent. But had Harrison more carefully studied the history of Congress's Association, he might have known better. Earlier that year, in Harrison's home colony of Virginia, the propriety of dancing had come into question. In January, a *Virginia Gazette* correspondent begged his representatives in Congress to clarify, "purely for the information of many well-meaning people," whether "a ball tending to an innocent and pleasing intercourse between the two sexes . . . calculated evidently upon a frugal plan, [would] be deemed extravagant, or fall under the description of dissipation?" Since that time, at least two patriot committees had answered that question decisively. In Marblehead, Massachusetts, a committee determined "that the meeting of the inhabitants of this town in parties at houses of entertainment . . . for the purposes of dancing, feasting, &c. is expressly against the Association." The Marblehead committee further forbade "extraordinary entertainments in private houses," and cautioned residents against even "the most distant appearance of a violation." Similarly, a Wilmington, North Carolina, committee concluded that "all private, as well as public dances, are contrary to the spirit of the 8th article in the Association."[109] Harrison and the organizers of the proposed ball either did not know that Americans had given up such festivities, or they believed that their station in Congress justified their behavior. Impatient with the "[m]any arguments" proffered against him, Harrison left in as foul humor as he came.[110]

The City Tavern crisis portended many of the social transformations that the coming Revolution would sweep across the Atlantic seaboard. By threatening to tear down the "most genteel" establishment in America, the people of Philadelphia demanded that ordinary folk and political leaders alike be held accountable to the Articles of Association. They insisted that the burdens of the imperial conflict be distributed fairly among all classes. And they tendered a penetrating critique against the material and ceremonial underpinnings both of polite society and, more pointedly, of a nascent congressional political culture. Notwithstanding Benjamin Harrison's grievances, the City Tavern episode brought about a temporary settlement in Philadelphia's social life. For the next two years, the people of that city honored the Association and kept the orders of their Committee of Inspection and Observation. They tolerated no theater or fairs and attended few if any balls. Congress, too, in all of its social affairs and civic events aspired to promote a spirit of simplicity and austerity. Not until September 1777, when the British army invaded the city, would Philadelphians again witness the gaiety and frivolity they had known before.

2

The Continental Congress Unmanned

WHEN, IN THE FALL OF 1774, the Continental Congress published the Articles of Association, announcing a scheme of nonimportation, nonexportation, and nonconsumption to be enforced by extralegal committees of local patriots, many British North Americans felt betrayed. Colonists who bristled at the prospect of economic resistance—either because they feared that aggressive political posturing would widen the breach between the colonies and Great Britain or simply because they dreaded the baneful financial consequences of yet another boycott—had expected the Continental Congress to embrace more conciliatory measures, much as had the Stamp Act Congress ten years before. "The hopes of all moderate and considerate persons among us . . . were long fixed upon the general *American Congress*," wrote the Reverend Thomas Bradbury Chandler, rector of St. John's Church in Elizabethtown, New Jersey. "But the poor *Americans*," he despondently concluded, "are doomed to disappointment."[1]

Among the most vociferous of these disappointed Americans were three Anglican clergymen from New York and New Jersey. In addition to Chandler, these included Samuel Seabury, rector of St. Peter's Church in Westchester, and Myles Cooper, president of King's College in New York. Over the past ten years, these clerics had watched with alarm as a nascent American resistance movement developed momentum. Deeply devoted to

the Church of England and to the Crown that sustained it, these clergymen blamed much of the era's political agitation on dissenting churches,
which they believed threatened monarchy and bred civil discord. "Independency in Religion," protested a committee of Anglican churchmen,
"will naturally produce Republicans in the State."[2] During the Stamp Act
Crisis of 1765, this Episcopal trio championed the Anglican Church as a
bulwark against "Clamour & Discontent." At decade's end, they began to
lobby for the appointment of an American bishop, provoking the ire of
Congregationalists and Presbyterians, and clashing in the pamphlet war
that ensued with a number of strident Whigs, including a few—Samuel
Adams, William Livingston, and John Morin Scott—who later served as
delegates to the Continental Congress.[3] In the late 1760s or early 1770s,
Chandler, Seabury, and Cooper entered a pact: fearing that republican
dissenters would dash their hopes for a bishopric, or worse, that they would
overwhelm royal administration, these clergymen agreed to "watch and
confute all publications that threatened mischief to the Church of England and the British government in America."[4]

After the Continental Congress circulated its Articles of Association,
these clergymen sprang to action. Taking up their pens, they drafted numerous
essays, poems, and plays denouncing Congress's boycotts. Joining these writers
in opposition to Congress were the New York assemblyman Isaac Wilkins,
Boston loyalists Harrison Gray and Jonathan Sewall, and a host of pseudonymous and anonymous pamphleteers.[5] During the sixth-month adjournment
between the First Continental Congress and the Second, these "disappointed"
Americans published nearly two dozen oppositional tracts.[6] Their titles—*Pills
for the Delegates*, *The Two Congresses Cut Up*, *What Think Ye of the* Congress
Now?—announced their authors' aim to undermine the Continental Congress and thwart its Association.

Many of these writers tendered sound constitutional, political, and economic arguments.[7] Chandler and his loyalist contemporaries claimed that
colonial assemblies and provincial conventions did not possess the authority
to appoint delegates to a general congress. They asserted that Americans owed
no obedience to such an irregularly assembled body. They challenged the legal
right of local committees to monitor the business activities of merchants,
traders, and other private persons. And they warned that a trade boycott
would bring ruin to American farmers.

Yet, in addition to disputing the legality of Congress and the wisdom of its
resolutions, these authors also poured a great deal of scorn on the delegates
who had gathered in Philadelphia. Numerous writers inserted derogatory

comments about the congressmen into their pamphlets: contemptuous dicta amid more formal arguments against the Association. But a few went further, penning humorous and bounding satires wholly dedicated to smearing the members of Congress. These writers almost never singled out congressmen for attack; some, in fact, expressly denied any intention to do so. Chandler opened his essay *What Think Ye of the Congress Now?* by asserting, "I mean to avoid all personal reflexions upon the members of the Congress; for I never had any personal objections to any of them."[8] But though these writers rarely slurred particular individuals, they relentlessly assailed the Congress as a group or order of men.

One of the foremost strategies by which loyalist pamphleteers and poets attempted to delegitimize the Continental Congress was by attacking the masculinity of its members. Directly targeting a faction of Massachusetts and Virginia radicals supposed to have prevailed in the Congress, these authors invoked an array of bigotries, including bigotries of region and religion as well as of class and race. Quite often, though, these authors couched such attacks in, or bundled them with, equally or even more damning imputations of gender inadequacy or deviance. The Continental Congress, in fact, had invited this gendered political rhetoric. By predicating the American resistance on the opposition of manly virtue to effeminate luxury, and by staking its institutional legitimacy on the delegates' stature as genteel white men, the Continental Congress made gender a matter of public discourse and controversy. Whereas the crowd that threatened to tear down the City Tavern feared that members of Congress were too rich to fairly represent the interests of ordinary Americans, the loyalist pamphleteers who wrote in the winter of 1774–75 believed that those delegates were the wrong sort of men to rule: undisciplined, weak willed, not worldly enough, not wealthy enough, not even white enough.

These writers depicted New Englanders in Congress as a crush of raving, fanatical zealots incapable of masculine self-control. They portrayed Southern congressmen as cuckolded or domineering husbands intemperate in their relations with women. These authors decried the Congress as a band of boorish and provincial colonists. They slighted the congressmen's social stature and professional accomplishments, describing them as lowborn, oafish laborers or, at best, bungling lawyers who had never traveled to England and who understood little of the world's affairs. They questioned the delegates' claims to the authority of white Englishmen, suggesting that life among "savages" and slaves had racially debauched the American gentry and rendered it ill-suited to govern. In short, these authors held Continental

Congressmen to a standard of white, aristocratic, and imperial masculinity and found them desperately wanting.

A careful analysis of numerous anticongressional essays, as well as two particularly contemptuous poems, *A Dialogue between a Southern Delegate and His Spouse on His Return from the Grand Continental Congress* and *The Patriots of North-America: A Sketch*, reveals that loyalist writers attacked the Articles of Association not merely by challenging its legal and economic merits, but also by censuring the men who had made it.[9] By calling into question the delegates' gender, as well as their class and race, these critics struck at the political legitimacy of the Continental Congress. Members of Congress seldom responded directly to these attacks. But as Congress began to invent a material and ceremonial identity for the United Colonies, the delegates self-consciously asserted the rightfulness, respectability, and manliness of their authority.

"[A] rational Man acts better"

Loyalist writers claimed that a cabal of New England republicans had gained the upper hand in Congress, foisting their radical agenda on more moderate delegates. Thomas Bradbury Chandler explicitly accused these New England conspirators of plotting for independence. "It has been long suspected," Chandler declared, "that a set of people in the Colonies, whose head quarters are at Boston, have for many years been aiming at, and preparing the way for, a government of their own modelling, independent of Great Britain."[10] To bring Congress and its program of economic resistance into disrepute, Chandler and his fellow penmen appealed to deeply engrained regional prejudices. They played on New Yorkers' disdain for their neighbors to the east. Samuel Seabury, for example, depicted New England delegates as miserly Yankees. He decried the "suspicious, jealous, parsimonious, stingy, contracted disposition" by which Congress refused to pay British taxes.[11] Seabury further alluded to long-standing territorial conflicts that pitted honest New Yorkers against covetous New Englanders, most recently in the disputed Green Mountain region. He implied that Massachusetts congressmen secretly schemed to establish an eastern republic carved out of New York lands.[12] Seabury even balked at Congress's recommendation that the colonies raise funds to relieve the distressed Bostonians. "Must they command the wealth of the continent?" he fumed. "Do they expect a *literal* completion of the promise, that the *Saints shall inherit the earth?*"[13] Seabury's allusion to

Scripture was not mere wordplay, but rather snide sectarian derision. In addition to castigating the New England "Saints" for their avaricious ways, Seabury and other Anglican pamphleteers alluded, acerbically, to the low-church origins of the American resistance. To mobilize readers against the Articles of Association, these writers drew upon a gendered discourse of mental illness and bodily disorder that dated to antiquity but that had been revitalized decades before during the so-called Great Awakening.[14]

During the mid-eighteenth century, a succession of evangelical revivals unfolded across many parts of British North America, popularizing new modes of religious expression and destabilizing the authority of established churches.[15] Old Lights—as skeptical clergymen such as Charles Chauncy, Samuel Mather, and Mather Byles came to be known—charged that the hordes of persons who flocked to these revivals had been deluded by ardor or zeal. These critics accused New Light ministers of exciting worshippers' emotions, rather than appealing to reason. As one correspondent to the *Pennsylvania Gazette* complained shortly after the charismatic itinerant George Whitefield toured Philadelphia in 1740, "Such whining, roaring Harangues, big with affected Nonsense, have no other Tendency, but to operate upon the softer Passions, and work them up to a warm Pitch of Enthusiasm."[16]

Old Lights noted with particular contempt the ecstatic bodily movements by which New Light evangelicals expressed repentance and experienced salvation. Enthusiasts, one alarmed observer protested, "*cried out, fell down, swooned away*, and, to all Appearance, were like Persons in *Fits*."[17] To the Old Light imagination, this sort of convulsive behavior suggested mental disorder. Old Lights frequently described religious enthusiasm as a form of madness. The author of an "Essay upon Enthusiasm," printed in the *Boston Post Boy* in 1741, cautioned readers, "Of all sorts of Madness, a religious Delirium is that which calls for the most Pity. . . . Religion and Reason are, and ought to be good friends, but . . . *Enthusiasm* is an enemy to both. A *mad Man* may mean well, but a *rational Man* acts better."[18] William Hooper, pastor of the West Church in Boston, objected more emphatically: "[H]ow base and unmanly is it . . . to give our selves up to the blind and mad Suggestions of an heated and disorderly Brain!" As Hooper's condemnation of "base and unmanly" forms of worship reveals, Old Light clerics described and decried religious enthusiasm in explicitly gendered terms. They denounced New Light ministers for the particular influence they bore on the supposedly weaker minds of women and children. They distinguished "*a rapturous Kind of Joy*" from the "much more desirable . . . manly, solid, stable Satisfaction of Soul." And they demanded "more manly things" of Whitefield's supporters.[19]

CREDULITY, SUPERSTITION, and FANATICISM.
A MEDLEY.

Believe not every Spirit but try the Spirits whether they are of God, because many false Prophets are gone out into the World.

1. John. C.4. V.1.

Design'd and Engrav'd by W.m Hogarth.

Publish'd as the Act directs March .r 15.th 1762.

Foes of the Continental Congress attributed to its members the same emotional and bodily excesses that William Hogarth vividly ascribed to a congregation under the enthusiastic sway of a Whitefieldian preacher. William Hogarth, "Credulity, Superstition, and Fanaticism. A Medley" (London, 1762). © The Trustees of the British Museum.

Like those Old Light clerics, the Anglican churchmen who opposed the Continental Congress espoused a liberal and rational theology. They disdained impassioned or mystical conversion experiences. Chandler himself once even refused to lend his pulpit to the itinerant George Whitefield.[20] To discredit the Continental Congress, Chandler and other loyalist critics likened radical New England delegates to religious enthusiasts and fanatics. A character in Jonathan Sewall's play *The Americans Roused*, for example, lamented that since the publication of Congress's Association, "civil war is openly talked of, with a blind, enthusiastic zeal, equal to that which in former days, crowded friend Whitefield's lectures."[21] Samuel Seabury likewise faulted the congressmen of New York for not more stridently opposing the New Englanders' "fiery intemperate zeal."[22] By accusing New England delegates of zealotry, loyalist pamphleteers suggested that these radicals had given themselves over to unmanly emotional excess.

To further disparage the Massachusetts representatives and their collaborators, loyalist writers invoked the Old Lights' rhetoric of madness. In the epigram of his essay *The Congress Canvassed*, Samuel Seabury asked his readers whether the proceedings of Congress more closely resembled "the Deliberations of Wisdom, or the Ravings of Phrenzy?" In yet another hostile pamphlet, *A View of the Controversy*, Seabury answered that question directly, proclaiming that the Association was the work of "Virginia and Massachusetts madmen." "Virginia and Massachusetts madmen?" he rhetorically protested:

> Aye, *madmen;—mad* beyond all doubt;—so *mad*, that an acre of Hellebore a piece will not cure them. . . . They *talked* like madmen: They *acted* like madmen: They *raved* like madmen: They *did every thing* like madmen:—Then why not *call* them madmen?—Why not? Why! they were the *representatives* of the people. And very fit representatives too. It could not be expected that *mad* people would send any other than *mad* representatives;—and *mad* work they made when they got together.[23]

Thomas Bradbury Chandler likewise urged his readers to resist "the madmen of *New-England* in their scheme of an *Independent Republic*."[24] Chandler proclaimed that he abhorred the Congress because it had behaved like "a perfect monster,—a *mad, blind* monster!"[25]

Representing the New England delegates' supposed madness in graphic, bodily terms, Seabury, Chandler, and other loyalist writers attributed to congressional radicals the same sort of bodily fits and contortions that had so disgusted a generation of Old Light ministers. Myles Cooper, for example, asserted that American patriots defied the "Laws of God, and Man" with a "furious Mein, and Blood shot Eye."[26] Grotius, the pseudonymous author of *Pills for the Delegates*, claimed that Congress endorsed the inflammatory Suffolk Resolves in a "paroxism of epidemic madness."[27] Isaac Wilkins likened Congress's course of resistance to the "unaccountable freaks of a madman."[28] These slurs—"Phrenzy," "paroxysm," and "freaks"—connoted violent spasms symptomatic of mental derangement. With this rhetoric, loyalist critics portrayed members of Congress as men who could discipline neither their bodies nor their minds.[29]

None of these accusations bore a semblance of reality. Rather, the charge of blind enthusiasm and fiery zeal functioned as a powerful metaphor of a kind of unmanly behavior that many contemporary readers found repugnant. Eighteenth-century British society counseled would-be gentlemen to act with a high degree of self-restraint, to govern their bodies and to regulate their passions on almost every occasion. Anglo-Americans countenanced well-moderated displays of sentiment among men, including weeping, embracing, and kissing. They also tolerated measured displays of anger and indignity, particularly in defense of personal honor or reputation. But they generally frowned on emotional caprice and physical abandon.[30] By representing New England delegates as immoderate, undisciplined, and irrational men, loyalist writers overtly impugned the congressmen's masculinity. In opposition to congressmen's lack of manly self-restraint, loyalist writers celebrated the virtues of temperate manhood: "prudence, firmness, and moderation." These admirable masculine qualities, loyalists claimed, were not to be found among "Enthusiastic delegates and brain-sick committee-men."[31]

"Wou'd! instead of Delegates, they'd sent Delegates Wives"

Foes of Congress portrayed New England delegates as fitful radicals who could not govern their emotional or rational faculties. In the same breath, they disparaged Southern congressmen as henpecked husbands and enfeebled patriarchs who could not govern their wives. In December 1774, shortly after the First Continental Congress adjourned, the loyalist newspaperman James Rivington published *A Dialogue between a Southern Delegate and His Spouse on His Return from the Grand Continental Congress*, written by the pseudonymous Mary V. V.[32] A brazen attack on congressional masculinity—the Philadelphia patriot William Bradford deemed it "grossly scurrilous"—this satire offered readers a glimpse of marital discord in one Southern congressman's household.[33] Across fourteen pages of versified dialogue, the delegate's wife chides Congress and its radical measures. The wife accuses Congress of usurping the powers of government; she proclaims that Congress's Articles of Association fall "little short" of high treason; and she protests that the committees Congress had empowered to enforce the Association would have shamed a Roman inquisitor or a Moroccan despot.[34]

The rhetorical power of *A Dialogue between a Southern Delegate and His Spouse*, however, derived less from its allegations of *political* malfeasance than from its allegations of *gender* malfeasance, that is, from its central assertion that this frail and irresolute congressman had surrendered his rightful domestic authority to his bride. The very action that shapes the *Dialogue*'s dramatic structure—a wife rebuking her husband—fundamentally challenges the southern delegate's command over his household. From the first page, the author makes apparent that this "dialogue" is no mere conversation, certainly no welcome-home greeting. Rather, the dialogue is a contentious dispute, and the congressman-husband is getting the worst of it. Futilely urging his wife to pipe down, to "be a little discreet" lest she "alarm the whole Street," the delegate reveals himself to be an emasculated husband whose scolding wife has publicly repudiated his claim to the head of their house.

Neighbors already know that the congressman's wife wears the pants in his family. They call him "Jerry Sneak," after the submissive, cuckolded title character whom a whimsical mob elected to office in Samuel Foote's popular play, *The Mayor of Garratt* (1763). But though the neighbors consider his wife's bossiness "Sport," the congressman moans that to him, "[I]t is Death."[35] By this lament, the congressman acknowledges that his patriarchal command, especially as performed in the community eye, is the essence of his life. His wife's usurpation thus amounts to murder, a figurative petit treason, abhorrent both to the family and the state.[36] And yet she refuses to relent. She expresses mock concern that her husband had been bitten by a mad dog, he so "foam[s]" and "slaver[s]." When her husband commands her not to "dabble" in politics, she laughs in his face.[37]

The lesson for readers was clear: this congressman is a weak man who cannot control his wife. Such would have been an unflattering accusation for any male head of house in early-modern Anglo-America. The sanctity of a husband's authority over his wife found pretext in the Bible, in prescriptive literature, and in centuries of European folk custom. Well before the late eighteenth century, the henpecked husband—and his even less manly kinsman, the cuckold—emerged as stock characters for the derision of

English audiences.[38] But in singling out a Southern delegate, the *Dialogue* offered an especially ruinous critique. As many scholars have demonstrated, the reputation and social cachet of the Southern planter derived not only from his wealth, but in large part too from his mastery over dependents, namely his family, servants, and slaves.[39] Perhaps for this reason, Virginia almanacs of the 1770s repeatedly ranted against henpeckery. "He who marries a wife whose tongue rings like a bell," admonished the *Virginia Almanack* in 1770, "had better have his brains knocked out with the clapper. To such a henpecked fellow his wife's tongue is as terrible as thunder; her presence shakes the house like an earthquake."[40] The *Dialogue's* Southern congressman married just such a bell ringer. Sounding throughout the neighborhood, her "clapper" rattles the very foundations of his social stature. Just as disparagingly, the wife asserts that her planter-husband's supposed dominion over his dependents is not equal to that which will be required of him in Congress:

> Thou born! thou! the Machine of an Empire to wield?
> Art thou wise in Debate? Should'st feel bold in the Field?
> If thou'st Wisdom to manage Tobacco, and Slave,
> It's as much as God ever design'd thee to have.[41]

The author thus contended that not even the great planters of Virginia and the Carolinas, for all their wealth and power, were qualified to represent the American colonies in their controversy with Parliament.[42]

After his wife's harangue, the Southern delegate pathetically apologizes for his conduct in Philadelphia. He admits that Congress took rash measures; indeed, he implies that members of Congress endorsed the Suffolk Resolves only because they were drunk. In a Congress "o'er heated with Wine," the Southern delegate shamefully explains, "Stark Fools" became "Sages" and "rank Cowards" grew "valiant." Himself but "a meek Husband," who "dares not" speak against his own wife, the Southern delegate felt powerless to "Oppose such a Torrent."[43] On the day that Congress voted its support for the Suffolk Resolves, the Massachusetts representative John Adams exulted in his diary, "In Congress We had generous, noble Sentiments, and manly Eloquence."[44] But the *Dialogue* told a different story, one in which *un*manly timidity imperiled the British nation.

Humiliated by his powerlessness and abashed by his behavior in Congress, the Southern delegate becomes angry. As the *Dialogue* progresses, the delegate reveals himself to be not merely a weak husband but, no less despicable, a would-be tyrant. Like Jerry Sneak, the character in Foote's play, the

One loyalist writer caricaturized Southern congressmen as weak, wife-ridden husbands, much like the spiritless fellow depicted here. "The Hen Peck'd Grocer" (1778). The Colonial Williamsburg Foundation. The verse reads: "Bred in the Learn'd Schools of Billingsgate / Behold this Beauty Cudgeling her Mate / Hoarse Grown with Rhetorick, she now Assists / The want of that, by Potent use of Fists. / Fierce as a Tygress, to his Back she Flies / & at his head the well known Cudgel Plys."

congressman attempts to reassert his authority over his wife. Though in the past he has suffered his wife to lead him "by the Nose," he now insists, "[F]or once I will speak." Reminding his wife of her place as a "Woman of Fashion," he chastises her "indecent" behavior. When she expresses her dread that the Association will bring not redress, but rather "Perdition and Murder," the delegate dismisses her fears as "Rant" and "Bombast." He belittlingly accuses his wife of "heating" her brain by reading "Romances, and Plays."[45] At last fed up with his wife's harangue, he admonishes her not to interfere in affairs of state, but rather to return to her proper confinement within the domestic sphere: "Mind thy Household-Affairs, teach thy Children to read, / And never, Dear, with Politics, trouble thy Head." Making a bitter mockery of his wife's meddling in politics, the husband exclaims, "You're so patient, so cool, so monstrous eloquent / Next Congress, my Empress, shall be made President."[46]

This oxymoronic epithet, "monstrous eloquent," suggests that the delegate-husband sees something grotesque in his wife's oratorical abilities. A woman who can speak articulately and persuasively on political subjects represents, for the husband, a perversion of the proper gender order, much as would a female president of Congress. But for contemporary readers of the *Dialogue*, it was the congressman-husband, more so than his spouse, who transgressed gender norms. The author of the *Dialogue* portrayed the Southern delegate as both unmasculine and hypermasculine. The delegate veers wildly from one extreme of immoderate husbandly behavior, his piteous submission to his wife, to another, his despotic lording over her. At either extreme, he deviates from the eighteenth-century norm of a firm and assertive, but not domineering, husband. His very lack of restraint ran afoul of the ideal of well-tempered manhood.[47] Through the delegate's efforts to dominate his wife, no less than the condescension with which he speaks to her, the author of the *Dialogue* suggested that members of Congress were cruel and oppressive men. That the *Dialogue* represented congressmen simultaneously as both servile and overbearing need not be understood as a contradiction, for both of those attributes signified an aberration from normative masculinity.

By accentuating the congressman's domestic tyranny, the author of *A Dialogue between a Southern Delegate and His Spouse* artfully rehabilitates the character of the wife. Casting the delegate as an object of contempt and disdain, the author renders his spouse an object of sympathy. At the *Dialogue*'s end, the wife emerges not as an obnoxious, overbearing nag, as Jerry Sneak's wife does, but rather as a dedicated helpmeet who feels a strong concern both for her family and for the welfare of her country. She also stakes her ground as an admirable advocate for the rights of women. In response to her husband's insistence that she butt out of state affairs, the wife challenges the patriarchal underpinnings of his gendered-sphere ideology. "Because Men are Males, are they all Politicians?" the wife asks. "Why then I presume they're Divines and Physicians." The wife further asserts that the women of America could have done a much better job in Congress than did the men. "Wou'd! instead of Delegates, they'd sent Delegates Wives; / Heavens! we cou'dn't have bungled it so for our Lives!"[48]

The wife's retort served as a strong commentary against masculinist assumptions about women's roles in eighteenth-century society. It will be recalled that the author of this *Dialogue* adopted a female pseudonym, Mary V. V. In so doing, the author signaled his or her sympathy for the feminist or proto-feminist views expressed by the Southern wife. Notably, Mary V. V. dedicated her *Dialogue* "To the Married Ladies of *America*," thus inviting female readers to critically reflect on the gendered balance of power within their own households. But this dedication also served as a call to arms in the imperial dispute. The author of the *Dialogue* beckoned women readers to dissuade their "patriotic" husbands from rushing hastily into war. For, as becomes increasingly apparent through the *Dialogue*'s progression, this wife is not such a carp after all. She confesses that she "may be sometimes too pert," but she maintains that she always spoken and acted with sincere regard for her husband's "true Interest," "Health," and "ease." She deplores Congress's measures in large part because she does not wish to see her husband imprisoned or hanged.[49] With this display of affectionate concern for her husband's happiness and safety, the wife redeems herself for the reader. The author thus enables the audience to value her counsel rather than to dismiss it as mere caterwauling. At the *Dialogue*'s end, the wife proclaims, "Let Fools, Pedants, and Husbands, continue to hate / The Advice of us Women, and call it all Prate." Wise persons, the reader must conclude, will hear, and heed, her somber warning: "Make your Peace:—Fear the King:—The Parliament fear. // Repent! or you are forever, forever undone."[50] With this note of caution, the congressman's wife literally gets the last word.

"Men to Atlantic Empire Born"

By representing New England congressmen as zealous enthusiasts and Chesapeake congressmen as spineless pushovers, the king's friends constructed a politically potent narrative of the First Continental Congress. They suggested that a faction of rabid Massachusetts delegates had forced its will on their craven Virginia colleagues. At the same time, to further discredit the Articles of Association, loyalist writers articulated a sweeping critique of colonial masculinity and American provincialism. Ridiculing Congress's pretense to social and politically authority, they argued, invidiously, that low-born colonists were not qualified to govern within the British Empire. Myles Cooper voiced this critique most forcefully in his *Patriots of North-America: A Sketch*. Addressed to "English Readers," Cooper's *Sketch* spanned forty-seven pages, including thirty-five pages of raucous and far-ranging verse denouncing resistance leaders, and twelve pages of expository notes explaining, justifying, and expounding on that denunciation. Across these many pages, Cooper attacked the Continental Congressmen not only on the basis of their gender, but also on the grounds of their race, their class, and their humble rank within British society, which is to say, on their status as colonials.

In an extended allegory of the American rebellion, Cooper represented members of Congress as "giddy" Eton schoolboys. Cooper described how pupils at that academy, when frustrated by "College Rules" and "Studies hard," would run away to a local inn and there "in Congress meet." These rebellious students would "cabal, harrangue, [and] resolve" to drive the schoolmaster out of business.[51] Here was the force of Cooper's criticism: like the unwhiskered Eton upstarts, American congressmen possessed little understanding of the world and even less familiarity with affairs of state. Cooper explicitly asserted that members of Congress—"Less fit for Senates, than for Toys, / in politicks, at best but Boys"—had not matured politically. With the naive self-assurance of adolescents, congressional delegates mistook provincial politics, their Eton College, for the "Cock-pit," that is, the sitting chamber of the British Privy Council. Only by returning to school, repenting, and receiving their flogging—at King George's "fond, paternal hand"—would these schoolboys grow wiser and learn to accept their "just Subordination."[52]

Cooper further traduced the *Patriots of North-America* by suggesting that they belonged to an impure race. Historians of British national identity have demonstrated that by the mid-eighteenth century, if not earlier, inhabitants of the British Isles had come to think of the American colonists as a separate and distinctly inferior people.[53] Many metropolitan Londoners imagined Britain's North American holdings as rustic, frontier outposts, where the exiles of Europe mingled promiscuously with "savages" and slaves. As the historian Bernard Bailyn has written, "the common European, and indeed British, conception of America [was that of] an uncivil place on the distant margins of civilization—a place where the ordinary restraints of civility could be abandoned in pell-mell exploitation, a remote place where recognized enemies and pariahs of society—heretics, criminals, paupers—could safely be deposited, their contamination sealed off by three thousand miles of ocean, and where putatively inferior specimens of humanity, blacks and Indians, could be reduced to subhuman statuses."[54]

Loyalist pamphleteers attacked members of Congress and local committeemen by suggesting that these self-styled patriots were, indeed, a racially mixed lot. The anonymous author of the scathing lampoon, *The Triumph of the Whigs*, pointed contemptuously to the "motly" crowds of patriots that gathered in New York City. This author disparaged the Whig throng as "People of all sizes and of all hues! red-skins, yellow-skins, green-skins, grey-skins, bay-skins, black-skins, blue-skins!" He or she sarcastically contrasted the "Enchanting variety" of the "sons of freedom" with the racial uniformity of the "sons of loyalty and order": "Hateful sight! no variety in their appearance; all of one colour—*white* as the unsullied snow!" This author further asserted, bitterly, that the Sons of Freedom aimed to establish a "Grand American Republic" in which all creatures would enjoy perfect representation. By electing provincial congressmen "from every colour," the author alleged, colonial Whigs ensured that "every man, woman, boy, girl, child, infant, cow, horse, hog, dog, and cat, who *now* live, or ever *did* live, or ever *shall* live in this province . . . will be fully, freely, and sufficiently represented in the next Grand Continental Congress."[55] With this caustic, reductio ad absurdum reasoning, the author of *The Triumph of the Whigs* defended the political supremacy of white Englishmen and deprecated the resistance movement for its democratic impulses.

Myles Cooper and Samuel Seabury also used race to condemn the American resistance. Cooper insinuated that life among "savage" neighbors had morally and politically corrupted patriot leaders. Men born to the "Atlantic Empire," Cooper explained, in mocking reference to British colonists, disdained the great civilizations of Greece and Rome and disavowed the wise teachings of classical history. Such men "Prefer their Mohawks, and their Creeks, / To Romans, Britons, Swiss, or Greeks." Cooper asserted that Native cultural influences had rendered provincial Americans "savage fierce," "savage raw," and "Savage rude."[56] Samuel Seabury likewise compared American patriots to "savages," but not to the Indians of North America. In *The Congress Canvassed*, Seabury compared the delegates who convened in Philadelphia to a party of New Zealand aborigines gathered for war. Before attacking their enemies, Seabury asserted, members of Congress first "animate[d] themselves

"A Tête-à-Tête between the Premier & Jno Hancock Esqr." (1778). © The Trustees of the British Museum. Printed in 1778, this cartoon depicts a fictitious meeting between British prime minister Lord Frederick North, a proper English gentleman, and past president of the Continental Congress John Hancock, a wild American rustic. Whereas North wears a powdered wig, Hancock's hair hangs loosely. Whereas North is attired in a fine suit, Hancock appears in a leopard-skin coat and fur-trimmed breeches and boots. The palm-tree that shades Hancock symbolizes the supposedly tropical American environment, while the puma that lurks behind him signifies the ferocity of its inhabitants, both animal and human. In the print, Hancock offers a carrot to North, a curious gesture the significance of which is explained in the inscription: "Hancock and N—th, Suppos'd to meet, / And thus, the first, his thoughts repeat, / Let some, like Spaniels, own the plan, / In me, behold a different Man / Who ee'r he'd call thy House his Home, / Wou'd with the mountain Tyger, roam, / Live on the Roots, pluck'd from the Earth, / From whence Himself, like Thee, had Birth."

by singing their war song, exercising their lances, and brandishing their patoopatoos, that they might work themselves up into . . . a state of frenzy."[57] Presumably, these exotic allusions to the South Seas were not lost on Seabury's New York readers, who, earlier that same year, bought up an inexpensive edition of Captain Cook's voyage, published by James Rivington.[58]

Finally, Cooper and other writers challenged colonial resistance leaders by attacking their class and colonial status. Cooper specifically alleged that the local committeemen whom Congress brought to power hailed chiefly from the laboring ranks. According to Cooper, these were common laborers, "Coblers, Tinkers, Butchers"; men formed by nature to work "the Oar, the Sledge, the Saw" (in his endnotes, Cooper added "the Awl, the Trowel, and many other Tools").[59] In making this claim, Cooper conceded no hyperbole, but rather encouraged his readers to "See the Names in the Lists of Committees, in the Several Districts of North-America; and enquire, what are their Callings?"[60] Cooper held the many lawyers who served in the Continental Congress in little higher esteem. Deriding their professional stature, Cooper announced that these lawyers were merely, "what they call in England, Attorneys at Law." Here, Cooper alluded to a distinction in the British legal profession, not generally recognized in the colonies, between attorneys or solicitors, who performed preparatory and procedural work, and barristers, who ultimately represented clients in England's high courts.[61] Jeering at Congress's putative legal expertise, Cooper proclaimed that the "Scriv'ners" in Congress were "Form'd at most, to scrawl a Lease." As for the Congress's "Code," that is, the Articles of Association, Cooper predicted that "the great and little Vulgar of England will laugh over [it], . . . every Man in Europe, of Sense and Benevolence, will read [it] with Grief and Indignation."[62]

Exploiting British imperial notions of American inferiority, Cooper argued that the delegates to Congress were ill-born, poorly educated, and untraveled provincials. The writings of colonial Whigs proved, in Cooper's opinion, "how frequently Men are led by Youth, Inexperience, Confinement to narrow Scenes, Want of Leisure, and general enlarged Knowledge, to form false and fatal Conclusions." Insinuating that American patriots had forgotten their place, geopolitically speaking, within the British Empire, Cooper alleged that these rebels had spent little time abroad. Unlike more cosmopolitan Americans, they had not compared the "Arts, Sciences, Knowledge, Accomplishments, Wealth, Power, [and] Dignity" of the colonies with those of Great Britain. In consequence, American resistance leaders esteemed their colonial lives much too highly. They suffered an "overweening Conceit of the Importance of this Country, and a very inadequate Knowledge, or a total Ignorance of the Parent Country." This was no idle insult, as Cooper saw it, but rather a "fatal" source of the "dreadful Calamities" that now afflicted the empire. "There is a very remarkable Difference," he declared, "between the Opinions, Principles, and Conduct in general, of the Natives of this Country, who have resided in Europe, or have conversed much with Europeans, and of those who have never passed the Limits of their own, or of some neighbouring province." Despite their humble stations, despite their supposedly uncultured worldview, American patriots had the nerve—galling to Cooper—to rebel against the greatest empire in the world.[63]

In all of this calumny may be found the writers' preconceptions not only about masculinity, but about social and political authority within the British Empire. For in the course of discrediting the Continental Congress, loyalist pamphleteers and poets articulated their own measure of statesmanly bearing and demeanor. The proper persons to rule the nation, they suggested, were well-bred, cosmopolitan elites, men who acted with reason and restraint, men capable, at least, of governing their own households. As portrayed by loyalist antagonists, members of the Continental Congress not only failed to meet these standards, but deviated wildly from them. Notwithstanding the ancestral commonalities of Briton and British American, that is, the many bloodlines that united metropolis and marchland, Congress's foes asserted that the North American environment, particularly its abundance of black and tawny peoples and its dearth of "civilization," debased colonial men and rendered them unsuitable for leadership. Yoking notions of American manhood to discourses of colonial inferiority, loyalist writers thus promoted an imperial model of masculinity. They embedded gender in the colonists' subaltern status. In their calculus, American statesmen were lesser statesmen because American men were lesser men. Less white, to be sure, but also less propertied, less educated, less mannered, and thus less qualified to rule.

It is impossible to gauge the precise extent to which loyalists' attacks on congressional masculinity swayed public opinion. But these writings do appear to have influenced Revolutionary politics. In New York, where much of this prose and poetry first appeared in print, the colonial assembly voted not to consider the proceedings of Congress, not to thank the merchants of New York City for abiding by the Association, and not to appoint delegates to the Second Continental Congress to be held the following May.[64] Writing from as far away as Pennsylvania, Maryland, and Delaware, grateful loyalists credited the Anglican pamphleteers with this "happy effect."[65]

The extraordinary acrimony with which American patriots greeted anti-congressional pamphlets further suggests that these authors had struck a raw nerve. In New York and Virginia, the people out of doors made a ritual of burning loyalist publications.[66] The inhabitants of Monmouth County, New Jersey, tarred and feathered one of Seabury's tracts and nailed it to the pillory, "there to remain as a monument to the indignation of a free and loyal people."[67] Whig leaders in New Jersey and Pennsylvania organized boycotts of Rivington's press and swore not to conduct business with post-riders who carried his publications. In November 1775, patriot militiamen at last arrested

Seabury and confiscated Rivington's types. By that time, Chandler and Cooper had already fled to England.[68]

A handful of Whig essayists took up their pens in support of Congress and the Association. The future congressmen James Wilson of Pennsylvania and William Henry Drayton of South Carolina, as well as the future continental general Charles Lee, wrote in favor of steadfast economic resistance and military preparations. A few of these patriot pamphleteers strove to vindicate members of Congress from loyalist assaults. Alexander Hamilton, still just a nineteen-year-old student at King's College, authored a rejoinder to Samuel Seabury entitled *A Full Vindication of the Measures of the Congress*. Hamilton celebrated Congress as "an august body of men, famed for their patriotism and abilities," "an assembly truly respectable on every account!"[69] The New York congressman Philip Livingston likewise defended Congress in an essay entitled, *The Other Side of the Question*. Embarrassed by his fellow Anglicans, Livingston apologized for the "rude and opprobrious terms" with which Thomas Bradbury Chandler had libeled the dissenting churchmen in Congress.[70]

Members of Congress, however, mostly refrained from participating in this pamphlet war. Upon returning home from Philadelphia, delegates to the First Continental Congress found themselves pressed with political business and personal affairs. Some, too, apparently believed that it was beneath their dignity, both as congressmen and as private individuals, to respond to generalized character attacks. The North Carolina congressman William Hooper (son of the Old Light cleric) deemed Chandler's *Friendly Address* "the most trifling performance that the publick have yet been insulted with." He insisted that such pamphlets were best received with "Neglect."[71]

Yet, the Continental Congress did respond to attacks on its legitimacy. After war erupted in the spring of 1775, the Second Continental Congress began to exercise executive and legislative powers. Very much like a national government, it created an army and printed a paper currency; it organized days of fasting and thanksgiving; it commissioned monuments to commemorate the dead, and medals and swords to honor the heroic. In doing all of these things, the Continental Congress produced material artifacts and ceremonies that not only justified the American resistance but that also affirmed its own merit and dignity. The necessity of vindicating its authority, a necessity born in part of the scathing attacks leveled by skeptics in the winter of 1774–75, gave shape and substance to many of Congress's inventions. And yet, every new object, ritual, or holy day that Congress fabricated to validate the cause of liberty provided loyalists additional fodder with which to condemn it.

Part II

THE OUTCOME IS IN DOUBT

Obverse of Benjamin Franklin's three-dollar bill, featuring a crane and eagle locked in mortal combat. Reproduced from the original held by the Department of Special Collections of the University Libraries of Notre Dame.

Shortly after it first convened in the fall of 1774, the Continental Congress received the "horrid" but mistaken news that British naval vessels had bombarded the city of Boston. Delegates responded vehemently. Some proposed transforming the Congress into a "Council of War" and moving closer to the seat of battle. "WAR! WAR! WAR! was the cry," reported John Adams. "If [rumors of the bombardment] had proved true, you would have heard the Thunder of an American Congress."[1]

By the time the delegates reconvened in the late spring of 1775, war had in fact erupted, and a similar spirit of urgency and bellicosity governed the Congress's proceedings. The British assault on Lexington and Concord antagonized the American public, muted opposition to Congress and the Articles of Association, and motivated tens of thousands of patriots to turn out for military service. Indignant at the British offensive and inspired by Americans' militant volunteerism, the Second Continental Congress moved quickly to put the colonies "into a state of defence." Within a matter of weeks, Congress voted to establish a continental army, to launch a preemptive assault against Quebec, and to publish a Declaration on Taking Arms.[2]

Despite these swift and decisive measures, there persisted feelings of grave apprehension, both within the Pennsylvania State House, where the Second Continental Congress sat, and among the people out of doors. Would the skirmishes in Massachusetts escalate into full-blown war? Could American forces defend themselves against a professional British army? If war did come, what would be the fate of the American colonies? Or of the British nation?

John Dickinson, congressman from Pennsylvania, felt a range of political sentiment. Famed throughout the colonies and in London as author of the *Letters from a Farmer in Pennsylvania* (1767–1768), Dickinson balked at Parliament's efforts to tax the colonists for the purpose of raising a revenue. He likewise resented, perhaps as forcefully as any colonist, the British incursion in Massachusetts. In July, Dickinson drafted Congress's Declaration on Taking Arms, in which he boldly declared, "We are reduced to the alternative of chusing an unconditional submission to the tyranny of irritated ministers, or resistance by force.—The latter is our choice." Yet, impelled though he was to defend American rights, Dickinson feared that armed resistance would tear the empire apart. Dickinson dreaded the prospect of civil war and worried for the future of liberty and constitutional order in British North America. At nearly the same moment that he wrote the Declaration on Taking Arms, Dickinson also composed, and insisted that Congress adopt, a petition to King George III, beseeching his majesty's merciful intervention and praying for his "long and prosperous reign."[3] Dickinson carried the sword in one hand and the Olive Branch in the other.[4]

Benjamin Franklin did not share Dickinson's reconciliationist politics. As a colonial agent in London, Franklin witnessed firsthand the North ministry's determination to subdue the colonial rebellion. To plead for the king's interposition was, Franklin believed, to pin Americans' hopes on chimerical prospects of peace and to divert precious energies from defensive preparations. So long as the colonists continued to vest faith in "a Speedy Reconciliation," Franklin cautioned, "[t]hings will be done by Halves."[5]

That summer, as he designed Congress's new paper dollars—a continental currency to finance a continental army—Franklin offered a pointed rejoinder to Dickinson's Olive Branch Petition. Franklin adorned his three-dollar bill with an emblem of an eagle "pouncing upon a *crane*." Writing pseudonymously in the *Pennsylvania Gazette*, Franklin explained that the eagle, possessed of "superior strength," represented Great Britain, while the crane, a weaker bird, stood for the American colonies. Though the eagle clutched the crane in its sharp talons, the crane pierced the eagle with a thrust of its long beak.[6]

Much like the clash of these deadlocked birds, the contest between Britain and the American colonies remained in doubt, as the Latin motto that accompanied Franklin's emblems suggested. But much like the small yet capable crane, the American colonies, Franklin understood, possessed vital protective features: a wide ocean separated them from their British enemies, an extensive sea coast gave shelter to their commerce, and a vast territory made room for their rapidly expanding populations.[7] So, Franklin counseled the American people to take a lesson from the crane: rather than depending upon their "*endeavors to avoid* the contest (by petition, negotiation &c.)," they ought to "prepare for using the means of defence God and nature had given [them]" (italics in original). Franklin's three-dollar bill thus circulated not merely as a monetary instrument, but also as a political commentary, a repudiation of Dickinson's Olive Branch politics.[8]

As hopes of reconciliation crumbled in the summer of 1775, dashed by the Battle of Bunker Hill in July and again by George III's rejection of the Olive Branch Petition in August, Franklin's point of view—that the colonists should mind their business—came quickly to prevail in Congress. Already, the militarization of the American resistance had fundamentally altered the objectives and powers of that assembly. Whereas the First Continental Congress committed Americans to nothing more than collaborative economic resistance, the Second Continental Congress raised a military establishment and bound Americans to its financial support. In so doing, this Congress began to exercise unprecedented executive and legislative authority.

To mobilize the "United Colonies" for war and to justify its assumption of federal powers, the Continental Congress began to create new patriotic material, iconography, and ceremony. Benjamin Franklin embellished the continental currency with emblems of industry and economy, in the spirit of Poor Richard. Franklin sought not simply to safeguard Congress's bills against counterfeiting, not simply to rouse public enthusiasm for this novel and precarious paper money, but more importantly, to prepare Americans for the hard work and thrift necessary to safeguard their political rights. In the meantime, Congress endeavored to sanctify the American resistance and to imbue it with a sense of righteousness. Toward this end, Congress began to proclaim days of fasting and thanksgiving, to publicly and solemnly commemorate the deaths of civil and military leaders, and to commission medals in honor of American military triumph. By these means, Congress sought to rally the colonists for war and, at the same time, to present itself as a staid and dignified assembly, not the "pack of banditti" its adversaries had portrayed.

In all of these measures, Congress unwittingly provided grist for persons who opposed the American resistance or who wished only to remain aloof from it. Loyalist poets lampooned the pretentious decorations on Congress's rag bills. Conscientious Quakers refused to honor the continental fast and instead opened their shops. An Anglican minister who wished desperately for political accommodation tempered the spirit of independence at one congressional memorial service. Even confirmed patriots, forlorn by the progress of war, found it difficult to be thankful merely because Congress had commanded it. Despite Congress's best efforts to modulate the economic, moral, and spiritual tenor of the American resistance, the people out of doors found ways to make their voices heard.

3

"[A]n Impression upon the Mind"

THE OUTBREAK OF WAR forced the Continental Congress to contend with an awkward constitutional dilemma. To ready the colonies' defenses—to raise soldiers; to shelter, feed, and clothe them; and to fit them with arms—required vast sums of money. But Congress possessed no power to tax. And so, on June 22, 1775, Congress made the momentous decision to print two million dollars worth of paper currency. For want of means to generate a revenue, Congress instead ran up a debt.[1]

Colonial authorities had begun to experiment with paper money nearly a century before. In 1690, the Massachusetts Bay Council issued the first public currency in British North America.[2] Other colonial assemblies soon followed suit, emitting bills of credit, loan certificates, treasury notes, and other forms of legal tender to pay for military campaigns, to finance public improvements, and to stimulate local economies in times when specie, or gold and silver coin, was scarce.[3] Nevertheless, the printing of paper dollars remained a perilous and controversial venture. These instruments generated considerable public anxiety. Many colonists distrusted "soft" paper money because it lacked the intrinsic value of "hard" specie. Experience taught, too, that paper currencies depreciated over time. Colonial merchants particularly objected to paper money because they could not pass it along in payment of debts to British manufacturers and exporters.[4] But precisely because money flowed across the Atlantic, Britain's North American colonies suffered chronic, trade-stifling shortages of specie. Extraordinary financial exigencies—expenses arising from military expeditions, for example, or from urgent public works—compelled colonial legislatures to circulate bills and notes in spite of public apprehensions and in spite of Parliament's repeated efforts to regulate the circulation of paper money.[5]

Congress's currency suffered all the shortcomings traditionally associated with paper money, as well as from certain imperfections entirely its own. Before the war's end, Congress printed more than $240 million, an enormous sum that vastly exceeded previous colonial emissions and that depreciated at a dizzying pace.[6] Historically, colonial assemblies sustained the value of their bills by receiving them in payment of taxes. But, again, Congress wielded no authority to levy taxes, so it could not "sink" its currency in this manner. More problematically still, the Continental Congress issued its paper currency for the express purpose of financing war against Great Britain. Yet hundreds of thousands of colonists remained loyal to the British Crown. Persons who considered the war a rebellion, rather than a defensive campaign, believed the continental currency to be a treasonous medium of exchange. Pacifists, too, including many prominent Philadelphia Quakers, protested the continental currency as an instrument of war. Even for those colonists who championed American resistance and later embraced independence, continental currency made for risky tender. Congress backed its paper money with nothing more than the loose promises of rebel governments to redeem the bills at some unspecified future date. An enterprising individual might reap financial benefit from a depreciating currency in any number of ways: by using it to pay off creditors, for example, or by purchasing it cheap in expectation of a future redemption at greater value. But in 1775 no patriot could have put faith in the long-term value of continental currency unless he or she believed, first, that the frail United Colonies would defeat the British Empire, and second, that members of Congress and their constituents would all make good on their word. Continental currency was thus a partisan money whose worth was most uncertain. And yet, the cause of liberty depended on its vitality.

To craft this fateful currency, to design the bills and oversee their printing, Congress called on Benjamin Franklin.[7] Franklin recognized the necessity of creating a visually appealing currency, one that would hearten and enthuse persons who received it. He imagined that, despite its weaknesses, continental currency had the potential not only to pay for the war, but, far more ambitiously, to reshape Americans' political and economic behaviors. Never before had the various colonies united to issue currency. This unprecedented continental enterprise would naturally generate a great deal of interest. Hundreds of thousands of these bills would pass through the colonists' hands. Here was a far greater circulation than Franklin's *Pennsylvania Gazette* or Poor Richard's almanac had ever enjoyed. Here, too, was a captive audience. Because the faces of Congress's bills would set forth their unique terms of value and redemption, cautious bearers would actually have to read the various denominations they tendered.[8] Continental currency might thus serve not merely as a medium of exchange, but also as a medium of patriotic values. Seizing this opportunity, Franklin produced the most elaborately didactic paper money the world had ever known.

Franklin adorned the continental currency with emblems of righteousness, industry, and fortitude. His paper money warned the colonists to brace for the escalating war and urged them to work diligently in anticipation of hardship. It assured them that they could and should defend their rights against the mighty British Empire. It even promised that the war would bring prosperity to the American people. Franklin's continental currency designs roused patriots and came to serve, during a brief but critical moment, as symbols of the American resistance movement. But in so doing, Franklin's designs also attracted the scorn of British sympathizers. More than simply financing the war, the continental currency opened a public dialogue about Congress, resistance, and the political and economic future of America.

Freshly returned from years of service in London, Franklin was the obvious pick to devise the continental currency. He firmly believed in the utility of paper money and he possessed many years' experience printing it. When the colony of Pennsylvania fell into a trade slump in 1729, Franklin, then only twenty-three years old, responded by publishing a pamphlet, *A Modest Enquiry into the Nature and Necessity of a Paper Currency*. In that tract, Franklin endorsed soft money as an essential catalyst to active labor, easy credit, and vibrant business. Franklin's *Modest Enquiry* swayed public opinion in favor of a new emission. Soon after, the Pennsylvania assembly rewarded Franklin with a contract to print its paper bills. Franklin continued to win Pennsylvania's currency contracts; he later obtained New Jersey's and Delaware's too. For more than three decades, Franklin made his money by making money.[9]

Much of the currency printed in early America bore some proprietary or royal insignia. Franklin, in fact, helped to establish this numismatic tradition. He decorated Pennsylvania's bills, for example, with the Penn family coat of arms, and New Jersey's and Delaware's with the British arms of dominion.[10]

Such imprints became standard for the paper money of British North America.[11] The Revolution inspired Franklin to abandon that convention. No single provincial emblem could fairly represent the thirteen united colonies. And now that war had erupted with Britain, royal emblems would not do. Writing years later, Franklin expressed disdain for currency that perpetuated "the dull Story that everybody knows, and what it would have been no Loss to mankind if nobody had ever known, that Geo. III. is King of Great Britain, France & Ireland etc. etc."[12] Franklin abandoned monarchical currency because he no longer wished to glorify a tyrannical king. But more significantly, he invented a republican currency because he perceived an opportunity to deliver moral instruction. In designing new continental denominations, Franklin aimed at nothing less than the reformation of human behavior.

Franklin long believed that visual images possessed the power to influence their beholders' moral, ethical, and political principles.[13] When describing that power, Franklin often employed the concept of impression.[14] Sometime around midcentury, for example, Franklin wrote to Dr. John Mitchell, a member of the Royal Society of London, proposing that he create and sell ornamental chimney tiles for the decoration of private homes. Franklin recommended that Mitchell adorn these tiles with didactic images inspired by the Roman poet Horace.[15] "[C]onstantly in the Eyes of Children when by the Fire-side," these chimney tiles, Franklin suggested, would "give Parents an Opportunity in explaining them, to impress moral Sentiments."[16] Later in the Revolutionary War, after the New York and New Jersey campaigns, the Continental Congress called on Franklin to commission a booklet of engravings that depicted British war atrocities. Writing to David Hartley, son of the pioneering associationist psychologist, Franklin explained that these engravings were intended "to impress the minds of Children and Posterity with a deep sense of [Britain's] bloody and insatiable Malice and Wickedness."[17] Franklin believed that continental currency, as it passed through the colonists' hands, might function in the same way as these edifying chimney tiles and "horrid" war engravings. Writing in 1779, Franklin explicitly set forth his aims for U.S. currency and coin: "[P]ut on one side some important proverb of Solomon, some pious moral, prudential or economical precept, the frequent Inculcation of which, by seeing it every time one receives a piece of money, might make an Impression upon the Mind, especially of young Persons, and tend to regulate the Conduct."[18] Continental dollars, Franklin believed, could transform American thought and habit.

This conviction impelled Franklin to design the continental currency with great care. Rather than with seals or arms, he chose to adorn his bills with emblems, an early-modern fine-art form closely associated with engraving, heraldry, the medallic arts, and architecture.[19] Emblems were narrative images: they told moralistic stories, the lessons of which were amplified or explicated by accompanying Latin mottoes. In the mid-sixteenth century, Europe's newly established printing presses began to churn out emblem books containing dozens and even hundreds of didactic engravings. More than two hundred years later, the emblem book remained a popular genre. To ornament Congress's money, Franklin consulted two: the 1702 Mainz edition of *Symbolorum ac Emblematum Ethico-Politicorum*, a compendium of plant and animal emblems published by the German botanist Joachim Camerarius, and the 1660 Amsterdam edition of *Idea Principis Christiano-Politici Symbolis*, a collection of moral emblems created by the Spanish political theorist Diego de Saavedra Fajardo.[20] From these compendia, Franklin selected more than a half dozen emblems to appear on the faces of the continental bills. Others he designed from scratch. During the summer of 1775, Franklin created ten unique denominations. By August, $3,000,000 worth of this currency had passed into circulation.[21]

Early-modern emblems were intended to be cryptic, their meanings intelligible only to highly learned persons who could read Latin and comprehend arcane allusions.[22] Not so with Franklin's currency. In September, Franklin submitted a letter, published on the front page of the *Pennsylvania Gazette*, in which he explained exactly what each design meant.[23] That Franklin took the time to write and publish this key, amid frenzied preparations for war, attests to his optimistic faith that his currency would mobilize the public. The nature of Franklin's letter to the *Gazette* further reveals his intention to make these emblems accessible to broad segments of the American readership. Franklin did not identify himself as the designer of the continental currency or even as the author of the letter to the *Gazette*.[24] Rather, he signed the letter Clericus, an appellation befitting a clergyman or perhaps a clerk or scribe. But "Clericus" was no mere pseudonym. Rather, it may more properly be understood as a persona. A much younger Benjamin Franklin first introduced Clericus to readers of the *New-England Courant* decades before. Franklin's famous widow, Silence Dogood, boarded a minister whom she called Clericus for the sake of "Distinction." In Franklin's gentle lampoon, Clericus represented the Harvard-educated ministry. Dogood "now and then" appealed to Clericus to "beautify [her] Writings with a Sentence or two" of Latin. "[T]he learned Languages," Dogood quipped, were "very ornamental" and "pleasing to those who do not understand it."[25] By adopting the moniker "Clericus" in 1775, Franklin assumed that bookish parson's benignly pedantic voice. As Clericus,

Franklin managed to expound on his emblems in plain and simple English, without seeming pretentious or condescending.[26] Drawn from European texts and adorned with heraldic Latin, Franklin's emblems may well have engaged the educated gentry, but Clericus placed them within the grasp of common folk.[27] Meanwhile, colonial printers aided in this cause by distributing Clericus's letter far and wide. In the fall of 1775, no fewer than eight colonial newspapers reprinted Franklin's key to the continental currency. The Delaware printer James Adams also reproduced Clericus's letter in his *Wilmington Almanack* for the year 1777.[28]

Clericus disingenuously professed not to know the intended meanings of the continental bills. Rather, he presented "Conjectures" because no official explanation had yet been made. As interpreted by Clericus, Franklin's bills offered political assurance and economic counsel to a people confronting an escalating war.[29] Clericus prefaced his remarks by casting the imperial crisis as a struggle between the "tyrant state," which stood for "absolute power and plunder," and the colonies, which championed "liberty, property, and safety." Many of Franklin's bills sought to persuade the colonists that Britain, not America, was rightly to blame for the conflict. Franklin's five-dollar bill, for instance, depicted a gardener's hand "attempting to eradicate" a thorny bush. Clericus explained that the hand represented Britain and the bush America. He translated the motto, *Sustine Vel Abstine*, as "Either support or leave me."

Other bills took up this same theme. The twenty-dollar bill featured a design of Franklin's own creation, a "tempestuous sea" roiled by strong winds. Clericus provided a lengthy explanation: "From the remotest antiquity, in

Obverse of Benjamin Franklin's five-dollar bill, featuring a hand struggling to uproot a thorny bush. Reproduced from the original held by the Department of Special Collections of the University Libraries of Notre Dame.

figurative language, great waters have signified the people, and waves an insurrection." Like the sea, Clericus continued, the people are "naturally inclined to be still." But now "Boreas, the North wind," blew "violently" and whipped up the waves. Clericus's readers would have immediately grasped the pun on "North wind." The British prime minister Lord Frederick North warmly advocated the Tea Act and the Coercive Acts, both of which greatly agitated the American colonists. Clericus affirmed the double entendre, writing, "The black cloud perhaps designs the British Parliament . . . Britain seems thus charged with being the sole cause of the present civil war."[30]

Franklin's four-dollar bill, which portrayed America as a wild boar charging against a hunter's spear, similarly faulted the British. The boar, Clericus informed, is an "inoffensive" creature so long as he is left to "enjoy his freedom." But if "roused and wounded by the hunter," the boar "well knows" how to use his "long and sharp tusks . . . in his defence." By reiterating the defensive nature of American resistance, Franklin sought to justify the war to his countrymen. In 1775, many colonists felt qualms about waging war against a nation to which they had long paid allegiance. Some lobbied desperately for reconciliation and accused the Continental Congress of fomenting a rebellion. On July 6, Congress explicitly rebuffed this charge in its Declaration on Taking Arms. In this declaration, addressed to the inhabitants of Great Britain, Congress delineated a long history of imperial abuses and asserted that a "cruel and impolitic" Parliament had driven the colonies to force. Franklin's currency emblematized this same perspective: Britain's oppressive administration provoked a people who by nature were as still as the seas and as inoffensive as the wild boar. Justifying the colonists' military efforts, Franklin's currency also gave good reason for its own existence:

Obverse of Franklin's twenty-dollar bill, featuring a North wind whipping up waves. Reproduced from the original held by the Department of Special Collections of the University Libraries of Notre Dame.

Congress had printed paper money not as a weapon of aggression, but rather of self-defense. Colonists—scrupulous Quakers in particular—need not suffer pangs of conscience for accepting it.

The continental currency asserted overemphatically that the colonists had already united in opposition to Great Britain. Ignoring the pleas of loyalists, reconciliationists, and pacifists, Clericus claimed that the malevolent North wind had blown the waves all in "one direction." Franklin's professions of unity were critical, for the success of the American resistance depended on widespread if not universal participation. As the scholar Lester C. Olson has observed, through the fall of 1774 into the summer of 1775, congressional delegates filled their letters with sentiments of accord and consensus.[31] Franklin's paper money likewise promoted the illusion of solidarity. His eight-dollar bill carried a symbol of colonial unanimity, a thirteen-string harp, whose motto, *Majora Minoribus Consonant*, Clericus translated as, "The greater and smaller ones sound together." He speculated that the "strings of different lengths and substance" represented "the several colonies of different weight and force," now joined in perfect harmony by the harp's "strong frame," the Continental Congress. Understood in this manner, the eight-dollar emblem served to rebuff detractors of American resistance who charged that Massachusetts and Virginia radicals had roped more moderate colonies into rebellion. But Clericus also provided a second interpretation: the strings might also signify "the various ranks of people . . . now united by that government." As the continental currency would have it, landed gentry and laboring farmers, wealthy merchants and poor tradesmen, all stood together in opposition to

Obverse of Franklin's four-dollar bill, featuring a wild boar, inoffensive until roused. Reproduced from the original held by the Department of Special Collections of the University Libraries of Notre Dame.

British despotism. Franklin designed his money not only to speak to "various ranks of people" but to ensure that they would fight together.

In addition to these political assertions—that an arbitrary government had driven the colonists to defend their liberties, that Americans should act swiftly to prepare for war, and that all manners of people supported Congress and its measures—Franklin's bills also imparted earnest economic instruction. Franklin imbued the continental currency with the same economic sensibility that had inspired Poor Richard's almanac for more than three decades. Franklin perceived early in his career that the growth of the transatlantic trade and the maturation and expansion of intercolonial markets demanded considerable financial savvy, especially of merchants and investors but increasingly, too, of ordinary producers and consumers.[32] In the eighteenth century, a rising number of British colonists, particularly in urban seaport communities, began to take part both as buyers and sellers in extended networks of trade.[33] These colonists came to depend less on neighborhood bartering for life's necessities and more on market exchange. But in the process, they found themselves traversing unfamiliar financial terrain. Face-to-face exchanges with friends and acquaintances slowly but steadily yielded to impersonal business transactions; the swapping of goods and services gave way over time to the extension of credit and the charging of interest. Innovations in financial instruments, such as the paper money that Franklin himself had promoted and printed, left bearers vulnerable to fluctuations of value. Participation in distant trade networks subjected the colonists to risk, while

Obverse of Franklin's eight-dollar bill, featuring a harp with thirteen strings. Reproduced from the original held by the Department of Special Collections of the University Libraries of Notre Dame.

unstable markets and new speculative investment opportunities exposed them to cycles of boom and bust.[34]

In part to protect against these market perils, Franklin began publishing Poor Richard's almanac in 1732. His pages offered sage advice not merely to entertain his readers, but to edify them. Many of Poor Richard's proverbs instructed how to accumulate personal wealth. Hard work, Poor Richard advised, was the surest path to prosperity. "*[P]lough deep, while Sluggards sleep, and you shall have Corn to sell and to keep,*" he wrote. "Industry gives Comfort, and Plenty, and Respect."[35] In addition to commending the virtues of diligence and industry, Poor Richard also provided detailed monetary counsel. To protect his readers from financial enslavement, Franklin compared for them the costs and benefits of purchases made on credit with those paid in "ready Money." In his short essay "Hints for those that would be Rich" (1737), Poor Richard advised, "*Consider then*, when you are tempted to buy an unnecessary Housholdstuff, or any superfluous thing, whether you will be willing to pay Interest, and Interest upon Interest for it as long as you live; and more if it grows worse by using."[36] To achieve prosperity, the British colonists would have to earn, to save, and to manage their credit wisely. Not buying on interest, and preferably, not buying at all, would spare them from the shackles of indebtedness.[37]

Much like the pithy maxims that filled the leaves of Poor Richard's almanac, the emblems that adorned Franklin's continental dollars admonished bearers to increased productivity. Franklin, in fact, lifted one of his currency mottoes directly from Poor Richard's pages. For the continental fractional notes, including the one-half and one-third dollar bills, Franklin designed an emblem of the sun shining on a sundial as it passed through its orbit. This emblem contained two mottoes, one in Latin, and the other, notably, in English. The first motto, *Fugio*, suggested that time flies. The second advised colonists, Mind Your Business, a charge that appeared in the final edition of Poor Richard's almanac.[38] Written in the readily accessible vernacular, this motto offered immediate counsel for the working poor who handled Congress's small bills.

Other denominations expounded on the theme of industry. Franklin's six-dollar bill depicted a beaver gnawing down a large tree. Clericus explained that the tree represented "either the enormous power Britain has assumed over us . . . or the exorbitant profits she makes by monopolizing our commerce."[39] The "assiduous and steady" beaver of course signified the American colonies. The motto, *Perseverando*, suggested that colonists could regain their liberties "by perseverance" in their present measures of economic resistance.

Obverse of Franklin's half-dollar bill, featuring a sundial and the motto, Mind Your Business. Reproduced from the original held by the Department of Special Collections of the University Libraries of Notre Dame.

By that same perseverance, Clericus asserted, the colonists would establish "the most necessary manufactures" and "abolish the British monopoly." The imperial controversy was a struggle not simply for political rights, but for economic autonomy as well.

Evoking Poor Richard's wisdom on diligence, credit, and indebtedness, Franklin's bills implicitly counseled bearers to forego consumer expenditures and to manage their money shrewdly. Franklin particularly worried that the marketing of luxurious manufactured goods and imported comestibles threatened to rob the colonists of their hard-earned wealth. In the voice of Poor Richard, Franklin warned that the ill-advised purchase of superfluous goods—"*Finerie* and *Knicknacks*," "*Silks and Sattins, Scarlet and Velvets*"—cost many families their very liberty.[40] In much the same spirit, the Articles of Association of 1774 called on patriotic citizens to forego British goods and to withhold their own produce from export markets. Members of Congress understood that the total cessation of transatlantic trade would work a hardship on British North Americans. To offset the loss of imported goods, especially textiles, and to compensate for the decline in personal income, Congress entreated the colonists to "encourage frugality, economy, and industry, and

Obverse of Franklin's six-dollar bill, featuring a beaver perseveringly gnawing a large tree. Reproduced from the original held by the Department of Special Collections of the University Libraries of Notre Dame.

promote agriculture, arts and the manufactures of this country, especially that of wool."[41]

Franklin himself expressed tremendous optimism that such measures would alleviate the burdens of war. Writing in October 1775, Franklin declared, "I am not terrified by the Expence of this War, should it continue ever so long. A little more Frugality, or a little more Industry in Individuals will with Ease defray it . . . Forbearing to drink Tea saves three fourths of the Money; and 500,000 Women doing each threepence Worth of Spinning or Knitting in a Week will pay the rest."[42] Now, as the designer of the continental currency, Franklin likewise championed personal sacrifice and fiscal restraint. His *Perseverando* and *Fugio* emblems summoned individuals to work devotedly. His motto, Mind Your Business, instructed them to make sound economic decisions. By urging the colonists to industry and thrift, Franklin's bills thus promoted the economic imperatives of Congress's Association.

Franklin's bills even aspired to safeguard the financial integrity of the United Colonies. Historically, emissions of paper currency encouraged spending, not only because they increased the amount of money in circulation, but also because the risk of depreciation motivated bearers to exchange chancy paper dollars for more dependable investments. Franklin's money, by contrast, trumpeted a penny-saved, penny-earned ethos. By encouraging colonist to hold their dollars rather than to spend them, Franklin endeavored to limit the quantity in circulation and thus to stave off depreciation. In this way, his continental currency worked, though ultimately in vain, to sustain its own value.[43]

All of these themes—industry, sacrifice, and thrift—achieved their fullest and most controversial expression in Franklin's two-dollar bill, which featured a hand threshing sheaves of wheat. An uninformed holder of this two-dollar bill might have mistaken its design for an admonition to hard work, an agrarian Harvest Your Fields to match the mercantile Mind Your Business. But Clericus offered a much different interpretation. Clericus explained that the sheaves of wheat represented the America colonists, while the flailing hand stood for the British army, or more generally for the trials of war. The two-dollar bill thus gallantly asserted that a vigorous thrashing would be good for the country. Translating the motto, *Tribulatio Ditat*, as "Threshing improves it," Clericus proclaimed, "Threshing . . . often improves those that are threshed." Specious though it seemed to contemporaries, Clericus optimistically claimed that the blows of war, however so hard, would be more "advantageous than hurtful" to the colonists. Like the hand threshing wheat, they would bring forth "every grain of genius and merit in arts, manufactures, war and council." Clericus observed that "many an unwarlike nation have been beaten into heroes." He explained that the "public distress . . . that arises from war, by increasing frugality and industry, often gives habits that remain after the distress is over." Herein resided the ultimate meaning of Franklin's emblems. The war would make Americans wealthy; tribulation would strengthen and imburse the nation. As Clericus contended, war "naturally enriches those on whom it has enforced those enriching virtues."

Before concluding his letter to the *Pennsylvania Gazette*, Clericus turned his attention to the thirty-dollar bill. On this, the largest denomination of continental currency, Clericus discerned a lesson for members of the Continental Congress. Franklin adorned the thirty-dollar bill with an engraving of a laurel wreath resting on a marble altar. The motto, *Si Recte Facies*, read, "If you act rightly." Clericus understood the wreath to signify a "crown of honour" held forth to encourage "brave and steady conduct in defence of our liberties." But Clericus quoted a "learned friend" who interpreted the emblem differently.[44] Clericus's friend believed that the device was "more particularly addressed" to the Continental Congress itself. Clericus explained that "the ancients" wove wreaths for their heroes of laurel, oak, and olive twigs. Each of these plants signified the chief virtue of the Roman god associated with it: laurel stood for the "knowledge and prudence" of Apollo, oak for the fortitude of Jupiter, and olive for the peace of Pallas, "the whole to show, that those who are intrusted to conduct the great affairs of mankind should act prudently and firmly, retaining, above all a pacific disposition." Clericus's friend went on to suggest that the wreath had been placed

Obverse of Franklin's controversial two-dollar bill, featuring a hand threshing grain. Reproduced from the original held by the Department of Special Collections of the University Libraries of Notre Dame.

on an altar as a reminder "that true glory is founded on and proceeds from piety."

Clericus found supporting evidence for his friend's interpretation in the classical texts that had inspired its motto. Clericus quoted Horace for the proposition, *Rex eris, aiunt, / Si recte facies*, which may be translated as, "You shall be king, they say, if you act rightly." Similarly, Clericus turned to Ausonius, a fourth-century Gallic poet, for the assertion *Qui recte faciet, non qui dominatur, erit Rex*, or, "He who acts rightly, not he who tyrannizes, will be king." But for the present occasion, Clericus offered his own loose translation: "Not the King's Parliament, who act wrong, but the People's Congress, *if it acts right*, shall govern America" (italics in original).

By designing an emblem for Congress and by expounding on that emblem in the public gazettes, Franklin offered a trenchant commentary on Congress's shifting stature and authority. When the First Continental Congress convened the previous fall, it acted as a sort of diplomatic council, a gathering of emissaries from the various colonies, empowered only to advise.[45] By contrast, the Second Continental Congress had begun to function much more like a national government, exercising executive power to raise an army and legislative authority to issue a currency.[46] Though the delegates carried instructions from their provincial assemblies, conventions, and congresses authorizing them, either explicitly or implicitly, to take all necessary measures for the restoration of colonial rights, the fact remained that Congress had assumed a great deal of power. Not every British colonist approved. Franklin's thirty-dollar bill counseled Congress to win the public's faith by governing

Obverse of Franklin's thirty-dollar bill, featuring a laurel wreath upon an altar, the reward for a righteous Congress. Reproduced from the original held by the Department of Special Collections of the University Libraries of Notre Dame.

with wisdom, courage, pacifism, and piety. By tendering this advice in the colonial newspapers, sharing it with all who would read Clericus's letter, Franklin invited the public to bear witness to Congress's dealings. In so doing, Franklin worked to legitimate both the United Colonies and the Continental Congress.

Benjamin Franklin's currency designs gave Congress's money an impressive and distinguished look. His emblems imparted sophistication, even gentility. The Latin mottoes, as well as Clericus's allusions to Corinthian architecture and to the classical poets Horace and Ausonius, lent the currency an air of erudition and eloquence. In sum, Franklin's emblems made a fine substitute for the royal coat of arms and the colonial seals that adorned the earliest British American currencies. Yet Franklin strived for much more than this. Wishing his emblems to "regulate the conduct" of his fellow colonists, Franklin decrypted their meanings and published them throughout America. He condemned the despotic British ministry and defended the colonists' decision to take up arms. He brashly asserted that Americans could repel British military forces. His plant and animal emblems—the small crane wounding the robust eagle and the diminutive beaver felling a sturdy tree—naturalized the triumph of the meek over the mighty. Franklin's emblems admonished the colonists to labor with industriousness equal to the beaver's, to mind their business before it was too late. Melding republican and Protestant virtues of sacrifice and austerity with liberal principles of economic self-determination and public spiritedness, these emblems primed Americans to participate in a disrupted wartime economy. Franklin anticipated and sought to lessen the depreciation of Congress's bills by counseling the public to save its dollars. He would have urged them to save their pennies too. Writing in 1779, Franklin suggested that Congress mint copper coins bearing Poor Richard's mottoes: "He that by the plough would thrive, himself must either lead or drive . . . [K]eep they shop, & thy shop will keep thee . . . A Penny sav'd is a Penny got . . . He that buys what he has no need of will soon be forced to sell his Necessaries . . . Early to bed & early to rise, will make a man healthy, wealthy & wise; and so on, to a great Variety."[47]

Early to bed, early to rise: this sort of well-regulated conduct would serve a revolutionary people well. As a reward for their sufferings, as an incentive for their diligence, Franklin pointed to a peaceful and prosperous future. War with Great Britain would invigorate the colonies; it would break them of their dependence on frivolous imported goods and force them to establish their own manufactures. War would also draw forth the most talented persons, elevating them to positions of prestige and authority. For these meritorious individuals, Franklin's money promised enduring glory, provided that they ruled not in the manner of British tyrants, but rather with prudence, firmness and devotion. The continental currency stopped well short of calling for independence, but by foretelling the ascendancy of the "People's Congress," it hinted toward a new political order in which worthy persons, regardless of birth, governed in accordance with popular will.

We cannot measure with certainty the extent to which Franklin's emblems transformed Americans' political and economic behaviors. But though their exact influence may not be quantified, anecdotal evidence suggests that his currency designs greatly inspired colonial patriots. An inventory of Continental Army standards in Philadelphia, prepared by the commissary of military stores Jonathan Gostelowe in the late summer of 1778, lists thirteen regimental standards. Seven of these standards featured devices and mottoes taken from Franklin's continental currency. Possibly belonging to the thirteen regiments raised in Pennsylvania in 1777, these standards may have flown at the Battles of Brandywine, Germantown, and Monmouth. Similarly, in 1780, the state of Connecticut ordered its army regiments to decorate the reverse of their colors with the wreath-and-altar design that appeared on Franklin's thirty-dollar bill.[48] In the earliest years of the republic, before the eagle or the stars-and-stripes had gained purchase as symbols of U.S. independence, Franklin's emblems served to rally Americans in defense of their liberties. Adorning dollars and battle flags alike, these emblems melded the economic and military aims of American resistance.

Franklin's currency also set a new, more ambitious standard of ornamentation for paper money printed in the various colonies. New York, South Carolina, and Georgia all decorated their revolutionary dollars with emblems
inspired by Franklin's bills: sheaves of wheat, angry wild boars, and plants
flourishing through adverse conditions.[49] The Maryland woodcutter Thomas
Sparrow and printer Frederick Green also followed Franklin's lead, casting
aside the Calvert family arms that had embellished the colony's bills for more
than forty years. These craftsmen aspired to create a more overtly propagandistic currency than even Franklin's. Whereas Franklin made use of small,
single-themed emblems, Sparrow and Green contrived an intricate allegor-
ical panorama that spanned the length of their bills. Their panorama features
a meeting between Britannia and America, the latter represented by the
Goddess Liberty crushing slavery beneath her foot. Though America offers a
petition to Britannia from the Continental Congress, perhaps the Olive
Branch, King George tramples on Magna Carta and extends a lit torch
toward a coastal village besieged by the British navy, presumably an allusion
to the burning of Charlestown or Norfolk. On the reverse of these bills,
Sparrow and Green depicted Britannia and America reunited: the two hold
an olive branch, a ship in the background signifies the restoration of trade,
America grasps a cornucopia of abundance. The motto, *Pax Triumphis Potior*,
proclaims, "Peace is preferable to victory." This rich iconography offered a
political and economic perspective much different from Franklin's. Despite
the king's cruelty, peace still represented the surest path to bounty, or so the
Maryland currency declared.[50]

The most popular and influential of all Franklin's emblems proved to be
the simple chain that he created for the reverse of his Mind Your Business
fractional notes. Comprised of thirteen interwoven links, each labeled with
the name of a colony, this chain formed a circle, in the middle of which
appeared a radiant sphere, similar to a sunburst, bearing the words, American
Congress. Modified versions of this chain design subsequently appeared on
an eight-dollar note issued by Georgia in 1777 and on a battle flag adopted by
the 2nd New Hampshire regiment that same year. After the war, Franklin's
chain design emerged as an icon of the confederated United States. It graced
the masthead of Isaiah Thomas's *Massachusetts Spy*; it distinguished a peace
medal struck after the war, and it adorned a variety of early U.S. coins. It
likewise ornamented housewares, carpets, portraiture, jewelry, and similar
paraphernalia. Josiah Wedgwood reproduced Franklin's chain on a set of
china that he created for Robert Morris. In 1781, the Vermont assembly
printed a provocative adaptation of Franklin's chain design on its treasury

Obverse of Sparrow and Green's panoramic sixteen-dollar bill, featuring a meeting between Britannia and America. Reproduced from the original held by the Department of Special Collections of the University Libraries of Notre Dame.

bills. These bills styled the contested Green Mountain region the "State of Vermont" in spite of the fact that the Confederation Congress had not formally admitted Vermont to the union. The face of these contentious bills bore a chain similar to Franklin's, but near the top, a fourteenth link remained unattached. The English motto exclaimed, "Vermont calls for justice."[51] Franklin's emblems thus provided symbols by which the people of the United States could rejoice in their nation and contest its boundaries.

In the meantime, Franklin's designs also enabled Congress's enemies to voice their political opposition. The continental currency sparked a great deal of interested conversation among loyalists and British sympathizers. A British officer, for instance, introduced the Salem loyalist William Browne to the "devices upon the denominations of the continental bills." Browne in turn wrote brief descriptions of Doctor Franklin's latest "inventions" and forwarded them to exiled loyalists in London.[52] Perhaps because Congress's paper money excited the patriot imagination, and aroused the curiosity even of "disaffected" persons such as Browne, loyalist satirists worked diligently to discredit it. In October 1776, for example, the British-sponsored *New York Gazette and Weekly Mercury* printed a scornful mock advertisement implying that the continental bills were better fit to decorate walls than to circulate as a medium of exchange: "Wanted, by a gentleman fond of curiosities, who is shortly going to England, a parcel of congress notes, with which he intends to paper some rooms."[53] Similarly, in March 1778, a Pennsylvania editorialist lamented that Congress, "like a set of giddy mad-caps, entered the *dance*, without money to *pay the piper*." This writer—perhaps a Quaker for he or she wrote under the pseudonym "Pacificus"—disparaged the continental currency as a "droll kind of money . . . [that] consisted of nothing but *brown paper*."[54]

Obverse of Franklin's one-third dollar bill, featuring his chain design, a popular but contentious emblem of American unity. Reproduced from the original held by the Department of
Special Collections of the University Libraries of Notre Dame.

Numerous of the writers who attacked Congress's paper money explicitly
lampooned Franklin's designs. In February 1778, the *Pennsylvania Evening
Post* printed a poetical satire of Franklin's two-dollar bill, whose hand-and-
flail emblem suggested that a good threshing would improve the country.

> That thrashing [*sic*] makes rich the congress do know,
> Or else on their money they would not say so;
> But what kind of thrashing they do not explain,
> Whether beat by the English or beating out grain:
> And since we're left dark, we may fairly conclude,
> That both will enrich them, and both do them good.[55]

Signed by "A Maryland Loyalist," this poem lambasted a notion that must
have struck many colonists as dubious and dangerous: that the war would
somehow strengthen or enrich the people of British North America.

The most detailed and contemptuous censure of Franklin's emblems
flowed from the pen of Joseph Stansbury, a loyalist Philadelphia shopkeeper.
Stansbury opposed the American resistance movement and welcomed the
British capture of Philadelphia in 1777. He later served as an intermediary
in Benedict Arnold's treasonous correspondence with the British high

command. Throughout the war, Stansbury composed verses, which he presumably circulated among loyalist acquaintances, that celebrated the British Empire and ridiculed colonial patriots. In 1776, Stansbury wrote a disdainful satire of the continental currency entitled "The History of Peru." The depth and vigor of this poem suggest that the author carefully scrutinized both Franklin's emblems and Clericus's letter to the *Pennsylvania Gazette*.[56]

Stansbury opened by suggesting that Congress possessed no more virtue than any other government:

> Most Authors describe Man
> A covetous Elf
> That Health, Fame, and Honour
> would barter for Pelf,
> Assemblymen, Convention,
> or Congress or King,
> It is Money suits all—
> and of Money I sing.

Stansbury particularly blamed Congress for issuing an unbacked and unreliable paper currency. The title of his poem, "History of Peru," alluded to the fabled silver mines in the Andes Mountains, a source of extraordinary wealth for the Spanish Empire in the late sixteenth and seventeenth centuries. Stansbury sarcastically likened Congress's printing press to those vast Peruvian lodes, declaring, "Our Wealth knows no End." Alluding to many colonists' refusal to accept Congress's paper money, Stansbury chided that assembly for continuing to emit "Blackball'd Paper."

Turning his attention to the bills, Stansbury first suggested that Franklin's decision to abandon colonial motifs was itself emblematic of the sad state of British American affairs. Early in his career, Franklin stamped Pennsylvania currency with the Penn family coat of arms, which bore the mottoes "Mercy" and "Justice." "Mercy and Justice," Stansbury rued, "are now left behind, / for Mercy is dead, / and poor Justice is blind." Stansbury likewise scoffed at the haughtiness of Franklin's Latin: "The Latin, besure, / strikes the Ear somewhat Grand O, / For what is plain English / to Perseverando!" To Stansbury's mind the worst fault of these bills was their affectation. Much like the new American "State," Franklin's bills tried pretentiously to "cut a figure." In poking fun at Franklin's thirty-dollar emblem, Stanbury belittled the honors that Congress chased after: "The Laurel awaits us, / if we do not falter, / But it's Pasteboard, not Marble / that fashions the Altar."

Stansbury dreaded that Franklin's dizzying array of metaphors had baffled and duped the colonists.

> Then We were a Crane
> and Great Britain a Spear
> Then We were the Corn
> which She thrash'd most severe
> Or We were the Harp
> that was ever in tune—
> Then We were the Beaver
> And now We're the Spoon!

Used here in a colloquial sense, "Spoon" referred to a simpleton or dunce.[57] Only a person so naive could be tempted by the promise of an "enriching" threshing. Only a person so gullible could believe, as Franklin's emblems insisted, "that Thirteen are but One." By vilifying members of Congress and other prominent patriots with epithets connoting foolishness—"Spoon," "Folly," "Puppet show"—and irrationality—"raving," "Madness"—Stansbury cast aspersions on their mental faculties and self-control. Stansbury further accused the Continental Congressmen of tyrannical ambition. He sarcastically commended Franklin's linked-chain motif, implying that it was an apt emblem of the slavery in which Congress conspired to bind the colonists. Stansbury warned that these self-appointed rulers, enthralled with their newfound public stature, would never relinquish power or return to their proper rank as brewers, candlesnuffers, and schoolmasters.[58]

Stansbury concluded his satire by appropriating Franklin's most famous motto and proposing an alternative economic vision for America: "Mind your Business, good folks, / of this raving give o'er // Return to your Duty, / Great Britain is kind, / And all past Offenses, / She'll give to the Wind." Whereas Franklin urged industry and frugality as the path to political and economic autonomy, Stansbury promoted allegiance as the proud obligation of British subjects. By beckoning his countrymen to their "Duty," Stansbury demanded that they give up their trade boycott and return instead to their traditional posture of mercantile subordination. For their reward, the colonists would once again enjoy the blessings of Englishmen:

> Peace, Freedom, and Safety
> Again is your Lot,
> And Stand, till in ruin

> Old Nature is hurl'd,
> The Glory, the Envy,
> and Pride of the World.

Franklin had called on the American people to envision themselves as members of a new polity. Stansbury, by contrast, reminded his fellow colonists of their place within the British nation. The imperial conflict thus waged across the faces of Congress's bills.[59]

Franklin's currency emblems did little to sustain the value of the continental currency. Or didn't they? At least one contemporary critic believed that Franklin had given force to Congress's money. "There is a great plenty of rag money," wrote a captain in the British army in March 1777, a few months after Franklin departed for Paris on diplomatic mission. "[B]ut since old Franklin went to France, there is no one left to argue it into the favor of Jerseymen, who, though justly called republicans, are not willing to give even bad provisions for Congress notes, or mere rebel promises to pay."[60] If Franklin managed to argue his money into favor—if only to a limited degree and if only for a brief time—he did so by persuading the colonists of the righteousness of their resistance and by helping them to imagine themselves as part of a new political and economic community. Franklin's monetary designs dignified the continental currency, rendering it a decorous medium of exchange for a budding confederation. But more than mere ornamentation, Franklin's bills propelled Americans toward economic autonomy and marshaled their energies in support of war. His emblems served potently as the earliest symbols of American resistance and confederation. At the same time, however, Franklin's money invited criticism, not only of its aesthetic qualities, but also of the vision it offered for the United Colonies. Franklin's emblems provided a shared iconographic vocabulary by which even those persons who opposed the war, persons such as Joseph Stansbury, could give expression to their opinions. Pennsylvania soldiers marching into battle, loyalists protesting the Continental Congress, Green Mountaineers calling for statehood: these and other Americans used Franklin's emblems to make their own meanings of the Revolution and the disordered world in which they lived. Therein lay the value, if not the worth, of the continental.

4

The Pride and Pomp of War

DURING THE WINTER OF 1774–75, many American communities began to exercise militias or to organize independent companies of volunteer soldiers in anticipation of armed conflict. In January, for example, George Washington reported that Virginians had begun "forming themselves into independent Companies, chusing their officers, arming, Equipping, & training for the worst Event. The last Appeal!" The outbreak of war at Lexington and Concord greatly intensified the colonists' efforts. As the Virginia congressman Richard Henry Lee declared, "The shameful defeat of General Gages Troops near Boston . . . roused . . . a universal Military spirit thro out all the Colonies." America's commons and greens burst forth in a boisterous pageant of war.[1]

As they journeyed to Philadelphia in the late spring of 1775, delegates to the Second Continental Congress not only witnessed this martial splendor, but by their presence also inspired and animated it. Local militia units turned out as a matter of pride to escort congressmen as they traveled from town to town. Writing to his son, the North Carolina delegate Richard Caswell described the militant scenes that unfolded in Virginia and Maryland, where independent companies treated passing congressmen to "all the Military honors due to General Officers":

Here [at the Potomac River] were part of the Militia of three Counties under Arms & in the Uniform of hunting shirts. . . . [At Port Tobacco] the Independants made a Most Glorious Appearance. Their Company consisted of 68 Men beside officers all Genteelly drest in Scarlet & well equiped with Arms & Warlike Implements with drum & Fife. . . . The next Morning We all set out together & were Attended by the Independants to the Verge of their County, where they delivered us to another Company of Independants in Prince George's & they in like Manner to a second and that to a Third which brot us through their County. . . Arrived at Baltimore at the enterance of Which Town we were received by four Independant Companies who Conducted us with their Colours Flying, drums Beating & Fifes playing to our Lodgings at the Fountain Tavern.[2]

These military escorts represented a novel distinction for members of the Continental Congress. Ten months earlier, private citizens, not armed soldiers, had welcomed the delegates and conducted them along their way. The congressmen's safe passage did not now necessitate such large contingents of troops. It did, however, provide an opportunity for provincial militias and independent companies to display their proficiency and their devotion to the cause. It also enabled them to demonstrate a heightened measure of respect for Congress. After the eruption of hostilities in Massachusetts, these militiamen and independents began to view Congress in a new light. They rightly anticipated that Congress would undertake responsibility for mobilizing the colonists and readying their defenses. Though these volunteer soldiers answered only to their provincial authorities, they recognized that the fate of the American war effort rested in Congress's hands.

In the weeks that followed, the Second Continental Congress did indeed take momentous steps, creating an army and issuing a paper currency. In so doing, Congress began to wield substantial executive and legislative authority. To legitimize its exercise of governmental powers, Congress assumed a prominent place in the military spectacle that unfolded across the summer of 1775, making appearances, for example, at the drills and parades of Philadelphia's independent associators. Congress also began to devise new rituals—and to creatively adapt older British traditions—by which to steel the colonists for war. Congress feted the new army commander George Washington on his departure for camp; it set aside days of fasting, humiliation, and prayer; it displayed the trophies garnered by continental forces at Montreal;

it commissioned a medal to celebrate the liberation of Boston; and it robustly commemorated the lives of civil and military officers who died in the service of the United Colonies.

By these means, Congress worked to justify Americans' participation in a defensive war. It labored to harness the public's militancy and to channel its energies into a disciplined campaign. It worked to unify the British colonists as a common people and to delineate the boundaries of their American community. By these same means, Congress also endeavored to vindicate its exertion of extraordinary powers. Most delegates to the Second Continental Congress carried broad grants of discretionary authority—from their home assemblies, conventions, or other appointing bodies—for obtaining the redress of American grievances.[3] Yet, as these delegates well understood, many segments of the colonial population not only blamed Congress for exacerbating the imperial crisis, but looked on the prospect of civil war with profound dismay and regret. By placing itself conspicuously at the fore of a sober, devout, and well-regimented resistance, Congress sought to win favor both for its scheme of military preparations and for its assumption of continental authority. Congress further strove, in keeping with republican mandate, to assert its supremacy, as the civil authority, over the army that it had created.

In its efforts to recast American resistance as a holy war, as in its efforts to enlist the memory of the dead in the fight for liberty, Congress met with considerable opposition. Some individuals resented Congress's attempts to sanctify the American rebellion. Others insisted that Congress hew its politics not toward independence, but rather toward reconciliation. The rituals and observances that Congress inaugurated after the outbreak of war did not fix the meaning or purpose of colonial protest. Rather, they provided opportunities for persons of divergent political beliefs to express their own ideas about the supposed righteousness of the American cause.

Comitia Americana

Delegates to the Second Continental Congress arrived in Philadelphia to discover that their host city had been swept up, like much of the countryside through which they had traveled, in a *rage militaire*. "Warlike Musick" broke the Quaker silence. "Uniforms, and Regimentals" swarmed "thick as Bees."[4] Immediately after the delegates assembled, Congress began to prepare for war. On May 11, the delegates reviewed the depositions of persons who had witnessed the skirmishes at Lexington and Concord. Two weeks later, Congress determined to put the colonies "into a state of defence." In early June, Congress passed a series of resolutions for provisioning "the American army before Boston"—which is to say, the New England militias that had gathered in response to the hostilities in Massachusetts—and on June 14, Congress resolved to augment those militias by raising ten companies of riflemen from Pennsylvania, Maryland, and Virginia. On June 16, Congress appointed the Virginia congressman George Washington to command this new "American continental army." Before summers' end, Congress would authorize an invasion of Canada, issue the Declaration on Taking Arms, and direct the organization of a military hospital.[5]

Though the Continental Congress moved quickly to create an army, the delegates did not take that action lightly. Real Whig ideology—a tradition of political thought that greatly inspired the American resistance—taught that professional, standing armies tend to accumulate dangerous power. Consuming vast quantities of public resources, comprising large numbers of armed men, commanded by officers whose every battlefield victory further endeared them to a grateful populace, an army would, if left unchecked, devour the society it was established to defend. Such were the lessons of Greece and Rome and such were the grim and still-fresh legacies of the English Civil War. Mindful of these histories, Real Whig thinkers of the seventeenth and eighteenth centuries—writers such as James Harrington, Robert Molesworth, John Trenchard, and Thomas Gordon—warned that the preservation of liberty depended on the subordination of military forces to civil authority.[6]

By compelling Congress to establish an army, the outbreak of war in Massachusetts provoked Whig concerns about the accumulation of power by a military force. Members of Congress did not expect that the Continental Army would become a permanent, standing institution; rather, they anticipated that it would disband soon after the resolution of the imperial conflict. Nevertheless, as royal authority continued to disintegrate in the British colonies, some delegates began to fear that an army of Congress's own creation would encroach on American rights. Counseling his friends in Massachusetts, Samuel Adams declared,

> A standing Army, however necessary it may be at some times, is always dangerous to the Liberties of the People. Soldiers are apt to consider themselves as a Body distinct from the rest of the Citizens. They have their Arms always in their hands. Their Rules

and their Discipline is severe. They soon become attachd to their officers and disposd to yeild [*sic*] implicit Obedience to their Commands. . . . Men who have been long governd by military Laws, and inurd to military Customs and Habits, may lose the Spirit and Feeling of Citizens. And even Citizens, having been used to admire the Heroism which the Commanders of their own Armies have displayd, and to look up to them as their Saviours, may be prevaild upon to surrender to them those Rights, for the Protection of which against an Invader, they had employd & paid them.[7]

To prevent such ruin, Congress worked diligently to assert its supremacy over America's armed forces.

One way that Congress accomplished this was by participating conspicuously in the military fanfare of 1775. On the morning of June 8, the delegates attended "a grand review of the Militia of this City." Weeks before, after receiving word of the British offensive against Lexington and Concord, thousands of Philadelphians had turned out to defend their "Property, Liberty, and Lives." Since that time, these volunteers had mustered twice a day "to learn the military discipline." This, their first exhibition, a moment of pride and accomplishment, made a sensational show. Three battalions, consisting of two thousand men—including a unit of artillery equipped with brass field pieces, as well as "a troop of lighthorse, several companies of light infantry, rangers, and riflemen"—assembled in brigade and together performed "manual exercise, firings, and manoeuvres, with a dexterity scarcely to have been expected from such short practice."[8] The Continental Congress was not obliged to attend this "grand review." These battalions did not fall directly under Congress's command; they answered, as they saw fit, to Philadelphia's revolutionary committees.[9] But that fact made the delegates' attendance all the more symbolically significant. By appearing on the field of exercise, Congress expressed its support for and admiration of these volunteer soldiers. Congress further signaled its intention to closely superintend America's armed forces. In a brief account of the event, subsequently reprinted throughout the colonies and in London, the *Pennsylvania Evening Post* reported that the battalions conducted their exercises "in the presence of the gentlemen of the Congress, and several thousands of spectators." Making no specific mention of provincial or local officials who may have been present that morning, the *Pennsylvania Evening Post* gave the impression that those battalions had in fact exercised at Congress's pleasure.[10]

In the months that followed, some members of Congress, including Patrick Henry and John Dickinson, did in fact assume places of command in their provincial militias. John Adams believed that these statesmen had an important role to play in rallying American forces. Noting the "Ardor and Pathos" with which Dickinson "harangue[d]" his Pennsylvania battalions, Adams declared, "In the Beginning of a War . . . where the martial Spirit is but just awakened and the People are unaccustomed to Arms, it may be proper and necessary for such popular Orators as Henry and Dickenson [*sic*] to assume a military Character."[11]

Because Congress aspired so earnestly to preserve the subordination of America's armed forces, the selection of a general to lead the army was a decision of paramount importance. In the tradition of the British monarchy, supreme command of military forces resided in the king or queen. For this reason, Britons invested the Crown with all the accoutrements of military glory. In the words of the eminent jurist William Blackstone, the British nation exalted its monarch "as the generalissimo, or the first in military command, within the kingdom."[12] The Continental Congress did not intend to supplant the king, but it had created an army. As a plural executive, Congress stood at best but awkwardly at the head of that new institution. Consequently there arose a risk that whomever Congress appointed to lead the army would glean the accolades of war and emerge as an object of popular adulation. Over the course of the Revolution, the staunchest republicans in Congress came to fret over Americans' idolization of their commander in chief, but in the summer of 1775, they took comfort in the appointment of George Washington.

One of the wealthiest planters in Virginia, owner of thousands of acres and hundreds of slaves, Washington was nevertheless humble and reserved. He carried himself with extraordinary self-discipline, befitting his stature as one of the British colonies' most senior and experienced officers. A veteran of the Seven Years' War, he had served with distinction at the Battle of Monongahela in 1755 and again in Forbes's expedition against Fort Duquesne in 1758. As commander of the Virginia militia, he had also defended Virginia's interests against France and its Native American allies in the Ohio River Valley. In 1774, Washington's reputation as a bold champion of American resistance preceded him to the Continental Congress. Before he had even set foot in Philadelphia, Washington's fellow Virginians spread the story of a "most eloquent Speech" in which he, as a delegate in their provincial convention, pledged to raise one thousand men, outfit them at his own expense, and march them "for the Relief of Boston." Along his journey back to Philadelphia in 1775, Washington stopped in Baltimore, where, in testament to the high regard in which he was held even outside his native colony, local authorities called on him to review their militia. At the Second Continental Congress, which Washington attended in dress uniform, delegates frequently consulted him for "his great Experience and Abilities in military Matters."[13]

For all his qualifications and martial demeanor, Washington's appointment also made shrewd political sense. Unlike other potential candidates for the command, Washington had been born and raised in the American colonies, not in the British Isles. No less significantly, he hailed from the Chesapeake, rather than from New England. His appointment was expected to gratify Virginians and to persuade the colonists that British tyranny posed a threat not only to the people of Massachusetts but to all Americans. As the Connecticut congressman Eliphalet Dyer explained in a letter to his governor, the installation of Washington would "more strongly Cement the Southern with the Northern Colonies, & serve to the removing all jealousies [against an] Army composed principally of New Englanders."[14]

In accepting his commission, Washington exhibited all of the virtues that members of Congress desired in the commander of a republican army. Disavowing his own merits, Washington declared "with the utmost sincerity" that he did not think himself "equal to the Command" with which he had been honored. Refusing to accept a salary, Washington assured, "[N]o pecuniary consideration could have tempted me to have accepted this arduous employment."[15] In the days that followed, Washington also penned numerous letters—to his wife, to his brother and brother-in-law, and to the captains of the Virginia militia—all disclaiming any interest in or fitness for his new post: "I assure you in the most solemn manner, that, so far from seeking this appointment, I have used every endeavor in my power to avoid it." He expressed dread that the generalship was "a trust too great for [his] capacity," and he lamented that it would rob him of the "real happiness" of retirement with his family. Indeed, Washington asserted that he had accepted the post only to save his loved ones from embarrassment: "[I]t was utterly out of my power to refuse this appointment without exposing my Character to such censures as would have reflected dishonor upon myself, and given pain to my friends." Washington promised to return safely to his family, but he nevertheless enclosed in his letter to Martha a freshly drafted will and testament.[16]

Washington's correspondence exemplified both the refined characteristics of a landed gentleman and the keen sensibilities of an officer steeped in the British military tradition. His stoic repudiation of "every kind of domestick ease" recalled the selfless patriotism of Cincinnatus, even as his will, providing for Martha in the event of his death, gave full satisfaction to the masculine ideals of a Southern patriarch. His humble expressions of self-doubt, however sincere, suggested to readers—both the designated recipients of his letters and the Virginia gentry among whom they were sure to circulate—a measure of ennobling modesty. And yet, for all his professions of "inadequacy," Washington's letters conveyed his abundant sense of honor. It was honor that compelled Washington to forego the "felicity" of retirement, honor that compelled him to assume the command in spite of his "want of experience," and honor that compelled him to disregard the harm his public reputation would "probably" sustain. Washington, his readers were to believe, accepted his commission not because he wished to be an officer once again, but rather because his honor had demanded it. This is not to suggest that Washington's humility was feigned or insincere. As a careful student of gentility, he instinctively suppressed any outward display of ambition and he may very well have doubted his qualifications for command on a continental scale. But Washington's farewell letters must also be understood as self-conscious appeals to the norms and traditions of the Anglo-American military establishment. Making masterful displays of heroic, Cincinnatean virtue, Washington's letters particularly suggest the influence of classical republicanism on the British army and colonial militias.

Because Washington so epitomized the republican ideal, members of Congress, particularly the New England delegates, extolled his appointment. John Adams could not help but romanticize the new commander: "There is something charming to me in the conduct of Washington," Adams proclaimed. "A gentleman of one of the first fortunes upon the continent, leaving his delicious retirement, his family and friends, sacrificing his ease, and hazarding all in the cause of his country!" Working to quiet apprehensions about the appointment of a Southern commander, other New England congressmen explicitly praised Washington's humility and self-possession. Thomas Cushing described the new general as "a compleat gentleman . . . sinsible, amiable, virtuous, modest, & brave." Similarly Eliphalet Dyer portrayed him as "discret & Virtuous, no harum Starum ranting Swearing fellow but Sober, steady & Calm." Writing to the governor of Connecticut, Dyer assured, "We esteem [Washington] . . . much better Suited to the Temper & Genius of our People than any other Gent not brought up in that Part of the Country."[17]

To herald the commander, but also to present their native colonies in the fairest possible light, New England delegates instructed local officials to prepare fanfare for Washington's arrival. "I hope the utmost politeness and respect will be shown to these officers," John Adams declared. "The whole army, I think, should be drawn up upon the occasion, and all the pride, pomp, and circumstance of glorious war displayed;—no powder burned, however."[18]

Pennsylvania authorities and members of Congress likewise organized a bit of informal ceremony for the general's departure. On the morning of June 20, the battalions of Philadelphia once again drilled, this time under the superintending eye of the commander in chief, in the first public appearance since his appointment. John Adams deemed the spectacle—with its precision "Wheelings and Firings"—a "great shew" for "Our great Generals."[19] The *Pennsylvania Evening Post* reported that General Washington, "who is appointed Commander in Chief of all the North-American forces by the honorable Continental Congress," had reviewed the associators. In notable contrast with its coverage of the associators' previous exercise, the *Evening Post* did not indicate that members of Congress had attended.[20] Transpiring less than two weeks apart, these two military drills gave ceremonial expression to the transfer of military authority from Congress to the commander in chief.

Three days later, Washington and a handful of subordinates set out on horseback for "the American Camp" outside of Boston. To see the general off, several members of Congress rode out in their carriages, accompanied by a large troop of light horse and numerous uniformed militia officers, while musicians played a tune.[21] Upon returning to the city, members of this entourage ventured to Christ Church, at the invitation of Philadelphia's third battalion, to hear a sermon delivered by Reverend William Smith. An Anglican clergyman and provost of the College of Philadelphia, Smith figured prominently, but not always agreeably, in the city's Revolutionary civic ceremony. Many Philadelphia patriots distrusted Smith. Benjamin Rush, a local physician and future member of Congress, warned the New England delegates that Smith aspired to "an American Episcopate and a Pair of lawn Sleeves." John Adams warily noted that the "[s]oft, polite, insinuating, adulating, sensible, learned, industrious, [and] indefatigable" Smith "had Art enough and Refinement upon Art to make Impressions" even on ardent and sober patriots.[22]

Though Rush and Adams harbored misgivings, Philadelphia's third battalion put their faith in Smith, with some good reason. Nearly two decades before, at the height of the Seven Years' War, Smith had delivered a well-received sermon entitled *The Christian Soldier's Duty*, which justified the lawfulness and dignity of war against "*popish* Perfidy, *French* Tyranny and *savage* Barbarity."[23] More recently, Smith had established himself as a vocal supporter of American rights. That spring, he invited members of the recently reconvened Congress to attend graduation exercises at the College of Philadelphia. There, students performed a patriotic dialogue—written for the occasion by the provost himself—that heaped accolades on the congressmen and urged them to stay the course of resistance:

> Attend! be firm! Ye fathers of the state!
> Ye chosen bands, who for your country's weal
> With rigid self-denial, sacrifice
> Your private ease,—let wisdom be your guide,
> And zeal enlightened feed the ardent flame,
> Which yet shall purge and renovate the land.

At that same graduation ceremony, Smith's eldest son, a member of the graduating class, delivered a speech entitled "The Fall of Empires." Though the younger Smith made no explicit reference to Congress's Articles of Association, he railed against the imported luxuries that had corrupted the world's great civilizations. The most earnest republicans in Congress could not have scripted a more rousing commencement.[24]

On the day of Washington's departure, Smith inspired once again. Urging his fellow Anglican clergymen to champion the cause of religion and liberty, Smith proclaimed that "continued submission to violence" was no tenet of his church. Beseeching Philadelphia's associators to "cultivate the spirit of Liberty," Smith looked forward to the day when their country would rise as "a chosen seat for freedom." Then and there Smith erased any lingering doubt about his patriotism. The Connecticut congressman Silas Deane wrote that Smith's sermon "exceeded in style and sentiment anything I ever heard on the subject." Relinquishing old suspicions, Deane acclaimed the provost as a model of clerical conscience: "As the Doctor has been called an high churchman, and one that had a bishopric in expectation, I hope his thus publicly sounding the pulpit alarm on the subject of liberty will be an example to the church clergy elsewhere." In coming months, members of Congress would come to regret placing their confidence in the "insinuating" Reverend Smith.[25]

Reflecting back over the spectacle of the day, particularly the cavalcade of civil and military officials that had escorted Washington out of town, John Adams mused, "Such is the Pride and Pomp of War."[26] At times during the summer of 1775, the Continental Congress found itself swept up in that pride and pomp, and the manner in which it chose to participate helps to illuminate the paradoxical relationship between Congress and the Continental Army. On the one hand, Congress wished to celebrate American military might, to encourage enlistments, and to engage the public in a vigorous war effort. On the other hand, Congress sought to uphold the civil authority, elevating neither the army nor its commander to a place of veneration. Though the delegates enthusiastically trumpeted Washington and exhorted Pennsylvanians to lively military preparations, Congress made a point of asserting its supremacy over the army.

John Adams felt this imperative more urgently than most. Adams, who came of age during the imperial wars of the mid-eighteenth century, had long pined for a military career. As a schoolboy at the height of King George's War in 1746, he marveled at the thousands of New England militiamen who marched to Boston to defend their shores against the Duke d'Anville. As a drudging young lawyer at the opening of the Seven Years' War, he felt "a flow of Spirits, and an Effort of Imagination, very like an Ambition to be engaged in the more active, gay, and dangerous Scenes."[27] As a delegate to the Continental Congress, Adams vowed that he would turn out "in Rank and File" if the war should take a desperate turn. "Oh that I was a Soldier!" Adams declared, "I will be. I am reading military Books. Every Body must and will, and shall be a soldier."[28]

Adams's boyish longing for the soldierly life, his Whiggish instinct to preserve the supremacy of the civil authority, and his hope that the regiments of his native New England would outperform General Washington's low expectations all fixed his mind on army affairs.[29] He begged his associates in Massachusetts to keep him apprised of the army's innermost workings. "It is of vast Importance," Adams explained, "that I should be minutely informed of every thing which passes at the Camp, while I hold a Place in the Great Council of America." Throughout the summer and fall of 1775, Adams brooded over the most mundane operations of the army. In June, he implored James Warren to see that Massachusetts soldiers bathed frequently and kept "their Linnen washed and their Beds clean." In July, he demanded that his former law clerk William Tudor provide him with the name of every engineer to be found in the province. In September, he advised Abigail to instruct their children in "Geometry, Geography, and the Art of drawing," the "utility" of those sciences having been forcefully impressed on him in recent days. In November, he entreated the Boston bookseller and future artillerist Henry Knox to stock Harvard's library with "a compleat set of Books upon the military Art in all its Branches." Most of all, Adams demanded to know the

"Character of every Man" who appeared at camp. Fearing that the officer corps might be corrupted by persons of low virtue or dubious political principles, Adams entreated his friends to "make the most minute Enquiry" of every would-be aide, secretary, or deputy. "I will know that Army," Adams resolved. "I swear, I will be a faithfull Spy upon it for its good."[30]

Determined to uphold the civil authority, Adams at times peevishly defended the dignity of Congress. In October 1775, he censured William Tudor for inadvertently belittling Congress in the eyes of General Washington. Recently appointed to the post of judge advocate general, largely on the basis of Adams's recommendation, Tudor wrote to the commander seeking clarification of his duties. "The Congress," Tudor confided, "were wholly unacquainted with the Duties of a Judge Advocate, especially in the continental Army." Tudor may have drawn this conclusion fairly and innocently, for not two months before, Adams specifically instructed him to "make Enquiry" about the "Duties and necessary attributes" of similar officers, including "the Quarter Master General, the Muster Master General, the Commissary of Artillery &c." Nevertheless, Tudor's unguarded expression greatly "alarmed" Adams, who feared that it would "excite a Disgust" in Congress. Censuring Tudor, Adams explained that even if the charge of congressional ignorance had been true, "yet it was indecent to tell them of it, because they ought to be presumed to know all the Duties of this officer, but most especially in their own Army." Adams would not have the ineptitude of Congress complained of to the commander in chief.[31]

Adams's concern for the civil authority, Congress's desire to commend the army to the American people, and Washington's characteristic humility all found emblematic expression, in the spring of 1776, in the first medal commissioned by the Continental Congress. Early that March, the Continental Army fortified Dorchester Heights, which looked out over the Boston peninsula, and thereby compelled British forces to evacuate the Massachusetts Bay. To honor Washington and to celebrate the memorable liberation of Boston, John Adams prevailed on Congress to award the triumphant general a medal. Establishing a tradition that it would maintain throughout the war, Congress ordered the medal struck and appointed a committee to fabricate an emblem of the American victory.[32] As a member of that committee, Adams wrote to Washington to solicit the general's recommendations for a suitable design. With the modesty that had so endeared him to Congress, Washington responded, "What ever Device may be determined upon, by the respectable committee they have chosen for that purpose will be highly agreeable to me."[33]

Washington's medal would not be executed for another fourteen years. Whether Benjamin Duvivier, the French engraver who ultimately completed the device in 1790, fully appreciated the sentiments of Congress in 1776 is not known. He very well may have, for he designed the medal in consultation with Thomas Jefferson, who attended Congress through much of that summer. Duvivier's creation, which came to be known as the "Washington before Boston" medal, adroitly symbolized Congress's solicitous regard for its authority. The medal featured a bust of the general, encircled by the Latin inscription, *Georgio Washington Svpremo Dvci Exercitvvm Adsertori Libertatis,* or, "George Washington, Supreme Commander of the Army, Champion of Liberty." Below, in exergue, appeared the important words, *Comitia Americana.* A reference to the institution that had granted the medal, this inscription signified that the power to bestow laurels, like the power to establish an army or appoint its commanders, resided in the American Congress. Congress, the medal instructed, was the foundation of Washington's command.[34]

"[T]o cajole the godly Party"

Assuming a role in the military spectacle of 1775 and 1776 was but one of the ways that the Second Continental Congress strove to promote the American war effort. In the same week that Congress established the Continental

The medal awarded by the Continental Congress to General George Washington for the liberation of Boston, 1776. "Washington before Boston, 1776." Obverse. Bronze medal engraved by Benjamin Duvivier. Reproduced from the original held by the Department of Special Collections of the University Libraries of Notre Dame.

Army, it also appointed a day of "humiliation, fasting, and prayer" throughout the continent. Endeavoring to consecrate the American resistance and to promote defensive preparations as the sacred obligation of every colonist, Congress established a practice that it would keep throughout the war. In so doing, however, Congress subjected itself to charges of hypocrisy, abuse of religion, and, later in the war, incompetence. Days that Congress set aside for worship became occasions of political protest and dissent, both for loyalists and patriots alike.

The keeping of fast days and thanksgivings was a longstanding tradition whose colonial origins may be traced to the English Civil War.[35] After the convention of the Long Parliament in 1640, Puritan authorities began to appoint days of humiliation, fasting, and prayer. On the Restoration of Charles II in 1660, fast days and thanksgivings fell somewhat out of favor in England, but they remained popular in the Puritan colonies. During the seventeenth and early eighteenth centuries, civil officials in Massachusetts, Connecticut, and New Hampshire commonly proclaimed fasts in response to catastrophic events that they interpreted as manifestations of God's displeasure: the outbreak of illness, the eruption of war with Native Americans, or the devastation of crops by droughts, floods, or pests. Likewise, they appointed thanksgivings upon the restoration of good health, the smiting of enemies, and the reaping of bountiful harvests.[36] Enabling New England communities to beg forgiveness for their wayward behavior and to express gratitude for divine blessings, fast days and thanksgivings made rituals of covenant theology.[37]

During the taxation controversies of the 1760s and 1770s, these occasions began to reflect the colonists' political tensions with Great Britain. In 1771, for example, Governor Thomas Hutchinson ordered the people of Massachusetts to give thanks for the "continuance of our civil and religious privileges." This order irked colonists who noted a distinction between privileges and rights and who believed that an overreaching Parliament threatened both. To protest Hutchinson's offensive proclamation, Massachusetts ministers refused to read it to their congregations. After the imposition of the Coercive Acts, fast days and thanksgivings grew more politicized still. The president of the Massachusetts provincial congress John Hancock's December 1774 thanksgiving proclamation appeared without the customary royal arms or the legend, "God save the King." In response, James Rivington's *New-York Gazetteer* published a derisive satire, "Thanks upon Thanks":

> Thanks to H[ancoc]k for *thanksgiving*,
> Thanks to G-d for our *good-living*;

> Thanks to Gage for hindering evil;
> And, for source of discord civil,
> Thanks to [Samuel] Ad[am]s and—the Devil![38]

Meanwhile, in Virginia, the Coercive Acts provoked the House of Burgesses to proclaim that colony's first fast day in nearly three decades. In a demonstration of Virginians' sympathy for the plight of Massachusetts, the burgesses scheduled their fast for June 1, 1774, the day on which the Port Bill was to go into effect. Rummaging through a dusty volume on the English Civil War, Thomas Jefferson, Patrick Henry, and Richard Henry Lee uncovered "the revolutionary precedents and forms of the Puritans of that day," and "cooked up" a suitable proclamation. Virginia's royal governor Lord Dunmore seized on that proclamation as a pretense for dissolving the House.[39]

By the summer of 1775, the colonists' tradition of public fasts had thus become thoroughly entangled in imperial politics. When, after the Battles of Lexington and Concord, the Continental Congress set aside the twentieth of July as a day of fasting, it sought chiefly to promote American piety and godliness, but it also engaged in conspicuous revolutionary partisanship.[40] Congress's choice of dates, like Virginia's in 1774, was significant: Parliament had marked the twentieth of July for implementation of certain provisions of the New England Trade and Fisheries Act, a punitive law that prohibited American colonies from trading with other nations and from fishing in the rich waters of the North Atlantic.

To announce the fast, Congress appointed William Hooper, John Adams, and Robert Treat Paine to draft a proclamation. Published in newspapers and printed on handbills, this proclamation entreated "Christians, of all denominations, to assemble for public worship." Aimed at the revival of "virtue and true religion," Congress's proclamation adhered to the conventions of the Jeremiad. It warned of "impending danger and public calamity" and called on Americans to "unfeignedly confess and deplore [their] many sins." The proclamation promised that the colonists would "soon behold a gracious interposition of Heaven," if God so willed it. Congress's fast day proclamation thus infused congressional resistance with Christian religiosity and hinged the fate of the American colonies on the piety of their inhabitants.

Congress's fast day served a number of other ends, both sacred and secular. It reaffirmed the moral sensibilities of the Association by urging colonists to refrain from "recreation" on the day of the fast. It suggested that members of Congress—far from the frenzied dissenters portrayed by their enemies—were sober, upright, and moral men. It also permitted Congress to clarify its political

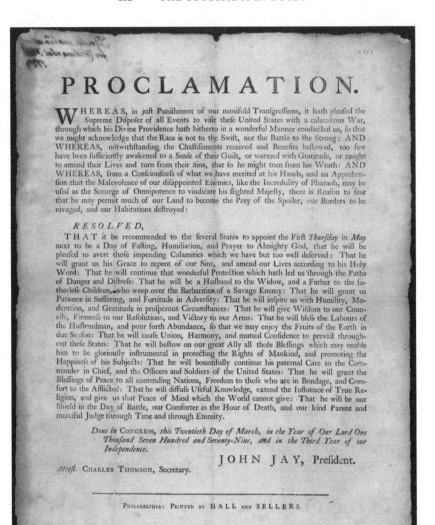

Broadside proclamation of a continental fast, issued by President John Jay, 1779. *Whereas, in Just Punishment of our Manifold Transgressions . . .* (Philadelphia, 1779). Library of Congress, Rare Book and Special Collections Division, Continental Congress and Constitutional Convention Broadsides Collection.

intentions after the Battles of Lexington and Concord. Though war had broken out in Massachusetts, few, if any, congressmen had set their minds on independence. In its fast day proclamation, Congress reasserted the imperative of securing American liberty while at the same time preserving the British Empire.

Acknowledging the "many grievances" the colonists had suffered, the proclamation nevertheless articulated Congress's desire for "reconciliation with the parent state, on terms constitutional and honorable to both." The continental fast even afforded Congress an occasion to position itself, in the public view, as a duly constituted governing body. In the colonial period, the prerogative of appointing fast days and thanksgivings belonged to colonial governors and assemblies. By adopting that prerogative as its own, the Continental Congress signaled its intention to take up the mantle of government.

Perhaps most significantly, members of Congress hoped this first continental fast would unify the American people. Rarely if ever had so many American colonies observed a common fast; never had they done so independently of the British Crown. Congress's proclamation underscored this sacred collaboration, inviting "the inhabitants of all the English colonies on this continent" to pray with "united hearts and voices . . . and offer up our joint supplications."[41] In a letter to Abigail, John Adams exulted, "Millions will be upon their Knees at once before their great Creator, imploring his Forgiveness and Blessing, his Smiles on American Councils and Arms."[42] Echoing this sentiment in an essay published in the *Pennsylvania Magazine*, the future congressman Francis Hopkinson delighted at "the thousands and ten thousands inhabitants of a country eighteen hundred miles in extent united in one important cause."[43] Not only did the continental fast join British colonists in shared acts of worship, but by the logic of covenant theology, it also allowed them to imagine themselves as part of a distinct, American community. In the Jeremiadic tradition, God held whole societies accountable for the sins of their individual members. Congress's fast day stretched the covenantal bond beyond the boundaries of a single colony, expanding it across the entire seaboard. Congress's proclamation suggested that God would deal with Americans together, as one people.[44]

To make the most of the continental fast, to hallow it both with and for the American public, Congress observed the day with high reverence. Members of Congress could have kept the fast privately, each delegate worshipping according to his own conscience. Instead, Congress resolved to worship as one body. To avoid the appearance of sectarianism, Congress agreed to go to both "Church & Meeting."[45] In the morning, Congress attended Christ Church, to hear the preaching of Reverend Jacob Duché. Having prayed with the delegates in the fall of 1774, Duché knew the temper of Congress well. His sermon, entitled *The American Vine*, an allusion to the eightieth Psalm, brilliantly articulated Congress's hopes and expectations for the continental fast. Duché spoke of the American colonists as a single people. In his opening prayer, Duché exclaimed that God inflicted "national punishments upon national guilt." In the spirit of the Articles of Association, Duché called on "Christian Patriots" to embrace "honest industry, sober frugality, simplicity of manners, plain hospitality and Christian benevolence." Before concluding, Duché complimented the Continental Congress for proclaiming the fast and urged his congregants to "adore, then, the divine wisdom and goodness, for putting it into the hearts of that Honourable Assembly, now entrusted with the great cause of American Liberty, to call upon the whole people, whom they represent, in the most solemn and affectionate manner."[46]

Later that day, Congress visited First Presbyterian, where Reverend Francis Alison delivered the sermon. The *Journals* reveal that the delegates first met at the state house and from there embarked to their morning and afternoon worship services.[47] From this fact we may infer that the delegates walked the few short blocks to Christ Church and First Presbyterian. Congress's appearance in the street, as a solemn and penitent processional, epitomized the fast day's melding of civic and sacred purpose. It might also have brought to spectators' minds a passage of Congress's fast day proclamation that called on Americans to pray for their civil rulers.[48]

Much to the gratification of Congress, the continental fast prompted widespread observance. Writing to his wife Abigail, John Adams rejoiced, "The Fast was observed here with a Decorum and solemnity, never before seen ever on a Sabbath. The Clergy of all Denominations, here preach . . . Politicks and War in a manner that I never heard in N. England."[49] Outside of Philadelphia, a variety of individuals, institutions, and governments also honored the day. The Presbyterian Synod of New York and Philadelphia, for example, postponed its previously appointed fast in June to coincide with the continental fast in July. More impressively, the provincial congress of Georgia recommended that inhabitants of that colony observe the fast that it had slated for July 19 *in addition to* the fast that Congress had scheduled for the following day.[50]

The Continental Army and numerous colonial militias likewise strictly observed the fast. Here it must be noted that though Congress proclaimed the continental fast before the clash of British and American forces at Bunker Hill, the appointed day did not arrive until after that bloody battle. The escalation of war cast a martial pallor over the continental fast. General Washington, who had by this time arrived at camp in Cambridge, ordered the officers and soldiers under his command to observe the occasion.[51] In Philadelphia, Lieutenant Robert Taylor reported that nearly "two hundred" of his fellow volunteers attended church in their uniforms.[52] At York, Reverend Daniel Batwell preached a fast-day sermon before Captain Daniel Morgan's company of riflemen, while at Christiana Bridge and Newcastle, the minister Joseph Montgomery orated to a crowd of Delaware militiamen. Finally, in Tredyffrin Township in Chester County, Reverend David Jones assured his congregants that a defensive war, fought for a just cause, was sinless.[53] Looking back over the summer of 1775, Samuel Ward, a congressional delegate from Rhode Island, concluded that the appointment of the continental fast was one of the most important achievements of the Second Continental Congress. Ward ranked the event alongside such "Great Objects" as the establishment of an army, the emission of paper money, and the scheme to import gunpowder and arms.[54]

Yet, in spite of Ward's and Adams's enthusiasm, not all British Americans participated in the fast. Some opposed it as a matter of religious scruple. The Society of Friends refused to participate in programmatic religious ceremonies. Exhibiting "a perverse spirit of obstancy [sic]," as the radical committeeman Christopher Marshall saw it, some Philadelphia Quakers breached the peace by opening their shops. To put an end to this "ill behaviour" and to force recalcitrant Quakers into "Complyance," Philadelphia patriots smashed "some few of their windows."[55] Other persons opposed the fast as a matter of political partisanship. To keep the congressionally appointed holy day was to align oneself with the American resistance, much as it had been to subscribe to the Articles of Association and much as it would soon be to accept the continental currency. To ignore the fast was thus an expression of protest. In New York, the Anglican cleric and caustic penman Samuel Seabury refused to keep the fast day in his parish. When the Sons of Liberty arrested Seabury several months later, they charged him with a number of crimes, including the failure to open his church in observance of that day.[56]

In spite of such opposition, Congress continued to proclaim fast days, most commonly during the spring months, throughout the course of the war. In the fall of 1777, after the triumph of continental forces at Saratoga, Congress also inaugurated a tradition of appointing thanksgiving days (see table 4.1). These occasions imbued the American resistance movement with sacred purpose and bound patriots in a sense of shared national destiny. But they also provided fodder for British and loyalist critics who accused Congress of false piety. In 1777, Ambrose Serle, secretary to Admiral Richard Howe, claimed that Congress ordered days of fasting and prayer simply "to cajole the godly Party" (a charge he borrowed verbatim from the English historian Thomas May's damning narrative of the Cromwellian Protectorate). It was an "Abuse" of religion, Serle maintained, to direct it toward "Sedition & Rebellion . . . an Abuse, the more diabolical as it pretends to be the more sanctimonious."[57] Similarly, in response to the particularly repugnant congressional thanksgiving of 1781, celebrated only weeks after the British surrender at Yorktown, the *Royal Gazette* proclaimed, "[I]t seems, for the benefits that have flowed from their past losses and sufferings, the Americans are commanded to rejoice! Obdurate Hypocrites! forbear to pervert the genuine devotions of grateful piety to your barbarous and destructive policy."[58]

Even patriots at times had difficulty swallowing Congress's mandatory solemnities. As early as 1776, some Americans began referring to the continental fast as "Congress Sunday." Perhaps because this phrase articulated such

Table 4.1   Fast Days and Thanksgivings Proclaimed by the Continental and Confederation Congresses

Year	Fast Days	Thanksgivings
1775	July 20	
1776	May 17	
	December 11	
	the date of congressional resolution; the fast date was determined by the individual states	
1777		December 18
1778	April 22	December 30
1779	May 6	December 9
1780	April 26	December 7
1781	May 3	October 24
		a congressional thanksgiving voted in response to the surrender at Yorktown
		December 13
1782	April 25	November 28
1783		December 11
1784		October 19
		voted in response to news of the definitive peace treaty

Source: Worthington C. Ford et al., eds., *Journals of the Continental Congress, 1774–1789*, 34 vols. (Washington, D.C., 1904–1937).

forceful cynicism toward Congress and its annual holy day, the North Carolina delegate Joseph Hewes denounced it as "Vulgar language."[59] "Vulgar"
though it may have struck Hewes, this language captured the disheartenment
of those who bore the brunt of the war. In December 1777, as the hungry and
fatigued Continental Army marched toward its encampment at Valley Forge,
Congress's first thanksgiving proclamation struck some soldiers and officers
as painfully out of season. Private Joseph Plumb Martin bitterly described
the holiday that he and his fellow soldiers were made to keep:

> While we lay here there was a Continental thanksgiving ordered
> by Congress; and . . . we were ordered to participate in it. We had
> nothing to eat for two or three days previous, except what the trees
> of the fields and forests afforded us. But we must now have what
> Congress said—a sumptuous thanksgiving to close the year of
> high living, we had now nearly seen brought to a close. Well—to
> add something extraordinary to our present stock of provisions,
> our country, ever mindful of the suffering army, opened her sympa-
> thizing heart so wide, upon this occasion, as to give us something
> to make the world stare. And what do you think it was, reader?—
> Guess.—You cannot guess, be you as much of a Yankee as you will.
> I will tell you: it gave each and every man *half* a *gill* of rice, and a
> *table spoon full* of vinegar!! After we had made sure of this extraor-
> dinary superabundant donation, we were ordered out to attend a
> meeting, and hear a sermon delivered upon the happy occasion.[60]

Major Henry Dearborn, also with the army en route to Valley Forge, likewise
found it difficult to rejoice on the occasion. "[T]his is Thanksgiving Day thro
the whole Continent of America—but God knows We have very little to
keep it," Dearborn declared. "I think all we have to be thankful for is that we
are alive & not in the Grave with many of our friends."[61]

"[F]or the Indulgence of Griefe"

In the months that followed the creation of the army, as hostilities between
British and American forces accelerated, and the prospect of independence
drew more clearly into view, a grievous and unforeseen turn of events enabled
Congress to further solemnize the war effort both with and for the American
public. The deaths, in rapid succession, of three prominent patriots—Peyton

Randolph, past president of Congress, speaker of the Virginia House of Burgesses, and chair of Virginia's provincial conventions; Richard Montgomery, a Continental Army general killed during the failed invasion of Quebec; and Samuel Ward, a Continental Congressman and former governor of Rhode Island—stirred Congress to organize three public memorial services. Spanning the momentous winter of 1775–76, these commemorations permitted Congress to promote the Articles of Association, to inaugurate a somber but stately civic culture for the United Colonies, and to assert its own institutional legitimacy as a governing authority. Pregnant with political significance, these mourning occasions at times became moments of controversy, much as Congress's first fast day had.

The earliest funeral took place in late October 1775 after Peyton Randolph's sudden death of an "Apoplectic fit." Not yet in the short history of the Continental Congress had a member died in office; consequently, the delegates had no official precedent for Randolph's commemoration. By colonial tradition, the funerals of distinguished persons, especially ranking statesmen, were highly ritualized public events. Had Randolph died in Williamsburg, he would have been commemorated grandly. Members of Congress were too sensible of Randolph's stature, too grateful for his service as their president, and too dependent on Virginia's political and military support not to honor his memory in the fullest possible manner. To coordinate Randolph's funeral, Congress appointed a three-man committee consisting of Henry Middleton of South Carolina, Stephen Hopkinson of Rhode Island, and Samuel Chase of Maryland. In consultation with Randolph's wife and friends, this committee arranged for a funeral service at Christ Church, to be performed by Jacob Duché.[62]

Randolph's funeral provided Congress a keen opportunity to model its compliance with the Articles of Association.[63] In many regions of British North America, funeral services were often sumptuous and expensive affairs, particularly among the affluent. By convention, surviving family members honored their deceased loved ones and displayed their own generosity by giving gloves, scarves, and rings, as well as wine and rum, to officiating clergymen, pallbearers, mourners.[64] The nonimportation and nonconsumption agreements of the late 1760s, however, called on Americans to refrain from the practice, not merely for the sake of frugality, but for the promotion of American industry. Gloves, scarves, and rings were precisely the sort of luxurious "baubles" that colonists imported in large quantities from Great Britain, much to the impediment of their own manufacture. In 1774, the First Continental Congress sought to end extravagant mourning. Subscribers to

Congress's Association pledged to "discontinue the giving of gloves and scarves at funerals." They further agreed that, "on the death of any relation or friend," they would not attire themselves in "any further mourning dress, than a black crepe or ribbon on the arm or hat, for gentlemen, and a black ribbon and necklace for ladies." In keeping with this provision, Congress resolved to mourn Peyton Randolph by wearing the crepe for a period of one month.[65] At Randolph's funeral, gloves, scarves, and rings passed conspicuously ungifted.

Randolph's funeral also enabled the Continental Congress to stake a new place in the American body politic. To escort Randolph's remains to the burial ground, the congressional committee organized a large funeral procession. In the British colonies, funeral processions for public officials and other eminent persons functioned as rituals by which the civic community reconstituted and reaffirmed itself. Typically, members of every branch of government, of the militia, of the clergy, of the professions, and of local voluntary associations marched in these processions, as did private citizens. Their presence, alongside the decedent's loved ones and mourners, attested to the community's sense of loss. By filing these participants according to social and political rank, funeral processions fortified hierarchies of power and prestige. And by entwining those hierarchies with the hallowed ceremonies of death and mourning, funeral processions sacralized relations of authority within the community.[66] A letter to the editor of the *Providence Gazette*, written by the pseudonymous Sinceritas in 1769, helps to illustrate this dynamic. Funerals, explained Sinceritas, cause mourners to reflect on their mortality and to contemplate their spiritual condition. These are "important lessons" that bring "real and lasting Advantages to Mankind." But when "Order and Decorum are wanting to compleat the Solemnity," these lessons are lost. For this reason, Sinceritas asserted that the "Virtue and Morality" of funerals depended on "Regard to Seniority, and Respect to Superiors."[67]

Viewed in this light, Peyton Randolph's funeral procession must be recognized as an assertion of congressional political legitimacy. At the head of Randolph's procession marched nearly two thousand Philadelphia soldiers, artillerists, and riflemen, their "Standards and Colours . . . furled with black Gauze: their Drums muffled." Next came ministers of "all Denominations in this city," followed by Randolph's pall, borne by six magistrates. Then, at the middle of this somber procession, in the privileged position immediately behind the pall, walked members of Congress, led by their president, John Hancock. Behind Congress moved a lengthy train that included the city physicians, the Pennsylvania assembly, the committee of safety, the mayor and corporation of Philadelphia, the committee of the city and liberties, Anglican vestrymen, and an enormous crowd of inhabitants estimated at twelve to fifteen thousand persons.[68] As the imperial order crumbled, Randolph's procession conjured a *novus ordo seclorum* in which Congress inhabited the foremost place. The multitude of spectators who bore solemn witness lent credence to Congress's authority. The New Hampshire delegate Josiah Bartlett proclaimed Randolph's "the greatest funeral that Ever was in America."[69]

As it happened, Randolph's funeral was but the first in a remarkable triptych; its greatness was soon eclipsed by Congress's memorial service for the fallen continental general Richard Montgomery. Born in Ireland in 1738, Montgomery served as an adjutant in the British army. A veteran of the Seven Years' War, he immigrated to New York in 1772 and married into the prominent Livingston family. On account of Montgomery's military experience, his powerful New York political connections, and his warm support for the American cause, Congress appointed him among the first brigadier generals in the Continental Army.[70] During his brief service in the Continental Army, Montgomery won a reputation for heroism. In mid-October, American forces under his command captured Fort Chambly in the Richelieu River. As trophies of that victory, Montgomery delivered "Two Pair of Colours" belonging to the 7th Royal Fusiliers to General Philip Schuyler, who in turn forwarded them to Congress.[71] The congressional president John

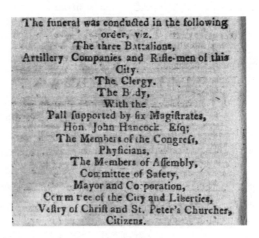

The funeral procession for Peyton Randolph, as illustratively typeset in the *New-York Journal*, October 25, 1775. The Historical Society of Pennsylvania.

Hancock exultantly hung these flags "with great Splendor and Elegance" in his quarters. There, he and his wife, Dorothy Quincy Hancock, entertained a succession of congressmen and local patriots who wished to behold the spoils of war.[72]

News that Montgomery had been killed during an ill-fated assault on Quebec reached Congress in mid-January 1776, at a moment of dire public sentiment. In recent days, rumors of Lord Dunmore's bombardment of Norfolk had outraged Philadelphia patriots, while the publication of Thomas Paine's *Common Sense* had roused them for independence. Amid this political ardor, word of Montgomery's demise evoked an outpouring of sorrow: "The whole city of Philadelphia was in tears," reported the South Carolina congressman Thomas Lynch. "Every person seemed to have lost his nearest relative and heart friend."[73] Members of Congress felt this loss with particular poignancy. One month earlier, Congress had promoted Montgomery to major general; he died without having received the word. Making matters worse, Congress had until this time harbored bright expectations for a successful capture of Quebec. An expedition commanded by Benedict Arnold had overcome wretched conditions to join forces with Montgomery's troops. To members of Congress it seemed as if Heaven had interposed to sustain the American army, so that it might "compleat the grand work of the subduction of Canada." The failure of Montgomery's invasion shattered congressional hopes. The fact that Montgomery had staged the fatal assault on December 30—in a desperate bid to conquer the city before his soldiers' enlistments expired on the last day of the year—gave Congress its first hint that the Canadian campaign would meet a dismal end.[74]

The sad news of Montgomery's death presented Congress with a novel scenario. No continental general had yet been killed in the line of duty, and so the question arose, how should Congress mourn the fallen hero? Thomas Lynch proposed that Congress order "a Public Monument" to Montgomery's memory.[75] William Hooper of North Carolina delivered a "florid Speech" in which he suggested that Congress organize a memorial service and wear black crepe for one month, much as it had done for Peyton Randolph. Salutary as these proposals may seem, they did not pass uncontested. Samuel Ward and other delegates objected "that no Mourning [was] ever worn by any Courts on such Accounts." This fragment of an objection—preserved only in the diary of New Jersey congressman Richard Smith—offers a tantalizing glimpse into Congress's invention of tradition. It suggests that at least some members of Congress wished to cut American civic protocol closely to the customs of nations. To deviate from the practice of European "Courts" would be to invite international scorn on the United Colonies. Ward's protest that no mourning was ever worn "on such Accounts" further illuminates the distinction that many congressmen wished to maintain between civil and military authorities. The delegates had not hesitated to mourn the death of congressman Peyton Randolph, but the death of an army officer was another matter. To back his objections, Ward admonished that excessive mourning might "cause too much alarm at such a critical Juncture." The American cause should not be thought lost simply because a single officer had been slain. It was enough, Ward proclaimed, that the general's memory had already been "embalmed in the Heart of every good American."[76]

Unpersuaded by Ward's objections, Congress appointed a special committee to "consider a proper method of paying a just tribute of gratitude" to the general. The committee agreed that a monument should be built as a testament to Montgomery's "patriotism, conduct, boldness of enterprize, insuperable perseverance, and contempt of danger and death."[77] The committee further recommended that the monument be erected in the very chamber in which Congress sat, as a tribute to the sacrifices Americans were making to preserve their liberties.[78] To pay for it, Congress allocated a remarkable sum of money, £300 sterling. Presumably because no American artist was thought equal to the important task, Congress authorized Benjamin Franklin to contract for the monument's design in Paris.[79]

The memorial committee also recommended an oration in Montgomery's honor to be delivered by William Smith, the Anglican clergyman and provost who had preached with such spirit on the occasion of Washington's departure. Finally, to complete the commemoration, the memorial committee organized a grand processional, very similar to Randolph's. Despite the fact that Montgomery's remains lay in Canada—there was no body to escort or bury—Congress assembled at the state house on the morning of the memorial service. From there it marched to the German Calvinist Church, flanked by light infantry and riflemen and followed by the Pennsylvania assembly, local authorities, and several battalions of soldiers. As the procession moved along Fourth Street, it came to the home of William Smith, and there was joined by the provost, by other clergymen from around the city, and by the faculty and students of the college, all attired in their academic gowns. Inside the church, a small orchestra of bass viol, violins, organs, flutes, and French horns performed "very solemn and mournful" music.[80]

Though spacious, the church galleries could not accommodate every mourner in the city. Consequently, a local committee distributed tickets in advance to a few hundred "principal ladies" and out-of-town guests. These audience members performed a vitally important role in the ceremony. The women who attended Montgomery's memorial service personified the domestic obligations for which American patriots supposedly fought and died. Insofar as these women's expressions of sorrow had the power to enkindle popular sympathy, their mourning must be understood as a political act.[81] At Montgomery's commemoration service, Samuel Adams noted that a "Circle of Ladies" seated themselves in a prominent place where they could "see as well as hear the orator, that they might take every Advantage for the Indulgence of Griefe on so melancholy an Occasion."[82] Adams's observation suggests that Philadelphia's female patriots appreciated their influence and actively sought a role as arbiters of public sentiment.

The stage was thus set for a heartrending panegyric, full of pathos and patriotic emotion. Reverend Smith, who had solicited biographical information from Montgomery's family so that he might expound on the general's noble character, gave Congress high hopes for the eulogy. New York congressman James Duane confidently predicted that Smith's address would be "read with avidity not only in America but Europe."[83]

Smith, however, proved a grave disappointment, as least to those members of the audience who had already turned their minds toward independence. Contrary to the spirit of the wildly popular *Common Sense*, Smith preached reconciliation. Rather than describing Montgomery as a valiant hero who had given his life in the fight against tyranny, Smith portrayed him as a reluctant soldier, wary of letting loose "the stroke which should sever the ancient bond of union." In lauding Montgomery's military talents, Smith disparaged the continental forces under his command. It required "the highest abilities," Smith proclaimed, to command America's "ill-supplied" and "worse disciplined" army.[84] Many spectators thought Smith's oration a brazen and insidious performance. More radical members of Congress sat aghast. The problem was not that Smith had turned apostate; he continued to care deeply about American rights. But Smith had failed to keep political pace with the avant-garde of the American resistance. Smith's tepid eulogy reflected his own persistent wish for a peaceful and constitutional settlement. Smith hinted that Congress should continue along a path of dependency. He even quoted the Olive Branch Petition as evidence of Congress's shared desire to restore "the former harmony" in imperial relations.[85] But political sands had shifted since Congress extended the Olive Branch seven months before. Many patriots now took exception to Smith's point of view. Samuel Adams observed that the "Circle" of grieving ladies appeared "disappointed and chagrind" by Smith's remarks.[86] Two days after the memorial, the New York delegate William Livingston, who was related to Montgomery by marriage, moved that Congress thank Reverend Smith for his oration and pay for its publication, but this motion met such stubborn opposition that Livingston at length chose to withdraw it rather than submit it for a vote.[87]

Unwilling to be silenced, Smith privately arranged for his oration to be printed. In the pamphlet version, Smith assumed an even more stridently reconciliatory tone than he had in his spoken address. As if to insinuate an endorsement, he prefaced his pamphlet with the resolution, extracted from the minutes of Congress, inviting him to speak. Smith also appended a footnote in which he justified his quotation of the Olive Branch Petition, arguing that it would have been *"indecent"* of him to "impute to [Congress], or even suspect the least change of sentiment before they themselves have declared it."[88] Smith even added a new paragraph, "forgot in the delivery," in which he heaped praise on the "magnanimity" of General Guy Carleton, the British army commander who had ordered his troops to bury Montgomery, with honors, in Canada. Smith's oration was published in at least four American and two British editions. Whether the oration's popularity owed to Smith's conciliatory politics or rather to Montgomery's posthumous fame is impossible to determine. Whatever the case, radical members of Congress fumed to see Smith's tract reach such an audience. John Adams, who had promised before hearing Smith's oration to pass along copies of the published edition just "as soon as it is out," subsequently refused, proclaiming, "I have too much Contempt and Indignation, at that insolent Performance to meddle with it."[89]

In this way, the "soft, polite, insinuating, adulating" Smith engaged proponents of independence in a contest for the memory of the slain general. That contest did not end with the printing of Smith's sermon. In May 1776, Thomas Paine published an enlarged edition of *Common Sense*, to which he appended *A Dialogue between the Ghost of General Montgomery . . . and an American Delegate*. In this tract, Paine imagined a meeting, "in a wood, near Philadelphia," between Montgomery's ghost and a moderate congressman who, like John Dickinson, still clung to hopes of reconciliation. Paine's Montgomery claimed that he had returned from the dead to warn Congress against "listening to the terms of accommodations" with Great Britain. In protest, Paine's delegate trotted out a number of arguments against American independence, including "the destructive consequences of war," the ruin of trade, domestic conflict between the colonies, and a dread of "innovation" in government. In the plain and artless language that made

Common Sense such a success, Paine's spectral Montgomery answered the timid congressman's every objection. The tract climaxed with the apparition's dramatic proclamation, "For my part if I thought this Continent would ever acknowledge the sovereignty of the Crown of Britain again, I should forever lament the day in which I offered up my life for its salvation."[90] Paine thus reclaimed Montgomery's memory for radical resistance. He also reformulated the question of independence in terms sure to sway Americans bereaved by the general's death: if the colonists did not pursue and achieve independence, would not the general have died in vain? Like the monument that Congress sought to erect in the Pennsylvania State House, Paine dreamed up an otherworldly Montgomery to haunt reconciliation-minded delegates onto the righteous path.

While Congress and Thomas Paine clashed with William Smith over the legacy of General Montgomery, yet another prominent patriot passed away. Samuel Ward, the eminent former governor of Rhode Island and an active member of the First and Second Continental Congresses, died of smallpox on March 26. Ward's death aggrieved members of Congress who believed that it could have been prevented. Before the First Continental Congress convened in the fall of 1774, Philadelphia physicians halted their practice of inoculation so as not to jeopardize the health of delegates arriving from out of town.[91] But by the summer of 1775, "[t]he small Pox [was] extremely thick" in Philadelphia and local doctors had no choice but to resume the practice.[92] Smallpox inoculation—whose symptoms were typically limited to headache, fever, swelling of the inoculated arm, and a mild outbreak of pox—became a rite of passage for congressmen new to Philadelphia. Still, despite assurances that they could be inoculated "without keeping House an Hour, and without absence from Congress four days," some delegates opted not to take the risk. Samuel Ward, in particular, refused the treatment despite the constant advice of his friends. In January 1776, Ward wrote his wife that though he could find no time for inoculation, she should not worry, because there was "very little of the Small Pox now in the city." Less than two months later, friends observed that "the small pox appeard plainly and very full upon him." Ward's face soon swelled "excessively," his breathing became difficult, and his throat "much obstructed by Phlegm." He died shortly thereafter. By that time, Congress and the people of Philadelphia had grown accustomed to their Revolutionary mourning rituals. On March 27, Congress, wearing black crepe, took its place in procession, marched to the Arch Street meeting house where the Reverend Samuel Stillman delivered a eulogy, and then escorted Ward's body to the burial ground.[93]

These three funerals, in a span of only a few short months, served important political and cultural purposes. They allowed Congress to promote the Association and to institute a new, dignified civic ceremony for the United Colonies. They provided occasion for what the historian Michael Meranze has called the necropolitics of the Revolutionary Era; that is, the politics of the dead and their commemoration.[94] The memorial services for Randolph, Montgomery, and Ward enabled Congress to rechannel the public's sorrow into patriotic support for the American cause. These services had the capacity to transcend Americans' sectarian conflicts. Congress celebrated Randolph's life at Christ Church, honored Montgomery at the German Calvinist Church, and laid Ward to rest in the Baptist cemetery. These funerals even had the capacity to smooth over regional differences. The deaths of Randolph, a Virginian; Montgomery, a New Yorker; and Ward, a Rhode Islander, distributed the emotional burden of war evenly throughout much of the continent, while newspaper accounts and private letters invited the rest of America to share in Congress's anguish. In performing all of these functions, the memorial services also helped to legitimize Congress as a governing assembly, of equal dignity to, if not greater than, the colonial legislatures. Not only did these services elevate Congress to the prominent places traditionally reserved for the highest-ranking civil authorities, they also exalted the offices of those who had passed away. As an obituary notice for Samuel Ward published in the *Pennsylvania Packet* proclaimed, "So highly was he esteemed by his countrymen, that they conferred on him their greatest honors. . . . [W]hen a Continental Congress became necessary, he was appointed one of the Delegates. A striking proof this, of the esteem of his fellow citizens, seeing every thing dear to America was at stake."[95]

In late April 1776, as radicals in Congress began to push earnestly for independence, John Adams declared, "There is one Thing . . . that must be attempted and most Sacredly observed or We are all undone. There must be a Decency and Respect, and Veneration introduced for Persons in Authority, of every Rank, or We are undone. In a popular Government, this is the only Way of Supporting order."[96] For more than a year, the Continental Congress had taken every opportunity to instill such high regard for the civil powers: superintending the rich military pageantry that erupted after Lexington and Concord, proclaiming a continental fast, consecrating the memory of persons who had given their lives in defense of American liberties, and bestowing a medal on the commander in chief for his triumph over British forces. These measures may have contributed to the preservation of order at the beginning of the Revolution. As American patriots cast off British authority and began to establish new state constitutions, they preserved a remarkable degree of political, social, and economic stability. And yet, if the ceremonies and civic traditions that Congress inaugurated in 1775–76 helped to build "Decency and Respect, and Veneration . . . for Persons in Authority," they also served to erode them, for Congress could not fix the import of its commemorations and observances. As evident in Quaker refusals to keep the continental fast or in Provost Smith's scandalous abuse of Montgomery's memory, Congress's endeavors, far from defining the meaning and purpose of the Revolution, rather provided occasion for the contestation thereof.

Part III

E PLURIBUS UNUM

Pierre Eugène Du Simitière, September 20, 1776, Proposal for United States Coat of Arms. The Thomas Jefferson Papers Series 1. General Correspondence. 1651–1827. Library of Congress, Manuscript Division.

In the months that followed the outbreak of hostilities at Lexington and Concord, the Continental Congress dedicated its material and ceremonial energies chiefly to the justification of a defensive war and to the validation of its own legislative and executive authority. After declaring independence on July 4, 1776, Congress immediately redirected those energies toward the fabrication of a national identity for the newborn republic. That very afternoon, Congress appointed John Adams, Benjamin Franklin, and Thomas Jefferson "to bring in a device for a seal for the United States of America."[1]

Evidently dissatisfied with their own proposals—Adams's Hercules, Franklin's Moses, and Jefferson's Hengist and Horsa—the committee turned for assistance to Pierre Eugène Du Simitière, a Swiss-born artist who, since settling in Philadelphia in 1774, had devoted his talents to the patriot cause. Trained in Geneva, Du Simitière had read works on the heraldic arts and studied the designs of ancient coins and medals.[2] In consultation with the seal committee in late July or early August, Du Simitière submitted a composition

129

of his own making: an American coat of arms. These arms consisted of a shield supported on the left by the "Goddess Liberty" and on the right by a buckskinned rifleman. Divided into six panels, the shield bore emblems of six countries said to have "peopled" the United States: England, Scotland, Ireland, France, Germany, and Holland. Encircling the shield, thirteen scutcheons, linked by a chain of gold, bore the initials of the states. From a crest above, the "Eye of Providence" looked out in radiant glory, while below unfurled a scroll bearing the inscription, *E Pluribus Unum*.[3]

The Continental Congress tabled Du Simitière's proposal and ultimately adopted very few of its particulars. Nevertheless, his "American" coat of arms has much to tell us about the incipience of national identity in the Revolutionary United States.[4] Du Simitière's shield contained no commonly recognized symbols of the American people or of their new nation. Declared into existence only weeks before, the United States could not easily be distilled into a single distinctive emblem. As a result, Du Simitière was forced to patchwork an American coat of arms out of European swatches: the rose, the thistle, the harp, the fleur-de-lys, the imperial eagle, and the lion. The only elements of Du Simitière's design that properly belonged to America—the buckskinned rifleman and his tomahawk—the seal committee rejected in favor of the "Goddess Justice," a classical figure to balance the Goddess Liberty.[5] Fittingly, Du Simitière represented the United States not as a single polity, but rather as thirteen separate entities. In 1776, the individual states remained jealous of their rights and distrustful of their neighbors' ambitions. Du Simitière's arms aptly signified the looseness of their union.

Yet, though the American republic knew not how to emblazon itself, though state interests and regional cultural differences continued to promote local attachments, the collective experiences of revolution enabled many former colonists to envision themselves as members of a new, national community. Nearly a decade of collaborative nonimportation, nonexportation, and nonconsumption agreements conditioned American patriots to recognize that their mutual political and economic concerns transcended provincial boundaries. Nearly two years of congressional encouragement caused them to look on the cause of liberty as a "continental" cause. More than twelve months of war forced them to reimagine Great Britain as a foreign enemy. The Declaration of Independence formally severed the political ties that bound the colonists to their once beloved nation and compelled them to rethink their national identities.

The Continental Congress labored—at times concertedly, at times haltingly—to facilitate the transfer of Americans' loyalties to the infant republic. To ensure the broadest possible dissemination of the Declaration of Independence, Congress ordered it read and posted throughout the United States. In so doing, Congress prompted weeks of popular festivity and political demonstrations in July and August of 1776. Gathering to hear the Declaration of Independence and rallying to destroy vestiges of monarchy—the king's coat of arms, for example—former colonists ceremoniously repudiated their allegiances to Great Britain. In the years that immediately followed, Congress also organized public celebrations on the anniversaries of independence. On those occasions, Congress began to introduce new rituals and emblems of nationhood, both to nurture affection for the American union and also to boost morale after two traumatic seasons of war. Out of doors, American patriots seized these festivities as opportunities to establish and to police the boundaries of their nation. On the earliest holidays of the United States, they discovered ways to ostracize and to punish loyalists, pacifists, and other persons deemed inimical to American liberty. Du Simitière created a coat of arms that, in spite of its inclusive motto *E Pluribus Unum*, emblematically excluded vast numbers of persons from the United States, particularly African Americans and Native Americans, who also peopled the continent. Crowds of Philadelphians likewise endeavored to define the limits of their imagined community. They committed acts of vandalism and performed malicious street theater not simply to celebrate the Revolution but to draw lines of national inclusion and exclusion.

The founding of the republic also necessitated the creation of new ceremonies of state. After the Declaration, the individual states agreed to function in important ways as a nation, the imperfect and unfinished nature of their confederation notwithstanding. Most significantly, the states pursued diplomatic relations as a corporate entity. The execution of treaties with King Louis XVI in 1778 obliged the United States to implement new diplomatic protocols for the reception of a French minister. In devising those protocols, members of Congress deliberated how most effectively to situate the United States as a nation among nations. This process gave rise to contentious debate. Some delegates wished to preserve the simple republican virtue of the United States against the corrosive monarchical extravagance of France. Others very much desired to dignify the United States and to impress the representatives of the ancien régime.

In November 1776, Silas Deane, an American commissioner in France, wrote to Congress to announce his receipt of the Declaration of Independence. Deane expressed disappointment that it had come so late to hand, after all of Europe had heard the news, and so informally, with no proper introduction to the French king. "[S]omething is due," Deane declared, "to the dignity of old and powerful states, or, if you please, to their prejudices in favor of long accustomed form and etiquette." Deane particularly objected that the Declaration had arrived without proper authentication, Congress having not yet settled upon a design for the Great Seal. The use of such seals, Deane counseled, was "a very ancient custom, in all public, and even private, concerns of any consequence."[6]

In the early years of independence, and in spite of the wishes of more ardent republicans, Congress imitated many of the "ancient customs" of European nations, and of Native American nations too. The earliest symbols and ceremonies that Congress manufactured for the United States testify to the conflicting aesthetic and political imperatives by which Congress operated, to the inchoateness of national identity in the infant republic, and to the limitations of material and human resources in war-torn Philadelphia. They also stand as evidence of the meaningful influence exerted by persons out of doors, including some who possessed no representation in Congress: disappointed Britons who sniggered their contempt for independence, crowds of patriots who dressed down Tory women by dressing up a notorious "strumpet," loyalist penmen who ridiculed the pretense of U.S. diplomacy, and Delaware Indians who seemingly paid greater deference to the minister of France than to the president of Congress. From the inception of the United States, the honor, merit, and reaches of the new nation proved to be matters of negotiation and dispute.

5

"The spirits of the whigs must be kept up"

ON JULY 2, 1776, the Continental Congress resolved, "That these United Colonies are, and, of right, ought to be, Free and Independent States." Soon after, John Adams ebulliently predicted that the second of July would "be celebrated, by succeeding Generations, as the great anniversary Festival." Adams declared that the day "ought to be commemorated . . . by solemn Acts of Devotion to God Almighty. It ought to be solemnized with Pomp and Parade, with Shews, Games, Sports, Guns, Bells, Bonfires and Illuminations from one End of this Continent to the other from this Time forward forever more." As Adams conjured it, the anniversary of Independence would serve many of the same functions as the newly proposed Great Seal. It would supplant a now-outmoded monarchical device, or in this case, tradition, the celebration of King George's birthday on June 4. It would mark the creation of a new sovereign republic, the United States. And it would unify the American people in shared appreciation of their nation's momentous beginnings. In short, to borrow Adams's euphoric language, it would perpetuate "the most memorable Epocha, in the History of America." Toward those ends, Adams envisioned celebratory roles for all ranks of society: sacred worship directed by the new nation's clergy, stately processions conducted by its civil and military authorities, and mirthful frolic made by the people out of doors.[1]

Yet, in July 1777, when occasion first arose to celebrate this "great anniversary Festival," Congress very nearly lost the opportunity. As Adams explained, "The thought of taking any notice of this day, was not conceived, until the second of this month, and it was not mentioned until the third." Having forgotten his reverie of the previous year, Adams and his fellow congressmen found themselves in the middle of an anniversary for which they had made no preparations. By then it was too late to commemorate the second, as Adams had anticipated. Nor was there time to prepare a sermon, "as every one wished." Only by hastily arranging a display of boats and ships anchored in the Delaware River and a review of continental forces that happened "accidentally" to be passing through Philadelphia did Congress and Pennsylvania officials manage to engage the city, on the Fourth of July, in a suitable measure of festivity.[2]

This ironic bit of Independence Day history illuminates the rudimental development of national identity in the Revolutionary United States. John Adams imagined that the anniversary of independence would be celebrated as an occasion of universal rejoice, from "one End of this Continent to the other." In fact, only a handful of American cities and towns commemorated independence in 1777 or 1778. Few communities yet felt the imperative, let alone knew the proper date. Adams, moreover, expected the slate of festivities to consist of "Games, Sports, Guns, Bells, Bonfires and Illuminations." But these were the same activities with which the former colonists had observed monarchs' birthdays in years past. By declaring independence, the Continental Congress breathed a new republic into existence. Yet the American people possessed no distinctive emblems or rites of nationhood. Consequently, the few patriots who did keep the anniversary began to experiment, tentatively and under the strain of war, with novel means of representing their polity. To consecrate the union of states and to affix on it a tangible identity, they devised new symbols, new ceremonies, and new acts of street theater and violence.

Despite their halting and irregular origins, the rituals with which patriots celebrated independence in 1776, and commemorated its anniversaries in 1777 and 1778, gave rich expression to the realignment of national identities in the young United States. They also bore ample witness to grievous social and political hostilities that bitterly divided the former British colonists. Adams anticipated that the anniversary of independence would promote harmony and cooperation among the inhabitants of the thirteen states. He confidently imagined that Congress, by waiting so long to formally declare independence, had prevented "Heats" and "Convulsions" among the American people.

Prudence and deliberation, Adams believed, had "cement[ed] the union," while the progress of war had extinguished "mistaken" hopes for reconciliation with Great Britain.[3] But Adams overestimated American consensus. The Revolution continued to sow dissension within American towns, churches, and families. Consequently, independence celebrations assumed a stridently partisan and often destructive tone.

Rather than promoting community cohesion, the anniversaries of independence induced many American patriots to intimidate persons deemed "disaffected" to the cause. The people out of doors claimed their streets and commons as American, not British, and as patriot, not loyalist, spaces. With the tacit approval of local authorities, they often directed their enmity against the persons and private property of supposed Tories. Nowhere was this truer than in Congress's host city, whose inhabitants reeled from a succession of evacuations and military occupations in 1777 and 1778. Punctuating the comings and goings of continental and British forces, the first anniversary celebrations prompted fierce assertions of authority and power. The resulting animosities and social conflicts accentuated differences of political allegiance and hardened the boundaries of Americans' imagined community. Fraught with enduring prejudices of gender, race, and class, they entangled a nascent U.S. national identity in the political and social subjugation not only of loyalists, but of women, persons of color, and the poor.

The Declaration of Independence

The Declaration of Independence prompted splurges of festivity throughout the United States. The momentous and long-anticipated repudiation of King George III provoked a binge of destructive jubilation. Across the summer of 1776, American patriots demolished the vestiges of British authority and tumultuously rejoiced in the sovereignty of their free and independent states. In large measure, these popular responses resulted from the ceremonious manner in which independence was declared.

Within Congress, proponents of an immediate separation from Great Britain perceived many advantages to making a public declaration of independence, rather than simply voting for it. Ideologically speaking, Lockean notions of the social contract compelled the delegates to articulate the "long train of abuses and usurpations" that justified the breach with Great Britain.[4] But John Adams counted other "very numerous, and very great" advantages to "Such a Declaration." Adams predicted that a declaration would "arouse and unite the Friends of Liberty," that it would motivate the colonies to frame new constitutions, that it would provide legal justification for the prosecution of treason, and that it would inspire "a Vigour, hitherto unknown" in civil governments and military operations. Perhaps most significantly, a declaration would enable foreign nations to treat with the Americans "upon equal Terms."[5] As the historian David Armitage has demonstrated, prevailing notions of international law obliged Congress to assert the United States' intention to do "All Acts and Things which Independent States may of right do." These included making war, concluding treaties, and establishing trade. Only by affirming this intention could the United States stake a fair claim to sovereignty; only by communicating it to other nations could the United States signal its openness for diplomatic and commercial business.[6] Without a declaration, the ends of independence might never be achieved.

The political and legal expediency of making a formal declaration of independence created magnificent opportunities for public celebration. After the January 1776 printing of Thomas Paine's *Common Sense*, British colonists began to wonder whether and when they might hear "an open and determined declaration."[7] Members of Congress sensed the public's anticipation. Prodding his congressman, Samuel Adams, the Massachusetts radical Joseph Hawley urged, "The Peoples blood is too Hot to admit of Delays." Not even John Dickinson, who opposed independence in the summer of 1776, could deny that the "Spirit of the People" demanded a declaration. "The People expect it."[8]

Making the most of the public's excitement, the congressional president John Hancock forwarded broadside copies of the Declaration to state officials, with instructions that they be circulated far and wide. "The important Consequences resulting to the American States," Hancock asserted, "will naturally suggest the Propriety of proclaiming it in such a Mode, as that the People may be universally informed of it."[9] State officials readily obliged. In Virginia, the governor's council ordered sheriffs to read the Declaration at local courthouses on the next court day. In Massachusetts, legislative authorities directed ministers to read it from their pulpits on the following Sabbath. By the end of the month, at least thirty American newspapers had published the Declaration, including Henrich Miller's German-language *Pennsylvanischer Staatsbote*. Meanwhile, in the Continental Army, General Washington commanded his junior officers to assemble their brigades and pronounce the Declaration before them in "an audible voice." Throughout the month of July—and continuing even into August as the Declaration wound its way through back roads to distant regions of the infant nation—Americans gathered on commons and in town squares to hear the spoken word.[10]

Thomas Jefferson, in fact, intended the Declaration to be consumed in precisely this manner. As the literary scholar Jay Fliegelman demonstrated in his creative analysis of diacritical marks scribbled throughout the rough draft of the Declaration, Jefferson wrote the document to be read aloud.[11] Jefferson believed that oratory—like music, in the words of a playwright whom he admired—hath charms to soothe the savage breast.[12] In eloquence lay the power of both rational and affective persuasion. Words could evoke a compelling emotional response, not only in the meanings they conveyed but in the drama or pathos of their utterance. By composing a mellifluous Declaration, Jefferson hoped to stir listeners to a sympathetic engagement with the American cause. A devoted violinist, Jefferson even inserted "rhythmical pauses" into his text, contemplating as he chose his breaks how they might more harmoniously strike the ear. Years later, John Adams recalled his delight at the result, noting particularly the "high tone and the flights of oratory with which [the Declaration] abounded."[13]

The many public readings of the Declaration enabled proponents of independence to ceremonialize the birth of the United States. Rapt in the momentousness of the occasion, spirited revolutionaries extolled the Declaration with joyful noise and light. John Adams noted that the crowd that gathered to hear the Declaration read on the lawn of the Pennsylvania State House "rended the Welkin"—that is, tore open the sky—with its cheers. Later that afternoon, the city's battalions paraded on the common and fired a *feu-de-joie*, "notwithstanding the Scarcity of Powder." The church bells rang "all Day, and almost all night. Even the Chimers Chimed away." That evening, townsfolk illuminated the city by building bonfires and lighting candles in their windows.[14] Scenes such as this unfolded across the new nation. In Princeton, New Jersey, for example, "Independency" was proclaimed by a "triple volly of musketry." Similarly, at Fort Liberty, in Rhode Island, a brigade of soldiers "drew up and fired in thirteen divisions . . . agreeable to the number and situation of the United States." In Savannah, the governor, council, and militia drank a toast to "the United, Free, and Independent States of America."[15] Throughout the continent, newspaper accounts of local celebrations echoed the patriotic glee.[16] In this manner, the Declaration inaugurated a season of partisan festivity that carried on for several weeks.

American patriots heralded their new republic with much the same fanfare by which they previously exalted the British monarchy. The ringing of bells, the lighting of candles, the firing of salutes, and the drinking of toasts were all activities by which British colonials feted royal birthdays and other imperial anniversaries during the Hanoverian reign. Reliance on these monarchical traditions need not be understood as a failing of the patriot imagination. By appropriating older modes of celebration, supporters of independence found means to enact their transference of national loyalties. They signaled their conviction that the United States merited the same honor and glory as Britain. One newspaper correspondent gave rhapsodic expression to this very sentiment. Describing the faces of American soldiers at Ticonderoga as they reacted to the Declaration, the writer reported, "[T]he language of every man's countenance was, Now we are a people! we have a name among the states of this world."[17] By utilizing customary forms of national jubilation to hail the birth of the United States, American celebrants asserted their belief that the newly confederated republic deserved their filial affection.

Exhilarated patriots also began to adapt older traditions of British rule to include what few icons of United States nationhood had begun to attain purchase. Most commonly, they incorporated into their independence festivities the number thirteen: thirteen toasts, thirteen volleys, and thirteen units of soldiers, for example. (One congressman later boasted that his inoculated daughter erupted in thirteen patriotic pustules, "one for each of the united States.")[18] They also invoked liberty trees, Revolutionary battle flags, the fame of President Hancock and General Washington, the memory of the heroic war dead, and the simple, novel appellation, the United States of America.[19] By embracing these emblems, American revolutionaries took small but important steps toward the articulation of a national identity.

Not every American, however, partook in this fanfare, for in its day the Declaration was a highly partisan document. In many colonies, the struggle for independence generated intense political conflict, particularly during the late spring and early summer of 1776. On May 15, several weeks before the Continental Congress voted for independence, it first recommended that "every kind" of royal authority "be totally suppressed." By this measure, Congress empowered local patriots to extinguish their ancient charters, to dismantle their colonial governments, and to cast out of office all persons who had labored for reconciliation.[20] In Pennsylvania, where radical demands for a decisive breach from Great Britain threatened to nullify William Penn's Charter of Liberties, the resolution of May 15 provoked a great deal of acrimony. For those who endeavored to protect the empire, as well as for those who fought simply to sustain Pennsylvania's historic assembly, the Declaration proved a bitter draft.[21]

On July 8, the congressional secretary Charles Thomson, himself fraught with mixed emotions, witnessed Philadelphians' reactions as they heard the Declaration read aloud on the state house lawn. Though Thomson once stood at the fore of city's resistance, he had since briefly occupied a seat in the Pennsylvania assembly, and his politics had cooled. Like fellow moderate John Dickinson, Thomson wished to protect the assembly and to reconcile it to independence, so that the duly established legislature—not some factious provincial convention—would determine Pennsylvanians' political fate. But as the campaign to dismantle the proprietary government gathered momentum, and the prospect of a constitutional convention came more clearly into view, Thomson relinquished hope of preserving the assembly and yielded to independence earlier than he might have otherwise wished.[22] In his account of the public reading of the Declaration, Thomson expressed a pang of misgiving. Contrary to Adams's cheerful narrative, Thomson observed that the "boldness" of the Declaration "frightened, and appalled, even its wellwishers." "[T]he citizens," by whom Thomson presumably meant persons of property and stature, "mostly kept aloof—the crowd that assembled at the state house was not great and those among them who joined in the acclaimation were not of the highest order, or the most sober and reflecting."[23] Other observers corroborated Thomson's rendition of events. The Quaker patriot Charles Biddle noted, "There were very few respectable people present . . . many of the citizens who were good Whigs were much opposed to it." Similarly, the Quaker Deborah Norris Logan, fourteen years of age in the summer of 1776, later remembered, "The first audience of the Declaration was neither very numerous [nor] composed of the *most respectable* class of citizens."[24]

Thomson's, Biddle's, and Norris's perceptions of the day may have been soured by feelings of political loss or by a sense of anxiety for Pennsylvania's uncertain future, for the Declaration received a much fuller and more coordinated welcome than would seem possible if only the "lower sort" had embraced it. Nevertheless, their accounts offer a valuable reminder that the Declaration was not universally applauded in the summer of 1776. To the contrary, numerous Americans, including many well-to-do persons who had formerly held positions of authority and public trust, grimaced at its enunciation. In at least one community—New Brunswick, New Jersey—Whig organizers anticipated that the Declaration would provoke a hostile response from local "Tories," including "men of wealth and influence" who were "active" in political affairs. To "overawe" these "disaffected" persons and to "resent any interruption of the meeting that they might attempt," Jersey patriots rallied numerous "staunch friends of independence" to their public reading. Their loyalist adversaries, however, would not be intimidated. "[P]rudent enough not to make any demonstration," they nevertheless "sneered" at the Declaration "and looked their dissatisfaction in other ways."[25] In this instance, and perhaps others untold, the Declaration of Independence functioned not to promote American harmony, as Jefferson, Adams, and other members of Congress might have wished, but rather to fuel internecine discord.

Public readings of the Declaration enabled triumphant patriots to profess allegiance to the United States. At the same time, they also permitted former colonists to sever, ritualistically, the ties that bound them to Great Britain. Celebrants of the Declaration made a point of disavowing the British Empire, often brashly and violently. In numerous instances, the Declaration of Independence motivated patriotic crowds to engage in sprees of antiroyal iconoclasm, including the mock execution or burial of King George III and the physical destruction of Hanoverian arms, insignia, and statuary. In some colonies, the process of renouncing the king had begun many months earlier.[26] In Philadelphia, for example, George III's birthday passed almost entirely uncelebrated in 1774. "[N]ot one of our bells suffered to ring," the committeeman Christopher Marshall observed, "and but very few colours were shown by the shipping in the harbour; no, nor not one bonfire kindled."[27]

Independence channeled American's festering disdain for the Crown into a variety of destructive acts. Some American communities responded to the Declaration by defiling the king's effigy or burying it in theatrical funerals. Effigies and mock funerals figured prominently in Anglo-American folk culture. Colonial crowds deployed both traditions to protest the Stamp Act and the Townshend Revenue Act.[28] Almost invariably, those earlier crowds targeted royal advisors or ministers for symbolic execution. After the Declaration of Independence, patriots turned their ritualized vengeance on the king. On the evening of August 10, for example, the inhabitants of Savannah, Georgia, assembled in a "very solemn funeral procession" and marched to the local courthouse to witness the burial of an effigial George III. The crowd committed the king's "political existence to the ground," as the eulogist remarked, "in sure and certain hope that he will never obtain a resurrection."[29]

Other patriots signified their renunciation of monarchy by tearing down statues of the king or by setting Hanoverian insignia ablaze. After the proclamation of independence in Philadelphia, patriots marched to the state house to dismantle the royal arms displayed therein.[30] In New York, a crowd of soldiers and Sons of Liberty pulled to the ground a large equestrian statue of King George and laid it "prostrate in the dirt." Only six years before, New Yorkers erected the statue in gratitude for the repeal of the Stamp Act. After its destruction, patriot gazettes looked back on that gesture as one of "Tory pride and folly." They reported the statue's fall as "the just desert of an ungrateful tyrant!"[31] Meanwhile, in Boston, the Declaration prompted townsfolk to build a bonfire on King's Street, onto which they piled "every King's arms . . . whether lion and crown, pestle and mortar and crown, heart and crown."[32] Here was an unmistakable irony: the street named for monarchy now flickering in an antimonarchical firelight. A similar conflagration raged in Dover, Delaware, where the committee of safety "sent for a picture of the king," marched it around the town square to the beat of an infantry drum, and then committed it to flames, the committee president announcing, "[W]e destroy even the shadow of that king who refused to reign over a free people."[33] That diverse patriotic crowds targeted emblems and signs—even "the shadow of the king"—suggests how heavily the former colonists depended on symbols to denote their sense of belonging to the British nation. As loyal subjects, they predicated their national allegiance upon mementos of the Crown.[34]

By destroying those mementos, American patriots made a ritual of independence. Whereas the Continental Congress repudiated King George III on paper, the people out of doors repudiated him in the streets. In at least one instance, a crowd of patriots drew explicitly from Jefferson's text to dramatize the king's crimes. In a richly figurative pageant, the people of Huntington, Long Island, crafted a crude effigy of George III "out of the basest materials." Before hanging this effigy from the gallows, the crowd first blackened its face in likeness of the runaway slaves fighting in Lord Dunmore's Ethiopian Regiment. The crowd also stuck feathers in the king's head to resemble the "savages" whom the British general Guy Carleton allegedly loosed on innocent American women and children.[35] In this motley, blackfaced and befeathered effigy, the Long Islanders constructed a perfect tableau of Jefferson's Declaration, for in that document, Jefferson specifically accused King George of exciting "domestic insurrections" and rousing "merciless Indian Savages." This mock execution thus translated Jefferson's legal document into material and performative folk vernacular. Both productions signified the political death of King George, and like the first proposal for a Great Seal, both productions defined the American nation as a community of Europeans and their descendents, distinct from the African American and Native American peoples with whom they shared the continent.

Though wrong in important details—the statue featured George III on horseback, not stand-ing; a crowd of soldiers and Sons of Liberty, not slaves, tore it down—this French print cap-tures the iconoclastic energy unleashed by the Declaration of Independence. *Die zerstorung der koniglichen bild saule zu Neu Yorck / La destruction de la statue royale a Nouvelle Yorck*, by Chez Bassett. Paris, 177–. Library of Congress, LC-USZCV-1476.

The First Anniversary of Independence

The twelve months that passed between the Declaration of Independence in 1776 and its first anniversary in 1777 witnessed tremendous political and social upheaval. In September, the Pennsylvania provincial convention drafted an alarmingly radical constitution, establishing a unicameral legislature and imposing stringent loyalty and religious oaths that disenfranchised conscien-tious Quakers, Moravians, and Mennonites.[36] Later that fall, war came to the Delaware Valley as British forces under the command of Charles Cornwallis hounded Washington's army through New York and New Jersey and ulti-mately across the river into Pennsylvania.[37] To defend Philadelphia against imminent invasion, General Israel Putnam implemented a curfew, confis-cated arms, ordered shops closed, and directed all adult males to turn out for service. Rumors abounded of the two armies' movements, thrusting people "of all ranks" into "confusion."[38] On December 11, Congress denounced a "scandalous report" that it would soon abandon Philadelphia and instead proclaimed its bold intention to remain until "the last necessity shall direct it." One day later, Congress lost its nerve and adjourned to Baltimore, at a safe distance from the enemy.[39]

This abrupt flight, necessary though it may have appeared to safeguard the rebel government from the advancing British army, greatly embarrassed Congress.[40] For the next ten weeks, the delegates sat in miserable and humiliated exile in the "dirtyest Place in the World," as John Adams experienced Baltimore.[41] Worrisome reports from Philadelphia—of the capture of General Charles Lee, of the faithlessness of John Dickinson, of the defection of the prominent Allen brothers—Andrew, a former Continental Congressman, and William, a lieutenant in the Continental Army—deepened Congress's discouragement.[42] Washington's daring offensive against the Hessian garrisons at Trenton and Princeton greatly revived patriot morale. Yet, by foreclosing the possibility of a British invasion of Philadelphia, Washington's triumph made Congress's flight appear all the more craven. Congress had fled a city that did not in fact fall.[43]

After the Battles of Trenton and Princeton, General Howe drew his forces back to New York and life in Philadelphia began to normalize, but slowly and with trepidation that the British army would return once the winter had passed. In February, the executive committee that Congress appointed to conduct business in its absence began to cajole the delegates to return to the city, if for no better reason than to restore faith in the continental dollar.[44] When the delegates at last ventured back in early March, they discovered that the threat of a British invasion had sapped Philadelphia of its energy and spirit. "This City is a dull Place, in Comparason of what it was," wrote John Adams. "More than one half the Inhabitants have removed into the Country, as it was their Wisdom to do—the Remainder are chiefly Quakers as dull as Beetles."[45] To restore vigor to the city, local officials sponsored two public festivities that spring. On March 5, the Pennsylvania assembly celebrated the inauguration of the Supreme Executive Council—the first council elected under the state's new constitution—by organizing a parade, hosting a dinner at the City Tavern, and arranging bells to be rung throughout the city. On June 28, Philadelphia Whigs commemorated the Battle of Sullivan's Island, in which Carolina forces defended Charleston Harbor against British incursion in 1776. Those events suggest a desire on the part of patriot organizers to fete the American resistance and the revolutionary governments it spawned.[46] Surprising, then, that the notion of celebrating the anniversary of independence struck Adams and the rest of Congress so late.

More understandable is the confusion that surrounded the anniversary's date. The cities of Boston, Providence, and Charleston all scheduled festivities for the Fourth of July, likely because the printed copies of the Declaration that circulated in 1776 prominently featured that date.[47] But in Congress, where independence had been accomplished not in a single day but rather through weeks of motions, preambles, votes, declarations, and signings, the Fourth apparently seemed a less obvious choice. Writing to his father on July 4, 1777, the Maryland congressman Charles Carroll of Carrollton reported, "This day the Congress dine at Smith's Tavern. You will see by the inclosed paper it is to be celebrated as the anniversary of Independance." Similarly, in a letter to the former congressman Richard Caswell, the North Carolina delegate Thomas Burke added a parenthetical aside to explain that the Fourth had been celebrated as "the Anniversary of the declaration of Independence." That Carroll and Burke felt obliged to explain the significance of the date suggests how little meaning had yet been fixed on it.[48]

Once the notion of commemorating independence did strike Congress, the delegates moved swiftly to coordinate a proper demonstration of joy. On the afternoon of the third, the *Pennsylvania Evening Post* invited readers to celebrate the anniversary of their deliverance from "the worse than Egyptian bondage of Great-Britain."[49] The following day's events—evidently coordinated by members of Congress in collaboration with local officials—offer glimpses of the hopes and apprehensions that preoccupied American revolutionaries in the summer of 1777. They reveal a precarious sense of optimism about the force of continental arms. They expose intense distrust toward loyalists and pacifists who refused to embrace the cause of liberty. Perhaps most clearly, they lay bare real uncertainties about the American nation and the precise manner in which it ought to be symbolized by and for the people.

With little moment to prepare a grand anniversary pageant, organizers drew on the limited naval and military resources available to them. On the morning of the Fourth, and with the apparent cooperation of Congress's Marine Committee, planners arranged for the armed vessels stationed along the Delaware River to be "hawled off" and "dressed in the gayest manner." These craft included the frigate *Delaware*, one the first ships commissioned by the Continental Congress, as well as several U.S. and Pennsylvania galleys and guard boats jointly patrolling the river. At noon, this small, "beautifully dressed" flotilla was "drawn up before the city" and soon all hands "were ordered aloft, and arranged upon the tops, yards, and shrowds."[50]

So many sailors and marines scampering about the heights must have dazzled the spectators who gathered on Philadelphia's wharves, but of perhaps even greater fascination may have been the ships' decoration. Unfortunately, the exact mode in which Congress decked out this fleet is a matter of historical uncertainty. But either of the novel possibilities would have captivated and excited the audience. The *Pennsylvania Evening Post* reported that each vessel appeared "with the colours of the United States and streamers displayed." Such an exhibition would have been timely and fitting, for not three weeks earlier, on June 14, the Continental Congress formally adopted the Marine Committee's recommendation of a new naval flag, which consisted of thirteen red and white stripes and "a new constellation" of thirteen white stars on a field of blue.[51]

In order to comprehend just how remarkable Congress's Fourth-of-July naval display may have been, it is first necessary to appreciate the confusion that arose from the want of a unique American flag.[52] In the early months of the Revolutionary War, the United Colonies possessed no official standard. During the winter of 1775–76, continental military forces modified the British Union Flag by dividing its red field with six white bars, thus creating a total of thirteen stripes to represent the American colonies. This so-called Continental Union, however, did not gain wide recognition. Left to pick and choose from a dizzying array of regimental flags, ensigns, jacks, and bunting, army and naval officers hoisted whatever standards best suited "their own fancies and Inclinations," as the New York congressman John Jay lamented.[53] This lack of regularity exacerbated concerns about security on the high seas and obliged Congress's Naval and Marine Committees to dictate minute instructions for the signaling of vessels in the American service.[54] To bring order to this chaos, Congress's Marine Committee began to press for the adoption of a uniform banner in the spring of 1777.[55] The Fourth of July would have provided a spectacular opportunity for the Marine Committee to unfurl the newly designed stars-and-stripes.[56] Months before, a ship displaying "the flag of the Independent States of America"—presumably the Continental Union described above or possibly a simple field of thirteen red and white stripes—sparked such curiosity in Saint Domingue that the gawking crowd was reported to have "almost Sunk" the vessel.[57]

Curiously, John Adams's personal account of Philadelphia's Independence Day celebration differed from the *Pennsylvania Evening Post*'s report. In contrast to the *Post*'s assertion that the ships on the Delaware raised "the colours of the United States," Adams asserted in a letter to his daughter that the vessels displayed "the colours of *all nations*" (italics added). By "all nations" Adams presumably meant the nations of Europe, particularly those whose coats of arms graced the escutcheon first proposed for the Great Seal: England,

Scotland, Ireland, Holland, Germany, and France. The very fact that any confusion could arise about what flags had flown that day reveals just how inchoate the emblems of the United States remained. But what if Adams were correct? What if the Delaware ships did hoist the flags of "all nations"? Such a display might best be understood in one of two ways: first as a gesture of outreach or accommodation, an invitation to all European Americans, regardless of ancestral heritage, to join the fight for independence and to feel themselves a part of the infant republic; or, alternatively, as a symbolic representation of a new international order, one in which the United States had indeed taken a name among the states of this world. Whatever the case, Congress's Fourth-of-July naval panoply bespoke the incipience of U.S. national identity in the summer of 1777. Britain's former colonists did not yet know a better way to represent their confederated republic.

The only symbol that *had* attained widespread recognition as a mark of the United States was the number thirteen. This simple integer, which began to accrue significance not long after Georgia joined the Continental Congress in 1775, bore irresistible appeal. Prejudicial to no particular state or region, suggesting nothing more concrete than union, it proved both indisputable and inoffensive. For all of these reasons, and for lack of a symbol more compelling, anniversary planners put the number thirteen to shrewd use. After the seamen took to the air, a delegation consisting of President Hancock, members of the Marine Committee, and other congressmen rowed out by barge to the *Delaware*. Upon stepping aboard, they were hailed by a succession of thirteen-gun salutes: first from the *Delaware*, then from other armed vessels, then from the galleys, and finally from the guard boats. After this booming tribute to the United States, the entourage returned to shore, greeted by loud shouts and huzzahs.[58]

When this naval exhibition concluded, members of Congress retired to a celebratory dinner at the City Tavern, joined by the president and council of Pennsylvania and a handful of officers from the Continental Army, including Generals Gates and Arnold. John Adams basked in the "excellent company" and "good cheer," but it was not until after the meal, in the raising of toasts, that the afternoon's entertainment reached a climax.[59] Early American cultural historians have recognized the importance of the toast as an eighteenth-century rite of consensus. By drinking toasts, British North Americans articulated shared values, recollected sacred events, and exalted beloved heroes. The turning up of glasses thus functioned to establish and to reinforce the boundaries of Americans' affective communities.[60] The toasts imbibed at Congress's Fourth of July repast worked toward those same ends: "all breath[ed] independence, and a generous love of liberty, and commemorate[ed] the memories of those brave and worthy patriots who . . . fell gloriously in defence of freedom."[61]

But Congress's toasts proved distinctive as well, for organizers of the day's events arranged for a band of Hessian musicians, mostly oboists, to play "a suitable piece of music" after each cup.[62] In the wake of General Washington's assaults on Trenton and Princeton, Whig leaders made repeated, propagandistic displays of their German spoils of war. On January 30, victorious continental forces marched nine hundred German prisoners into Philadelphia and lined them up for a humiliating exhibition on Front Street, in the heart of the city.[63] On March 5, state officials dragged out thirteen Hessian cannon to fire a salute for the inauguration of Pennsylvania Supreme Executive Council president Thomas Wharton Jr.[64] On June 28, patriot organizers hired a Hessian band to perform for the anniversary celebration of the Battle of Sullivan's Island. Now, on July 4, the Continental Congress put that Hessian band to service once again.[65]

In keeping with European military tradition, these Hessian musicians likely retained their civilian status. They were neither compelled to fight as soldiers nor subjected to military discipline.[66] At the Continental Congress's independence banquet, they probably played for money.[67] Yet, congressional delegates crowed over these "taken" Hessians all the same.[68] More than a year before, in early 1776, when King George III first contracted German auxiliary troops to suppress the provincial rebellion, the American people, many of whom still felt strong devotion to the Crown, took profound offense. The hiring of mercenaries, as British colonists considered these German soldiers and conscripts, vindicated popular suspicions of a ministerial plot and convinced many Americans that the king had forsaken his loyal subjects.[69] By defeating the Hessian garrisons at Trenton and Princeton, American forces wrought a stunning and inebriating reversal of fortune. The "pleasure" of Congress's anniversary celebration, as the North Carolina congressman Thomas Burke exulted, was "not a little heightened by the reflection that the [Hessian musicians] were hired by the British Court for purposes very different from those to which they were applied."[70] To punctuate that afternoon's toasts even more forcefully, banquet hosts employed a corps of British deserters to fire the *feux-de-joie*. Drawn up on Second Street, just outside the City Tavern, these former British soldiers "filled up the intervals" with their fusillade.[71]

Congress's independence banquet thus evinced a spirit of triumph. The performance of the Hessian band vouched for the mettle of continental forces, just as the participation of British deserters bespoke the depravity of His Majesty's army. And yet in Congress's celebration might also be discerned a hint of desperate bravado. On balanced assessment, the trotting out of enemy noncombatants and capitulatory soldiers suggests an underlying insecurity about the strength of the U.S. military, or perhaps a pent-up frustration with the dismal progress of the war. To be sure, Washington's crossing of the Delaware greatly invigorated the Continental Army and restored much of New Jersey to patriot rule. By these eleventh-hour heroics, Washington and his troops managed not merely to salvage an otherwise disastrous season, but more importantly to cast grave doubts on Britain's presumed military supremacy.[72] Nevertheless, the victories at Trenton and Princeton, the Continental Army's greatest achievements to date, could only ease—they could never undo—the suffering of eleven hundred casualties at Long Island, the abandonment of New York City, or the capture of nearly three thousand American soldiers at Fort Washington.[73] Whatever glee Congressman Burke may have derived from the "mercenary" musicians who performed on the first Fourth of July must surely have been sobered by remembrance of the Americans' near-devastating defeats in New York and New Jersey.

To further inspire faith in the strength of continental forces, members of Congress concluded their afternoon's celebration by filing out of the City Tavern onto Second Street to review a parade of Maryland light horse and North Carolina infantry. Were it not for the fortuitous presence of these cavalrymen and soldiers, who happened to have stopped over in Philadelphia while traveling to join forces with Washington's army, Independence Day organizers might have been obliged to call an early end to the day's events. Instead, these troops provided an afternoon's entertainment by performing firings and maneuvers on the common.[74] In part by accident, then, and in part by intention, the prowess of American arms became a central theme of the day's festivities, as sounded in the roar of the *Delaware*'s guns, in the music made by enemy prisoners, and in the rhythmic footfall of infantrymen marching in the street. For some, this must have been a rousing display. The Declaration of Independence explicitly claimed for the United States the power to levy war; this was a prerogative of autonomous nations. The Continental Army and Navy thus represented both the ends and means of U.S. sovereignty. In these living, breathing, fighting continentals marched proof of American independence. And yet for others, the prospect of America's military forces inspired greater doubt than confidence. One spectator noted that many of the soldiers who paraded on the Fourth marched barefoot and "looked very unhealthy."[75] Though the celebration hearkened back, exuberantly, to Washington's crossing, it also looked ahead, uncertainly, to the summer's imminent campaign. (Indeed, within a matter of days, Philadelphians received the dismaying news that General Burgoyne had driven American forces from Ticonderoga.)

That evening, the city's formal Fourth of July observances drew to a close with "a grand exhibition of fireworks," culminating in a burst of thirteen rockets.[76] But though official festivities had come to an end, popular festivities had only just begun. Nighttime belonged to Philadelphia's out-of-door patriots, who marked the occasion with rich but destructive and intimidating folk tradition. Whereas Congress had emphasized the force of American arms, the city's townspeople made the persecution of suspected Tories the thrust of their independence celebration. One year earlier, John Adams had expressed his wish that Americans would light up the anniversary with "Bonfires and Illuminations." Prior to the eruption of hostilities, Britain's North American colonists commonly illuminated their cities and towns to celebrate joyous events, such as the accession of a new monarch, the birthday of a king or queen, or the proclamation of a peace. By building bonfires and placing candles in windows, inhabitants signaled their good cheer and their love of the nation. In 1765, American colonists celebrated the repeal of the Stamp Act with an illumination, thus engaging that custom in the politics of resistance. On the anniversary of independence, 1777, the illumination for which John Adams hoped did in fact come to pass. Walking about Philadelphia's streets that night, Adams marveled at the "most splendid illumination" he had ever seen: "the whole city lighting up their candles at the windows."[77]

Here, however, Adams overstated the case: the *whole* of the city had *not* placed candles in its windows and those who refused to do so had suffered considerably. In 1777, many Quakers—bound by conscience to abstain from the public celebration—felt obliged to leave their windows dark. In so doing, they placed themselves outside the community of revelers and gestured a seeming disregard for American independence. As often happened during these sorts of illuminations, Philadelphia's patriots responded by smashing their neighbors' unlit panes. Anticipating such acts of vandalism, the Pennsylvania Council issued a resolve on July 3 urging Philadelphians to "shew moderation and forbearance toward those persons who, either through their religious principles, or on any other account, may not for the present join with them in those expressions of joy."[78] The Council also ordered constables, watchmen, and a patrol of soldiers to keep the public peace. Nevertheless, the Council apparently considered Quaker and loyalist glass expendable to patriot morale. As Council vice president George Bryan confided, "Perhaps some disorders may happen, but we were willing to give the idea of rejoicing its swing. The spirits of the whigs must be kept up."[79] Given this attitude, it was perhaps to be expected that independence revelers shattered dozens, perhaps hundreds, of windows that night. The diarist Sarah Fisher, whose own family lost fifteen windows, noted that the Quaker minister Nicholas Waln suffered fourteen smashed, Thomas Wharton "a good many more," and George Logan as many as fifty windows "cracked & broken." "[A]ll this," Fisher sardonically reflected, "for joy of having gained our liberty."[80]

The destruction of so much private property naturally provoked considerable dismay and resentment. Rallying around the community of aggrieved Quakers, the Monthly Meeting of Friends at Philadelphia for the Southern District condemned the perpetrators as a "licentious mob."[81] The victim Daniel Humphreys took his grievance one step farther. A printer by trade, Humphreys was reputed to be "well affected to the cause," but this fact saved neither him nor his father from "assault and abuse." Posting a notice in the local gazette, Humphreys explained that an "unlawful banditti," "attended with a band of music," had broken all of his third story windows "except *thirteen* panes of glass." (Here, as italicized in the original, was that patriotic cipher once again, now used to isolate and menace rather than to unite.) Humphreys claimed to know the identities of his chief assailants—"*certain persons, who call themselves gentlemen*"—and he boldly threatened to "publicly advertise them" if they did not "make satisfaction . . . within three days." True to his word, Humphreys named these "*nocturnal insurgents*" later that week: James Mease, clothier general, and Richard Peters, secretary of war.[82]

Humphreys's allegation—that two of Congress's high-ranking appointees celebrated the birth of the United States by making rough music and hurling rocks through windows—blackened Congress's eye. By linking Congress to the petty violence committed against peaceable Quakers, Humphreys's charges belittled that assembly and the republic for which it stood. Worse still, Humphreys's assertions threatened to reframe the official narrative of Independence Day, a red-letter day in the making, from one of widespread felicity to one of rancor and disorder. Sensible of the embarrassment both to Congress and himself, Peters published an immediate denial. "Some disaffected persons," Peters avowed, must have concocted the story and targeted Mease and himself precisely because of their "public stations under Congress." Dismissing the allegations as "false and scandalous," Peters dared Humphreys to bring the matter before a magistrate.[83]

The true facts of the case may never be uncovered, but rumors persisted that these two congressional officers spearheaded the window-breaking mob.

Months later, after the British army took Philadelphia, a loyalist poet looked back on the evening of the Fourth, when patriots waged their "daring war against the unenlightened windows of the Quakers." Likening "Jimmy Mease" and "Dicky Peters" to Cervantes's famously misguided hero, the poet lampooned,

> Our true Don Quixotes, by false guessings,
> Direct their calls, and lead the van,—
> Mistook the Tories—for the Hessians,
> And Quakers for—pah—Englishmen.[84]

With the simple mock interjection, *pah*, this satirist expressed something essential about the first anniversary of independence. Not so long ago, and still for many British Americans, the title of Englishman had been a source of tremendous pride. But for partisans of independence, it had become a category of derision, worthy of the contemptuous, *pah*. As this poet understood, the Revolutionary War worked a momentous but uncertain shift in Philadelphians' national identities and loyalties. The city's Fourth of July celebration enabled Whigs to rope off from their community those "disaffected" individuals who, like the author of the poem above, still put stock in their status as Englishmen.

Members of Congress and local patriots not only recognized this opportunity, but truly reveled in it. Recounting the evening's vandalism, continental officials suggested that Quakers and other nonilluminators deserved their fate. John Adams, who characterized darkened houses as "surly," spitefully exulted that patriot "shouting and huzzaing" gave "the utmost terror and dismay to every lurking tory." Another patriot, unsympathetic to Quaker scruples, asserted that persons who refused to light candles had paid for their "Obstinacy."[85] In regard to loyalists, pacifists, and would-be neutrals, the South Carolina congressman Henry Laurens professed, "Our greatest enemies are within ourselves." Laurens blustered that the damage inflicted on the anniversary of independence could have been much worse. To "a rigid Tory" who complained of broken glass, Laurens replied, "[H]e might depend upon this as a type of broken bones . . . unless they soon reformed or removed out of the Country."[86] Laurens's bravado suggests the power of celebratory hostility to establish and reinforce the boundaries of the patriot community. Until they could be driven from the nation, America's enemies might be symbolically exiled by vandalism and threats of violence.

After Philadelphia's long independence celebration had come to an end, John Adams reflected contentedly on the day's affairs: "Considering the lateness of the design and the suddenness of the execution," Adams declared, "I was amazed at the universal joy and alacrity that was discovered." The *Pennsylvania Evening Post* articulated the same delight: "Everything was conducted with the greatest order and decorum, and the face of joy and gladness was universal."[87] But the truth was something considerably different. Far from uniting the community, the first anniversary of independence rather accentuated and even exacerbated dissension among its inhabitants. For many Philadelphians, the anniversary passed as an occasion of discomfort and distress. Indeed, not even every *patriot* rejoiced in the day's entertainment. Connecticut congressman William Williams, the son of a moderate New Light minister and himself deacon of Lebanon's First Congregational Church, was too much the puritan to condone the waste of precious time and resources: "Yesterday was in my opinion poorly spent in celebrating the anniversary of the Declaration of Independence," Williams demurred. "A great Expenditure of Liquor, Powder, &c took up the Day, & of Candles thro the City, good part of the night." Writing to the governor of Connecticut, Williams professed to have attended the public festivities only "to avoid singularity & Reflection upon my dear Colony."[88] Williams's disdain for the anniversary celebration, like his use of the outmoded term "colony," reveals just how newfangled and peculiar independence still felt to many Americans.

One year later, in the dazzling light of the recently concluded Franco-American alliance, independence may have felt more secure, but its ceremonies and rituals had not yet matured. The second anniversary of independence once again found American Whigs cobbling new symbols and rituals of nationhood. And it witnessed even keener and more pernicious efforts by congressmen, Pennsylvania officials, and patriot revelers to claim Philadelphia as their turf. For, fewer than three months after Congress celebrated the first Fourth of July, Howe's army returned to conquer the "Capital of America." When exiled rebels at last returned on the heels of the British evacuation in the late spring of 1778, they discovered a city much given over to vice. To their dismay, they also discovered a cadre of elite women—the Meschianza ladies and their ilk—infatuated with the genteel and sociable British officer corps. Consequently, Philadelphia patriots, desperate to reassert authority over the city, dedicated the second anniversary of independence to patriot honor, to republican virtue, and, perhaps most remarkably, to the restoration of gender order.

The Second Anniversary of Independence

Howe's forces, nearly fifteen thousand strong, landed at Head of Elk, Maryland, in late August 1777, and immediately began to push north.[89] Anticipating a British invasion, the Continental Congress prepared once again to evacuate the city. Among other emergency measures, Congress urged the Supreme Executive Council of Pennsylvania to arrest "disaffected" Quakers and other individuals "whose general conduct and conversation, evidenced a disposition inimical to the cause of America." In early September, Pennsylvania officials apprehended or confined nearly forty such persons and ordered those who would not affirm their allegiance to the commonwealth transported, without due process and at their own expense, first to Reading and ultimately to Winchester, Virginia, where they remained until spring of the following year. The removal of "Tories," for which Henry Laurens had wished only weeks before, thus came quickly and forcibly to pass.[90]

Soon after, the Continental Congress was also forced to depart Philadelphia. Days after Howe's army routed American forces at Brandywine, General Washington warned the congressional president John Hancock that "the Enemy had it in their power to throw a party that Night . . . into the City." Members of Congress began to decamp. A week and a half later, they reconvened for a brief stint in Lancaster, before pressing on to York, a small German-speaking town situated on the Susquehanna River, four days remove from Philadelphia.[91] Congress's second flight from Philadelphia in less than a year chagrined the delegates as greatly as did the first. Writing in early February, after nearly five months of congressional exile, the New York delegate Gouverneur Morris wryly lamented, "The Continental C[ongress] and C[urrency] have both depreciated."[92]

While the delegates struggled to sustain their value in York, William Howe endeavored to improve his stock in Philadelphia. The occupation did not sit easily on the city or its inhabitants. Howe's officers and soldiers took shelter in public buildings, private dwellings, and abandoned houses and barns. From the civilian population, they requisitioned—or looted—blankets, firewood, and other necessities. The British army also consumed a substantial quantity of foodstuffs, exacerbating wartime scarcities. Rising prices fueled contention over rapidly depreciating paper currencies and ever-scant specie. Meanwhile, the collapse of local government spawned a rise in crime and a decline in sanitation. Over the course of the British occupation, General Howe took steps to ameliorate Philadelphians' distress. To maintain the peace and to restore business, Howe appointed the Philadelphia native and onetime congressman Joseph Galloway to the post of superintendent general. Under Galloway's administration, the city regained many of its essential services, including street cleaning, ferries, and the night watch. For the sake of commerce, Howe ordered the *chevaux-de-frise* cleared from the Delaware River. Merchants and storekeepers began to open shop.[93]

Howe and his officers also endeavored to revive the city's sporting and social life. Indifferent to the Articles of Association, indeed as if purposefully to flout them, British soldiers organized cockfights, horseraces, and cricket matches. Under the direction of John André, a genteel army officer with an aptitude for the fine arts, the Southwark Theatre reopened, featuring weekly performances of comedies, farces, and Shakespearean tragedies.[94] On Thursday nights, the officer corps hosted balls at the City Tavern, the popularity of which attested to the total collapse of Congress's moral authority. The young loyalist socialite Rebecca Franks, daughter of a prominent merchant, delighted in the gaiety and amusement Howe brought to Philadelphia. Writing to her friend Anna Harrison Paca, Franks half-heartedly complained, "I've been but 3 evenings alone since we mov'd to town." With no apparent sense of impropriety, Franks urged Paca, wife of the Maryland Continental Congressman William Paca, to visit her in the occupied city. "Oh how I wish Mr. P. wou'd let you come in for a week or two!" Franks declared. "[Y]ou'd have an opportunity of rakeing as much as you choose either at Plays, Balls Concerts or Assemblys."[95]

The season of "rakeing" that so delighted Franks hastened to a spectacular climax in the Meschianza of May 18, 1778, an infamously extravagant farewell party hosted by British officers in honor of their retiring commander, Sir William Howe. Coordinated by John André and rumored to have cost more than three thousand guineas, the Meschianza took its name from the Italian words for "mixture" and "medley." But though the Meschianza did incorporate a variety of eclectic thematic elements, the long night's entertainment was unified by a single, overarching motif: the chivalric English romance. Imagining the occupation of Philadelphia as a heroic medieval crusade, the Meschianza cast British officers as gallant knights and "seven of the principle young ladies of the country" as Turkish maidens. Major André, who personally designed the evening's costumes, drew a sketch illustrating just how the Meschianza ladies should appear. Their attire consisted of a silk polonaise adorned with a bespangled sash, stockings, and veil, and trimmed in the color of one of two mock chivalric orders: the Blended Rose and the Burning Mountain. In their hair—arranged in high turbans by the "Ladies Hair-Dressers" who followed the wives and mistresses of the British army to

Philadelphia—the Meschianza ladies concealed gifts for their knightly suitors.

On the evening of the grand soiree, these Philadelphia "Turks" stepped aboard decorated barges and floated down the Delaware River, accompanied by music and cannonade, to Walnut Grove, the country estate of the late Joseph Wharton. Upon disembarking, they passed through a large square lawn "properly prepared for the exhibition of a tilt and tournament, according to the customs and ordinance of ancient chivalry." After the women had taken their seats in a nearby pavilion, a trumpet blast heralded the arrival of "knights," or British officers mounted in "ancient habits." Boasting of their respective ladies' wit, beauty, and accomplishments, and challenging all who dared deny them, the knights then jousted with lances, pistols, and swords. After four rounds, the master of ceremonies proclaimed a draw: each lady's honor had been nobly avenged. At last, the knights and their devotees proceeded to a lofty banquet tent bedecked with flowers, mirrors, arches and columns, Latin proverbs, and a painting of the Goddess Liberty bestowing laurels on the departing commander. There they partook of dinner and an exorbitant ball that lasted until sunrise.[96]

By presenting the women of Philadelphia as darling damsels, and the British officers as gallant knights, the Meschianza fancied the occupation of Philadelphia as a noble defense of female virtue. The lived experiences of the city's women, however, demonstrate that gender relations during the occupation were more complex, and less heroic, than the Meschianza suggested. Certainly some women enjoyed the social and presumably the sexual opportunities that resulted from the occupation. Rebecca Franks, for instance, thrived on the attention of British officers. "[E]ven I am engaged to seven different gentlemen," she boasted, "for you must know 'tis a fixed rule never to dance but two dances with the same person." For others, the occupation was a period marked by fear and vulnerability. The Revolution, like other wars, put civilian women into close and extraordinary interaction with hostile forces. Several months earlier, in anticipation of Howe's invasion, large numbers of Philadelphia men fled the city, either to fight with the army or to escape arrest or impressment. Of necessity, many of these male refugees left behind their families, such that Howe arrived to discover a city inhabited disproportionately by women. According to British census takers, Philadelphia women outnumbered men by 30 percent.[97] In the absence of fathers, husbands, and sons, the city's women had no choice but to fend for themselves. Propertied women struggled to stave off American and British soldiers who came to their homes to confiscate supplies or loot for pelf. Women with rooms to spare, such as Elizabeth Sandwith Drinker, were made to quarter British officers. Every such encounter bore the threat, implicit or explicit, of physical and sexual assault.[98] Drinker, left alone with her sister to care for five children after Congress exiled her husband to Virginia, agreed to house a Major Crammond only reluctantly, after he suggested the next officer to come along might be less mannered than he. Drinker also watched bitterly as a belligerent, sword-brandishing officer carried off her servant girl, "thief like."[99] Even when violence and coercion were not at hand, officers' and soldiers' sexuality still posed a threat, for male desire was imposed by false promises as well as by force. Sarah Logan Fisher was troubled by "[v]ery bad accounts of the licentiousness of the English officers in deluding young girls."[100]

On the eve of the British evacuation, the Meschianza told a different story about gender relations in occupied Philadelphia. Eliding the genuine experiences of sexual anxiety and confrontation that marked the winter of 1778, the jousting tournament reenvisioned the occupation as a fantasy of male conquest, in which noble British officers captured the hearts and hands of Philadelphia's ladies.[101] Both as enacted on the mock-Authurian stage at the Wharton estate, and as represented to Londoners later that summer in a *Gentleman's Magazine* article written by John André, the Meschianza supplanted "[v]ery bad accounts" of a dissolute and rapacious army with a quaint, Camelot narrative of chivalric masculinity.[102] Affirming British conceptions of colonial American inferiority, the Meschianza also trafficked in ethnicized and racialized discourses of imperial subjugation. The Meschianza's fabulous political geography conflated the New World with the Muslim world, imputing to the British North American colonies all of the decadence and vice that early modern Europeans perceived in the Ottoman Empire. Even as the officers' knightly heraldry betokened their familial honor and Christian virtue, the ladies' Turkish costumes hinted toward their sexual allure and colonial exoticism. Tellingly, the women were joined in their Turkish garb by "twenty-four black slaves," who donned "Oriental dresses, with silver collars and bracelets." When the Howe brothers entered the room, these slaves were made to bow low.[103]

Some Continental Army officers apparently felt stung by the attention Philadelphia women paid to their British counterparts. General Anthony Wayne, for example, responded to the Meschianza socialites and their effete suitors with bitter sarcasm. After the Battle of Monmouth, Wayne gloated, "Tell those Philadelphia ladies who attended Howe's assemblies and *levées* that the heavenly, sweet, pretty red-coats, the accomplished gentlemen of the guards and grenadiers, have been humbled on the plains of Monmouth. The

A Meschianza lady, her escort, and a slave, as sketched in watercolor by Major John André. Courtesy of Cliveden, a property of the National Trust for Historic Preservation in the United States.

knights of the *Blended Rose* and of the *Burning Mount* have resigned their laurels to rebel officers." Disregarding the real distress of persons left behind in occupied Philadelphia, Wayne instead bemoaned the ostensible betrayal of women who consorted with the enemy. His impulse to flaunt the American victory in the face of the Meschianza ladies reveals how begrudgingly mindful he had grown of their opinions and behaviors. It suggests that the women of Philadelphia, particularly the city's patrician ladies, exercised a measure of social power during the occupation.[104] Free to bestow their companionship and romantic favors on whomever they pleased, they became arbiters of masculine virtue and prowess. By doting on British officers, these women embarrassed the American men who had been exiled from the city. Resentful of their power, Wayne and other patriots resolved to withdraw their affections from supposedly faithless women. Wayne vowed to surrender the laurels he had won at Monmouth to the "virtuous daughters of America." Later that summer, after American forces returned to Philadelphia, a handful of army officers and local gentlemen hosted "an excellent entertainment" for those "young ladies who had manifested their attachment to the cause," presumably by spurning the company of British officers.[105]

Members of Congress, too, perceived a threat in the capriciousness of Philadelphia women, a perception that may have been heightened by their dolorous exile. For nine months, while the British officer corps besieged Philadelphia with gaiety, high living, and ostentation, members of Congress sat in a cramped courthouse in dreary York, a small, predominately German-speaking community that the North Carolina congressman Cornelius Harnett remembered as "the most Inhospitable Scandalous place I was ever in."[106] There, the delegates enjoyed little in the way of polite sociability. Very few delegates brought their wives to the Pennsylvania hinterland. Dorothy Quincy Hancock, who had actively hosted congressmen and other dignitaries in Philadelphia, did not join her husband-president in York. Congressman Gouverneur Morris of New York grumbled, "There are no fine women at York Town. Judge then of my Situation." The Massachusetts delegate James Lovell echoed Morris's complaint. Lovell, who joined Congress after serving a lengthy term in a Halifax prison, described his tenure in York as an "equally tedious" period of confinement, "in a narrow Circle, with He-Creatures, drudging, plodding Politicians."[107]

In their letters and diaries, members of Congress made almost no mention of the Meschianza or its participants, but upon returning to Philadelphia, some delegates strove, like Wayne, to distinguish patriot from loyalist women. In August, when the newly arrived French minister Conrad-Alexandre Gérard proposed to host a ball, a handful of congressmen urged him to refrain. "[T]hey wanted to draw an absolute line of separation between Whigs and Tories," Gérard reported, "especially among the ladies." Detailing the history of Congress's Association to his superiors in the French ministry, Gérard attributed the prejudice against genteel entertainments to "northern Presbyterians," who "fervently besought the aid of Heaven." Gérard explained that puritan moral sensibilities no longer prevailed in Philadelphia. "Things have taken another turn," Gérard declared, "quite a number of senators dance every night. Northern rigidity has become mollified in contact with Southern sensuousness."[108]

Perhaps encouraged by sensuous Southern congressmen, Gérard did host a ball, which provoked the expected outcry. A correspondent with the army at White Plains demanded to know, "What opinion . . . must the public entertain of the political principles of the honourable Congress of the United States of America, when some . . . who call themselves leading members, officiously undertake the management of balls, graced with Mescienza [sic] ladies, equally noted for their Tory principles and their late fondness for British debauchees and macaronies."[109] That the question of whether to embrace or to shun loyalist women arose as a matter of public controversy is indicative of the extent to which Philadelphians experienced the British occupation as a gendered phenomenon. Recognizing that women wielded real social and political power, some patriots took affirmative measures to thwart them. By socially rebuffing women perceived to have forsaken America, these Continental Army officers and congressional delegates endeavored to reassert their masculine authority over Philadelphia.

The second anniversary of independence figured prominently in patriot efforts to reclaim the city. Buoyed by news of the Franco-American alliance, the Continental Congress reentered Philadelphia on July 2, heralded by cannonade.[110] But unlike the previous year, Congress did not wait until that late date to plan its Fourth of July festivities. Two weeks before, news that British forces had at last evacuated the city reached Congress at its rural seat in York. Before adjourning, Congress appointed a three-man committee "to take proper measures for a public celebration of the anniversary of independence."[111] This committee faced a formidable task, for as it soon discovered, the city of Philadelphia had been heavily ransacked. British soldiers, who appropriated the state house for use as a hospital and barrack, tore the building "much to pieces" and left it "in a condition disgraceful to the Character of civility." Out on the lawn, they propped a number of dead fruit trees—ripped from Philadelphia's famous orchards—in an odd semicircle and hung lanterns about their branches. Nearby, they dug a large square pit for the disposal of the rotting carcasses of horses and men. So high had the "Filth & Dung" piled in Franklin's streets, so "exceedingly hot" had the summer grown, that the entire city now suffered from an infestation of black flies, a pestilence that New Hampshire congressman Josiah Bartlett remembered as "one of the Plagues of Egypt."[112] Against this fetid, fly-bitten backdrop unfolded a bizarre and carnivalesque Fourth of July, whose ceremony, rich street theater, and violence enabled long-frustrated patriots to reassert their political and cultural authority.

The second anniversary of independence opened, inauspiciously enough, with a gruesome duel, fought by two prominent military figures, John Cadwalader, a brigadier general in the Pennsylvania line, and Thomas Conway, an Irish-born French officer much despised for his outspoken criticism of the American commander, George Washington. That morning, the two generals met on the common, where at a distance of twelve paces, Cadwalader shot

Conway "thro the side of the face."[113] By besting Conway in their very public *affair d'honneur*, Cadwalader avenged Washington not only against that French officer, but against the many persons who had questioned Washington's failure to defend Philadelphia.[114]

In a similar way, the Continental Congress intended its official Fourth-of-July festivities to vindicate its own prestige and reputation. That afternoon, Congress treated the "principal civil and military officers and strangers in town" to a banquet at its old haunt, the City Tavern.[115] This celebration passed in a conspicuously humble fashion. Guests dined on a large baked pudding adorned with patriotic emblems.[116] They then exchanged toasts to the United States; to its new ally, the French king Louis XVI; and to the memorable conquests of the Continental Army and the patriot militias. Rather than celebrating these victories by name, Congress toasted them by date, thereby locating the anniversary of independence within a much fuller calendar of national holidays:

> The Glorious 19th of April, 1775 (the Battles of Lexington and
>   Concord)
> The Glorious 26th of December, 1776 (Washington's assault on
>   Trenton)
> The Glorious 16th of October, 1776 (Burgoyne's surrender at
>   Saratoga)
> The 28th of June, twice Glorious, 1776–1778 (The Battle of
>   Sullivan's Island and the Battle of Monmouth)

Congress rounded out its toasts by drinking to the future of the nation: the happy era of independence, the flourishing of the arts and sciences, and a free people forever. Finally, Congress toasted perpetuity to "the Union of the American States," an expression of hope that the Articles of Confederation would soon be ratified by the three holdout states: Delaware, New Jersey, and Maryland.[117]

The most distinctive quality of Congress's Independence Day celebration was its modesty. Congress's banquet came off vastly less ostentatious than any of the "assemblies and *levees*" by which gay Philadelphians had passed the British occupation. One year before, Congress had settled for stark anniversary festivities chiefly for lack of planning. Now, on the heels of the extravagant British Meschianza, Congress coordinated a resolutely sober event as a strident affirmation of republican moral economy. Determined to reestablish the austere mode of living that Howe's army had undone, Congress contented itself with a simple meal. No dancing, and certainly no jousting, consumed the day. Though a small "orchestra" played music, though fieldpieces fired despite the shortness of powder, Congress made no haughty show of prisoners of war or enemy deserters as it had the year before. In sum, Congress's banquet, a model of temperance and economy—virtues many believed essential to the republic's survival—served as an implicit condemnation of monarchical debauchery and dissipation. Savoring the reversal of military fortunes that had restored Philadelphia to American rule, the Rhode Island delegate William Ellery expressed his delight that British "rakeing" had come to an end: "What a strange vicissitude in human affairs!" Ellery proclaimed. "These, but a few years since, colonies of Britain, are now free, sovereign and independent States, and now celebrate the anniversary of their Independence in the very city where but a day or two before Genl Howe exhibited his ridiculous [*champêtre*]!"[118]

Yet, Congress's Fourth of July celebration was not the only one to carry the day. Philadelphia's out-of door patriots likewise harbored contempt for the ostentation of Howe's regime, and they too wished to mark the city as *their* territory. Late on the Fourth, after Congress's dinner had concluded, a crowd of Whigs gathered in the streets. As had been the case in 1777, it was their virulent out-of-doors activity that most potently defined the meanings of American independence. On this anniversary, the crowd did not attack Tory windows. A shortage of tallow, and presumably a concern for the public peace, prompted Congress to excuse inhabitants from illuminating the city.[119] And so, rather than smashing dark windows, this anniversary crowd—described variously in surviving diaries and correspondence as "the Whigs of the City," "the Citizens," "a mob," and "the vulgar"—found an alternative way to vent its spleen. It first dressed "a Woman of the Town,"—also reported to be "a demirep," "a strumpet," "a very dirty Woman," and "an old Negro Wench"—in "the most Extravagant high head Dress that Could be got," and then exhibited her about town. Her headdress, estimated to be "three feet high and of proportionable width, with a profusion of curls," parodied the "Monstrous" fashion that had been introduced by the British "Ladies Hair-Dressers" and popularized by "the Mistresses & Wh___s of the Brittish officers." By this ridiculous Fourth-of-July spectacle, Philadelphia patriots directed their enmity, figuratively if not literally, at the heads of women who sympathized, and socialized, with the British.[120]

By mock exaltation of this street heroine, Philadelphia patriots expressed derision for the outlandish fashions of loyalist women and of the men who failed to restrain them.[121] This Independence Day exhibition may thus best be understood as an incident of saturnalia, an early-modern folk tradition that drew symbolic power from the carnivalesque inversion of social rank and prestige. In saturnalia, the low was made high and the high was made low.[122] On at least one prior occasion, Philadelphians had utilized saturnine ritual to condemn audacious fashions and to establish sumptuary mores. During the colonial period, a Philadelphia crowd paraded the hangman's wife, draped in a voguish "trollopee" dress.[123] Similarly, in the present case, the crowd employed the most debased member of society, the black servant woman, to lampoon the most esteemed, the genteel lady. In so doing, the crowd subjected both working-class and elite women to its cultural authority.[124] By displaying this character on the Fourth of July, the crowd wove that very subjugation into its narrative of independence.

Refusing to fall casualty to this postoccupation gender warfare, several Philadelphia women devised strategies to ease the sting of the Whigs' pasquinade. Elizabeth Sandwith Drinker, who like many Quakers disdained the British army's social extravagance, distanced herself from the objects of Whig parody by commenting in her diary that ornate headdresses were a "very foolish fashion."[125] Rebecca Franks, upon observing that the overly coifed woman's feet were bare, offered a pointed repartee that recalled the dire conditions of Washington's army at Valley Forge: "[T]hough the style of her head is British, her shoes and stockings are in the genuine Continental fashion." Still another "Tory" lady, Rebecca Moore Smith—wife of the provost William Smith who had spoiled Richard Montgomery's memorial service two years before—took a different tack by participating in the farce, albeit from a distance. Smith "christened" the comical street heroine "Continella, or the Dutchess of Independence," and even "prayed for a pin from her head by way of relic." Joining in the satire, even at the risk of self-deprecation, Smith adopted for herself the subjective position of her would-be Whig satirists. By naming Continella, and by ridiculing that figure's significance for American independence, Smith laid bare the many patriarchal insecurities underlying the whole extraordinary episode.[126] Further, by bestowing on Continella a mock duchy, Smith jabbed at the want of a real American aristocracy. The simplicity of American manners, Smith suggested, owed more to impoverishment and the lack of gentility than to republican conviction.

The parade of the bewigged "strumpet" was thus layered with many meanings. The crowd's actions functioned as a critique of fashion, of women's roles, of polite society, and of political allegiance. The people in the streets endeavored to reclaim Philadelphia as a Whig cultural space, much as Congress did by hosting a simple banquet. They also sought to reconquer Philadelphia women from the Meschianza "knights." Members of Congress endorsed the crowd's agenda. One day after the appearance of Continella, Richard Henry Lee pronounced that the "droll" figure had "lessened some heads already," and would likely "bring the rest within the bounds of reason." "The Tory women," Lee declared, "are very much mortified." Josiah Bartlett of New Hampshire concurred, expressing his hope that "Ladies heads will soon be of a proper size & in proportion to the other parts of their Bodies."[127]

Lee's and Bartlett's statements suggest that more was at stake than simply the height of women's wigs. The "top-gallant-royal commode," as congressional president Henry Laurens dubbed the fashion, had come to be associated, in the patriot mind, with Tory women, which is to say, with treacherous femininity. For Whig leaders, both in and out of Congress, abandoning the city and its womenfolk to Howe's army had been an emasculating experience, a retreat that smacked of timidity and impotence. Women who consorted with British officers—"*women* prostitute in the service of *men* whose swords are still stained with the blood of their friends and relations"— effected a sort of symbolic cuckolding of male patriots.[128] In so doing, these women—however so unrepresentative of social relations during Howe's tenure—exercised considerable sway in the gendered politics of the occupied city. They had overstepped their place, usurping the prerogative of Whig men. Tall headdresses, as the preeminent, perhaps even gaudy, signifier of these women's social status, embodied both their presumptuousness and their faithlessness.[129] By ridiculing this fashion, the patriot crowd put such women back in their proper realm. As Lee's and Bartlett's rhetoric reveals, that realm was characterized by diminutiveness and restraint; it was a realm in which women's "heads" were "lessened" in accordance with the masculinist dictates of "reason" and "proportion."

Despite the ardor with which some patriots commemorated the anniversary of independence, the Fourth of July did not immediately take hold as a national holiday. In the latter years of the Revolution, most Americans ignored the occasion; not until after the war would they begin to celebrate the Fourth year in and year out.[130] It may be that the underdeveloped symbols and rituals of the United States proved uncompelling. Or it may be that the animosity and confrontation that marred these early celebrations strained too heavily the people's nerves. Certainly the dismal prosecution of the war and the altogether *uncertainty* of U.S. independence weighed heavily on the souls of congressmen who stood against the Fourth of July. In 1779, the "bombast" application of a French officer who claimed skill in "the Art of Artificial Fire Works" and who wished to create a grand exhibition in honor of U.S. independence prompted a furious debate about whether Congress really ought to fete the anniversary at all. Urging Congress to finance the Frenchman's pyrotechnics, the delegate William Henry Drayton observed that it was "the practice of all Nations ancient & modern to celebrate particular days of festivity." Drayton believed that marking holidays was a prerogative and function of sovereigns.

But Drayton's South Carolina colleague Henry Laurens objected on moral and ideological grounds. How, Laurens demanded to know, could Drayton think of "fooleries" and "mirth" at a time such as this? With Savannah in the enemy's grip, with Portsmouth and Norfolk reduced to ash, with the Continental Army hanging by a thread and paper money depreciated to an extreme, Laurens thought the anniversary should rather be spent in "fasting & mourning." Never in such times of trouble, Laurens argued, did the Dutch republics or the Swiss cantons debauch themselves with "expensive feasts." Lauren's "zeal" and his invocation of Europe's great republics seem to have swayed his audience, if only a bit. Three states voted not to keep the Fourth that year, and though a majority prevailed in favor of celebration, Congress consciously solemnized the occasion by attending a total of three worship services, at Christ Church, at the Catholic chapel, and at the Dutch Calvinist Church. Congress did sponsor the Frenchman's fireworks, which ascended to "amazing heights," but it preserved gunpowder by ordering that no cannon be fired.[131]

Twelve months later, in 1780, the war fared not much better, and Congress again downplayed the anniversary of independence. That year, the Fourth of July coincided with graduation at the University of the State of Pennsylvania, and Congress, rather than organizing its own Independence Day celebration, simply attended those commencement exercises. There, the delegates heard three graduates debate the morality of slavery, after which an arbiter, granting victory to the opponents of chattel bondage, declared it "the right of the Africans to equal liberty with the rest of mankind."[132] Here, in this refutation of slavery, was a declaration of independence that Congress had for six years now obstinately refused to consider. And here, ultimately, lay the potential of the Fourth of July: no congress or assembly possessed the power to fix its meaning.

6

"[U]ncommon and Extraordinary Movements"

ON THE THIRTEENTH DAY OF JULY 1778, there bloomed in Philadelphia an aloe "tree." This aloe, the only one of its kind in Pennsylvania, had been planted nearly half a century before. But not until the summer of 1778 did it shoot forth a spire, "which it never does but once in the course of its existence." Measuring thirteen inches round, the spire reportedly grew "thirteen feet in the first thirteen days." Here, concluded a correspondent to the *Pennsylvania Packet*, was something to "be observed, as something extremely observable": the earth offered "signs of gratulation." What force stimulated this joyous botanical rarity? To what "singular" event "in the political and rational system" did this "uncommon appearance in inanimate nature" correspond? One day before, as the *Packet* explained, Conrad-Alexandre Gérard, the minister plenipotentiary of his most Christian Majesty, King Louis XVI, set foot on Philadelphia soil. According to the *Packet* correspondent, who signed him- or herself Hary-Spex, after the Roman soothsayers who practiced divination, the Franco-American alliance filled "Heaven and Earth" with happy omens. Throughout months of treaty negotiations, the "most beautiful" auroras brightly illuminated the American heavens. At the appearance of the French navy off the Delaware Capes, "the artillery of the skies was discharged, and thirteen thunders were distinctly heard." And now, on the arrival of a French minister, this ancient aloe, which never in all its years sprouted more than four leaves, "spread forth thirteen." Many fine things, the *Packet* promised its readers, would be spoken "of the aloe-tree of America, and the *fleur de lis* of France."[1]

If perhaps less observant of omens and augurs than Hary-Spex, members of Congress nevertheless believed that the arrival of the French minister portended a glorious future for the United States. A fruit of the recently concluded Treaties of Alliance and of Amity and Commerce, Gérard's mission bore the heartening promise of much-needed financial and military aid. Just as importantly, Gérard's appointment signified that one of the great courts of Europe had at last recognized American independence. As the Rhode Island congressman Henry Marchant exclaimed, "The Scene brightens . . . We advance into the Circle and Standing of mighty Nations." Yet, Marchant also perceived that the opening of formal diplomatic relations called "for new and fresh Exertions of Senatorial Wisdom." One of those new and fresh exertions, the establishment and implementation of proper diplomatic ceremony, proved particularly demanding. European convention obliged Congress to grant the French minister an audience. For such a task, Congress possessed little practical experience. None of the delegates knew in precisely what manner a young republic ought to receive the representative of the ancien régime. As the congressional president Henry Laurens explained, the appearance of the French legation was a "novelty in these infant States." To pay the minister his "due attention" would "occasion some uncommon and extraordinary movements."[2]

Uncommon and extraordinary movements are the subjects of this chapter, both literally and figuratively. Literally, because eighteenth-century diplomatic ceremony relied heavily on bodily performance, including gesticulation and ritualized movement. At court, in state houses, and around council fires, physical acts such as sitting, rising, shaking hands, and bowing all assumed tremendous symbolic significance, as Congress quickly discovered. By these signals, the powers of the earth contended for honor, expressed indignation, claimed primacy, and paid deference. The reception of a French minister in 1778 thus opened a new theatrical medium by which Congress could assert rank for the United States while at the same time affirming its own institutional legitimacy.

Figuratively, too, uncommon and extraordinary movements are the subjects of this chapter, because Revolutionary diplomatic ceremony demanded that Congress make a number of awkward political and ideological contortions. As one of its highest diplomatic priorities, Congress strove to establish the sovereignty of the United States. The delegates refused, as a matter of principle, to negotiate with any power that impugned the honor of the American republic. In 1777, Congress rebuffed the conciliatory overtures of the Howe brothers, deeming it "beneath the Dignity of Congress to Treat with persons whose very Powers supposed them objects of their Dominion."[3] In the spring of 1778, Congress spurned the advances of the Carlisle Peace Commission on those same grounds. In its dealings with France, Congress likewise endeavored to preserve the dignity of the United States, instructing its commissioners in Paris "to obtain, as early as possible, a publick acknowledgement of the independency of these states . . . by the court of France."[4]

Yet, Congress's determination to vindicate the United States bent to a variety of diplomatic necessities, ideological conflicts, political machinations, and material circumstances. First, international custom compelled the United States, as the far less formidable party to the Treaty of Alliance, to flatter the French king. In his *Droit des Gens*, a treatise on the law of nations frequently consulted by Congress, the eighteenth-century Swiss jurist Emmerich de Vattel explained that in an "unequal alliance . . . to the more powerful is given more honour, and to the weaker, more assistance."[5] Congress thus faced the delicate task of showering praise on Louis XVI without compromising the integrity of the United States. Second, though members of Congress earnestly desired to celebrate their nation, they sharply disagreed over how best to do so. As a plural executive, the Continental Congress suffered grave disagreements over policy and protocol.[6] Plain-style republicans, including many who hailed from New England, demanded austerity and simplicity in Congress's ceremony; they insisted that legislative bodies should exemplify virtue and frugality in their public proceedings. More worldly congressmen, especially those drawn from the aristocratic Southern colonies, believed that the United States should present itself with greater splendor; they sought to elevate the new nation with pageantry and pomp and thereby to draw the United States into line with European practice. In its diplomatic ceremony, Congress struggled to reconcile these competing visions of national glory. Third, members of Congress approached their treating partners—not only the French but also the various Native American groups with whom the United States sought rapprochement—with a host of long-standing prejudices. Many congressmen dreaded the vice of the French court and fretted over the influence Gérard would exert on national affairs. At the same time, they recoiled from the primitiveness and heathenism they perceived among the indigenous peoples with whom they shared a continent. Congress strove to devise a diplomatic ceremony that distanced itself from both the debauchery of its "civilized" allies and from the brutishness of its "savage" ones. Finally, U.S. diplomatic ceremony became entangled in congressional politics, particularly after the so-called Deane-Lee affair, which intensified rancor among the loose factions that prevailed in the Pennsylvania State House. The French legation gravitated toward Deane and his powerful backer, Robert Morris, even going so far as to deem Lee's partisans, notably Samuel Adams, the "opposition."[7] Because diplomatic rituals touched on the dignity and politics of the United States and France alike, they provoked a good deal of controversy among members of Congress and other participants. No pure expression of national prestige or glory, U.S. diplomatic ceremony became both the means and ends of political manipulation.

Members of Congress labored mightily to accommodate the conflicting imperatives of diplomacy. In so doing, they evinced a remarkably keen regard for the character and reputation of the United States both at home and abroad. Precisely because Congress's diplomatic protocol bore such consequence for national honor, loyalists and other foes of Congress seized on it as a matter for ridicule. Congressional diplomatic ceremony thus became a highly contested phenomenon: contested by the friends of the United States, who questioned how best to glorify their nation, and by its enemies, who questioned whether the pretended nation merited any glory at all.

"[P]lain, grand, & decent"

Before turning to particular facets of the United States' diplomatic ceremony and language, it is useful to reflect first on the development of Franco-American relations during the Revolutionary period. The United Colonies began conducting secret, mediated negotiations with France in December 1775. The United States declared independence seven months later, in part because members of Congress believed that "European delicacy" prohibited France from formally treating with, or receiving an ambassador from, Britain's dependent colonies.[8] But not until February 1778, after continental forces had defeated Burgoyne's army in New York and by which time the French government has considerably strengthened its navy, did King Louis's ministry at last accede to a formal alliance. The United States requested a great deal of French military and financial assistance; in return, it offered little but trade, and that was badly hindered by war. Only because French officials perceived in the American rebellion an opportunity to weaken their ancient enemy, Great Britain, did they pursue this imbalanced relationship.[9]

Shortly after treating with the United States, the French government dispatched to Philadelphia a minister, Conrad-Alexandre Gérard. An experienced and high-ranking diplomat recently ennobled by Louis XVI, Gérard had conducted formal and informal negotiations with the American commissioners in Paris. The Franco-American alliance owed much to Gérard's labor; his mission to Philadelphia gave, in the understated words of President Henry Laurens, "a little fillip" to Congress.[10] Before Congress received the French minister in a public audience, it first had to welcome him to the American capital. This unofficial task, simple though it may seem, created a good deal of commotion. Upon receiving word in early July that the French navy had been sighted near the mouth of the Delaware, Congress, only recently returned to Philadelphia from its exile in York, moved quickly to prepare for the minister's imminent arrival. On Sunday, July 12, a barge—manned by twelve oarsmen "dressed in Scarlet trimmed in Silver"—rowed a congressional welcoming committee to the minister's frigate. Announcing their appearance with a volley of fifteen guns, the committeemen boarded Gérard's ship, exchanged "Compliments of Congratulation," and then accompanied the minister back to shore, where "four Coaches with four Horses" awaited. Heralded once again by the discharge of fifteen guns, the entourage paraded through the city to the High Street residence of General Benedict Arnold, the military governor of Philadelphia. Here, in the former home of the heiress Polly Masters and her husband Richard Penn, in a room most recently inhabited by the British commander William Howe, Gérard would stay until Congress made arrangements for his permanent lodgings. As the French minister descended from his carriage, the fire of thirteen cannons welcomed him to his temporary home.[11]

Big with pageantry, this reception provoked the derision of the king's friends, still smarting from the British evacuation of Philadelphia. The *Royal Gazette*, published in occupied New York, reported that the "ceremony observed at the landing of the French ambassador . . . has created a good deal of uneasiness in the minds of the spectators." The *Gazette* claimed that when Gérard set foot on American soil, the commissioner Silas Deane delivered seizin to him, that is, handed him a patch of turf as a symbolic gesture of property transfer. This, of course, was a bald fabrication meant to mock the United States' supposed independence and to play on fears of French despotism.[12] But, in fact, Congress's welcoming of Gérard had caused uneasiness, at least for one spectator. Neighbor Grace Growden Galloway, who looked out her window to discover eighty-two armed soldiers filed opposite her house, feared instantly for the safety of her loyalist husband, Joseph. Her

thoughts must have turned as well to her family home, as Pennsylvania officials had recently initiated confiscation proceedings against it. Soon, they
would take possession of her house and appropriate it for the residence of the
president of the Supreme Executive Council. Galloway would then know
exactly how it felt to see her property handed over, seizin-like, to a hostile
power. For now, as she beheld the array of soldiers and listened to the cannon
fire, she could only seethe at the "Contemptable sight."[13]

The welcoming of Gérard to Philadelphia marked only the beginning of a
new season of diplomatic fanfare. Congress now faced the exciting but daunt-
ing task of receiving the minister in a formal audience. This, as noted the
Rhode Island congressman Henry Marchant, was an "Important transac-
tion."[14] It required that members of Congress acquaint themselves with
European ceremonial forms and practices. As conducted among "the powers
of the earth," international diplomacy depended on an elaborate and highly
conventionalized etiquette. Historians have traced the origins of modern
diplomatic practice to the kingdoms, duchies, and republics of late medieval
Italy. Exported across the Alps after the French invasion of 1494, the Italian
practice, distinguished by its reliance on permanent residential ambassadors,
spread across Europe and ultimately to Russia and the Ottoman Empire. In
1648, the Treaty of Westphalia confirmed the principle of sovereignty in na-
tion-states and gave rise to a new class of professional diplomats. Across the
centuries there evolved a labyrinthine protocol to govern these emissaries and
the courts that received them.[15] Though numerous members of the Continental Congress had traveled in Europe, studied law, or served even as colonial agents abroad, Congress as a whole lacked familiarity with European
diplomatic ritual. As Gérard reported home to the French ministry, this was
"a totally new matter" for Congress.[16]

To master the intricate formalities of diplomacy, Congress consulted a
number of treatises on international law. At the delegates' fingertips were
dozens of legal, historical, and philosophical volumes held by the Library
Company of Philadelphia, including works by Grotius, Pufendorf, and Bur-
lamaqui.[17] The delegates also shared a copy of Emmerich de Vattel's *Droit des
Gens*, edited by Charles-Guillaume-Frédéric Dumas, a Swiss intellectual
who lived in The Hague and carefully observed the diplomacy conducted
there. Dumas presented his edition of Vattel to Benjamin Franklin in 1775,
and it passed "continually" through the delegates' hands ever after. As Franklin
gratefully acknowledged, Dumas's gift came to Congress "in good season,
when the circumstances of a rising state ma[d]e it necessary frequently
to consult the law of nations."[18] The dutifulness with which members of

Congress pored over these volumes reveals just how fully they desired their practices to comport with the established traditions of Europe. By contrast, fifteen years later, the French Revolutionaries purposefully cast aside their ancient compendiums. "The theory of revolutionary government," Robespierre proclaimed, "is as new as the revolution which brought it into being. It is not necessary to search for it in the books of political writers . . . or in the laws of tyrants."[19]

Though Congress wished to emulate European custom, at least one influential delegate, Samuel Adams, believed that U.S. diplomatic ceremony ought to reflect the simplicity of American manners. In July, Adams found himself appointed to a three-man committee to devise a protocol for Gérard's audience.[20] The irony of this appointment was not lost on the once-shabby statesman. In his private correspondence Adams demurred, "Would you think that one so little of the Man of the World as I am should be joynd in a Committee to settle Ceremonials[?]"[21] Despite his humble pose, Adams valued this appointment all the same, for he worried a great deal about public morality. Upon returning from York, Adams discovered that Philadelphians had abandoned American virtue in favor of British vice. He and like-minded delegates urged Congress to recommend "effectual measures . . . for the suppressing of theatrical entertainments, horse racing, gaming, and such other diversions as are productive of idleness, dissipation, and a general depravity of principles and manners." Adams hoped that such measures would restore "true religion and good morals" to the American capital, but he doubted whether either could take root so long as the ruling classes continued to flaunt them.[22] Adams ardently believed that the customs and social behaviors of governors, legislators, and magistrates swayed those of the public. Writing two years later to counsel temperance and humility in the administration of his home commonwealth, Adams explained:

> [I]f we look into the History of Governors, we shall find that their Principles & Manners have always had a mighty Influence on the People. Should Levity & Foppery ever become the ruling Taste of the Great, the Body of the People would be in Danger of catching the Distemper, and the ridiculous Maxims of the one would become fashionable among the other. I pray God we may never be addicted to Vanity & the Folly of Parade! Pomp & Show serve very well to promote the Purposes of European & Asiatick Grandeur, in Countries where the Mystery of Iniquity is carried to the highest Pitch, & Millions are tame enough to believe they

are born for no other Purpose than to be subservient to the capricious Will of a single Great Man or a few! It requires Council & sound Judgment to render our Country secure in a flourishing Condition.[23]

Adams felt it his earnest duty to safeguard the United States against parade, pomp, and show. Mindful that Gérard's audience would "be recurrd to as a Precedent in Futurity," Adams endeavored to tailor the ceremonials in accordance with "true republican Principles."[24]

Not every delegate shared Adams's moral aesthetics. When the ceremonial committee laid its proposals before Congress in mid-July, a lengthy debate erupted over diplomatic ritual and national honor. In his report to the French ministry, Gérard explained that more cosmopolitan congressmen, particularly those hailing from the wealthier and more aristocratic Southern states, objected that the proposed ceremony fell too far short of European standards. "*Les members méridionaux*," Gerard reported, had "beheld the king of England seated upon his throne."[25] Regrettably, Gérard did not name these particular Southern delegates, but a review of congressional voting records reveals that John Banister and Thomas Adams of Virginia and William Henry Drayton and John Mathews of South Carolina all voted in opposition to the proposed ceremony.[26] Each of these Southern congressmen spent portions of his adult life in London and could have feasibly gained entrance to the Court of St. James's. Drayton seems a particularly likely candidate, having been appointed by George III to the privy council of South Carolina in 1771.[27]

How did it feel to behold the king of England seated on his throne? How would that experience have shaped a congressman's expectations of a suitably dignified ceremony of state? The correspondence of Benjamin Rush, a Philadelphia republican and Continental Congressman who had once seated *himself* on the king of England's throne, provides a glimpse of the tremendous symbolic power of monarchical ceremony and artifact. After visiting the House of Lords in 1768, Rush confided,

> I felt as if I walked on sacred ground. I gazed for some time at the Throne with emotions that I cannot describe. I asked our guide if it was common for strangers to set down upon it. He told me no, but upon my importuning him a good deal I prevailed upon him to allow me the liberty. I accordingly advanced towards it and sat in it for a considerable time. When I first got into it, I was seized

with a kind of horror which for some time interrupted my ordinary train of thinking. "This," said I . . ., "is the golden period of
the worldly man's wishes. His passions conceive, his hopes aspire
after nothing beyond *this Throne*." I endeavored to arrange my
thoughts into some order, but such a crowd of ideas poured in
upon my mind that I can scarcely recollect one of them.[28]

Having experienced something of this awe and wonder, Southern congressmen balked at Adams's lackluster proposal. They demanded splendor for
the United States, if not equal to that of European courts, at least in some
discernible measure.

At the heart of this conflict lay a vital but unresolved question: how should
the United States present itself on an international stage? Here was the dilemma of a republic wishing to conduct affairs in a world of monarchies.
European diplomacy evolved in large part to suit the pride and prerogatives
of hereditary rulers. The law of nations recognized republican governments,
and during the early modern period, a handful of such polities—notably the
Swiss Cantons, the Netherlands, and certain small Italian states such as
Venice—carved unique niches for themselves in European courts. But the
existence of such republics presented a variety of challenges for a diplomatic
etiquette steeped in monarchical tradition. Powerful, landed, hereditary
rulers, whose sovereignty resided in their dynastic bloodline, did not enthusiastically deign to receive the representatives of feeble elected officials. Even
Vattel, who stridently asserted in his *Droit des Gens* that "elective kings and
princes," however so limited their authority, ought to be treated as full sovereigns, acknowledged that this point had historically been a matter of contention. "Great princes," Vattel conceded, "make a difficulty of admitting an
ambassador of a small state, from a repugnancy of paying him such distinguished honours."[29]

The Continental Congress now found itself in the opposite position, that
of an exceedingly weak confederation entertaining the minister plenipotentiary of a powerful monarch.[30] Congress faced the delicate task of adulating
the French king and dignifying the United States, all the while muting the
"European and Asiatick grandeur" that Samuel Adams so dreaded. National
pride thus clashed with republican principles. For four days the delegates
wrestled with this problem, quarreling over how best to elevate the republic
to its rightful place among the powers of the earth. They deliberated details
of the finest grain: whether the minister ought to be granted a public coach
for the day; whether, when, and in what manner the president of Congress

should be seated; and whether Congress and Gérard ought to bow to one another.[31] This, Richard Henry Lee sighed, was "a work of no small difficulty." That Congress should devote so much energy to these questions reveals two things: first, that the delegates fervently wished to vindicate the honor of the United States, and second, that they implicitly believed in the potency of ritual and ceremony not simply to communicate but even to mediate these relations of diplomatic power. The French minister apparently shared Congress's faith, for he flatly refused to appear before Congress until he had personally approved the final draft of the ceremony.[32]

The minister's audience unfolded in accordance with Congress's minute choreography: At noon on the appointed day, Samuel Adams and Richard Henry Lee waited on the minister at his residence.[33] Offering Gérard the privileged right-hand seat in the United States' coach-and-six, they proceeded to their destination, escorted by a detail of Pennsylvania officers of the peace.[34] At the door of the state house, Gérard received "such military honours as [were] paid to a general officer of the second rank in the armies of the United States."[35] Inside, Congress and its president Henry Laurens awaited.

Prior to this moment, the presidency of Congress had mostly been a titular position. An elected office with no fixed term, the presidency had come

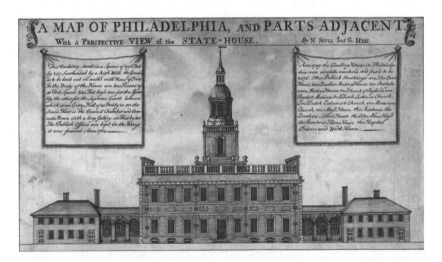

Upon returning to Philadelphia in early July 1778, the Continental Congress moved swiftly to clean and restore the Pennsylvania State House, much abused during the British occupation, in time for the audience of the French minister in August. Detail of *A Map of Philadelphia and Parts Adjacent: With a Perspective View of the State-House*, by Nicholas Scull and George Heap. Philadelphia, 1752. Library of Congress, Geography and Map Division.

by tradition to rotate among the states. The president's chief duties included chairing deliberations and writing and receiving much of Congress's official correspondence.[36] The opening of diplomatic relations with France did not bestow any greater authority on the president, but it elevated him, literally, as the ceremonial figurehead of the United States. At Gérard's audience, President Laurens personally embodied the sovereignty of the nation. The French minister faced the president, was introduced to the president, and delivered his credentials to the president. The president alone spoke the sentiments of Congress and he did do so from a perch. Here was the first of two compromises struck between Samuel Adams's ceremonial committee and the worldlier Southern delegates: the president of Congress sat, not on a throne exactly, but in a mahogany armchair raised on a platform two steps above the state house floor. The rest of Congress and the French minister sat beneath him. Laurens apparently recognized that these protocols would enhance the stature of his office, for when Congress voted on the ceremony, he tactfully requested and was unanimously granted permission to abstain. Gérard, on the other hand, objected to the eminence on which Congress placed its chief officer, but the Southern delegates would not yield.[37] Having seen the king of England on his throne, these congressmen would not relinquish the monarchical conceit that national glory resided in the exalted body of a supreme ruler.

This display of prestige and authority would have passed for naught had no one been present to behold it. From this fact arose the ceremonial committee's second concession to the Southern delegates. Though Congress had never before opened its proceedings, indeed had conducted them in sworn secrecy, on this occasion it flung wide its doors. In the back of the room, behind "the bar," crowded nearly two hundred Pennsylvania officials, Continental Army officers, and other distinguished gentlemen. In his official narrative of the event, Gérard bluntly attributed this arrangement to the vanity of Southern congressmen who insisted that the audience be made public.[38] Less vain delegates such as Samuel Adams could take heart: these spectators stood as living, breathing proof of the revolutionary ideal of popular sovereignty; their presence attested to the consent of the governed.

While these guests solemnly watched, Richard Henry Lee announced what everyone already knew: that the "Stranger" on the floor was the "minister Plenipotentiary from his most Christian Majesty." At that cue, Gérard, the president, and the Congress all stood, exchanged bows, and retook their seats. Gérard then rose to deliver a prepared speech, after which the entire house stood and remained standing while President Laurens gave his reply. When Laurens concluded, Gerard bowed to the president, to the Congress, and once again to the president, who "returned the Compliment" before the minister withdrew.[39] Strikingly, this ceremony incorporated several conventionalized elements of eighteenth-century European diplomacy. In its proffer of a state coach and in the acts of rising and remaining seated and of bowing and standing upright, Congress carefully imitated the stylized gestures by which European diplomats asserted the rank and stature of their sovereigns.[40] Yet, though Congress patterned Gérard's reception in the fashion of St. James's and Versailles, it adapted its protocols as well to the republican precepts of Philadelphia. Notably, Congress demanded that the French minister pay his respects to the entire house. The minister bowed not only to President Laurens but to all the assembled delegates. In so doing, Gérard acknowledged that the sovereignty of the U.S. properly resided in the states, not in their president. Further, Gérard addressed the assembled delegates simply as "Gentleman of the Congress," rather than with "sumptuous titles" such as *les hauts puissants*, that is, their high mightinesses, as was the usage in the Dutch republic.[41]

After the audience, Congress invited its guests to a dinner featuring a "Band of Musick and the firing of Cannon." Reporting the day's events, the New Jersey congressman Elias Boudinot perfectly captured the tension between the simplicity and the stateliness to which Congress simultaneously aspired. Without any sense of contradiction, Boudinot described the ceremony as "plain, grand & decent."[42] Gérard, too, commended the affair. Though he groused that "confused notions of the honor, dignity, and etiquette of a sovereign state" still prevailed in Congress, he praised the reception for its want of ostentation, ambition, pride, and luxury. The modesty of the event, Gérard believed, befitted a people committed to the avoidance of ceremony and pomp.[43] The *Pennsylvania Packet* proved less circumspect. "Thus has a new and noble sight been exhibited in this new world," declared the *Packet*, in its widely reprinted account of the reception: "the Representatives of the United States of America, solemnly giving public audience to a Minister Plenipotentiary from the most powerful Prince in Europe. Four years ago, such an event, at so near a day, was not in the view even of imagination." The magnificent ascendance of the United States, the *Packet* concluded, could only be attributed to divine intervention: "[I]t is the Almighty who raiseth up; he hath stationed America among the powers of the earth, and cloathed her in robes of Sovereignty."[44]

The Grand Council Fire at Philadelphia

The *Packet*'s triumphant account recalled the first sentence of the Declaration of Independence, wherein Congress proclaimed the new United States' foremost ambition: "to assume among the powers of the earth, the separate and equal station to which the Laws of Nature and of Nature's God entitle them." Historian David Armitage has demonstrated that this sentence must be understood as an appeal to natural and positivist international law. An assertion of sovereignty, it staked the United States' claim to all of the rights and privileges appurtenant thereto.[45] Yet, though rooted in legal axioms and principles, Jefferson's words ripened into something much more. The opening lines of the Declaration captured the imagination of American revolutionaries and, over the course of the war, came to represent their aspirations for the new nation.

Consider, for example, the New Hampshire congressman William Whipple's wish in 1779 that "the United States were fully sensible of their importance among the powers of the Earth." Or the Carolina congressman John Mathews's rhapsodic prophecy in 1781 that the United States' "arms" would soon "acquire the highest renown, and raise her into consequence among the nations of the earth." Or the New York congressman James Duane's assertion in 1782 that the merciful treatment of British prisoners would "give this Infant Republick a distinguished Rank among refined and civilized Nations." Or the Rhode Island congressman David Howell's exultation in 1783 that he had "lived to see the day when the U.S. are not only allowed rank among the nations of the earth; but from the renown of their atchievements [*sic*] all nations are ambitious of testifying their regard to us."[46] These statements demonstrate that Jefferson's language came to shape the congressmen's hopes for the future of the United States. But these statements also reveal that members of Congress did *not* believe that the earth's powers occupied equal stations. Inspired by the ideals of natural law, the first sentence of the Declaration posited a fraternity of independent nations, each on a par, each exercising the same fundamental rights. By contrast, members of Congress understood that nations assumed "rank" by degrees of "importance," "renown," "consequence," and "atchievements."

This disjuncture—between "the powers of the earth" as imagined in the Declaration of Independence and the "powers of the earth" as held sway in the world—raises intriguing questions about the Continental Congress's vision for the United States. Among which powers did Congress expect the former British colonies to take rank? Precisely what station did Congress intend its confederated republic to assume? What was hoped for the United States' place among nations, aside from independence from Great Britain? Answers to these questions may be found in the diplomatic etiquette of the American Revolution. Diplomacy was one of the few arenas in which the thirteen states, each jealous of its individual sovereignty, agreed to function as a nation.[47] Through diplomacy the United States' doubtful place in the world became slightly more certain. Treaties and conventions fundamentally defined relationships among nations, but so, too, did diplomatic ritual. Eighteenth-century diplomacy relied heavily on performative ceremony. As evident in Congress's reception of the French minister, nations exchanged courtesies and professed affection but also contended for honor and jostled for rank through ceremonial posture and address.

France, however, was not the only power with whom the United States conducted negotiations during the war. A full three years before the Continental Congress concluded treaties with Louis XVI, it first opened diplomatic relations with the indigenous peoples of North America. These peoples also ranked among the powers of the earth, however so little or much they might be recognized at international law.[48] And just as delegates to Congress measured the United States against France, so too did they adjudge their fledgling republic in relation to their Native American neighbors. The following pages offer a comparative analysis of the diplomatic protocols employed between the United States and its foremost treating partners: the nation of France, and various Native American peoples, particularly certain inhabitants of the Ohio River Valley and former constituents of the ruptured Iroquois Confederacy. This comparison focuses on four well-documented aspects of U.S. diplomatic ceremony and language: exchanges of gifts, rituals of salutation, bestowals of honorific names and titles, and idioms of friendship and alliance.[49] The similarities and differences between U.S.-French and U.S.-Native ceremony point up many of the prejudices and self-conceptions that these would-be allies brought to their negotiations. They further illuminate participant-nations' beliefs about their standing in the world. Contrary to the hopes expressed in the first sentence of the Declaration, members of Congress recognized that the United States did not yet occupy an equal station among the powers of the earth. Consequently, they took solace in the fact that it possessed a separate one.

Shortly after war erupted in 1775, Congress began making overtures to numerous indigenous peoples living east of the Mississippi River. In July of that year, Congress appointed commissioners to treat with Natives in each of three departments: the northern, middle, and southern. At that time,

Congress also drafted lengthy addresses urging Indian nations to disengage from the conflict and to "keep the hatchet buried deep."[50] Most Native groups ultimately rejected Congress's diplomatic overtures, both because Britain seemed more likely to protect their land claims and because British agents offered a steadier supply of trade goods and provisions than did the former colonists. Some nations, however, did respond positively to congressional outreach and of these, a few sent deputies to Philadelphia. Representatives of the Delawares and Shawnees, certain of the Six Nations, and several New England peoples visited Congress between October 1775 and December 1776. Gelelemend and other members of the Delaware nation returned in May 1779. Throughout this period, congressional commissioners treated with Native Americans in outlying entrepôts such as Albany and at borderland posts such as Fort Pitt.[51]

Whereas the United States negotiated with France as a decided inferior, it approached Indian peoples, at least initially, from a somewhat more equitable bargaining position. True, Native American military capacity was strong enough to shift the balance of war; equally true, the United Colonies, their trade disrupted by boycott and blockade, did not have much to offer those prospective allies. But in 1775 Congress asked relatively little of most Native groups; only for neutrality, not for financial or military assistance. As in its dealings with France, Congress endeavored to conduct its Native diplomacy in keeping with established convention. Across nearly three centuries of diplomatic encounters, European colonists and the indigenous inhabitants of North America forged an array of syncretic practices, blending elements of their diverse cultures to create a distinctive protocol for the middle ground.[52] The diplomacy of the council fire thus diverged in key aspects from that of the court, and Congress sought to display its mastery of the former no less than of the latter. Some members of Congress took part in earlier Anglo-Indian peace talks, observing firsthand the time-honored rituals, symbols, and idioms that governed these interactions. Congressional secretary Charles Thomson, for example, attended the Easton treaty of 1757 between Pennsylvania and the Delawares and even served on that occasion as clerk to the Delaware "king" Teedyuscung.[53] Congress also called on the advice of experienced cultural intermediaries, such as the Presbyterian missionary Samuel Kirkland and the Illinois trader George Morgan. Finally, Congress consulted numerous colonial treaties to discern "the Formalities practised with the Indians, and the Mode of Language adopted in Addressing them."[54]

European and Native American diplomacy shared certain basic objectives, most fundamentally the establishment of mutual trust and the creation of reciprocal obligations. Few customs did more to serve those purposes than a bountiful exchange of gifts. Gift giving had long been an essential component of Euro-Indian diplomacy. By presenting gifts, European and Native peoples honored their treating partners, expressed friendship and goodwill, and made conspicuous exhibitions of their generosity. The early governors of New France assumed the mantle of "Onontio," or "father" of their Algonquian-speaking allies, and thereby undertook an obligation to provide their "children" with a regular supply of gifts. The French furnished Native chiefs with wares, weapons, and ornaments for redistribution throughout their villages or clans, both as a means of brokering prestige and authority and of reconciling their communities to particular diplomatic accords.[55] After the Seven Years' War, the refusal of the British commander Jeffrey Amherst to keep this custom so greatly affronted *les gens du pays d'en haut* that it, along with other grievous policies, precipitated the uprising that came to be known as Pontiac's Rebellion.[56]

Unwilling to repeat British mistakes and eager to avail the United Colonies of every diplomatic expedient, Congress determined very early in the war to offer presents to its Native treating partners.[57] In July 1775, the Rhode Island congressman Samuel Ward ranked the preparation of "Presents[,] Talks[, and] Belts of Wampum" among a handful of measures necessary for the "Security of Our Frontiers." In December of that same year, Congress resolved that it was "both suitable and proper" to give presents to "the Indians of St. Francis, Penobscot, Stockbridge, and St. John's." In April 1776, Congress presented the Delaware alliance chief Quequedegatha with three hundred dollars and two saddled horses during his visit to Philadelphia. Two years later, when Quequedegatha appealed for "a Commission or Certificate" of the United States' approbation "to produce as a Testimony of his Services," Congress determined to bestow a silver medal on the Delaware captain, "to perpetuate the memory of that great esteem which Congress have for his Merit."[58]

In making these gifts, the United States treated with Native peoples not altogether differently than it treated with the French. In 1776, the Paris commissioner Silas Deane advised Congress to send presents for the queen, Marie Antoinette, who was believed to be a friend of the American cause. It would be "money exceedingly well laid out," Deane assured.[59] Prompted by Deane's recommendation, Congress began casting about for "American curiosities, to send across the Atlantic as presents to the Ladies." Among the gifts that Congress considered were "Mr. Rittenhouse's Planetarium, Mr. Arnolds Collection of [bird and insect] Rareties in the Virtuoso Way, . . . Narragansett

Pacing Mares, Mooses, Wood ducks, Flying Squirrels, Redwinged Black birds, Cramberries [*sic*], and Rattlesnakes." Here were mementos of American genius and nature sure to gratify the Enlightenment imagination.[60]

In the meantime, the French king bestowed gifts on his American allies, too. Upon the retirement of the American commissioners Deane, Lee, and Franklin, the French Crown presented each with a diamond-encrusted gold box adorned with a portrait of Louis XVI. These gifts fulfilled a variety of purposes. They functioned as tokens of esteem, as prestige items, and perhaps as petty bribes. Much like the medal that Quequedegatha begged of Congress, they also served as certificates of French approbation. Recalled from Paris under accusation of graft and abuse of office, Silas Deane defended himself by displaying for Congress his gold box, along with a "handsome testimonial" that the French ministry had written in appreciation for his service. Deane's detractors, notably Samuel Adams, partisan of Deane's rival Arthur Lee, dismissed the box as "mere etiquette and partiality." "Unthinking Men may be amusd with a Golden Snuff Box," Adams sneered. Such items, he declared, were "mere Things of Course, especially in the Honey Moon of National Matrimony."[61]

Other gifts performed substantive diplomatic functions, bearing material witness to the establishment of alliances. In the late fall of 1777, for example, representatives of the Creek Nation presented to Congress an eagle's tail and a "rattle trap." The Creeks further instructed the United States to carry these items—"the strongest mark of their sincere friendship"—to the Six Nations, as proof that the Creeks and the United States had buried the hatchet.[62] In a remarkably similar gesture tendered shortly after his arrival in Philadelphia, the French minister Conrad-Alexandre Gérard delivered to the congressional president Henry Laurens a "ponderous and beautiful silver Medal" as a token of the Franco-Helvetic alliance. One face depicted King Louis XVI, while the other bore a wreath of olive branches to emblematize the confederation of Swiss cantons and states. The French had only recently acknowledged Swiss independence, and Laurens believed the decision to do so may have been prefatory to France's recognition of the United States.[63]

Strikingly congruent in action and communicative intent, these gift exchanges underscore certain commonalities of diplomatic protocol in Revolutionary North America. French, U.S., and Indian deputies alike aspired to appease, to oblige, to express confidence in, and to win the confidence of, their respective allies. By making presents, these treating partners worked to endear other peoples and to bind them in reciprocal commitment. In this way, the custom of diplomatic gift giving bore the potential to cultivate mutuality and comity. Other aspects of U.S.-French and U.S.-Native diplomacy, however, tended to accentuate differences of rank and privilege. Such may be glimpsed in the discrepant rituals of salutation adopted by Congress in the company of the United States' allies.

Anglo-American and Native-American diplomats welcomed one another and bade farewell in accordance with a variety of hybridized customs. English and Iroquoian treating partners, for example, melded diplomatic tradition with social convention by exchanging gifts, offering condolences, smoking tobacco, making music, drinking toasts, eating feasts, and firing salutes.[64] During the Revolutionary period, Anglo and Indian negotiators also commonly partook of the "Ceremony of shaking hands." When the Delaware alliance chief Quequedegatha appeared before Congress in 1775, for example, he "shook all the Members heartily by the Hand, beginning with the President & used the same Ceremony at his Departure." Likewise, the delegation of Iroquois, Delawares, and Shawnees that visited Philadelphia the following year "shook hands with every member of Congress." In January 1777, U.S. commissioners introduced themselves to a party of Six Nation and Ohio Indian chiefs at Easton, Pennsylvania, by declaring, "The great Congress of the thirteen united States . . . have sent us to shake hands with you and to hear what you have to say." The Seneca speaker replied, "When we come along the road to Wyoming, we sent our belt to Easton that our Brothers might know of our coming to shake hands with them." Both at the opening of closing of the Easton treaty, all participants "Shook Hands [and] Drank Healths."[65]

The "ceremony of shaking hands" is perhaps best understood as a fusion of English and Indian greeting rituals. Anglo-Americans shook hands to express good faith and trust. *The Refin'd Courtier*, a seventeenth-century courtesy manual that taxonomized the world's greetings, explained, "The *English* . . . *shake hands* to intimate a *league* and *contract* willingly to spend their fortunes and lives in a *mutual defense*."[66] Certain Eastern Woodland peoples, meanwhile, kept an indigenous diplomatic tradition that bore a strong gesticular resemblance to the English handshake. Members of the Iroquois Confederacy linked arms—that is, grasped one another by the hand or by the inside of the arm—to signify the conjointness and dynamism of their Covenant Chain.[67] Similarly, in the southeast, the Catawbas locked arms, each grabbing another's upper arm at full length, in testament to friendship and diplomatic accord.[68] Given the physical similarities between the Anglo-American shaking of hands and the Native American linking or locking of arms, it is little wonder that recombinant forms of those rituals emerged as commonplaces of Anglo-Indian diplomacy.[69]

Necessitating intimate bodily contact, the ceremony of shaking hands / linking arms lent a spirit of familiarity to diplomatic exchange. In this regard, the handshake that prevailed in Anglo-Indian encounters contrasted markedly with the bow that distinguished Franco-American interactions. An act of genuflection, even when returned, the bow preserved the physical, social, and political distance between European sovereigns and their supplicants. *The Refin'd Courtier* explained that the English only "*bow* the *body* in testimony of *submission*."[70] In Anglo-America, too, the bow was recognized as a gesture of extraordinary respect, most often reserved for one's superiors.[71] That Congress, which with its Native visitors kept the egalitarian tradition of shaking hands / linking arms, should in the company of its French guests yield to the more deferential custom of bowing, suggests its willingness, perhaps even its eagerness, to conform to European diplomatic norms. Though the monarchical traditions of the ancien régime were inimical to "true republican principles," the United States, newly arrived on the international stage, did not disavow them, but rather endeavored to comply. By contrast, the French Revolutionaries of the 1790s determinedly cast off "obsequious forms" of monarchical diplomacy, including the practice of bowing.[72]

Precisely because the act of bowing was freighted with connotations of power, Congress's reception of the French minister provoked scornful rebuke from British and loyalist adversaries. One prominent critic, George Johnstone, accused the delegates of paying obeisance to a foreign king. A commodore in the royal navy, member of Parliament, and most recently one of the Carlisle Peace Commissioners rebuffed by Congress on account of their powerlessness to recognize U.S. independence, Johnstone contemptuously noted that the delegates had "so far sull[ied] the principles upon which their first resistance was made as to bow to a French Ambassador." Johnstone's allegation provoked the ire of the South Carolina congressman William Henry Drayton, likely one of the Southern delegates who had insisted on grandiose diplomatic ceremonials in the first place. Obliged by a sense of national dignity to vindicate the Franco-American alliance, Drayton published a peevish retort, written in collaboration with the French minister Gérard: "[Johnstone] censures Congress for *bowing* to a French Ambassador!" Drayton proclaimed. "Did his Britannic Majesty *never bow* to a French Ambassador?" This riposte offers some measure of the extent to which national honor was bound up in richly symbolic diplomatic performance. For Drayton, Congress's bow signified not deference to a monarch, but rather equality among glorious nations; he believed it imperative that the American public understand the gesture in this way. If the king of England could bow without denigrating his sovereignty, surely the Continental Congress could as well.[73]

The loyalist newspaperman James Rivington also mocked Congress's bowing. Rivington fixed on the ritual not because it signaled fealty, but rather because it smacked of ceremonial pretense. Shortly after Gérard appeared before Congress, Rivington lampooned the stiffness and formality of his reception: "From Lewis, Monsieur Gérard came / To Congress in this town Sir. / They bow'd to him, and he to them, / And then they all sat down, Sir."[74] Later that same fall, Rivington printed "Intelligence Extraordinary" of a fanciful visit between Congress and Gérard:

> Three Members of Congress . . . approached his Excellency with three times three bows, to which his Excellency returned twelve; the deputies determined not to be out-done by French politeness, bowed thirteen times, the exact number of the United States, and then proceeded to business: Monsieur Gerard requested a moment for consideration . . . the deputies, in silent expectation, continued standing, for the representative of the *Grand Monarque* thought it inconsistent with his dignity to offer them chairs.[75]

Rivington's satire played on multiple levels. As an attack against the niceties and stylized gentility of eighteenth-century diplomatic protocol, it appealed to readers who harbored class prejudice against the elite would-be senators gathered in Philadelphia. But Rivington's lampoon of congressional diplomatic protocol also pierced the United States' aspirations to nationhood, much as did his mockery of the number thirteen. By adopting European diplomatic convention, Congress laid bare its ambitions for the American republic. Readers who doubted that the self-styled United States belonged among the fraternity of nations could chuckle at Congress's affectation.

As Johnstone's and Rivington's invective reveals, diplomatic rituals such as the handshake and the bow were laden with implications for national power and rank. So, too, were the honorific names and titles bestowed by the United States, France, and Native Americans on their treating partners. Shortly after ratifying the Treaties of Alliance and of Amity and Commerce in the spring of 1778, Congress formally bestowed on King Louis XVI the title "protector of the rights of mankind."[76] This sobriquet bore a twofold purpose. First and most obviously, Congress wished to compliment and pay homage to its benevolent ally. President Henry Laurens boasted that the new title, a "happy Tribute of America's sensibility," was "better founded than 'Defender of the

Faith,'" the formal appellation of the English sovereign, was "more lustrous than King of Navarre," a hereditary moniker of the Bourbon dynasty, and made "an excellent adjunct to 'Most Christian,'" a centuries-old papal designation for the French monarch. Laurens perceived that by granting the French king this new title Congress had worked an insult on "a certain deluded Prince." He delighted in imagining the mortification with which George III would receive the news, and he relished in predicting that, should Louis bring the United States to victory, "Then His illustrious Titles in plain English will read . . . Protector of the Rights of Mankind, who by the Magic of Policy, humbled . . . a powerful, haughty & much dreaded Rival & gave peace to both Shores of the Atlantic."[77]

Congress's second and less obvious purpose in thus honoring Louis XVI was to promote the alliance to the American public, whom a century of imperial wars and anti-Catholic propaganda had habituated to disdain and distrust the French nation. By way of announcing the new title, Congress urged the people of the United States "to consider the subjects of his most Christian Majesty as their brethren and allies and . . . behave towards them with the friendship and attention due to the subjects of a GREAT PRINCE, who, with the highest magnanimity and wisdom hath treated with these United States on terms of perfect equality and mutual advantage, thereby rendering himself THE PROTECTOR OF THE RIGHTS OF MAN-KIND."[78] Henry Laurens assured his friends among the French officer corps that this new title would make "proper impressions & effects." Likewise, the Massachusetts congressman Elbridge Gerry rejoiced that "every Whig in America" now applauded "the great protector of the Rights of Mankind."[79] Setting the example on the anniversary of independence in 1778, Congress toasted "The Protector" second only to "The United States of America."[80] Within days after his arrival in Philadelphia, Gérard could proudly report, "this is the most used toast among the well intentioned . . . they appear to be afraid of not rendering me enough honors."[81] All of this effusive homage stood in powerful contrast to the unembellished title with which Gérard greeted the delegates, "Gentlemen of the Congress." At the ceremonial committee's request, he purposefully eschewed "les hauts puissants." Such nomenclature likely pleased Samuel Adams, according as it did with his republican principles, but "[l]es députés du Midi plus vains que ceux du Nord" must have bristled at the disproportion of national prestige that such language conveyed.

Native American negotiators also granted distinctive names "in Token of their Friendship."[82] In 1776, a delegation of Onondaga Indians dubbed the president of Congress "Karanduawn," meaning "the Great Tree," a metaphorical nickname that for the Iroquois evoked notions of peace and shelter.[83] In addition to such honorifics, Indian diplomats often conferred adoptive names on their treating partners. The Iroquois who met with a congressional committee at Albany in 1775 gave the names "Terogha of the Oneida" to Robert R. Livingston; "Sanghradow one of the Mohawk" to John Langdon; and "Carwash, meaning good news given by the Onondaga" to Robert Treat Paine.[84] Similarly, in 1779, deputies of the Delaware people tendered on Conrad-Alexandre Gérard the name of a "revered chief" who had died three generations earlier.[85] These adoptive names established a fictive kinship to cement the diplomatic bond.[86]

This sort of kinship found further expression in the masculine familial titles that Native Americans and Europeans or Euro-Americans bestowed on one another. In their speeches and diplomatic correspondence, Congress and Native groups almost invariably addressed one another as "brothers." In so doing, Congress abandoned the convention of the French, and to a lesser extent that of the British who in their dealings with Native American peoples belatedly took the rank of father.[87] Congress may have preferred the fraternal title as an affirmation of republican egalitarianism; more likely Congress recognized that the United States could provide neither the military protection nor the trade goods that many native peoples had come to expect of their "paternal" allies.[88]

Whatever the case, these hierarchical familial titles at times made for awkward diplomatic exchange. In May 1779, fourteen members of the Delaware nation journeyed to Philadelphia to meet with Congress and, at Congress's invitation, with Minister Gérard and the Spanish agent Don Juan de Miralles.[89] According to Gérard, the Delaware captain Gelelemend took little comfort in the vague promises offered by the congressional president John Jay. Gelelemend repeatedly turned to Gérard for assurance and bluntly iterated how heavily the Delawares depended on French advice and friendship. Likely inadvertently, but no less embarrassingly for the United States, Gelelemend communicated greater respect for the French by the familial titles with which he addressed the various delegations. Styling the Delawares "les plus jeunes de ses enfans [sic]," or the youngest of Louis XVI's children, Gelelemend gave to the French king the title of father and to the Spanish king the title of "second father." To the United States and its president, however, Gelemend gave only the title of brother.[90] Gelemend presumably intended no slight by this distinction. Like other matrilineal peoples of eastern North America, the Delawares commonly employed "brother" to denote relative equality among linked peoples.[91] The Continental Congress itself employed the fraternal metaphor in all of its dealings with Native Americans. But in the ear of the French minister, "le titre de frères" rang of diminishment. To ameliorate the palpable discomfort, Gérard conspicuously deferred to Congress on all matters, a discretion that earned him "sharp acclamations." In his own speech, too, Gérard honored the Delawares as the ancient children of the French king, but he identified the citizens of the United States as the brothers of the French and of the Delawares alike.[92] In this manner, Gérard avoided any imputation of filial subordination on the part of the States.

On at least two occasions Congress vigilantly defended the fraternal nature of the Franco-American alliance. In November 1779, the Massachusetts congressman Elbridge Gerry objected to portions of a speech written for President Samuel Huntington to deliver at the public audience of Gérard's successor, Anne César de La Luzerne. Narrating the history of the alliance, the draft speech began, "His Most Christian Majesty by patronising the liberty and independence of America justly acquired the name of the protector of the rights of Mankind." This language, which portrayed King Louis's generosity as an act of condescension and suggested an unbecomingly paternalistic relationship, drove Gerry from his chair. Willing to hear the United States protected, but not *patronized*, Gerry moved that the offensive phrase be redacted. Lest anyone oppose, he called for the yeas and nays to be recorded.[93] Similarly, in September 1783, Congress scolded Benjamin Franklin, its minister to France, for speaking of King Louis as the United States' "Ally and Father." Congress—again at Gerry's urging—formally resolved that it disapproved "the use of any terms or measures that hold up the idea of their dependance on any foreign power as their Father, it being inconsistent with the dignity of the United States."[94] Congress's ear for national honor was thus very finely tuned: between "Protector of the Rights of Mankind," the title it readily granted, and "Ally and Father," the title it huffily refused, Congress heard subtle inflections of dependency and subservience.

The law of nations, in fact, amplified certain of these tonal distinctions while muting others. International custom obliged the United States, as the weaker party to the Treaty of Alliance, to honor the French king, but their imbalanced relationship was not perceived to have voided or in any way compromised the sovereignty of the United States. Indeed, Congress granted Louis XVI the epithet "Protector of the Rights of Mankind" for the express reason that "he had treated with these United States on terms of perfect equality and mutual advantage." "Patron" and "father," on the other hand, imputed too great a subjugation. In the law of nations, fatherhood served as a metaphor for sovereignty itself.[95] Vattel wrote that the sovereign "ought in every thing to appear as the father of his people." It was the sovereign's duty "as a tender, and wise father . . . to watch for the nation, to take care of preserving it, to render it more perfect, to better its state, and to secure it, as much as he is able, from every thing that threatens its safety, or its happiness."[96] Thus, while "protector" and "father" both signified an obligation to safeguard and defend, the latter also implied a right of parental governance, precisely the sort that the United States disavowed in its breach with "Mother" England. Much more than "protector," "father" carried notions of male dominance and hierarchy that Congress could not abide. On this matter, the French ministry indulged Congress's delicate sensibilities, but only to a point. In 1782, La Luzerne announced the birth of the dauphin in language that affirmed the paternal benevolence of the French throne while torturously eliding the suggestion of paternity: "The prince who is just born will one day be the friend and ally of the United States. He will in his turn support them with all his power, and while in his dominions he shall be the father and protector of his people, he will here be the supporter of your children and the guaranty of their freedom."[97]

Honorific names and titles belonged to the highly specialized languages spoken in eighteenth-century diplomacy. Taken as a whole, these diplomatic languages must be understood as lexicons of power and racialized identity. In addressing Native Americans, Congress purposefully employed a conventionalized argot that evolved out of nearly three centuries of Euro-Indian negotiations. This argot—which the Revolutionary historian David Ramsey later described as the "familiar Indian style"—incorporated a variety of middle-ground idioms and metaphors.[98] Congress referred to itself, for instance, as a "council fire, kindled for all the United Colonies"; it decried King George's efforts "to break the covenant chain" with "his children in America"; and it urged Native Americans not to "take up the hatchet." Congress utilized this language not only to facilitate diplomatic communication with its indigenous treating partners but also to express its regard for them. In its speeches and missives, Congress repeatedly emphasized commonalities among the Anglo and Indian inhabitants of North America. Congress, for instance, claimed a shared origin with its indigenous neighbors. "Brothers!" Congress asserted in its address to the Six Nations, "we live upon the same ground with you. The same island is our common birth-place." Conjuring an ancient and mutual history, Congress recalled the "strong tree of friendship, by our common ancestors planted in the deep bowels of the earth."[99] Some

Native peoples responded in kind. In 1780, Samuel Adams recounted the words of several representatives of the Creek and Chictaw [*sic*] nations: "We stand [on] the same Ground with you, we drink the same Water & breathe the same Air, we are the Trees, you are the Buds, & can there be Fruit if the Buds are nipped off[?]"[100] In proposing union with Indians, Congress seemed to suggest, remarkably, that diplomatic alliance would melt racial difference: "[W]e ought to be one people," Congress told the Six Nations. "Let us . . . join hand and heart in the defence of our common country. Let us rise as one man and drive away our cruel oppressors."[101] In one treaty, U.S. agents even held out the promise of future statehood, complete with representation in Congress, for the Delawares and other Indian peoples.[102]

Yet for all of this talk, it is illuminating to note that Congress couched its appeals for U.S. and Native American solidarity in the cold terms of geopolitical interest. "Let us, who are born on the same great continent, love one another," Congress implored. "What are the people who belong to the other side of the great water to either of us?"[103] Congress thus predicated its diplomatic relations with Native Americans on affinities of *geography*. By contrast, Congress couched its appeals for U.S. and French solidarity in the warm terms of magnanimity and affection. Invoking the conventionalized language of European courts, Congress predicated its diplomatic relations with the French on affinities of *sentiment*.[104] The first article of the Treaty of Amity and Commerce announced a "true and sincere friendship" between France and the United States. Likewise, Congress and successive French ministers characterized the alliance as a "constant friendship," founded on the admirable principles of "justice and humanity." Congress extolled the wisdom and generosity of the French king as well as the "benevolent pleasure" by which he gave succor to the United States.[105] Depicting the Franco-American bond as an affective bond, Congress assured the French nation that it "sensibly felt" the "beneficial effects" of the connection, that it "gratefully felt" the kindness of the States' "good friend and ally." Exalting the French soldiers who had sacrificed their lives on "the same field of glory" as the Americans, Congress declared, "A noble emulation . . . hath poured out the blood of the two nations, and mingled it together as a sacred pledge of perpetual union!"[106] This was a language of sensibility: it presumed on the part of both the French and the Americans a heightened emotional faculty, a capacity for sympathy that rendered irresistible the pleas of human suffering.[107] Whereas the language of Revolutionary diplomacy premised U.S.-Native American relations on shared territory, it premised U.S.-French relations on shared humanity.

In neither case should these idealized diplomatic languages be mistaken for the whole or even the prevailing part of American opinion. Members of Congress, like their constituents, harbored an array of prejudices toward their Native American "brothers," prejudices bound up in the ideological complex of noble savagery. While some delegates condemned Native Americans as "treacherous savages," complained that they were "very expensive and troublesome Confederates in war," and decried their "inhuman thirst of blood," other congressmen exalted Native Americans' sense of honor, deeming them far more trustworthy allies than the "Old Countries, hacknied in the vices & debaucheries of Courts."[108] The diplomatic language employed in the Pennsylvania State House, moreover, failed to capture the realities of human conflict on the North American borderlands. There, as the war unfolded, neutrality quickly proved an untenable position for most indigenous peoples. British and U.S. military leaders alike goaded, cajoled, and bribed Indian warriors to take up the hatchet. In so doing, they not only thrust Native communities into civil war, but also licensed American militias to commit acts of retributive violence and indiscriminate atrocity. As the historian Richard White has written, "Murder gradually and inexorably became the dominant American Indian policy," supplanting the policies of Congress.[109]

Similarly, the United States' professions of a "constant friendship" with France articulated but a portion of American sentiment. As one delegate's derisive comment about "Old Countries, hacknied in the vices & debaucheries of Courts" makes evident, members of Congress looked askance on the luxury and intrigue of Versailles. Though the French alliance buoyed Congress and marked the ascension of the United States, individual delegates warned against "French tyranny" and "French perfidy." They deprecated France as a "foreign crafty power" and railed against the "polluted Shrine of Monarchy" to which foreign affairs had exposed their impressionable republic.[110] The abruptness with which the United States unyoked itself from the Franco-American alliance after the war suggests the opportunism by which that alliance had been forged in the first place.

Still, despite the illusory or disingenuous qualities of Revolutionary diplomatic language, the distinctions between that which the United States employed with Native Americans and that which it employed with the French are suggestive. As revealed in its speeches and missives, Congress imagined the people of the United States of a *place* with Native Americans: their relationship, though of indisputable strategic consequence, arose primarily out of hemispheric circumstance, the accident of territorial proximity. By contrast, Congress imagined the people of the United States of a *kind* with Europeans: their relationship flowed from the loftiest, most refined attributes in human nature. Congress did not often ascribe such attributes to its indigenous allies. Indeed, some members of Congress suggested that Native peoples were stirred only by baser emotions such as greed and fear. The Pennsylvania congressman James Wilson counseled two newly appointed Indian commissioners that "[p]resents are the most prevailing Arguments that can be used with the Savages." Likewise, the North Carolina delegate Joseph Hewes approvingly reported that Congress had drummed out the Philadelphia militia in order to give a delegation of Six Nation Indians "some idea of our strength and importance."[111]

Some idea of the United States' strength and importance: establishing such through ritual and idiom was an important subtext of the Continental Congress's diplomatic ceremony and language. What may be gleaned from a study thereof? As founders of a republic, members of Congress upheld the principle of egalitarianism among nations. Preferring a nomenclature of brotherhood to that of fatherhood; happy to shake hands, if willing to exchange bows; swift to rebuke any insinuation of inferiority or subordinacy, Congress seemed intent, at times, on remaking the earth into the separate and equal stations that the Declaration had envisioned. At other times, Congress clearly apprehended distinctions of eminence and refinement among the United States and its allies. In its dealings with France, Congress signaled in a variety of ways that King Louis was the more glorious sovereign. And it evinced a strong desire to fashion U.S. diplomatic protocol according to venerable European practice. Yet, if deferential to the French king and to the law of nations, members of Congress distrusted the artifice and decadence of the ancien régime. Deploying the same republican ideology by which Americans had broken ties with Great Britain, Congress reconceptualized the deficiencies of the United States—its want of wealth, civility, and the arts—as virtues of modesty and sobriety.

In like manner, Congress dispensed with the unpalatable implications of the United States' alliance with Native Americans. Congress understood that the United States' fate, and to some extent its national character, were intertwined with those of the indigenous peoples with whom it shared a continent. Congress acknowledged as much by alluding, somewhat disingenuously, to the "strong tree of friendship by our common ancestors planted in the deep bowels of the earth." Though Congress's outreach toward Native Americans appeared amicable enough on its face, a sense of racial superiority pervaded the United States' diplomacy. Congress scorned the coarseness of indigenous peoples and leaned on civility as proof that Anglo-Americans and Native

Americans would not, as its diplomatic language proposed, become one people.

What sort of nation did Congress wish the United States to be? Not yet a powerful one, Congress took comfort in the belief the United States was a righteous one. Sharing ground with "savage" ones, Congress clung to its faith that the United States was a civilized one. The Massachusetts congressman Elbridge Gerry conveyed just these sentiments in 1783, when he declared of the new nation, "We are my dear sir happily placed at a distance from civilized stations; We are surrounded by barbarous ones, which if they could be humanized, would in my opinion be as far beyond some that boast of being civilized, as they conceive themselves to be above the others."[112] For Congress, a separate station among the powers of the earth—separate from European luxury and separate from, albeit proximate to, Indian "barbarity"—became as meaningful as an equal one.

"Gentlemen might despise etiquette as they pleased"

The opening of formal diplomatic relations with France, which raised so many questions about the United States' place in the world, greatly augmented the ceremonial life of Congress and the infant confederation. Providing fresh occasions for state festivity, the Treaties of Alliance and of Amity and Commerce necessitated the manufacture of new traditions. Infused with French flavor, these novel practices fostered a tendentious regard among patriots for the honor and prestige of the United States. In Congress, the alliance provoked the ire of delegates who possessed neither the savvy nor the wealth to keep pace with the polite diplomacy practiced by the French foreign ministers. More problematically, the Franco-American alliance and its many celebratory protocols became embroiled in the political hostilities that nearly debilitated Congress in the late 1770s, particularly the controversy that erupted between the American commissioners Silas Deane and Arthur Lee. Meanwhile, by binding the American republic to a Catholic monarch, the alliance attracted the hostile attention of British and loyalist satirists, who derided the unscrupulous accord and piled calumny on the United States' pretentious diplomatic etiquette.

The Franco-American alliance thickened Congress's calendar of state holidays and brought new customs to the Pennsylvania State House, particularly during its first year. Just days after his formal audience in the summer of 1778, Gérard invited members of Congress to celebrate the birthday of

Louis XVI.[113] A few weeks later, patriot gazettes carried a story from Martinique, the French sugar island, telling of a magnificent "concert, supper and
ball" hosted by the congressional agent William Bingham, where the female
guests dressed up their hair "*a la independance*," that is, in thirteen curls.[114] In
the spring of 1779, Congress and Gérard commemorated the anniversary of
the alliance by dining at the City Tavern, where they drank toasts to the
United States; to the king, queen, and princes of the house of Bourbon; and
to the perpetual friendship of all.[115] Upon receiving word in May that Marie
Antoinette had borne a princess, a committee consisting of one delegate from
each of the thirteen states waited on Gérard to offer well wishes "according
to form & etiquette." A second committee, meanwhile, wrote congratulations
to the monarchs and requested a portrait of the "royal consort" so that "the
representatives of these states may daily have before their eyes the first royal
friends and patrons of their cause." (Those portraits did not arrive until April
1784, at which time they were hung in the state house of Congress's new host
city, Annapolis.)[116] In September 1779, after Gérard announced that he would
retire from foreign service on account of poor health, Congress honored him
by hiring Charles Willson Peale to paint his portrait. Gérard further reported
that Congress requested Benjamin Franklin, in Paris, to commission a medal
in his honor, though no such motion is found in the *Journals*.[117] Soon after,
Congress welcomed Gérard's successor, Anne César de La Luzerne, with a
public audience very similar to that of the previous year.[118]

As this brief survey suggests, Franco-American diplomacy presented new
occasions for festivity and public ceremony in the Revolutionary United
States. More contentiously, the alliance obliged Congress to accommodate
the manners and customs of its Gallic treating partner. At times, French
sensibilities rested easily on members of Congress. In September 1778, for
example, the Massachusetts delegates savored at Gérard's table a "grand &
elegant" meal prepared "in the [F]rench taste."[119] But at other times, French
sensibilities weighed heavily on them. That Christmas, Oliver Ellsworth of
Connecticut attended worship services at "a romish chappel." There, "among
the papists," the one-time theology student beheld the mass with a mixture
of awe and disdain:

> I confess I was wonderfully struck with the shew of the place, the
> superstition of the ceremonies & devotion of the people. I did not
> arive in season to smell the burning of frankinsense, nor to see
> our saviour carryed about in a cradle under pretense of his having
> been born the very night before; but I saw him extended at full

length upon the cross, seven golden candlesticks burning upon an
Alter before him, & one in the midst with a candle as large as
a man's Arm . . . The priest administered the sacrement to a
number, but I observed after he had put a small wafer into their
mouths, he drank all the wine himself . . . I returned home to a
dinner which gave me more substantial entertainment.[120]

The trappings and rituals of the Catholic Church struck Ellsworth and
other members of Congress as foreign and distasteful. Likewise, they struck
a generation of British colonists, steeped in the antipapal rhetoric of the
Hanoverian settlement, as decidedly suspicious.[121] Nevertheless, Congress
had begun to court Catholic favor as early as its first, ill-fated campaign for
Quebec. In early 1776, Congress recruited two prominent Catholics—the
wealthy Maryland patriot Charles Carroll of Carrollton and his cousin, John,
a Jesuit priest—to join a delegation to Canada in hope that they might quiet
sectarian apprehensions about the colonial rebellion.[122] The Franco-American
alliance once again enabled Congress to solicit Catholic support both at
home and abroad. But this outreach entailed the incorporation into U.S. state
ceremony of the very sort of Catholic liturgical practices that so disconcerted
Ellsworth.

Such was the case on the Fourth of July, 1779, when the anniversary of
independence fell on a Sunday. Determined to celebrate the day but resolved
to keep the Sabbath as well, Congress attended three worship services, including one with Gérard at the Catholic chapel. There, members of Congress,
prominent military officers, and the executive council of Philadelphia joined
the French minister in the singing of a Te Deum. An early Christian hymn
central to the offices of the Catholic Church, the Te Deum must be understood as the "traditional symbolic centre-piece" of the French state. Adopted
by Charlemagne for his coronation in 800 AD and elevated by Henry III and
Henry IV to a prominent place in court ceremony in the late 1500s, the Te
Deum affirmed the paternal benevolence both of God and, by implication, of
His Most Christian Majesty, the French king. The Bourbon monarchs
ordered the singing of the Te Deum on military victories and peace treaties,
on the convalescence of the royal family, and on the birth of princes and
dukes. During the colonial period, the singing of the Te Deum came to map
the reaches of France's overseas dominions. At the direction of Versailles,
French colonists heard the Te Deum sung in Saint Domingue, in Martinique, in Louisiana, and in New France.[123] Gérard took great pride in introducing the hymn to Philadelphia, boasting to his home ministry, "This is the

first Te Deum that has ever been sung in the thirteen States." Gérard predicted, "[T]his brilliant act will have a good effect on Catholics, quite a large
number of whom are suspected of not being strongly attached to the American cause."[124]

Loyalist writers quickly pointed fingers at the strange bedfellows Revolutionary politics had made. They ridiculed the hypocrisy of the Continental
Congress, which having denounced the Quebec Act and its establishment of
"the Roman Catholick religion" just a few years before, now pledged fidelity
to a Catholic monarch. They charged that in declaring independence
and treating with the French, Congress had cast off one king only to subju-
gate itself to another. And they warned that French superstition and vice
would soon wash over America. "We are credibly informed," wrote one loyalist satirist,

> that the French vessel lately taken . . . brought a considerable cargo
> consisting of the following articles, viz.
>
> Mass Books, 50,000
> Racks and Wheels, 200
> Consecrated Wafers, 3,000,000
> Crucifixes, 15,000
> Rosaries, 70,000
> Wooden Shoes, 200,000
> Paint for the Ladies Faces, five Chests
> Pills for the cure of the French disease [i.e., syphilis], 10000 boxes.
>
> We also learn that the passengers on board were all priests, in
> the disguise of hair-dressers, tooth-drawers, fidlers, and dancing
> masters.

Originally published in New York by the loyalist newspaperman James Rivington, this lampoon was reprinted in at least one patriot newspaper in Massachusetts, where anti-Catholic sentiment historically ran high.[125] And
though this particular piece adopted a farcical tone, others appealed in earnest. "*Americans Attend!*" exclaimed the *Royal Gazette* in December 1781 after
Congress had gathered to sing yet another Te Deum. "Protestant Americans!
Did you imagine in so short a space as seven years, a Congress of your own
creating, would, *on your own ground* have exhibited that profligate apostacy
from the reformed faith, of publicly attending a Roman Catholic church, to
countenance that impious religion?"[126] Ancient prejudices such as these

obliged the ministers Gérard and La Luzerne to hire a handful of America's leading orators and penmen—Samuel Cooper, Thomas Paine, and Hugh Henry Brackenridge, among them—to propagandize on behalf of France and the Franco-American alliance.[127]

Perhaps because the United States' diplomatic relations and ceremony provided such rich fodder for British and loyalist penmen, delegates kept a watchful eye against expressions or gestures that might besmirch the legitimacy of the Continental Congress or the honor of the American republic. In October 1778, for instance, Samuel Adams chided Massachusetts authorities for the "Etiquet" with which they celebrated the French naval commander Comte d'Estaing on his recent arrival in Boston. "The Arrangement of the Toasts was not perfectly agreable to my Idea of Propriety," Adams declared, "Nations and independent sovereign States do not compliment after the Manner of Belles & Beaus." Adams particularly objected that the Massachusetts toastmasters first raised their glasses to the monarch and kingdom of France and only then to the Continental Congress, first to the French military and only then to the Continental Army. These indiscretions, he insisted, were not "Trifles light as Air," but rather bore the power to "do good or Hurt." "[T]here is no Appearance made by the Publick but [that] adds more or less to its Honor or Disgrace."[128]

State and local officials, however, faced a difficult balancing act. To elevate the United States was to risk affronting foreign allies. North Carolina authorities discovered as much when they welcomed the Spanish agent, Don Juan de Miralles, to "a great banquet" in celebration of the Franco-American alliance. Reporting to Cuba's governor Diego José Navarro, Miralles lodged his own complaint about the arrangement of toasts: "After dinner there followed thirteen toasts, each one followed by thirteen cannon shots. The sixth was for the health of Louis XVI, the Most Christian King of France, and the seventh for our Catholic Monarch Sire, Don Carlos III. It did not escape notice that they had placed in the middle those worthy sovereigns with whom they should have begun."[129] Masters of state ceremony were thus compelled to act with extraordinary care, for the primacy of nations depended on these slight punctilios.

Members of Congress scrupulously monitored U.S. diplomatic ceremony not only because it touched on the dignity of the United States, but also because they felt self-conscious anxiety about their own clumsiness in foreign affairs. Congress's want of diplomatic savoir faire obliged members to turn for tutelage to the very ministers they aimed to impress. Before Gérard's audience in 1778, Samuel Adams's ceremonial committee presented its proposed ceremonials to the minister, who confirmed that they adhered "to the general principles accepted in the Courts of Europe."[130] Likewise, after announcing the birth of a French princess in 1779, Gérard alerted Congress to the necessity of waiting on him with congratulations. Along with a notice of the princess's birth, Gérard delivered to President John Jay a note detailing how the Seven United Netherlands, perhaps the foremost republic of Europe, responded on such occasions.[131]

More embarrassing still was the lavish expense of polite diplomacy, which delegates incurred as they endeavored to reciprocate the French minister's hospitality. One eighteenth-century diplomatic treatise advised the ambassadors of France, particularly those on mission to democratic states, to keep an open house and "a well-garnished table" so as to attract the company of delegates.[132] Gérard possessed both the resources and the disposition to do just that. "The Minister of France is incessant in his Invitations to dine," lamented the congressman James Lovell, as he appealed for greater financial support from the Commonwealth of Massachusetts. "We have never invited him but once . . . We must either totally refuse his Invitations or be seemingly his Table Pensioners." As the wartime economy spiraled, members of Congress felt this strain all the more acutely. An empty purse prompted the congressional president Samuel Huntington to beg a cash advance from his home state of Connecticut in order that he might "receive the Company of all Foreigners of Distinction [and] appear decent in dress." As Lovell's and Huntington's pleas suggest, wealth was a congressman's political capital. Delegates who could not maintain the expense of entertaining foreign and domestic dignitaries lost valuable opportunities to politick.

The rapid depreciation of the continental currency rendered the obligations of diplomatic sociability all the more arduous. For this reason, the delegate Gouverneur Morris urged New York officials to send to Congress men of means: "For Heaven's Sake," Morris cried, "contrive if possible to have in the Delegation Men . . . who possess such Property that they can afford to sacrifice a few thousands to the general Cause . . . or they will content themselves to live in a Style which will deprive them of all Weight & Influence."[133] So financially strapped were members of Congress as a whole that the Virginian Cyrus Griffin entreated Benjamin Franklin to apologize to Gérard on his return to France. "The French are a gay people and entertain a good deal," Griffin observed with chagrin. "I am afraid Mon. Gérard has thought the Delegates in Congress were rather deficient in that respect; but really the expence of every article is so very enormous . . . that a person of a handsome American fortune could not entertain frequently without absolute ruin in the

period of two or three years . . . [Y]ou would do some of us a singular favor
to hint this matter to Mon. Gérard—since it has the appearance of not paying
proper Civilities to a man of his worth and elevated station."[134] In fact, Gérard
had taken note of Congress's poverty. "Not one member lives becomingly," he
wrote, "and none can give a dinner except at a tavern."[135]

Compromised by want of both knowledge and money, the diplomatic ceremony of the United States at times, too, became entangled in Revolutionary
politics. As already seen, the snuff box presented by Louis XVI to Silas Deane
became a prop in the commissioner's self-vindication. But there were other
ways that the lengthy political controversy that has come to be known as the
Deane-Lee affair subverted U.S.-French diplomatic ceremony. Greatly mor-
tifying to the United States—one congressman declared the whole matter
"disgraceful to the Country"—the affair resulted in large part from Congress's inexperience in diplomatic matters.[136] Instead of sending only one
commissioner to Paris, as was customary in Europe, Congress sent three:
Silas Deane, Benjamin Franklin, and Arthur Lee. The feud erupted after Lee
accused Deane of diverting public monies into his own pocket. Prompted by
these allegations, Lee's backers in Congress—notably, Lee's brother Richard
Henry Lee and his compatriot Samuel Adams—orchestrated Deane's recall.
Determined to exculpate himself, Deane returned to Philadelphia and marshaled his own political supporters, including one of his investment partners,
the congressman Robert Morris of Pennsylvania. Partisanship in the Deane-
Lee affair broke along preexisting factional lines, pitting a coalition of New
England and Virginia congressmen against a bloc of delegates from the Mid-
Atlantic states and their allies from the Carolinas. In so doing, the conflict
arrayed the plain-style congressman Samuel Adams and his "true" republican
colleagues against the "vainer" delegates of the South.[137]

Consuming long hours of congressional debate, sparking rancorous crimination among the delegates, and touching off a hostile war of words in
American newspapers, the Deane-Lee affair dragged on for more than a year,
resulting in the resignation of President Henry Laurens and opening a
number of political wounds that would not soon heal. The Deane-Lee affair
also embroiled the French minister, who was called on to vouch for Versailles'
confidence in the recalled commissioner. By this time, French concerns in a
number of regionally specific disputes had begun to skew Gérard's relationships with various constituencies in Congress. On behalf of his government,
Gérard resisted New England's interest in the North Atlantic fisheries and
opposed Virginia's claims to the Indiana and Illinois countries. The Deane-
Lee affair further aligned Gérard and his successor, La Luzerne, against

congressmen from New England and Virginia and with their rivals from the Mid-Atlantic and Deep South.[138]

Against this backdrop of disputation, and in consequence of the politicization of the French ministry, U.S.-French diplomatic ceremony became a matter of partisan contention. In May 1782, La Luzerne requested a special audience with Congress to announce the birth of the dauphin, male heir to the French throne. Moved by this joyous news, Congress called on Robert R. Livingston, secretary of foreign affairs, to organize a dinner at the City Tavern. Perhaps due to financial constraints or perhaps to mere oversight, Congress authorized Livingston to invite only "such General Officers and foreigners of distinction in town as the President shall approve." Those ranks did not include executive secretaries such as Livingston himself. Affronted by this slight, Livingston flatly refused to host the dinner. When pressed by Secretary Charles Thomson, Livingston objected that to coordinate an event to which he had not been invited would demean his office, placing him on the level of the "Presidents steward." "[T]here is a respect," Livingston opined, "which every Man owes to himself if he has been dignified by honorable Employments . . . which forbids him to take a new Charge derogatory to the former."[139]

Livingston's qualms thus appear to have been premised on notions of personal and professional honor. But Livingston's recalcitrance is further and perhaps better explained by his close working relationship with La Luzerne. Livingston, whom one historian has deemed a member of La Luzerne's "inner circle," in fact owed his secretaryship to the French minister; La Luzerne lobbied vigorously for the appointment of Livingston, in preference to Arthur Lee.[140] Livingston apparently wished to enlarge the entertainment for the gratification of his French backer, for in addition to his own admittance to the dinner, Livingston insisted that he be allowed to invite members of the executive departments, army officers, the president and council of Pennsylvania, and other "genteel Strangers." To deny him such discretion, Livingston asserted, would degrade his office "in the eyes of foreigners" and expose him to the contempt of persons who felt snubbed. Livingston's arguments prevailed and Congress granted the prerogatives he sought.[141]

As might be expected, La Luzerne made the birth of the dauphin an occasion of exorbitant celebration, hosting an extravaganza that far exceeded the Congress's modest supper. That summer, a handful of delegates began to grow weary of La Luzerne's ostentation and of the sway he exerted among their fellow congressmen. In August, the Pennsylvania delegate Thomas Smith protested a distinction that had arisen among the members of

Congress: certain delegates were "constantly" seen at the French minister's table, "while others were wholly excluded." Smith believed "that it would more comport with the dignity of Congress if the members were seldomer seen at his table." Short of that, he desired that a "rule of conduct" be established to ensure that no delegation enjoyed greater privilege than another. Smith's proposal spurred a lengthy deliberation. Tellingly, the Virginia congressman Arthur Lee rose in support of Smith's concerns. Lee—twice now scorned by the French ministry, first in his dispute with Deane and again in his bid for the secretaryship that Livingston won—argued forcefully for the establishment of a protocol to limit congressmen's interactions with La Luzerne. Declaring it "highly proper to establish a rule," Lee cited the example of the Venetian republic, which, to avoid the appearance of impropriety, forbade senators from dining with or being entertained by foreign diplomats. Secretary Charles Thomson reported that "[s]everal members treated the matter as trifling, & not deserving further attention," but Lee refuted them. "Gentlemen might despise etiquette as they pleased," Lee declared, "but it was so important as to be attended with very serious consequences. Every civilized nation had found it necessary to settle it."[142] Whether Lee's position was governed more by principle or by old political score we may only surmise, but had Congress adopted the rule he backed, it could only have mitigated the influence of Lee's adversaries in the French legation.[143]

Unlike the French revolutionaries of later years, the Continental Congress never renounced European diplomatic ceremony. The United States depended too heavily on French military and financial assistance and it wished too desperately to win Spanish and Dutch recognition for Congress to abjure the diplomatic etiquette of those nations. Yet, so long as the United States continued to emulate the diplomatic customs of Europe, there remained an awkward tension or incongruity between "true republican principles" and "the Mystery of Iniquity." At the beginning of the war, just after nonexportation had gone into effect, the Massachusetts congressman John Adams reflected on the measures Americans must take in order to achieve their independence: "We must change our Habits, our Prejudices, our Palates, our Taste in Dress, Furniture, Equipage, Architecture &c . . . [T]he Question is whether our People have Virtue enough to be mere Husbandmen, Mechanicks & Soldiers?" Six years later, Adams had indeed changed his habits and tastes: he had moved into a large, stately house; furnished it with silver, service, and linens of his own choosing; employed two servants; and hired a coach and coachman, whom he attired in blue livery, red cap, and waistcoat.[144] Why had Adams so diverged from the path of sacrifice and self-denial he prescribed just a few years before? Because now, in 1781, he was living not in Braintree, as a husbandman, mechanic, or soldier, but rather in Amsterdam, as the minister plenipotentiary to the United Provinces of the Netherlands. Or, rather, as the *would-be* plenipotentiary, for the States-General had not yet acknowledged U.S. independence or recognized Adams in his ministerial capacity. Adams determined to win that recognition. Though he professed that the dignity of the United States consisted not of "diplomatic ceremonials or any of the subtleties of etiquette," but rather of "reason, justice, truth, the rights of mankind, and the interests of the nations of [E]urope," Adams knew of no better way to assert the sovereignty of the American republic than by adorning himself, as its minister, with the most respectable furniture, equipage, and architecture.[145]

In Adams's ministerial self-fashioning may be glimpsed many of the ideological and material challenges that confronted Congress in its efforts to tailor diplomatic ceremonials for the United States. Some members of Congress wished to remake the world according to republican and liberal precept. But they were forced to yield that ambition to a more pressing concern, that of obtaining for the United States the acknowledgement and esteem of the earth's powers. Unlike the French revolutionaries of the 1790s, the American revolutionaries sought not to break with history but rather to find a place in it.

Part IV

"THE SYMBOL OF SUPREME POWER & AUTHORITY"

Charles Thomson and William Barton's design for the Great Seal of the United States, 1782; Reports of Committees of Congress; Records of the Continental and Confederation Congresses and the Constitutional Convention, 1774–1789, Record Group 360; National Archives.

On June 20, 1782, the Confederation Congress, successor to the Continental Congress, at last approved a design for the Great Seal of the United States. Since 1776, various congressional committees had tinkered with Pierre Eugène Du Simitière's original proposal, modifying his "American" coat of arms and introducing a variety of characters to support it: a "naked savage," a Roman warrior, the "Genius of America," a knight in armor, and a continental soldier.[1] But not until Secretary Charles Thomson and his consultant, the Philadelphia attorney and amateur heraldist William Barton, proposed the eagle and the shield did Congress at last reach a consensus.

Thomson and Barton's design incorporated much of the iconography popularized during the war, including the red and white stripes on a field of blue; the number thirteen, as manifest in the bundle of arrows; and the "new constellation" of stars. The eagle, however, was an innovation, and in certain respects a curious one. By selecting an eagle, Thomson and Barton deviated from the United States' very brief emblematic tradition. In 1775, on his three-dollar bill, Benjamin Franklin had depicted Britain as an eagle and America as a "weaker bird." From his post in France, Franklin expressed disappointment that the eagle, a scavenger, had been chosen to symbolize his country. The eagle, Franklin lamented, "is a Bird of bad moral Character. He does not get his Living honestly. You may have seen him perch'd on some dead Tree near the River, where, too lazy to fish for himself, he watches the Labour of the Fishing Hawk; and when that diligent Bird has at length taken a Fish, and is bearing it to his Nest for the Support of his Mate and young Ones, the Bald Eagle pursues him and takes it from him. . . . [H]e is generally poor and often very lousy. Besides he is a rank Coward: The little *King Bird* not bigger than a Sparrow attacks him boldly and drives him out of the District."[2]

Why had Thomson and Barton chosen a cowardly bird of prey to represent the United States? *The Columbian Magazine*, which printed an engraving of the seal complete with Thomson's "Remarks and Explanations," supposed that the eagle was "a symbol of empire."[3] Already, some members of Congress had begun to think of the United States in imperial terms. In 1779, for example, President John Jay urged Americans to consider the continent that sprawled before them as security for their national debt. Anticipating a later generation's faith in Manifest Destiny, Jay exulted, "Extensive wildernesses, now scarcely known or explored, remain yet to be cultivated, and vast lakes and rivers, whose waters have for ages rolled in silence and obscurity to the ocean, are yet to hear the din of industry, become subservient to commerce, and boast delightful villas, gilded spires, and spacious cities rising on their banks."[4] Now, having defeated the British and secured independence, the United States looked ever more confidently toward a glorious future. In fact, it may have been the opening of negotiations in Paris and the prospect of ratifying a formal treaty of peace that impelled Congress to finish its imperious Great Seal.[5]

William Barton, however, ascribed to the eagle a more particular meaning. Barton, who first proposed the bird, explained that it was "[t]he Symbol of supreme Power & Authority, and signifies the Congress."[6] Here was an appalling irony. The Confederation Congress was an exceedingly weak institution. Supreme though its authority in principle may have been, by 1782 Congress exercised very little power and was held widely in contempt. Together, the Continental and Confederation Congresses suffered a host of structural and procedural defects: persistent absenteeism, the halting development of a workable executive infrastructure, and the imposition of super-majority voting requirements, to name only a few.[7]

In the late 1770s, two of Congress's more egregious shortcomings further eroded its authority and dignity. First, Congress repeatedly failed to adequately clothe, provision, and pay the Continental Army and to credibly pension its officers. Since 1775, Congress had commissioned not only medals and monuments, but also presentment swords, to assert its supremacy as the civil authority over the military and to honor an officer corps that it could not justly reward. Yet by its mismanagement of the commissary and quartermaster departments and by its reluctance to establish an honorable pension, Congress broke faith with the Continental Army, driving soldiers to mutiny and alienating many officers.[8] In the meantime, over the course of the Revolution, the army had developed its own rich ceremonial and celebratory culture. In its uniforms, regimentation, camp life, and festivity, the army stood apart both from Congress and from the American citizenry.[9] At the end of the war, the continental officer corps emerged as a rival to what little prestige and influence Congress continued to wield. Organized into an exclusive brotherhood, the Society of the Cincinnati, American officers appropriated the eagle as a symbol of *their* power and authority and of the vital role that they had played in the creation of the republic.

The collapse of the continental currency also greatly embarrassed and weakened Congress. Lacking the power either to levy taxes or to regulate commerce, Congress managed to finance much of the war by printing paper money. The exorbitant expense of the Revolution, however, quickly exhausted the public credit. Confronted by rampant inflation and the grossly depreciated continental, Congress had no choice but to devalue its currency in 1780. Repudiating millions of dollars in Revolutionary war debt, Congress provoked a great deal of public scorn. By abandoning the continental currency, Congress also forfeited the chief instrument of its political authority, its spending power. In consequence, Congress could no longer afford to promote a material and ceremonial identity for the United States. In the final years of the war, an impoverished Congress turned away artists and artisans who wished to memorialize the nation. It likewise yielded the festivities of peace to another, better funded institution, the French embassy.

7

"[T]he most amiable Garbs of publick Virtue"

DURING THEIR LONG MARCH SOUTH to Yorktown in the late summer of 1781, continental forces under the command of General Washington and French forces under the command of the Comte de Rochambeau stopped briefly in Philadelphia. The appearance of these allied armies occasioned numerous formal and informal exchanges between military and civil authorities. Members of Congress devoted the better part of a week to "paying and receiving compliments from the General Officers and Army."[1] Shortly after midday on August 30, a dispatch of light horse escorted the U.S. and French commanders into town. That afternoon, Washington "paid his respects" at the state house, then returned to the home of Robert Morris, where he and his officers dined with the newly elected president of Congress, Thomas McKean. After dinner, the guests toasted the alliance, while vessels in the Delaware River fired in salute. That evening, Washington walked the city's illuminated streets, attended by "a numerous concourse of people, eagerly pressing to see their beloved general." (The Quaker Samuel Rowland Fisher, who denounced Washington as "an instrument of destruction and devastation," lamented that the general's followers broke windows as they passed.)[2]

The spectacle had only just begun. Four days later, the French divisions marched into town and treated both Congress and the people of Philadelphia to an unprecedented military display. As reported in the *Pennsylvania Packet*, King Louis XVI ordered his army to pay Congress "the honours due to a sovereign power . . . the same as himself." To receive the "royal salute," congressional delegates crowded at the state house door. As the French army filed by, each officer "let fall the point of the sword, likewise the colours." On instruction from the Comte de Rochambeau, President McKean returned each salute by removing his hat and bowing. Members of Congress likewise took off their hats; by contrast, Washington and Rochambeau remained uncovered throughout the parade.[3]

Writing to the New York governor and former congressman George Clinton, Ezra L'Hommedieu recounted the event: "Count de Rochambeau ordered his whole Army to march by the City Hall and to salute Congress as a crowned head, and the President as the first prince of the blood." Marveling at the honors accorded the American president, L'Hommedieu wondered, "How do you think friend Thomas felt?" In a letter to the Comte de Rochambeau, reprinted in *The Pennsylvania Packet*, McKean provided an answer: "Sir, I have the honour to express to your Excellency the satisfaction of Congress in the compliment which has been paid to them by the troops of his Most Christian Majesty under your command."[4]

This episode bears witness to the remarkable capacity of state rituals to establish and reinforce political authority in the late eighteenth century. As evident in the lowering of French officers' swords and in the removal of congressmen's hats, military and civil authorities alike depended on ceremonies and material objects to define and articulate their relationships with one another. The salute may have been the most visible manifestation of this process, but it was not the only one. During the American Revolution, the Continental Congress relied heavily on symbolic assertions of preeminence and will. It began by bestowing a variety of laurels on continental forces, most commonly swords, medals, and monuments. Originally intended to exalt the army by rewarding officers for their bravery and sacrifice, and also, simultaneously, to uphold the supremacy of the civil authority over the military, these awards came to serve numerous additional functions. They enabled Congress to negotiate its relationship with the army, to encourage enlistments, to inspire heroic acts, and to otherwise remunerate an officer corps that it could scarcely afford to pay.

As Congress cast about for artifacts and civic traditions by which to promote the war effort, the Continental Army meanwhile developed its own very abundant material, ceremonial, and festive culture. Uniforms, flags, and military rituals distinguished the soldiery, setting it apart from the rest of the public and underscoring the uniqueness of its political interests and concerns. The genteel sociability of continental officers, meanwhile, brought the army into conflict with Congress's republican moral sensibilities and ultimately situated the officer corps as a rival to the prestige and influence of the confederated government. The establishment of the Society of the Cincinnati, an organization of lavish manners and observances, sustained that rivalry well after the war had ended.[5]

The material objects and ceremonies by which Congress and the army endeavored to mediate their interactions bore tremendous political significance, in part because their meanings were never fixed or immutable. Consider, for example, derisive comments privately made by French officers after parading through Philadelphia in 1781. The Baron du Bourg implied that President McKean's ignorance of military etiquette reflected poorly on the head of a sovereign state. Likewise, the Comte de Deux-Ponts mocked Congress for its pitifully small numbers, alleging that "when the French troops paid the Congress the honors the King had commanded, the thirteen members took off their thirteen hats . . . which was all that . . . was either polite or extraordinary." Thus, the very ritual by which the French command intended to pay deference to Congress served only to erode certain officers' respect for that assembly. In like manner, the rites and ornaments adopted by Congress and the Continental Army to assert their prestige provoked as much scorn as admiration.[6]

Patriotism and Her Necessary Aids

The Continental Congress encountered innumerable political, logistical, and financial challenges in superintending the war. Though members of Congress possessed extensive legislative and executive experience, no American assembly had ever undertaken such a mammoth military endeavor. British colonial history provided no precedent for the cooperative efforts that the Revolutionary War demanded of the thirteen states. Those states, moreover, remained profoundly jealous of their autonomy. Never granting to Congress the authority to levy taxes, the states deprived that institution of the power most essential to the sustenance of a fighting force.

Historians have carefully documented the many ways in which Congress disappointed the army. It politicized the appointment of continental officers. It meddled in the army's command decisions and internal affairs. It did not pay wages in a timely manner. It did not provide medical care equal to the

A VIEW IN AMERICA IN 1778

In this print by M. Darly, the congressman's eye disorder suggests blindness to the sufferings of the shivering soldiers and the wounded African American at right. It also recalls the "freaks" of madness attributed to members of Congress by their loyalist foes in 1774–75. M. Darly, "A View in America in 1778," (London, 1778). © The Trustees of the British Museum.

suffering of the sick and wounded. Most notoriously and egregiously, it did not adequately feed, clothe, or shelter the soldiery through much of the war. Though Congress labored in earnest to remedy the defects of its administration—by reorganizing its Board of War; by revising its Articles of War; by hounding out corruption and abuse in its quartermaster, commissary, and hospital departments; and by calling on the states to procure specific supplies such as beef, pork, flour, and rum—it never established an effective system for provisioning American forces. Congress's failings outraged and alienated the army and ultimately threatened to destabilize the supremacy of its civil authority.[7]

One of the means by which Congress attempted to negotiate its often tendentious relationship with the Continental Army was bestowing laurels on its officers. An early opportunity arose in November 1775, shortly after American forces captured the city of Montreal. To carry news of this triumph, General Philip Schuyler dispatched a meritorious field officer, Captain Henry B. Livingston, to Philadelphia. In his report, Schuyler commended Livingston as "a Gentleman whose Alertness & Zeal has caused him to be distinguished in the Army." One month later, Congress voted to present Livingston a sword valued at one hundred dollars. Congress offered this gift as a reward for Livingston's "services to the country" and as a promise that it would "embrace the first opportunity of promoting him in the army."[8] By this simple gesture, Congress complimented both Livingston—who expressed gratitude for the "amazingly genteel" and "very Flattering" honor—and his superior officers.[9] Congress likewise acknowledged Livingston's claim to higher rank without immediately committing itself to the politically delicate task of granting him a promotion.[10]

By presenting Livingston a sword, Congress inaugurated a tradition that would continue throughout the war. Between 1775 and 1784, Congress awarded fifteen swords to Continental Army officers. Some of these swords Congress voted in recognition of valor in the field. In 1777, for instance, Congress granted a sword to Lieutenant Colonel Marinus Willett "for repeated instances of his bravery and conduct in the sally on the enemy investing Fort Schuyler." Others of these swords Congress voted in appreciation for distinguished service in camp. Baron von Steuben won a gold hilted sword for demonstrating "great zeal and abilities as Inspector General of the Army." As Steuben's case suggests, swords also made fine prizes for foreign officers whom Congress could not otherwise compensate as richly as they deserved. Thus in October 1778, Congress imparted "an elegant sword, with proper devices" to the Marquis de Lafayette, on account of the "disinterested zeal, courage and abilities" that the Frenchman, who fought without pay, had demonstrated "on many signal occasions."[11]

Swords were but one of the means by which Congress endeavored to compliment and to commemorate the army. One month after Congress presented a sword to Captain Livingston, it received the tragic news that his commander, General Richard Montgomery, had been killed at Quebec. Among other acts of mourning, Congress voted to erect a monument to commemorate the fallen general. The following year Congress voted to build two additional monuments: one in honor of General Hugh Mercer, who died of wounds sustained during the Battle of Princeton, and another in memory of General Joseph Warren, who had perished at the Battle of Bunker Hill nearly two years before. By commissioning these new monuments, Congress transformed what had in the previous year been a spontaneous act of grieving into an official protocol for the remembrance of slain generals. In so doing, Congress hoped to perpetuate the names "of those who have peculiarly distinguished themselves in the glorious cause of liberty" and "to inspire posterity with an emulation of their illustrious actions."[12]

The sword awarded by the Continental Congress to Colonel Marinus Willet for distinguished service in the defense of Ft. Schuyler, 1777. Smallsword of Colonel Marinus Willet.
Made by C. Liger (recorded ca. 1770–1793). French (Paris). 1785–1786. Steel, gold, silver, and
shagreen. Sword, L. 39 5/8 in. (100.63 cm). Sheath, L. 33 ¼ in. (84.46 cm). Bequest of George
Willett van Nest, 1917 (17.87.3). © The Metropolitan Museum of Art/Art Resource, NY.

Congress agreed to build Mercer's and Warren's monuments in April 1777,
shortly after returning from Baltimore. With that embarrassing exile still
fresh in mind, Congress determined not to place Mercer's and Warren's
monuments in the Pennsylvania State House, as was its original intention
with Montgomery's. Instead, Congress directed state officials to situate those
monuments prominently in the home towns of the deceased officers—in
Mercer's case, Fredericksburg, Virginia, and in Warren's, Boston, Massachusetts. This resolution was both pragmatic, for it spared Congress the necessity
of abandoning or hauling away monuments in the event of British invasion,
and politically savvy, for it promised to bind afflicted communities more
firmly to the cause. Once completed, these monuments would stand in testament to the generals' heroic sacrifices and to Congress's enduring gratitude.
For each memorial, Congress set aside five hundred dollars.[13]

One high-ranking continental officer expressed appreciation for these
monuments and deemed them shrewd political investments. Writing to

John Adams in early May 1777, Brigadier General Nathanael Greene assured, "The monuments you are erecting to the memory of the great heroes Warren, Montgomery, and Mercer, will be a pleasing circumstance to the army in general . . . and at the same time a piece of justice due to the bravery of the unfortunate generals. These things are attended with but little expense, but have great influence." In the same letter, Greene proposed an additional means of acclaiming the army. "I would beg leave to propose another species of honor," Greene wrote. "Let a number of medals be struck, of different figures emblematical of great actions, with a motto expressive of the same. These medals to be presented by Congress to such of the officers as shall perform some great and noble act." Greene believed in the potency of medals. By appealing to ambition and envy, medals bore the power "to animate the living to great and worthy actions," that is, to rally men who might not else rise to the perils of war. "Patriotism," Greene declared, "is a glorious principle." "But," he advised somewhat cynically, "never refuse her the necessary aids." Greene even asserted that the acquisition of medals would subordinate the army to Congress's will. Medals, Greene argued, would render "the honors of the army dependent upon the dignity of Congress." They would predicate the glory of military service on the sovereignty of the civil government. The bestowal of medals would thus "unite the wishes of the army with the views of Congress" and inspire officers to uphold the union.[14]

John Adams welcomed Greene's recommendation. It was Adams, after all, who first nominated General Washington for a medal after the British evacuation of Boston. Responding to Greene, Adams professed an ardent faith in the "Utility of Medals." For Adams, this utility derived from medals' remarkable influence over human behavior. Just as Benjamin Franklin believed that emblems could make impressions on the mind, Adams concluded that medals could excite the "passions." As Adams opined, "Pride, Ambition and indeed what a Philosopher would call Vanity, is the Strongest Passion in human Nature, and next to Religion, the most operative Motive to great Actions." Adams urged Congress to exploit "the Vanity of Men" and he clearly envisioned at least one medal that would serve the purpose. Describing a scene from the April 1777 Battle of Ridgefield, Adams wrote, "I wish We would make a Beginning, by Striking a Medal, with a Platone firing at General [Benedict] Arnold, on Horseback, His Horse falling dead under him, and He deliberately disentangling his feet from the Stirrups and taking his Pistolls out of his Holsters, before his Retreat. On the Reverse, He should be mounted on a Fresh Horse, receiving another Discharge of Musquetry, with a Wound in the Neck of his Horse . . . I believe there have been few such Scenes in the world."[15]

Congress never acknowledged Arnold for his daring at Ridgefield, but not long after Adams received Greene's proposal, Congress did initiate a custom of awarding medals to valorous officers. In the fall of 1777, Congress commissioned a gold medal to honor Horatio Gates for his defeat of Burgoyne's army. In the years that followed, Congress conferred twelve additional medals, for a total of fourteen, each dedicated to a particular victory or heroic event (see table 7.1). Newspapers and gazettes carried reports of Congress's accolades throughout the United States. At least eight papers, for example, printed the resolution by which Congress granted medals to Anthony Wayne, François-Louis Teissèdre de Fleury, and John Stewart after the storming of Stony Point in 1779.[16] News of these distinctions also spread throughout the Continental Army by word of mouth. Citizens and soldiers alike thus came to learn of Congress's presentment of awards.

Unfortunately, the United States possessed neither the artists nor the facilities for crafting fine swords or minting elaborate medals. Congress's failure to bring these honors to fruition greatly disappointed the continental officer corps. In December 1780, Brigadier General Henry Knox wrote to Samuel Hodgdon, deputy commissary general of military stores, to inquire about a sword that Congress had awarded but never presented to Colonel Return Jonathan Meigs, a Connecticut officer who commanded a successful raid against Sag Harbor, burning British vessels and capturing dozens of prisoners, more than three years before in the summer of 1777. Knox demanded to know "whether the Colonel is to be content with the resolution only; or whether he may expect to have the sword, to exhibit to his children and leave to posterity."[17] Hodgdon understood that Knox voiced the frustration of the continental officer corps. Forwarding Knox's grievance to the Board of War, he reported, "[M]any similar applications and some more pointed having been made . . . [T]he officers think themselves neglected." Hodgdon explained that the commissary had made efforts to complete the swords, but that the first productions were "too badly executed to be presented as a token of National approbation." Hodgdon feared that "present embarrassments"—that is, the depletion of the U.S. treasury—would prevent Congress from commissioning anything better. Accordingly, he urged Congress to purchase European swords on European credit.[18] Until those could be obtained, honorees would have to "content" themselves with "paper medal[s]" and "a consciousness of having merited one of a better quality," as congressional president Henry Laurens once begged of Horatio Gates.[19]

TABLE 7.1   Swords and Medals Issued by the Continental and
Confederation Congresses

Date of Issue	Swords Occasion of Distinguished Service	Medals Occasion of Distinguished Service
December 12, 1775	**Capt. H. Livingston** Montreal (also delivered news thereof)	
March 25, 1776		**Gen. G. Washington** Siege of Boston
November 19, 1776	**Maj. W. Stewart** Delivering news of Carleton's withdrawal to Quebec	
July 25, 1777	**Lt. Col. W. Barton** Norfolk raid **Lt. Col. J. Meigs** Long Island raid	
October 4, 1777	**Lt. Col. M. Willett** Defense of Ft. Schuyler	
November 4, 1777	**Col. C. Green** Delaware River defense **Cdre. J. Hazlewood** Delaware River defense **Lt. Col. S. Smith** Delaware River defense	**Maj. Gen. H. Gates** Saratoga
October 21, 1778	**Maj. Gen. G. Lafayette** "many signal occasions"	
July 26, 1779		**Brig. Gen. A. Wayne** Stony Point **Lt. Col. F. de Fleury** Stony Point **Maj. J. Stewart** Stony Point
September 24, 1779		**Maj H. Lee** Paulus Hook

TABLE 7.1 (continued)

Date of Issue	Swords Occasion of Distinguished Service	Medals Occasion of Distinguished Service
November 3, 1780		**J. Paulding** Capture of John André **D. Williams** Capture of John André **I. van Wert** Capture of John André
March 9, 1781	**Col. A. Pickens** Cowpens	**Brig. Gen. D. Morgan** Cowpens **Lt. Col. W. Washington** Cowpens **Lt. Col. J. Howard** Cowpens
October 29, 1781	**Capt. W. Pierce** Eutaw Springs **Col. O. Williams** Eutaw Springs **Lt. Col. T. Tilghman** Yorktown (also delivered news thereof)	**Maj. Gen. N. Greene** Eutaw Springs
November 7, 1781	**Col. D. Humphreys** Yorktown (also delivered British standards captured there)	
April 15, 1784	**Maj. Gen. F. von Steuben** "several duties of his office"	
October 16, 1787		**Capt. J. Jones** Capture of the *Serapis*

Sources: Worthington C. Ford et al., eds., *Journals of the Continental Congress, 1774–1789*, 34 vols. (Washington, D.C., 1904–1937); John Brewer Brown, *Swords Voted to Officers of the Revolution by the Continental Congress, 1775–1784* (Washington, D.C., 1965); Vladimir Clain-Stefanelli and Elvira Clain-Stefanelli, *Medals Commemorating Battles of the American Revolution* (Washington, D.C., 1973).

The medal awarded by the Continental Congress to Major General Horatio Gates for the defeat of Burgoyne's army, 1777. "Horatio Gates at Saratoga, 1777." Washington-Webster set, Comitia Americana medal. Reverse. Silver medal engraved by Nicolas Marie Gatteaux. Courtesy of the Massachusetts Historical Society.

In the meantime, Congress found other ways to laud the army. Most commonly, Congress delivered simple words of thanks to accomplished officers, formally expressing the United States' "high sense" of the officers' "merit and abilities." In some instances, Congress also promoted deserving officers to brevet, or honorary, commissions with no increase of pay.[20] But as with its unfinished swords and medals, Congress at times antagonized the continental officer corps by these good intentions. Since the inception of the army in 1775, Congress's appointment and promotion of military personnel had embittered officers who felt slighted or overlooked. The political necessity of distributing commissions equitably among the states, the failure of Congress to respect the seniority of officers within their state lines, and the seeming partiality of Congress for French officers all excited disgust within the Continental Army.[21] Writing to Nathanael Greene, John Adams vented, "This delicate Point of Honour, which is really one of the most putrid Corruptions of absolute Monarchy, I mean the Honour of maintaining a Rank Superiour to abler Men, I mean the Honour of preserving a single Step of Promotion to the service of the Public, must be bridled. It is incompatible with republican Principles."[22]

At least one of Congress's brevet promotions breached the "delicate Point of honour" of which Adams complained. In November 1777, Congress bestowed a brevet rank of brigadier general on Colonel James Wilkinson, a "gallant officer" and "promising military genius" who delivered the news of

Burgoyne's surrender at Saratoga. Wilkinson's promotion sparked consternation and jealousy among his fellow officers; some threatened to resign in protest. Unwilling to provoke such discord, Wilkinson relinquished his brevet in March. "I wish to hold no commission," Wilkinson wrote to Congress, "unless I can wear it to the honour and advantage of my country." To spare Wilkinson further discomfort and to mollify an aggrieved officer corps, Congress had no choice but to accept this embarrassing repudiation of its laurels.[23]

It should be noted that Congress almost invariably reserved its swords, monuments, and medals for officers. Only once during the course of the war did Congress order medals for enlisted men, the three New York militia volunteers who, by arresting Major John André, exposed Benedict Arnold's treasonous conspiracy.[24] Only once, after the war, did Congress order a monument for enlisted men, the American soldiers who died in captivity aboard the British prison ship *Jersey*, and whose bones, Congress learned in 1785, the tides of New York Harbor often exposed (see table 7.2).[25] Much more commonly, Congress rewarded enlisted men with cash bounties, as for instance in September 1779, when it placed in the hands of Major Henry Lee the sum of fifteen thousand dollars to be distributed "among the non-commissioned officers and soldiers of the detachment he commanded at the attack and surprise of Powles Hook."[26] So long as the continental dollar held its value, enlisted men may have appreciated present cash bonuses more than the promise of future medals. Still, Congress's practice of honoring officers and not soldiers perpetuated class distinctions in the Continental Army. Ultimately, the continental officers' preoccupation with rank and social stature would provoke resentment among republicans in Congress and fuel a rivalry between the United States' civil and military leaders.

The Brightest Ornaments of Civil Government

As the war progressed, the American officer corps continued to chaff at Congress's maladministration. Infrequent and unfinished gestures of public appreciation such as swords, monuments, and medals proved an ineffective balm. The historian Charles Royster has demonstrated that continental officers came to be bound by common hardship and a collective sense of indignation toward both Congress and the American people. Congress, these officers perceived, had failed the army, as evident in its inability to satisfy the soldiers' most basic needs. The people, they further determined, had lost all virtue, as manifest in their refusal to pay taxes for the defense of their country.

Table 7.2   Monuments Commissioned by the Continental and
Confederation Congresses for Continental Officers
and Soldiers

Date	Honoree Battle or Place of Death
January 25, 1776	**Maj. Gen. R. Montgomery** Quebec
April 8, 1777	**Maj. Gen. J. Warren** Bunker Hill **Brig. Gen. H. Mercer** Princeton
May 19, 1777	**Brig. Gen. D. Wooster** Danbury
October 4, 1777	**Brig. Gen. N. Herkimer** Oriskany
November 4, 1777	**Brig. Gen. F. Nash** Germantown
November 19, 1779	**Brig. Gen. K. Pulaski** Savannah
October 14, 1780	**Maj. Gen. J. de Kalb** Camden
September 20, 1781	**Brig. Gen. W. Davidson** Cowan's Ford **Brig. Gen. J. Screven** Sunbury, near Midway Church
April 29, 1785	**"American prisoners who perished in captivity" aboard the *Jersey*** New York Harbor
July 11, 1786	**Maj. Gen. N. Greene** Savannah (of natural causes in retirement)

Source: Worthington C. Ford et al., eds., *Journals of the Continental Congress, 1774–1789*, 34 vols. (Washington, D.C., 1904–1937).

In the late 1770s, the United States' increasingly professionalized officer corps began to think of itself as a discrete segment of society, singularly meritorious for the extraordinary sacrifices it had made to keep the public faith. Many officers believed that they alone bore the standard of American liberty.[27]

The army's unique material and ceremonial culture exacerbated the officers' sense of detachment. The traditional signifiers of military service—arms, uniforms, and flags—of course set continental forces apart from civil society. But the army's celebratory rituals also distinguished the officer corps as an insular and influential band. Military festivity helped to define the character of the Continental Army. It gave expression to the officers' social aspirations and to their vision of the American republic. In so doing, it strengthened and accentuated the officers' sense of shared identity. At the same time, however, it also provoked jealousy and suspicion among civil leaders. After the Franco-American alliance, the army's fanfare grew more extravagant, situating the officer corps as a rival to, rather than an instrument of, Congress.

The Continental Army instituted holidays and celebrations to promote patriotism, to give outlet to fatigue and frustration, to break up the monotony of camp life, and to divert soldiers' energies from more disruptive forms of recreation such as gambling and heavy drinking.[28] The Valley Forge encampment of 1777–78 provides several examples. Though the Valley Forge winter is most often remembered for the severity of the weather, for the impoverishment of the soldiers, and for the systematic drilling and discipline by which Baron von Steuben professionalized the Continental Army, the Valley Forge spring might just as well be remembered for the merriment and festivity by which the high command elevated spirits and instilled patriotism on the eve of its summer campaign.[29] On the evening of April 30, 1778, for example, every regiment at Valley Forge erected a May pole in its camp. The following morning, reveille sounded with three cheers: this was St. Tammany's Day, an adaptation of May Day most commonly celebrated by Pennsylvanians in honor of Tamanend, the Delaware sachem who first welcomed William Penn to "his" woods. Situated as Valley Forge was on the banks of the Schuylkill, St. Tammany's Day was a fitting holiday for the army sheltered there, for according to legend, it was Tamanend who first granted Philadelphians the right to fish that river.[30] Now that the arduous winter had come to an end, St. Tammany's Day provided occasion for vernal rejoice. George Ewing, a lieutenant in the New Jersey line, recorded that "[t]he day was spent in mirth and Jollity the soldiers parading marching with fife & Drum and Huzzaing as they passd the poles their hats adornd with white blossoms."[31]

Just a few days later, word of the Franco-American alliance reached Valley Forge and in response General Washington ordered a day of thanksgiving. On the morning of May 6, army chaplains offered prayers and sermons of gratitude for the treaties that had been signed. Later that morning, Washington assembled the troops for a grand ceremonial inspection. This review, an opportunity for the soldiery to demonstrate the precision and regularity they had learned from Steuben, was rendered all the more brilliant by the prospect that the Continental Army might soon march alongside, and yield nothing in point of discipline to, French forces. At the close of the performance, Washington ordered a *feu-de-joie* followed by a "running fire" of musketry in lines around the camp and a series of huzzas in honor of the king of France. That afternoon, Washington treated his officers and several local ladies to a picnic of "fat meat, strong wine, and other liquors."[32]

The camp at Valley Forge also enjoyed a makeshift theater. On May 11, just one week after the army celebrated its spontaneous thanksgiving, Washington's officers staged a performance of Joseph Addison's *Cato* (1713), an enormously popular tragedy devoted to virtue, tyranny, and the collapse of the Roman republic. "The scenery was in Taste," one officer reported, "& the performance admirable."[33] That continental officers should devote a few spare hours to a patriotic theatrical production would certainly seem innocent enough. The stage offered a necessary respite from the tedium of camp life, and no play could have more forcefully exalted the principles for which the Revolution was fought. As one scholar has written, "Addison's tragedy offered a salient version of national destiny characterized by self-sacrifice, republican virtue, and an almost boundless devotion to the principle of liberty."[34] In comparison to the extravagant Meschianza hosted by British officers just a few days later, the theater at Valley Forge appeared altogether sober and austere.[35]

That theater, however, had opened in brazen disregard of congressional authority. It represented a developing tension between the polite leisure embraced by the continental officer corps and the virtuous self-denial demanded by the Continental Congress. Nearly four years had passed since the First Continental Congress called on Americans to forego "exhibitions of shews, plays, and other expensive diversions and entertainments." Since that time, the outbreak of war and the Declaration of Independence had mooted the original purpose of the Association, to compel redress for American grievances, but Congress had not rescinded its ban on the theater. The Valley Forge *Cato*, moreover, was not a one-off production. The army had been staging plays for more than a month and was making plans to expand its repertoire. One officer reported that if the British persisted in Philadelphia long enough, Valley Forge audiences would be treated to Nicholas Rowe's *The Fair Penitent*, Isaac Bickerstaffe's *The Padlock*, and George Farquhar's *The Recruiting Officer*. These plays—a domestic tragedy of adultery and deceit, a comic opera of romantic liberation, and a comedy that likened military

recruitment to sexual seduction—would have surely run afoul of "true republican principles."[36]

The continental officers' affection for theater—as manifest both at Valley
Forge and in Benedict Arnold's Philadelphia, where American officers
had also begun to stage performances—dismayed republican stalwarts in
Congress. In October, Samuel Adams grumbled to a Boston correspondent,
"You must know that in humble Imitation, as it would seem, of the Example
of the British army some of the officers of ours have condescended to act on
the Stage while others, and one of Superior Rank were pleasd to countenance
Them with their presense."[37] Adams and likeminded delegates wished to
stem this profligate behavior. They particularly perceived a need to reassert a
republican political economy in the city that Howe's forces had worked so
hard to debauch. On October 12, Congress took up a motion to reiterate its
former proscriptions:

> Whereas true religion and good morals are the only solid founda-
> tions of public liberty and happiness:

> Resolved, That it be, and it is hereby earnestly recommended
> to the several states, to take the most effectual measures for the
> encouragement thereof, and for the suppressing of theatrical en-
> tertainments, horse racing, gaming, and such other diversions as
> are productive of idleness, dissipation, and a general depravity of
> principles and manners.

> Resolved, That all officers in the army of the United States, be, and
> hereby are strictly enjoined to see that the good and wholesome
> rules provided for the discountenancing of prophaneness and vice,
> and the preservation of morals among the soldiers, are duly and
> punctually observed.[38]

Members of Congress did not universally support these resolutions. In a
letter to the French ministry, Conrad-Alexandre Gérard reported, "It is the
northern members, called the Presbyterian party, that delight in passing
moral laws so as to keep their credit and rigor in full exercise." Gérard
oversimplified the sectional dynamics of congressional factionalism. He
likewise underestimated the ideological and religious concerns that motivated the staunchest republicans. But he was right to note that these "moral

laws" divided Congress. Delegates from Maryland, Virginia, and North Carolina resisted the measures, not because they opposed "true religion and good morals," not even because they wished to preserve the theater, but rather, as Gérard explained, because they "regard[ed] horse-racing as a national affair."[39]

The very night that Congress renewed its prohibition against the theater, the dramatists of Philadelphia performed another play. The Marquis de Lafayette's decision not to attend the production greatly pleased Samuel Adams. Adams proclaimed that Lafayette, who was then visiting the city, "has discoverd the Dignity of the Citizen in the Regard he so readily paid to the Sentiments of those in Civil Authority."[40] Later that week, the *Pennsylvania Packet* published a laudatory account:

> A play being . . . performed in the city last Monday evening, the Marquis de la Fayette being in company with his Excellency the President of Congress, asked him to accompany him to the play. The President politely excusing himself, the Marquis pressed him to go: The President then informed the Marquis that Congress having that day passed a resolution, recommending to the several states to enact laws for the suppression of theatrical amusements, he could not possibly do himself the honour of waiting upon him to the play. Ah! replied the Marquis, have Congress passed such a resolution! then I will not go to the play.[41]

Lafayette's deference to the will of Congress, however, only underscored the impudence of those who put on the play, and of those who attended, in spite of Congress's decree. Dismayed, Samuel Adams asserted that the theatrical performance appeared to have been made "in contempt of the Sense of Congress."[42] In response, Congress again voted its forbiddance of the theater, but this time in much stronger language. Whereas in its resolution of October 12 Congress merely enjoined officers to uphold all "good and wholesome rules," in its resolution of October 16 Congress explicitly prohibited officers from attending the theater, on penalty of their commissions: "Resolved, That any person holding an office under the United States, who shall act, promote, encourage or attend such plays, shall be deemed unworthy to hold such office, and shall be accordingly dismissed." Again, however, this motion met with opposition from the Southern states and sparked procedural wrangling. The New York delegate William Duer, who opposed the measure, demanded that the yeas and nays be recorded in the *Journals*, presumably to dissuade individual congressmen from voting to deprive the army its leisure. The motion passed in spite of Duer's tactic.[43]

Notwithstanding Congress's bid to suppress the theater, the military continued to develop its own material and ceremonial identity. As the army professionalized, as new campaigns nurtured a sense of camaraderie within the ranks, and as an influx of European officers brought elevated notions of prestige and distinction to the American service, the army's festivity grew more elaborate and expensive. This progression may be observed in a lavish celebration of the anniversary of the Franco-American alliance, hosted by Brigadier General Henry Knox at his artillery encampment near Pluckemin, New Jersey, on February 18, 1779. Over the course of the war, Knox's artillery earned a reputation for proficiency and esprit de corps.[44] The Pluckemin anniversary festivity of 1779, which came to be remembered as the Grand Alliance Ball, gave early evidence of the artillerists' verve. Talk of the event generated excitement and anticipation among the officer corps. Brigadier General William Maxwell, whose New Jersey brigade was stationed at Elizabethtown as the first line of defense against the British army in New York, wrote to Washington requesting permission to leave his post. But the commander, who himself planned to attend the ball, refused. "The enemy," Washington apologized, "may think our attention too much engaged in the exhibition of that day, and may be encouraged to some enterprise on that account. I must therefore beg you will remain at your post, and have a look out more vigilant than ordinary upon the occasion."[45] Maxwell's eagerness to take part in the event appears to have been widely shared, for as Knox later recounted, the guests included "above seventy ladies, all of the first *ton* [i.e., fashionable society, italics in original] in the State, and between three and four hundred Gentlemen."[46]

The festivities opened with the firing of thirteen cannon at four o'clock in the afternoon. The guests then assembled for dinner and toasts in a temporary academy Knox ordered built for the instruction of artillery officers. Afterward they stepped out to the lawn for a display of fireworks. At the center of this pyrotechnics display stood a large ornate "temple" constructed just for the affair. One hundred feet in length, this temple consisted of thirteen Corinthian arches, each of which contained "an illuminated painting emblematic of the Revolution." In proper deference to civil authorities, the central painting depicted "The Fathers in Congress" under the heroic motto, *Nil Desperandum Reipublicae.* The remainder of the paintings, from left to right, provided an illuminated history of the Revolution: beginning with the Battle of Lexington; proceeding through the Declaration of Independence, as represented by a "magnificent arch broken in the centre"; continuing with a portrait of Louis XVI, "supporter of the rights of humanity"; and ultimately culminating in a representation of Peace, here adorned with "emblems of an extensive empire, and unrestrained commerce." Together with fireworks, this grand temple captured the attention of country folk for miles around. As the *New Jersey Gazette* explained, "The barracks of the artillery are at a small distance from Pluck'emin, on a piece of rising ground which shews them to great advantage." Situated on this prominence, Knox's temple attracted "a vast concourse of spectators from every part of the Jersies." After the fireworks display, guests returned to an elegant ball at the academy where, Knox boasted, they "danced all night."[47]

By feting the Franco-American alliance in such high fashion, the army conspicuously upstaged the Continental Congress. The artillerists' spectacular temple shined with greater resplendence than did the familiar City Tavern, where Congress hosted its modest anniversary repast. And though the officers' ball may not have technically violated Congress's most recent "moral laws," it afforded greater diversion and entertainment than the Articles of Association would have admitted. Back in Philadelphia, Congress took no official notice of General Knox's anniversary celebration. If any of the delegates begrudged the affair, Congress was in no position to condemn it. As a tribute to the United States' ally, King Louis XVI, the event lay beyond political reproach. Furthermore, by the spring of 1779, Congress—having repeatedly failed to provision the army and having frequently slipped into arrears in the army's pay—possessed little political capital to expend on scolding the continental officers. John Jay, perhaps the only delegate to mention the Pluckemin festivities in his letters, so far from criticizing them, approvingly reported, "The fireworks and Entertainment at the Camp, are said to have been well concerted and well executed. The Number of Ladies who were present must have added greatly to . . . the Celebrity of the Occasion." Jay's correspondent, his sister-in-law Catharine Livingston, knew that to be true, for she herself attended.[48]

Through the remainder of the war, the political relationship between Congress and the Continental Army continued to deteriorate. The collapse of the continental currency greatly diminished Congress's power. The reluctance of Congress to pension the officer corps further estranged that body of men. During this same period, the officer corps continued to indulge its taste for gaiety and polite sociability. In the spring of 1780, for instance, thirty-five officers, including General Washington, formed a dancing assembly at their winter headquarters at Morristown.[49] This sort of entertainment provided levity, recreation, and social opportunity for the army command. As an outlet for frustration and weariness, it served an important function for the military.

But another, less utilitary consideration impelled the continental officer corps to pursue refined pastimes. In the eighteenth century, military authority depended on genteel social status.[50] American officers took to the stage and the dance hall for the same reasons that they hired servants and horse, packed trunks full of personal possessions, and dined in polite taverns: to do so distinguished them from the men under their command. The advent of European military figures, particularly after the Franco-American alliance of 1778, heightened class anxieties in the Continental Army. Some foreign officers possessed considerable wealth, manners, and / or titles of nobility, such as the Marquis de Lafayette. Others aggrandized their social status and military achievement in order to obtain commissions in the Continental Army. The appearance of so many gentlemen, be they genuine article or mere imitation, engendered self-consciousness among the American officer corps. Few continental officers could claim the prestige or fortunes of their most distinguished French counterparts.[51] By attending plays and subscribing to dance assemblies, they sought to demonstrate their gentility and to justify their rank.

Members of Congress grasped the relationship between social standing and military authority in the army. Very early in the war, the delegates agreed, at least in principle, that the highest continental ranks ought to be filled with well-bred and accomplished individuals. Writing to Nathanael Greene in August 1776, John Adams justified the apparent favoritism by which Congress promoted colonels from the middle and southern colonies ahead of those from New England. Defending Congress's appointment of men of "Family and Fortune," Adams declared, "A General officer ought to be a Gentleman of Letters, and general Knowledge, a Man of Address and Knowledge of the World. He should carry with him Authority and Command . . . It is not every Piece of Wood that will do to make a Mercury."[52] By insisting that the continental officers be men of cultivation and attainment, Southern delegates endeavored to preserve a military tradition premised on social hierarchy. Northern congressmen such as Adams, meanwhile, found ways to square Congress's expectations with true republican principles. In another letter of August 1776, Adams opined,

> An officer, high in Rank, should be possessed of very extensive Knowledge of Science and Literature, Men and Things. A Citizen of a free Government, he should be Master of the Laws and Constitution, least [sic] he injure fundamentally those Rights

which he professes to defend. . . . His Views should be large
enough to comprehend the whole System of the Government
and the Army, that he may accommodate his Plans and Measures
to the best good, and the essential Movements of these great
Machines.[53]

Whether premised on class preference or ideology, Congress's penchant for
an educated and cosmopolitan officer corps privileged candidates of wealth
and stature. To accentuate social distinctions in the army, Congress adopted
a new pay scale in 1778, widening the gap between officers' and enlisted
men's pay.[54]

Despite the ways in which Congress institutionalized class hierarchy in
the Continental Army, some delegates began to resent the social pretensions
that prevailed among the officer corps. Late in the war, the officers' pursuit
of refinement became a matter of political controversy. In August 1779,
Congress resolved to compensate army officers for the loss of real income
they sustained from depreciation of the continental currency. Toward that
end, Congress granted remedial pay raises to all officers below the rank of
general.[55] Three months later, twenty-six generals protested that they too
suffered from the failure of the United States' paper money. Citing the exorbitant costs of war—of horses, of table, of clothing—these generals beseeched
Congress to remunerate them for the "diminution" of their "fortunes." No
favorable reply forthcoming, sixteen major and brigadier generals composed
a second memorial, which Major General Alexander McDougall personally
delivered to Congress in the summer of 1780. In this second memorial, the
generals once again begged Congress to increase their pay in equitable
proportion to inflation. The generals also urged Congress to make allowance
for the widows and orphans of officers slain in the public service.[56]

In addition to these reasonable demands, the generals pressed a claim that
Congress could not abide. "[T]he establishment for the general officers," they
asserted, "is unequal to their stations, the honor of their country, and the good
of the service. They therefore request that, in addition to the rations they are
entitled to receive, a sum be allowed to each general officer, to enable him to
support a table suitable to the rank he holds." To justify their entitlement to
a table—that is, a budget for food, wine, and service necessary for the hosting
of other officers and distinguished guests—the generals observed that in the
coming campaign they would likely fight alongside the French army, whose
troops, being "liberally paid in specie," would command "all the produce
of the country." This circumstance, the generals objected, "will constantly

present a most disagreeable contrast, and render the situation of [the American generals], already irksome enough, altogether insupportable." In short, the general officers of the Continental Army now insisted that the honor of the United States required that they be granted funds to entertain as politely as their French counterparts did.[57]

Representatives in Congress knew all too well how expensive it could be to keep pace with the French. Having themselves been obliged by financial embarrassment to decline the French minister's lavish hospitality, members of Congress received the generals' request for a table allowance with indignation. "[T]he demand is reasonable," the South Carolina congressman Henry Laurens sarcastically remarked. "[A] Warrant moreover should be Issued for furnishing them with equipages, good breeding & education equally with the French Nobility . . . but we have not yet determined that Congress shall be enabled to live in splendor equal to that of the Minister of France, nor that the American Minister at Versailles shall cut as superb a figure as the Venetian Ambassador." Laurens thought it particularly egregious that the officers, so fully cognizant of Congress's financial woes, should "demand what they know cannot be granted." "O Virtue," Laurens wailed. "O Patriotism! whither are ye fled!"[58]

Determined "to do Justice to the officers without giving in to Whims," as the Massachusetts congressman James Lovell put it, Congress resolved to advance the generals two months' pay. Congress also voted pensions for the widows and orphans of officers killed in service. Congress even granted large tracts of land, proportionate to those it had previously awarded junior officers and enlisted men, to the generals as well. But Congress refused to subsidize the generals' banqueting. Instead, Congress exhorted the generals to greater self-discipline. "[P]atience and self-denial, fortitude and perseverance, and the cheerful sacrifice of time, health and fortune," Congress admonished, "are necessary virtues which both the citizen and the soldier are called to exercise, while struggling for the liberties of their country; and that moderation, frugality and temperance, must be among the chief supports, as well as the brightest ornaments, of that kind of civil government which is wisely instituted by the several states in this union."[59]

The Only True Fountain of Honor

Antagonism between Congress and the American military persisted throughout the war and well into the confederation period. To appreciate that fact, we must move forward in time, past the British surrender at Yorktown, to the disbandment of the army nearly two years later. That event gave rise to a new and threatening institution putatively characterized by "a Splendor exceeding any thing within the practice of Government." In November 1782, the United States signed a provisional peace with Great Britain. But rather than alleviating tensions between Congress and the army, the end of the war temporarily exacerbated them. Soldiers feared that Congress would disband the army without pay. Officers worried that Congress would refuse to fund a pension. Persuaded that the confederation could not settle its accounts, many believed that the welfare of the United States depended on a stronger central power. Out of these concerns—and out of the camaraderie that prevailed among the continental officers—arose a new organization, the Society of the Cincinnati, in the late spring of 1783. Founded by Henry Knox and a handful of high-ranking collaborators, the Cincinnati consisted primarily of American and European Continental Army officers. During the first year of its existence, rumors swirled about the society's intentions and about its scheme of hereditary membership. Republicans, both in and out of Congress, began to dread the Cincinnati as a lever of political authority. Bowing to public opinion, the society abandoned certain aristocratic practices and subordinated itself to the administration of government. Nevertheless, in the years that followed, the Cincinnati quickly overshadowed the enfeebled Confederation Congress as a fount of civic festivity. The often uneasy relationship between Congress and the Cincinnati came to be defined, in large measure, by the contrast in their political aesthetics, as manifest in the material artifacts and ceremonies by which they expressed their allegiance to the United States.[60]

Various proposals for a hereditary order of American officers had been chattered about for months, possibly years. The Rhode Island congressman William Ellery claimed that as early as 1777 or 1778 he had seen a manuscript proposing "that titles of nobility should be given to our principal officers." In June 1783, the *Connecticut Journal* reported plans for the creation of the "Order of Freedom," an American knighthood composed of civil and military officers. Later that same year, the Order of Divine Providence, a Polish "order of dignity," invited Congress to nominate thirty-six American officers for its knighthood. Congress declined this "obliging proposal," declaring it inapposite to the "principles of the Confederation."[61]

Though some form of hereditary organization had long been an object of contemplation, the Society of the Cincinnati arose out of immediate political and economic circumstances; namely, the mutinous Newburgh conspiracy of March 1783, Congress's subsequent determination to commute the officer

corps' pensions from half-pay for life to full pay for five years, and the imminent discharge of the continental soldiery. Cognizant that demobilization of
the army would diminish their political cohesion and influence, Knox and his
fellow officers resolved to establish a fraternal military order.[62] In April, the
former Boston bookseller drafted and circulated a preliminary constitution at
army headquarters in Newburgh. Weeks later, delegates from the various
state lines gathered to formulate revisions. At a conference in June, Knox and
a small group of officers elected George Washington, who was not in attendance, to serve as president of the society. Before adjourning, they agreed that
the first general meeting of the Cincinnati would take place on May 4 of the
following year.[63]

According to the terms of its Institution, as the first constitution of the
Cincinnati was known, the organization was founded on the "cordial affection" of the continental officers, the "national honor" of the United States, and
the "exalted rights and liberties of human nature." It aimed to perpetuate the
memory of the Revolution and to nurture friendships "formed under the
pressure of common danger, and in many instances, cemented by the blood of
the parties." The society extended membership to the present officers of the
Continental Army, to those who had previously resigned after three year's
service or who had been honorably dismissed by Congress, and to "their
eldest male posterity." It also granted honorary membership to civilians, men
of eminent "abilities and patriotism," but only in limited numbers and only
for the course of the honoree's lifetime; honorary membership did not
descend. To finance the society's proceedings and charitable operations, each
member agreed to pay one month's salary into his state society's treasury. The
Cincinnati also accepted voluntary subscriptions and private donations for
the relief of "unfortunate members, or their widows and orphans." Finally, as
detailed in the Institution of 1783, members of the Cincinnati adopted an
"Order" or badge: "a medal of gold, of a proper size to receive the emblems,
and suspended by a deep blue riband two inches wide, edged with white,
descriptive of the union of France and America."[64]

The formation of a hereditary society of continental officers provoked
considerable alarm, particularly in New England, where opposition to army
pensions ran high. But the most vocal critic of the Cincinnati hailed from
South Carolina. Aedanus Burke, a judge and state legislator who formerly
served in the Carolina militia, perceived in the Cincinnati the genesis of
an American aristocracy.[65] In October, Burke published a condemnatory
pamphlet entitled, *Considerations on the Society or Order of Cincinnati . . .
Proving that It Creates a Race of Hereditary Patricians, or Nobility.* The Cincin-

nati, Burke proclaimed, had been "planted in a fiery, hot ambition, and thirst of power." Determined to establish "an hereditary peerage," it would soon divide Americans into two ranks: "the patricians or nobles, and the rabble." Mocking the officer corps' claims to Cincinnatian merit, Burke demanded, "Did that virtuous Roman, having subdued the enemies of his country and returned home to tend his vineyard and plant his cabbages; did he confer an hereditary order of peerage on himself and his fellow soldiers? I answer, No; it was more than he dared to do."[66]

Members of the Confederation Congress reacted to the Cincinnati in mixed ways. Some delegates, themselves former army officers, took membership with pride. Congressman James Tilton, who served as a surgeon in the Continental Army, accepted the presidency of his state's society after he and fellow Delaware officers determined that the Cincinnati's purposes were "laudable." President Elias Boudinot not only accepted an honorary membership, but appears to have coyly pursued it. Once a colonel in the Continental Army, Boudinot resigned his commission after one year's service in order to accept a seat in Congress. Consequently, he was not eligible for regular membership. In September 1783, Boudinot wrote to Elias Dayton, president of the New Jersey chapter, asking, "Will you be good enough to explain to me the Terms of admission into the Society of the Cincinnati and who it is designed for." Within weeks of submitting his query, Boudinot received from Dayton a certificate of his election as an honorary member. Deeply gratified by this "unsolicited" compliment, Boudinot pledged to render himself "worthy" of the society's friendship and esteem. Still another member of Congress, the Delawarean Thomas Rodney later claimed to have first dreamed up the very idea of the Cincinnati. Sometime in the early 1790s, Rodney composed a retrospect of his service in Congress entitled, "Particular Instances wherein the leading Members & Congress followed my Counsels." In one of many entries under this heading, Rodney described an after-dinner conversation in which he and General Horatio Gates agreed that the American people would not long suffer an incompetent confederation. "[T]o perserve [*sic*] the Union and to Effect a reform in the Government," Rodney recalled, "I then proposed the plan and association of the Cincinnatti [*sic*]."[67]

At the same time, a small but strident faction of delegates received the Cincinnati with profound suspicion. These congressmen—mostly dyed-in-the-wool republicans from New England and Virginia—shared Burke's trepidation that the Cincinnati represented the first step toward an American aristocracy, perhaps even an American monarchy. "[H]ow easy the Transition from a Republican to any other Form of Government, however despotic?" wondered the Massachusetts congressman Elbridge Gerry. "Surely this Country will not consent to a Race of Hereditary Patricians," exclaimed his colleague Samuel Osgood, borrowing a pointed phrase from the subtitle of Burke's pamphlet. Summarizing popular antipathy toward the Cincinnati, Thomas Jefferson—recently returned to Congress following two terms in office as the governor of Virginia and a period of mourning after the death of his wife—explained that the Cincinnati's heritable privileges ran afoul of Revolutionary principles: "[T]he foundation, on which all [state constitutions] are built, is the natural equality of man . . . and particularly the denial of a preeminence by birth . . . [E]xperience has shewn that the hereditary branches of modern governments are the patrons of privilege and prerogative, and not of the natural rights of the people." From France, Benjamin Franklin questioned, too, why "private Persons should think proper to distinguish themselves and their Posterity from their Fellow Citizens, and form an Order of hereditary Knights, in direct Opposition to the solemnly declared Sense of their Country."[68]

Some congressmen also discerned in the Cincinnati an insidious design to overthrow the confederation. Gerry believed, with good reason, that the American officer corps aimed at the securement of the public debt. Though Gerry did not doubt the "Rectitude" of the officers' intentions, he dreaded that members of the Cincinnati might be slowly drawn to measures "which they would now shudder at the thot of." To Samuel Osgood, the officers appeared far more menacing. "The Eyes of the proposed Cincinnati are fix'd, & pointedly fix'd on [the Treasury] Department," he asserted. "I have heard some of the Officers say, 'Fulfill your Promises, pay us honestly & the Cincinnati will be a harmless Body.' This seems to me to have a plain Meaning." Both Gerry and Osgood suspected that the French ministry had hatched the Cincinnati as part of a plot to render the United States "subservient to their political purposes." Gerry predicted that if the Cincinnati ever attempted a coup, the French government would lend financial and military support to see it accomplished. "Would not these pursuits be dressed in the most amiable Garbs of publick Virtue," Gerry admonished, "patriotism, a Love of good Government, & aversion to the Anarchy of fœderal republican Governments?"[69]

Though freighted with chauvinistic fears of a Jesuitical conspiracy, Gerry's and Osgood's dire prognostications nevertheless gave voice to a real and immediate concern: that the Cincinnati would emerge as a political adversary to Congress. Aside from Congress, the Cincinnati was the only American institution capable of rallying a national constituency. Its charter established a sturdy state-by-state infrastructure and its members commanded high esteem within their local communities.[70] Because the Cincinnati aspired to promote "union," "national honor," and "the future dignity of the American Empire," some congressmen believed that it had assumed the prerogatives of government. Gerry deemed the society an "unconstitutional monster."[71] He and other members of government perceived in the Cincinnati's conduct an array of slights against the Confederation Congress. The foreign minister John Jay trenchantly observed that the Cincinnati had requested King Louis XVI's permission to extend membership to French officers, but had not paid Congress, its own sovereign, "the like Compliment." In a similar vein, the Rhode Island congressman David Howell indignantly noted in the spring of 1784, "Georgia has not sent forward any delegates to Congress tho' it is reported that the Cincinnati of that State were represented at their late general meeting in Philada."[72]

Jay's and Howell's resentment of the Cincinnati arose not only from their highly cultivated regard for congressional dignity, but also from a sense of wounded pride. A similar spirit of acrimony animated Samuel Osgood, who refused to sit in Congress with the Cincinnati watching over his shoulder: "If the Intention of this Institution is, to connect throughout the Continent a large & important Body of Men to watch over the Doings of Congress, or of the State Legislatures, if there is a real Necessity for this, let the last be dissolved, & let the first take the Helmn [sic]." Elbridge Gerry likewise balked at the ways in which the Cincinnati threatened to supplant the civil power. He took particular umbrage at the society's practice of awarding honorary membership to the holders of high public office, a practice that up-ended the proper relationship between the army and its rightful superiors: "[H]ow extraordinary the Measure, that the Officers of the Army who derived their Honor from the only true fountain, the Great Council of the united States, should now become the fountain itself." Perhaps most elementally, these congressmen begrudged the Cincinnati's efforts to claim credit for the triumph of American arms. Writing to John Adams, surely a sympathetic reader, Osgood proclaimed, "There are many others besides the officers whose Names ought & will be immortalized for their Conduct during the late War."[73]

The establishment of the Cincinnati at the end of the Revolution preserved a distinction between civil and military authorities, a distinction that, as Thomas Jefferson counseled, it was now "for the happiness of both to obliterate." The Cincinnati's adoption of a rich material, ceremonial, and celebratory culture forcefully underscored that distinction. The cofounder Henry Knox originally proposed that the Cincinnati convene its national meetings on April 19, the anniversary of Lexington and Concord, and its state meetings on July 4, the anniversary of independence. Had it done so, the society may well have usurped those national holidays, positioning its members as guests of honor and channeling popular remembrance of the Revolution toward its own political ends. Perhaps sensing this impropriety, the Cincinnati formally abandoned Knox's plan, but some local societies began to celebrate the Fourth of July in a fashion so grand as to preempt any public fanfare. And there were other ways that the Cincinnati set itself apart. In 1783, for example, members of the Cincinnati attended commencement exercises at the College of New Jersey, but sat as a discrete body, unmingled with Congress or other eminent guests. This, one of the Cincinnati's earliest public appearances, distinguished that society as an exclusive organization.[74]

The most visible marker of the Cincinnati, and consequently the one most scorned by its adversaries, was its badge of membership, as first described in the preliminary constitution drafted by Henry Knox. The desire for a badge of honor apparently motivated Knox to found the Society, at least in part, and it also enticed fellow officers to subscribe. Years after the war, John Adams recollected a chance encounter with Knox in a New York tavern, likely in September 1776, when Adams ventured to Staten Island to participate in an ill-fated peace conference. At that time, Knox expressed his wish that he might obtain "some ribbon to wear in his hat, or in his button hole, to be transmitted to his descendants as a badge and a proof that he had fought in defence of their liberties. He spoke of it in such precise terms as shewed he had revolved it in his mind before."[75] Another high-ranking officer, Major General William Heath, acknowledged the badge as his chief incentive for joining the Cincinnati. Heath initially doubted the society and felt disinclined to pursue membership. He reversed his position after reflecting on the weight that the society's badge would accumulate in posterity:

> [T]he descendent of one who was a member might happen to fall in company with the descendant of one who was not; that the latter, on observing the badge, might inquire what it was, and what its intention? upon his being answered, that it was the insignia of a Society, of which his ancestor, who had served in the American army during the Revolution, was a member—the other might reply, my ancestor too served during that war, but I never heard any thing of such a badge in our family; to which it might probably be answered, it is likely your ancestor was guilty of some misconduct which deprived him of it.

Mortified that he might inadvertently cheat his heirs of their familial honor, Heath promptly endorsed the Cincinnati. (He later reversed himself once again, withdrawing from membership in the 1790s, after the French revolutionaries denounced badges and other sorts of decorations and in so doing brought his former objections fresh to mind.)[76]

Critics of the Cincinnati roundly condemned the badge. Aedanus Burke and Benjamin Franklin both considered it a vanity. Burke lamented that the "all-grasping, infatuating ambition" of the continental officers would not be satisfied until they had "a *quaint title* stuck upon their family, and a badge or bauble dangling at their button-hole" (italics in original).[77] Franklin considered the badge a vestige of French corruption. American officers, Franklin regretted, had "been too much struck with the Ribbands and Crosses they have seen . . . hanging to the Button-holes of Foreign Officers."[78] In his *Defence of the Constitutions of the United States of America*, John Adams also denounced the Cincinnati's "baubles." Though Adams had years before identified vanity as the "Strongest Passion in human Nature," and though he had urged Congress to cultivate that vice among aspiring officers, he now chastised the Cincinnati for suffering from it. "[T]hat the disposition to artificial distinctions, to titles, and ribbons, and to the hereditary descent of them, is ardent in America," Adams proclaimed, "we may see by the institution of the Cincinnati." Echoing Gerry's concern that the Cincinnati had abrogated Congress's civil supremacy, Adams opined,

> There is not a more remarkable phenomenon in universal history, nor in universal human nature, than this order. The officers of an army, who had voluntarily engaged in a service under the authority of the people, whose creation and preservation was upon the principle that the body of the people were the only fountain of power and of honor; . . . the moment they had answered the end of their creation, instituted titles and ribbons, and hereditary descents, by their own authority only, without the consent or knowledge of the people, or their representatives or legislatures.[79]

Perhaps the most honest objection to the badge was not that the Cincinnati had adopted it in vanity, not even that the Cincinnati had taken it in disregard of congressional sentiment, but rather that by this badge the continental officers had claimed all the laurels of the Revolution for themselves. Warning a colleague against the society, the Rhode Island congressman William Ellery let slip his resentment toward the badge: "It is a medal of Gold in the figure of an eagle with an inscription on the face & reverse alluding to the time of establishing the order, *and to their having saved the republic*" (italics added). Ellery, who wearied himself "making extracts" of Aedanus Burke's *Considerations on the Society or Order of Cincinnati*, would not have that fraternity take so much credit.[80]

Congress never took a formal stance toward the Cincinnati, presumably because the delegates divided over the propriety and lawfulness of that organization. In fact, only once, in 1785, did Congress take official notice of the Cincinnati at all, and then in response to a French officer who appealed to Congress for membership, presumably "from a mistaken opinion that the Society of the Cincinnati was an Order of Knighthood similar to those Orders instituted by the Sovereigns of Europe." Congress was obliged to disabuse the applicant: "The Cross of the Cincinnati Congress have not a power to grant."[81] In the meantime, delegates who harbored misgivings toward the Cincinnati worked privately to quash its influence. Through the winter of 1783–84, Gerry, Osgood, and other delegates wrote letters to their political allies denouncing the Cincinnati.[82] Thomas Jefferson exerted his personal influence to persuade George Washington to decline the presidency of that organization or, failing that, to insist on its reformation. At the society's first general meeting in 1784, Washington instigated a series of amendments to render its constitution more amenable to republican principles and less threatening to government. At Washington's insistence, the Cincinnati agreed to forego hereditary membership, to reduce the frequency of its meetings, to request the permission of state legislatures for the organization of new chapters, and to relinquish to those legislatures control over its charitable funds. Washington might even have secured the outright abolition of the organization but for a fateful, and telling, occurrence. On May 10, 1784, at the height of the Cincinnati's deliberations, Major Pierre Charles L'Enfant returned from France with pocketful of freshly minted badges: golden eagles of his own design, along with an extravagant diamond-encrusted eagle for the commander Washington. As the historian Minor Myers Jr. has demonstrated, the novelty of L'Enfant's badges, coupled with news that French officers now wore them with pride, exhilarated the Cincinnati and put an end to all talk of dissolution.[83]

By the palliative measures adopted at the meeting of 1784, and by the members' self-disciplined determination to wear their new badges only on days of convention or commemoration, the Cincinnati assuaged much of its opposition.[84] The peril of an American military nobility passed. But throughout the Confederation period, the Cincinnati remained a thorn in the side of the most stridently republican members of Congress. In part, the Cincinnati continued to provoke antagonism because it continued to

Membership certificate of the Society of the Cincinnati, featuring the eagle and other emblems. Library of Congress, Prints and Photographs Division, pga 01184.

accumulate elaborate artifacts of membership: diplomas, certificates, booklets, even fine imported porcelain. "If you should be in want of a new set of china," wrote the congressman and Cincinnati Henry Lee to George Washington in July 1786, "it is in my power to procure a very gentell set, table & tea. What renders this china doubly valuable & handsome is the order of the eagle engraved on it, in honor of the Cincinnati. It has upwards of 306 pieces, and is offered at the prime cost, 150 dollars."[85] To match these conspicuous material accoutrements, the Cincinnati also continued to institute pomp and showy ritual. One day after Lee offered to outfit his commander with the most fashionable and patriotic chinaware, he joined the New York Society of the Cincinnati to celebrate the anniversary of independence. After visiting Congress to offer congratulations on this occasion, the Cincinnati partook in an elaborate investiture ceremony, patterned after those of European orders, in which the members gathered round an elevated and fringed "Chair of State," a throne of sorts, fabricated by Baron von Steuben. Writing to Elbridge Gerry, the Massachusetts congressman Rufus King reported that many of Gerry's fears had come to pass: "*The Cincinnati* are in the highest prosperity—they . . . of course draw the Huzzas and admiration of the Multitude . . . I was witness to the degredation of Government in seeing them rec[eive]d."[86]

That King perceived the Cincinnati's Fourth of July celebration as a degradation of government illuminates both the extraordinary power that he ascribed to public ceremony and the remarkable animosity and distrust that had arisen between republican congressmen and the officer corps. Notably, this acrimony never erupted in dramatic conflict. The mutinies of 1781 and 1783 were put down with little incident, and the soldiers who marched on the Pennsylvania State House in the summer of '83 did not set out to provoke Congress. In part the limits of continental mutiny attest to the patriotic sacrifice of the American soldiery: the army willingly endured extraordinary hardship for the sake of independence. In part those limits attest to the constitutional debility of Congress: its maladministration resulted not from indifference or cruelty, but rather from the weaknesses of a decentralized confederation. But precisely because the Continental Army chose to persevere rather than to revolt, precisely because little purpose could have been served by rising against a people's Congress, the United States' civil and military officers were compelled to hammer out their uneasy relationship through the course of their existence. For this reason, their material artifacts and ceremonies bore all the more significance. Through medals, toasts, badges, and banqueting, Congress and the army asserted their respective places in the new republic.

8

Naked and Unadorned

On November 16, 1779, the New Jersey congressmen Nathaniel Scudder penned a ruminative letter to Richard Henry Lee. "Our Life is a strange Kind of checquered Work," Scudder declared. "[O]ne day we rejoice, on another we lament . . . Indeed the same Day often exhibits a Medley of Mourning and Festivity, of Joy & Lamentation." A recent afternoon of discordant public observances—"the Day after we received the melancholly Confirmation of the Repulse of the allied Armies at Savannah"—brought Scudder to these reflections:

> On that Day the President of this State was elected and proclaimed, and on that Day the Funeral of our Friend & fellow laborer Mr. Hewes of North Carolina was attended with the usual mournfull Formalities. About 12 o'Clock the President of the State, Mr. Reed, was proclaimed from the Court House Steps, and a Feu de Joy fired on the Occasion; after which there was a Procession to & Collation at the City Tavern, the Bells chyming joyously &c. &c. About 4 o'Clock the funeral Procession of the Honble Mr. Hewes began, the Same Bells ringing muffled; and as we proceeded down Market-Street we had a fine View of the continental Colours displayed on Market Street Wharf in Honor

to the President. When we arrived at Christ's Church we were entertained with the usual Service, and a very solemn funeral Anthem, after which the Body was interred. Scarce had the Attendants reached their Homes, before the Bells again unmuffled resumed their festive Sounds, with firings as usual, and the Evening closed with a grand Serenade at the governor's Door. Sic eminet; & sic transit gloria Mundi.[1]

Scudder's letter gives words to the emotional dissonance that afflicted Philadelphians at times during the war. Here, all at once, was a rebel capital aggrieved by the failure of its army, a state political party exuberant in the triumph of its candidate, and a revolutionary assembly despondent at the death of one of its members. Here, consequently, was a vertigo of sorrow and jubilation. From "mournfull formalities" to "grand Serenade," from *feu-de-joie* to "solemn funeral Anthem" and back to "festive Sounds," public sentiment lurched forcefully at the turn of events and by the pull of ceremony and symbol.

Scudder's contemplation of the fleeting glory of the world offers an apt metaphor of the situation in which Congress found itself in the latter years of the war. At the time that Scudder wrote to Lee, the confederation remained incomplete, the continental currency tottered on the brink of collapse, rising food and fuel prices strained the American economy, and the U.S. army marched hungrily and poorly clothed toward what would be remembered as the coldest winter encampment of the Revolution. All of these circumstances contributed to the steady decline of Congress's authority and reputation, such that by the early 1780s it sat as but a cipher of the union.

This chapter investigates Congress's diminishing efforts to craft material artifacts and ceremonies for the United States in the final years of the war. It explores Philadelphians' use of street theater and folk protest to express their grievances with the economy and their dismay at the progress of Revolution. It also charts the activities of other institutions—most particularly the French embassy but also the army and the states—which rose to organize festivity and civic entertainment for the American confederation during the period of Congress's decline. In the late 1770s and early 1780s, an impoverished Congress seized what opportunities it could to promote a national identity for the United States. When the depreciation of the continental dollar necessitated the manufacture of fresh bills, Congress invited Francis Hopkinson to invent new patriotic designs. That same depreciation, however, drove prices skyward and strained Congress's relationship with the inhabitants of Philadelphia.

Frustrated by economic hardship, local radicals seized on the treason of Benedict Arnold as an opportunity to mobilize townsfolk against greedy and avaricious behaviors. In the process, they made a point to reproach Congress for failing to rein in the abusive general when it had the chance.

Ultimately, the failure of the continental currency prevented Congress from commemorating the Revolution and celebrating the United States in print and the fine arts, as some hoped Congress would do. It greatly dampened, too, Congress's enthusiasm for festive banquets and republican pageantry. Once a bastion of virtuous ceremony, Congress yielded festivities at the end of the war to the exultant people out of doors and to the lavish French ministry. At last in 1783, Congress departed Philadelphia in a huff, not because it had been insulted, but worse, because it had been ignored. As this chapter makes apparent, the political and ceremonial culture of the late Revolutionary period, was, to borrow Nathaniel Scudder's phrase, "a strange kind of checquered work": checkered with desperate political crimination and abuse, checkered with contrasting visions of virtue and public service, checkered by a popular exuberance that far exceeded Congress's ability to give it full expression, and checkered, ultimately, by an enfeebled Congress's inability to remedy the confederation's most pressing ills.

"Labours of Fancy"

The continental currency that Benjamin Franklin so thoughtfully designed in the summer of 1775 passed through Congress's hands at an alarming rate. Within a year, Congress had printed more than twenty-million dollars. Over time, the emission of such large sums worked a tremendous depreciation, driving up prices and fueling speculation in foodstuffs and other commodities. To generate revenue in support of the continental dollar, Congress implemented a variety of schemes. It borrowed vast quantities of money from France, it sold interest-bearing certificates similar to bonds, it called on the states to levy taxes, it authorized privateering against British merchant vessels, it even launched a lottery for the inhabitants of the United States. None of these measures kept pace with the burdensome expense of war. As a result, Congress repeatedly determined to print more money. Between April 1778 and November 1779, Congress emitted the monumental sum of $195 million, more than quadrupling the quantity of continental paper already in circulation.[2]

These new dollars necessitated fresh emblems, in part because British counterfeiters had mastered Franklin's old designs. Once again, paper bills provided a medium by which the Continental Congress could speak directly to the hopes and anxieties of American patriots. In 1775, the invention of continental currency had enabled Congress to rally aggrieved colonists in defense of their liberties. Now, three years later, the renovation of that currency permitted Congress to assure the inhabitants of the United States that their confederation, though not yet complete, possessed a bright future. By then, Franklin had long since journeyed on a diplomatic mission to Paris. In consequence, the task of creating new currency emissions fell to the treasurer of continental loans, Francis Hopkinson. Hopkinson's paper bills are instructive, not only for the symbols of confederation that appeared on their faces, but for a bitter controversy that erupted when Hopkinson sought credit for his work. After the departures of Franklin, Adams, and Jefferson, few members of the federal government appreciated the capacity of emblems and mottoes to make impressions on the mind. Some in power seemed also to doubt whether devices, seals, and similar works of nationcraft made fit work for manly statesmen. Hopkinson's pursuit of acclaim, and the hostile response it provoked, reveal class- and gender-based resentment toward the fine arts within the Revolutionary administration. More fatal to the material culture of the union, however, proved the collapse of the continental dollar. Though artists and artisans continued to offer their services in the forging of a national identity, Congress lost the means to afford them.

A close friend of Franklin's, Hopkinson made a fitting surrogate to design the continental currency. Though he earned his living by the practice of law and held several public offices in Delaware and New Jersey, Hopkinson's heart lay in *belles lettres* and the arts. The first student to enroll at the College of Philadelphia, Hopkinson was liberally educated. He shared Franklin's scientific curiosity and he evinced too a strong interest in painting, poetry, and music. The owner of the finest harpsichord "that ever came to America," Hopkinson wrote numerous operas and psalms. He also penned allegories and satires—most famously *A Pretty Story* (1774) and "The Battle of the Kegs" (1778)—in support of the American resistance.[3] Elected to the Continental Congress in 1776, Hopkinson is most often remembered for his role in creating the United States flag. It was likely he, who as a commissioner of the naval board, proposed the stars-and-stripes adopted by Congress in 1777. But among his contemporaries, Hopkinson also earned renown for his expertise in heraldry. The American Philosophical Society and the State of New Jersey both turned to Hopkinson for assistance in making their seals. In 1780, the Continental Congress's Great Seal committee adopted Hopkinson's suggestion of a blazon striped in red and white. During the war, Hopkinson also devised seals for the Boards of Treasury and Admiralty and for U.S. ship papers.[4]

Summoning all his literary and heraldic talents, Hopkinson refashioned the continental currency to celebrate the union of states and to hearten a people weary of war. Hopkinson utilized earthy motifs to establish thematic consistency with Franklin's earlier bills. Evoking a spirit of industry reminiscent of Franklin's moral economy, Hopkinson adorned the thirty-five dollar bill with a plough and the forty-five with a hive of bees. Hopkinson likewise exhorted Americans to give thanks for divine intervention, which had carried them safely through the war thus far. The motto on his sixty-dollar bill, *Deus Regnat Exultet Terra*—"God reigns, let the earth rejoice"—promoted the same worshipful sentiment that Congress sought to cultivate on its fast and thanksgiving days.

In designing the continental currency, Hopkinson also endeavored to emblematize the American union. Whereas Franklin attuned bearers to the harmony of large and small colonies, Hopkinson pointed them to the splendor of the United States. Toward that end, Hopkinson created two original devices that have endured as symbols of nationhood. On his forty-dollar bill, Hopkinson arranged a circle of thirteen stars. After Congress adopted its flag resolution on June 14, 1777, the metaphor of constellation—"the rising Constellation" as James Lovell saw it—captured the imagination of American patriots, likely because it so aptly represented the nascent federal order: thirteen individual states, each shining in perfect sovereignty, but formed together to make a more glorious whole.[5]

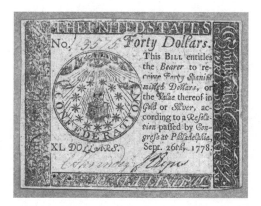

Obverse of Hopkinson's forty-dollar bill, featuring the eye of Providence and a circle of thirteen stars. Reproduced from the original held by the Department of Special Collections of the University Libraries of Notre Dame.

Hopkinson's stars and the stripes of his flag, too, made for festive metaphor and pun. On the first anniversary of the Franco-American alliance, members of Congress toasted, "May the new Constellation rise to the Zenith," and "May the American *Stripes* bring Great Britain to Reason." On the second anniversary of independence, they raised glasses to the sentiment, "May the ensuing campaign give . . . *fresh luster* to our *stars*."[6] In addition to the stars and stripes, Hopkinson employed a pyramid, comprised of thirteen steps, to represent the American republic. Unfinished at the top, the pyramid that decorated Hopkinson's fifty-dollar bill alluded to the incomplete work of confederation. Its motto *Perennis*, or "Everlasting," foretold an enduring American union.[7]

Finally, for his seventy-and eighty-dollar bills, Hopkinson selected a large, healthy tree, an emblem that presaged a stout and hearty future, much as did his everlasting pyramid. Hopkinson had employed the tree as a metaphor of American independence once before. In "A Prophecy," a political allegory written about the year 1776, Hopkinson promised readers that the American tree, "young and vigorous" would "grow and flourish and spread its branches far abroad: and the people shall dwell under the shadow of its branches, and shall become an exceeding great, powerful, and happy nation."[8] By the time it appeared on the seventy-dollar bill, Hopkinson's American tree had matured. The bill's motto, *Vim Procellarum Quadrennium Sustinuit*, observed that the tree had withstood the storm for four years. Extending this metaphor, the motto of Hopkinson's eighty-dollar bill, *Et In Secula Seculorum Florescebit*, assured bearers that the United States would flourish for ages and ages.[9]

Obverse of Hopkinson's fifty-dollar bill, featuring a thirteen-stepped pyramid, unfinished at top. Reproduced from the original held by the Department of Special Collections of the University Libraries of Notre Dame.

Here, however, was a painful irony that Hopkinson, the author of numerous sharp-barbed satires, could hardly have missed. Despite their comforting messages of fortitude and resilience, these seventy- and eighty-dollar bills themselves offered material witness to the derangement of American affairs. Only in consequence of rampant inflation and speculation had Congress been forced to print these large-denomination bills.[10] Despite their assurances of future prosperity, Hopkinson's seventy- and eighty-dollar bills bought no more in 1779 than did five or six continentals but a few years before.[11]

Notwithstanding the diminished value of the bills they adorned, Hopkinson took considerable pride in his emblems. Many months earlier, in a private letter to Benjamin Franklin, Hopkinson confessed that his literary and artistic talents were all that he had to give to the Revolution: "I have not abilities to assist our righteous cause by personal Prowess and Force of Arms, but I have done it all the service I could with my Pen, throwing in my Mite at Times in Prose and Verse, serious and satirical Essays &ca."[12] Perhaps sensible of the historical consequence of his efforts—the world, after all, would know the United States by *his* flag, devices, and seals—Hopkinson began to crave the recognition of a grateful republic. In the late spring of 1780, he launched a bid for commendation of his service. His efforts not only met with humiliation, they also provoked a heated political controversy that dragged on for weeks, embroiling numerous members of Congress and threatening a destructive schism within the Treasury Department. A careful examination of this controversy discloses a clash of opinion within government about the place of genteel arts in the Revolutionary United States. It further demonstrates how conflicting notions of masculinity and statesmanship frustrated the work of Congress and its administration. Remarkably, this controversy turned not only on the merits of Hopkinson's claim, but seemingly too on the size and shape of his body.

In May 1780, Hopkinson wrote a letter to the Board of Admiralty, whose seal he had recently designed. In that letter, he listed the numerous "ornaments" he had fashioned for the United States, including those that now appeared on the continental currency. Explaining that he had "yet made no Charge" for these handiworks, Hopkinson submitted to the board's consideration "whether a Quarter Cask of the public Wine will not be a proper & a reasonable reward for these Labours of Fancy and a suitable Encouragement to future Exertions of a like Nature."[13] Depreciation of the continental dollar had reduced Hopkinson to meager circumstances, but the fact that he begged recompense in wine rather than money, and in a modest quantity at that, suggests that what he truly sought was credit, some sort of public acknowl-edgment of the creative services he had performed for his country.[14]

Instead of praise, Hopkinson received cold poetic justice. His petition first languished in bureaucracy. The Board of Admiralty forwarded it to the congressional president Samuel Huntington, who, either incognizant of or indifferent to Hopkinson's true purpose, mechanically passed it along for payment to the Board of Treasury. That board treated Hopkinson's petition like any other account payable. Per the mandate of a cash-strapped Congress, it demanded an itemized bill for Hopkinson's services. Either in a spirit of charade, or perhaps in earnest expectation that a monetary payment would validate him as the genius behind the confederation's symbols and emblems, Hopkinson obliged, assigning monetary values for his "sundry Drawings & Devices": £9 for the naval flag, £7 for the currency designs, £3 for the Treasury seal, and so forth. Only then did the Chamber of Accounts certify that Hopkinson's claim was "reasonable and ought to be paid." The auditor-general agreed and presented Hopkinson's charges for allowance.[15]

The Board of Treasury, however, firmly resisted Hopkinson's claims. Noting that Hopkinson had produced no vouchers or receipts for his work, the board remanded Hopkinson's account to the auditor general. When the account came back a second time, the board tabled it, refusing to take any action at all. Outraged by this dilatory conduct, Hopkinson accused the board of "a design to injure" him. He then submitted a formal complaint, charging the board with negligence, obstruction of office, and fraud. At some point in the affair, the Treasury Board member Ezekiel Forman shut an office door in Hopkinson's face. What began as a bid for his countrymen's appreciation thus billowed into a contentious matter of honor. To resolve the dispute, Congress was forced to appoint an investigatory committee. Condemning the "Demon of Discord" that prevented a ready adjustment of Hopkinson's account and decrying the "great Jealousies & Animosities" that had arisen within the Treasury, the committee recommended that three members of the board be dismissed and the entire department restructured. Before Congress could act on that recommendation, and as if to add injury to insult, the board resolved that Hopkinson's claim should be denied. In the meantime, Hopkinson and Forman both embarrassedly resigned their posts.[16]

This episode illustrates not merely the cantankerousness and administra-tive inefficiencies that baffled Congress in the early 1780s, but more importantly the contradictory attitudes toward gender, public service, and genteel masculinity that inhibited the creation of a material and ceremonial culture for the United States. Not content to reject Hopkinson's claim on the technicality that he failed to produce vouchers for his work—as "Printers [and] Tradesmen" were required to do—the board proffered three additional reasons for denying payment: first, that "Francis Hopkinson was not the only person consulted on those exhibitions of Fancy, and therefore cannot claim the sole merit of them"; second, that "the public is entitled to these little assistances given by Gentlemen who enjoy a very considerable Salary under Congress without Fee or further reward"; and finally, that Hopkinson did not actually expect to be paid, as the board had heard it, but rather considered the wine "a compliment due him for these works of Fancy."[17]

The language of this dispute and its gendered connotations indicate that matters of masculinity were at play. Hopkinson was the first to describe his designs as "Labours of Fancy," in a letter to the Board of Admiralty. In its most common eighteenth-century usage, the word "fancy" suggested whim or imagination. Hopkinson's use of that word to describe his devices and seals was somewhat esoteric; nowhere else in the *Letters* or *Journals* of Congress is "fancy" employed in a comparable manner. Yet other parties to Hopkinson's dispute seized on the term and invoked it repeatedly throughout the lengthy quarrel. During one committee hearing, for example, the board member John Gibson interrogated Treasurer Michael Hillegas, "Did you ever charge for any of these works of fancy? . . . Did you ever do any labours of fancy for the public?"[18] As employed in this context, "fancy" implied artistic inventiveness. It signified cerebral, rather than physical labor, and it suggested a fastidious attention to fine-grain details. It thus conveyed a sense of delicateness.

When paired with "work," the term "fancy" explicitly denoted a kind of labor traditionally associated with women. The *Oxford English Dictionary* defines "fancy work" as "ornamental, as opposed to plain work, *esp.* in needlework, crochet, knitting or the like," and it dates such usage to the early 1800s. In fact, "fancy work" had developed its association with women's needlecraft some decades before, as evident in an advertisement for Hannah Barker's "genteel Day-School," published in the *Pennsylvania Packet* in February 1783, nearly contemporaneously with Hopkinson's case: "For the Instruction of Twelve Young Ladies . . . Tambour, Embroidery, every kind of Needle and Fancy Work, Lace making, etc."[19] By deeming the fabrication of flags, seals, and devices "fancy work," Hopkinson self-deprecatingly, and his detractors more malignantly, suggested that such efforts were not manly. In his letter to Franklin, Hopkinson himself apologetically juxtaposed his "prose and verse" against "personal prowess" and the more vigorous "force of arms." His request to be paid in wine coupled whimsical compensation with whimsical, and womanly, work.

In rejecting Hopkinson's claim, the Board of Treasury both affirmed and negated these gender preconceptions. On the one hand, the board demanded, rhetorically, "Do not [the Treasury commissioners] require Certificates and Vouchers from Printers, Tradesmen, &C to establish their Charges? . . . Why then are these Requisites dispensed with in the Honourable Mr. Hopkinson's case?" At first blush, this demand appears to be a legitimate objection grounded in concern for class equity and administrative uniformity. But the board's demand appears far more pointed and insinuative when viewed in light of the small physical stature for which Hopkinson was often ridiculed. Throughout Hopkinson's life, friends and acquaintances commented on his size. They also drew a notable linkage between Hopkinson's diminutive frame and his predilection for the arts. John Adams, for example, ruthlessly caricatured Hopkinson as "one of your pretty little, curious, ingenious Men. His Head is not bigger, than a large Apple . . . I have not met with any Thing in natural History much more amusing and entertaining, than his personal Appearance." Adams spoke of "your pretty little, curious, ingenious Men," as if they were a type, as if daintiness and creativity went commonly hand in hand. Political foes likewise derisively associated Hopkinson's artistry with his physique. One rival disparaged Hopkinson as a "pretty, little, musical, poetical, witling." He crowed that Hopkinson had lost a judicial appointment to "a gentleman of *manly figure* and *approved abilities*" (italics in original).[20] Feminizing the "pretty little" Hopkinson, this opponent expressly distinguished the "fancy work" of musicians and poets from the "approved abilities" of "manly figures." In the same manner, the Board of Treasury denigrated Hopkinson's heraldic efforts, characterizing them as but "little assistances." Understood in this way, and read in the context of door-slamming hostility, the board's insistence that "the Honourable Mr. Hopkinson" be held to the same standard as "Printers [and] Tradesmen" seems rather sneering. The "Honourable" reads sarcastically; it imputes aristocratic effeteness in contrast to the egalitarian, shirt-sleeve masculinity of manual laborers. The board thus subtly but invidiously distinguished Hopkinson's fancy work from the journeyman's virile toil.

On the other hand, the board characterized Hopkinson's fancy work as an obligation to be fulfilled by "gentlemen" officeholders. It scorned the suggestion that a public servant, under salary, should be rewarded or even complimented for such efforts. It censured Hopkinson, too, for taking more credit than was his due. Other persons, the board observed, had contributed to the seals and devices of the United States. The board thus intimated that this "fancy work," though minute, exquisite, even womanly in nature, was the

This portrait of Francis Hopkinson, sitting at his writing table, obscures the diminutive physical stature that so unsettled Hopkinson's contemporaries. *Francis Hopkinson*, Robert Edge Pine. Courtesy the Atwater Kent Museum of Philadelphia, the Historical Society of Pennsylvania Collection.

rightful duty of selfless statesmen. Uncompensated, uncomplimented, these labors of fancy were, properly understood, labors of republican virtue.

That Hopkinson's simple plea for recognition could consume months of Treasury Department energy, spawn a congressional investigation, and bring about the huffy resignations of two civil officials suggests just how contentious the making of a national material and ceremonial culture could be. Some members of Congress believed that emblems and rituals were frivolous and perhaps even effeminate concerns, while others considered them essential projects for the making of a sovereign nation. Congress never reconciled these incongruous beliefs. Indeed, it never had to, for the precipitous collapse of the continental currency prevented Congress from pursuing new opportunities to craft symbols of the American confederation. By the fall of 1779, the dollar had plummeted to one-twentieth of its original value.[21] In September, in a desperate bid to prop its currency, Congress announced that under no circumstances would it emit more than $200 million. Still, depreciation continued apace. Having all but exhausted the United States' foreign and domestic credit, Congress essentially bankrupted the union. In March 1780, after months of deliberation, Congress took the drastic measure of repudiating its debt. Revaluing the dollar at one-fortieth its original worth, Congress can-celled nearly two hundred million dollars in outstanding obligations.[22]

Never particularly esteemed, the continental currency now fell into base contempt. The Quaker loyalist Anne Rawle revolted at the "Dirty stuff." The Connecticut congressman Oliver Wolcott declared that it was fit "for little Else but to Make the Tail of a Paper Kite." The pseudonymous editorialist "Hard Money" denounced it as "rag-born" and "paper wasted."[23] By the spring of 1781, the continental dollar had dropped out of circulation entirely. Phila-delphia sailors marked its collapse by parading through the city with old bills stuffed in their hatbands and wrapped around the necks of their dogs.[24]

The decline of the dollar, which made Francis Hopkinson's currency designs possible, prevented Congress from pursuing at least three other "fancy works" that would have promoted a civic identity for the United States. In July 1779, Pierre Eugène Du Simitière—the Swiss artist who had con-sulted with Franklin, Adams, and Jefferson on a design for the Great Seal in 1776—proposed to write a natural and civil history of the United States. Congress, however, had so far depleted its treasury that it could not finance the work.[25] Subsequently, in 1781 or 1782, Du Simitière offered to compile a medallic history: a "Work intended to illustrate the Revolution in North America by Medals, Seals, Coins, Devices, Statues, monuments, Badges, &c." (Here was an idea that John Adams would have surely embraced.) But again, Congress possessed no means to contract it.[26] As Du Simitière bitterly com-plained, "[O]ur paper currency is knock'd in the head . . . it plays hell with everybody except those that have species [*sic*]."[27]

Lack of money likewise compelled Congress to deny funding for an Eng-lish-language Bible. The Revolutionary War disrupted the importation of Bibles from England and Ireland, as Congress was well aware.[28] To remedy this problem, the Philadelphia printer Robert Aitken offered to publish the Old and New Testaments. Insofar as English law licensed only the King's Printers and the universities at Oxford and Cambridge to print English-language editions of the Bible, Aitken's project offered Congress another op-portunity to assert the independence of the United States. In soliciting congressional aid, Aitken appealed to all manner of national and sovereign pride. "[E]very well regulated government in Christendom," Aitken asserted, had published the Holy Bible. "[T]he Monarchs of Europe," he observed, "have hitherto deemed the Sacred Scripture worthy of the Royal Patronage." Eager to complete this project before the conclusion of hostilities reopened American ports to British Bibles, Aitken even offered to extend credit to the United States, but Congress simply could not entertain the expense. Unable to provide monetary assistance, Congress could do nothing more than *endorse* Aitken's Bible. In September 1782, it commended his American Scripture in "the interest of religion, as well as an instance of the progress of the arts in this country."[29]

The Art of Treason

In 1779–80, the Continental Congress fell rapidly from the public's esteem. Long enervated by administrative inefficiencies, procedural impediments, and absenteeism, Congress often proved unequal to the demands of the war. Its failure to provision the army, most notoriously during the winter encampments at Valley Forge and Morristown, provoked resentment among the ranks. Its embroilment in partisan feuding, most scandalously in the dispute between Silas Deane and Arthur Lee, engendered widespread contempt. Now, its inability to curb rampant inflation and to regulate prices exacerbated popular scorn. Disheartened by the progress of war and aggrieved by a spiraling economy, the people out of doors articulated their grievances by demonstrating in the streets.[30]

Two of the more sensational episodes of revolutionary protest took place in Philadelphia in late September 1780. On the twenty-seventh of that month, news of Benedict Arnold's treason reached the capital city. The following evening, a crowd of townspeople constructed an effigy of the traitorous general and paraded him about the streets, ultimately hanging their papier-mâché villain on a gallows. Had the commotion ended there, we might look back on this event as a warrantable expression of Philadelphians' animosity toward Arnold, the duplicitous turncoat who bargained for the surrender of West Point. Treason was a particularly vexing problem in Philadelphia, where pacifist and loyalist sentiment remained strong throughout the war and where Lord Howe had hoisted the Union Flag for many months. As the highest ranking American, military or civil, to cross the lines, Benedict Arnold epitomized the faithlessness of loyalists and fence-sitting opportunists. His arrest afforded Philadelphia patriots an occasion to vent long-simmering animosities, as they did on the night of the twenty-eighth.

But the commotion did not end there. Charles Willson Peale, an active member of Philadelphia's radical Constitutionalist Society, insisted that the apostate Arnold be shamed again, in much more dramatic fashion. Over the next two days, Peale—sometimes remembered as the "artist of the Revolution"—designed and supervised the construction of an elaborate likeness of Arnold. Peale first crafted a life-size representation featuring two, Janus-like faces that turned continuously. Peale dressed his Arnold in military uniform, seated him in a cart ("emblematical of his usual position on account of his wounded leg"), and placed in his hands two mementos of deceit: a mask and a letter from Beelzebub. Taking his inspiration from colonial Pope Day processions, Peale then constructed a mannequin of the devil seducing Arnold with a purse of gold. (One observer described it "the most grotesque figure I ever beheld.") Finally, at the head of the cart, Peale hung a lantern, whose lengthy, illuminated inscription decried Arnold's "HIGH TREASON" and gave thanks for the "interposition of bounteous Providence" by which his plot had been discovered. Peale finished his handiwork on Saturday, September 30, and that evening Arnold was for the second time paraded in Philadelphia. A line of Continental officers, a guard of the city militia whose members all carried candles in the end of their muskets, and "Sundry Gentlemen" escorted Arnold and the devil, while a band of drums and fifes played the rogue's march. According to the *Pennsylvania Packet*, "a numerous concourse of people" followed, and "after expressing their abhorrence of the Treason and the Traitor, committed him

A Representation of the Figures Exhibited and Paraded through the Streets of Philadelphia, on Saturday, the 30th of September 1780 (Philadelphia, 1780). Library of Congress, Rare Book and Special Collections Division, rbpe 1460020a.

to the flames, and left both the effigy and the original to sink into ashes and oblivion."[31]

This agitation cannot be comprehended solely by reference to Arnold's treason. On the contrary, Peale's determination to cart Arnold a second time, and the townspeople's eagerness to restage a ritual they had enacted only two nights before, hint toward much deeper agendas than the mere condemnation of a traitor. Viewed in the context of postoccupation Philadelphia's social and economic turmoil, the second Arnold parade may be seen as an expression of numerous fervent political sentiments, each related to, but distinct from, Arnold's treachery. Peale's effigy took shape simultaneously as a manifestation of the artist's personal ill will toward Arnold, as yet another salvo in an ongoing jurisdictional conflict between Pennsylvania and the Continental Congress, as the last gasp of Philadelphia's faltering Constitutionalist faction, and perhaps above all else, as one of several popular demonstrations against high prices and economic distress.

Two years earlier, in the spring of 1778, even as Howe's officers had begun to make arrangements for their fanciful Meschianza, Benedict Arnold visited General Washington and his troops at Valley Forge. Arnold, still severely hobbled by the leg wound he received at Saratoga, arrived at camp at the very height of his popularity. Washington quickly honored him with an appointment as military governor of Philadelphia, pending the British evacuation. On June 19, one day after Henry Clinton's forces withdrew, Arnold entered the city, where he received a hero's welcome, particularly among triumphant Whigs eager to reassert their presence in Philadelphia. James Duane of New York quipped that the city's ladies were as fascinated with and "perplexed" by Arnold's injured leg as the fictional *Tristram Shandy*'s Widow Wadman had been with Uncle Toby's injured groin.[32]

Philadelphia's love affair with Arnold did not last long. As both the Continental Congress and the Pennsylvania government attempted to reestablish their authority in Philadelphia, a conflict quickly arose, pitting Arnold against Charles Willson Peale. After the British evacuation, Pennsylvania's Supreme Executive Council deputized Peale to confiscate the property and effects of loyalists who fled with the British army. Meanwhile, General Washington, acting on instructions from Congress, issued a conflicting order to Arnold: that he prevent the removal or sale "of any goods, wares, or merchandise" in the city. Arnold initially threatened to bar citizens, Peale included, from returning to Philadelphia until all such items could be secure. Only after Peale protested at Washington's headquarters did Arnold relent, but the antagonism did not cease. Washington further ordered Arnold to "give security to individuals of every class and description," that is, to protect loyalist citizens from Whigs bent on vengeance. When Peale attempted to evict the loyalist Grace Growden Galloway—wife of the one-time congressman and more recent superintendent of occupied Philadelphia, Joseph Galloway—from her home, Arnold ordered a guard to protect her.[33]

The flap with Peale augured larger controversies to come. In October, Arnold infringed on Pennsylvania authority and violated an explicit congressional order by directing his aide to issue the suspected loyalist Hannah Levy a pass to British New York. About the same time, Arnold embroiled himself in an admiralty case that hinged on the sticky matter of Congress's authority over Pennsylvania.[34] Both matters highlighted a developing jurisdictional tension between Congress and the commonwealth. Yet Arnold's difficulties did not arise solely from those disputes. Local officials came increasingly to suspect Arnold of abusing his position for personal emolument. Allegations abounded that Arnold "made considerable purchases for his own benefit" after closing Philadelphia's stores and shops.[35] In October 1778, Arnold fueled these suspicions by commissioning army wagons to retrieve a cargo of his privately owned goods from New Jersey, in flagrant contradiction of a Pennsylvania council resolve.[36] Arnold's conduct smacked of venality and aligned him, in the opinion of his detractors, with those who sought to make money even at the sake of the commonweal.

Arnold's haughty manner of living, which affronted both the moral economy and the communal sensibilities of local patriots, gave credence to such opinions. Shortly after arriving in Philadelphia, Arnold took residence in the former Penn mansion, where General Howe had lived during the occupation, leaving city folk to wonder whether they had traded one *bon vivant* for another. Arnold hired a number of servants, traveled about town in a lavish chariot, and hosted extravagant parties. At a time when Pennsylvania radicals took pains to eradicate loyalists from their society, Arnold hosted "not only Tory ladies but the wives and daughters of persons proscribed by the state and now with the enemy in New York," as the council president Joseph Reed exasperatedly proclaimed. In the late fall Arnold began to court one such woman, the Meschianza socialite Margaret Shippen. In the meantime, Arnold earned a galling reputation for mistreating the Philadelphia militia under his command, including the son of the radical council secretary Timothy Matlack, who was made to fetch a barber for Arnold's aide.[37] By January 1779, Pennsylvania leaders had lost patience with the commandant. On the twenty-sixth of that month, the council president Joseph Reed lodged a formal complaint with Congress. In early February the council took its grievances public, publishing eight allegations against Arnold in the *Pennsyl-vania Packet* and printing them for distribution, as well, in handbill form. Indignant, Arnold demanded a congressional investigation or court-martial to clear his name.[38]

By this time, Arnold had lost much of his luster in the eyes of Congress. His disregard of the congressional order against passes to New York might have been forgiven easily enough, but more problematic was his conspicuous high living. By Arnold's sufferance, American officers had begun to sponsor plays and dramatic performances, a transgression that prompted more aus-tere-minded congressmen to redouble their campaign against the theater.[39] Still, Congress did not wish to prosecute Arnold. An investigation would divert congressional energy from more pressing business. The mere prospect of such an inquest had already dredged up old, petty grievances between Pennsylvania officials and members of Congress.[40] Many congressmen pre-sumably shared the New York delegate Francis Lewis's fear that high-run-ning animosities between Arnold and the council would catalyze the formation of "parties in the Congress" and "injure the public Weal." Already entangled in a protracted, factional dispute between the French commis-sioners Silas Deane and Arthur Lee, members of Congress winced at the prospect of further acrimony. For weeks the delegates dragged their feet. Only at the insistence of an embittered Pennsylvania council did Congress at last order Washington to court-martial Arnold on a number of charges.[41]

Arnold's court-martial waited almost a year for adjudication. In the in-terim, the Pennsylvania government struggled to contend with stupendous wartime inflation. Through 1779–80, the assembly passed a series of acts for the purpose of suppressing prices. Meanwhile, the council and its backers among the Pennsylvania Constitutionalist faction blamed runaway prices on unscrupulous speculators and merchants who monopolized goods. By these strategies, Pennsylvania leaders for a time deflected popular acrimony. Ulti-mately though, the administration failed to curb inflation or to fix prices. Protracted economic hardship eroded the Constitutionalists' political credi-bility. Under the weight of a grievous economy, the radical Constitutionalist order, which had prevailed in Pennsylvania politics since the abrogation of the old colonial charter, began to collapse. When Peale and his collaborators determined to parade Arnold a second time, they did so in dim prospect of salvaging their hold on government. Personal grudges harbored by Peale and Matlack against Arnold, and lingering discord between Pennsylvania and Congress provoked their spleen, but the chance to mobilize voters and pre-serve their hold on government moved them to action.

For more than two years Philadelphians suffered as the prices of goods and foodstuffs rose dramatically, if unevenly.[42] In January 1779, their frustration turned to violence when a large crowd of sailors rioted in demand of higher pay, dispersing only after General Arnold dispatched troops.[43] Political leaders were quick to assign blame for the commonwealth's financial emergency. Most Republicans—moderates such as Robert Morris, Benjamin Rush, and James Wilson, who opposed Pennsylvania's liberal constitution—insisted that inflation resulted from the deluge of paper money pouring from congressional and state presses. Constitutionalists, on the other hand, whose ranks included men such as Thomas Paine, James Cannon, Charles Willson Peale, and Timothy Matlack, instead pointed to the avarice of wealthy merchants.[44] Through the spring, Constitutionalists touted a moral economy of plain dealing and honest prices. Shortly after the sailors' riot, the council issued a ban on the monopolistic practices of engrossing and forestalling. In April, the assembly empowered local justices to fix bread prices as well. In May, a mass meeting of Philadelphians appointed a committee to regulate prices and to investigate the business dealings of Robert Morris, who was suspected of selling flour to the French navy at prices higher than established.[45]

Though some tradesmen opposed price controls and balked at what they perceived to be the undervaluation of their goods, many of the city's poor continued to lay blame for their economic woes at the feet of merchants and traders. Like the nonimportation and nonconsumption campaigns of the late 1760s and early 1770s, price control could only succeed if all members of the community adhered to the established price structure.[46] Now, as during those earlier trade boycotts, the people out of doors resorted to ostracization and the threat of violence to coerce compliance. Hostilities erupted in October 1779 when a crowd of militia who supported price controls clashed with Republican opponents holed up in the home of James Wilson. In the ensuing melee, which came to be known as the Fort Wilson Riot, numerous persons were wounded and at least six killed before the city cavalry arrived to disperse the crowd. Congressman Henry Laurens, fearing that a revolution would break out within the Revolution, cautioned, "We are at this moment on a precipice, and what I have long dreaded and often intimated to my friends, seems to be breaking forth—a convulsion among the people."[47]

At this turbulent moment, Benedict Arnold rekindled his feud with Pennsylvania authorities. Many Philadelphians still resented their former commandant for having lived so opulently in a period of want, for having abused his office for profit, and for having ordered soldiers to break up price-control demonstrations on at least two occasions. In the aftermath of the Fort Wilson clash, as protestors gathered at the courthouse and jail in support of imprisoned militiamen, a "Mob of Lawless Ruffians" assaulted Arnold in the streets. On October 6, Arnold demanded that Congress appoint him a guard, claiming there was "no protection to be expected from the Authority of the State for an honest man." Congress by this time had grown weary of Arnold's quarrel with local officials and rejected his request, scolding him for insulting Pennsylvania authorities and referring him, half-mockingly it would seem, to the Supreme Executive Council.[48]

In that October's elections, which took place in the wake of the Fort Wilson unrest, Constitutionalists again carried the assembly, but in coming months they struggled mightily to ameliorate Pennsylvania's financial crisis. In the spring of 1780, the Constitutionalist Thomas Paine devised a voluntary subscription fund to help defray the costs of war, but it floundered for lack of subscribers. About the same time, price-control advocates called for a convention of delegates from New England, the middle states, and the Chesapeake to regulate the sale of commodities, but this plan also proved abortive as representatives from New York and Virginia failed to attend. In March, the Continental Congress's decision to devalue the continental currency forced Pennsylvania authorities to cancel that medium as legal tender. Increasingly, Philadelphia's laboring poor came to realize that the Constitutionalists' price-control measures had failed to rein in inflation. Through the spring and summer of 1780, Constitutionalists in the Pennsylvania assembly and council increasingly adopted the fiscal policies of their Republican foes, authorizing the export of flour and permitting market behaviors formerly denounced as grasping and acquisitive. In May, the Constitutionalists attempted to divert popular attention from the collapse of price control and win public support by launching a desperate campaign against Tories. By summer's end it was apparent that the party had lost its sense of purpose. Republicans, who had fought since the ratification of the Pennsylvania constitution to regain control over the state government, cautiously hoped for a strong showing in the October elections.[49] Less than two weeks before the polls opened, Philadelphians got wind of Arnold's treason. This news offered Constitutionalists a glimmer of hope.

In Congress, the response to Arnold's treason was measured. Several months earlier, the long-awaited court-martial had convicted Arnold on two counts: permitting entry of a vessel having sailed from an enemy port and appropriating public wagons for private use.[50] At that time, Congress affirmed the court's decision and ordered fifty copies printed and circulated. In so doing, Congress endeavored to mollify the Pennsylvania officials who had brought charges against Arnold. Now matters stood differently: Arnold's disloyalty had been exposed. To celebrate his capture would be to acknowledge a deeply embarrassing betrayal by a high-ranking and once celebrated officer. Instead, Congress quietly directed the Board of War to erase Arnold's name from the register of United States army officers. It rewarded the soldiers who captured John André, Arnold's co-conspirator, with silver medals and pensions for life. And in that year's annual thanksgiving proclamation, Congress listed among its reasons for rejoicing that the "Father of all mercies" had rescued "our Commander in Chief and the army from imminent dangers, at the moment when treason was ripened for execution." Beyond this, Congress took little official notice of Arnold's defection.[51]

Out in the streets, the people of Philadelphia made much greater ado. The journal of the Quaker Samuel Rowland Fisher describes the first parading of Arnold most fully: "Last Evening we were alarmed with the noise of Drums & Fifes & much shouting by the Mob in the Street . . . This morning we're informed the Mob had an Effigy of Arnold hanging on a Gallows, the Body of which was made of paper hollow & illuminated & an inscription in large letters thereon, which they conveyed thro' many parts of the City."[52] This apparently spontaneous event suggests that many townspeople and militiamen harbored a genuine enmity toward their former governor, either for his abuse of office, for his treason, or for both.

Charles Willson Peale's determination to parade Arnold in effigy a *second* time suggests that he and fellow Constitutionalists not only shared the crowd's animus for Arnold, but also saw in his treason an opportunity to promote agendas both personal and widely political. For Peale, designing a humiliating effigy of the man who once wronged him offered the reward of comeuppance. For councilmen who had pressed charges against Arnold before a disinclined Congress, the parade served a double-edged purpose: on the one hand, it provided a cathartic moment in which patriots in and out of Congress could unite in detestation of the villainous traitor. On the other, it vindicated those members of the Executive Council who had long, unavailingly protested Arnold's faithlessness. The second parade afforded an opportunity for self-congratulations and thinly veiled gloating in the face of an embarrassed Congress.

Beneath the radicals' glee, however, lurked an element of despair. The second Arnold parade also, and perhaps most significantly, functioned as a last-ditch bid for popular support by Pennsylvania's flailing Constitutionalist faction. On the eve of the annual election, radical leaders saw an opportunity to once again herald the sort of moral economy that underscored their failed price-control efforts. Arnold had long embodied the avarice of forestallers and monopolizers; he now too stood for the untrustworthiness of those "Tories," "Suspicious Characters," and other public enemies against whom the Constitutionalists had recently launched a crusade. Immediately after word broke of Arnold's plot to sell West Point, the Executive Council ordered a search of his papers and effects. Within the week, the *Pennsylvania Gazette* reported evidence of "such a scene of baseness and prostitution of office and character, as it is hoped this new world cannot parallel." Local authorities seized Arnold's estate as well as his ornate chariot and ordered his "Tory" wife to leave Pennsylvania. To symbolize Arnold's depravity and greed, Peale adorned his effigy with three evocative props not witnessed in the first parade: the Devil, the mask, and the purse. Contemporary observers fixated on the purse. The *Packet* explained it was a "thirst for gold" that inspired Arnold's crimes. The New Jersey congressman William Churchill Houston speculated that Arnold committed treason in hope of securing "Money from the Enemy." "His dissipated and expensive Course of Living in this City," Houston wrote, "has so involved and impoverished him that money was probably become very necessary to him."[53]

Writing in his journal, Samuel Fischer explained that the second Arnold parade "appear'd not as a frolick of the lowest sort of people but as the Act of some of the present Rulers here . . . They think [Arnold's treason] a matter of consequence to them . . . it chafes them much."[54] Arnold's treason chafed Pennsylvania authorities because their warnings against him had gone unheeded. Demonizing the general allowed them to vent their frustrations. By appropriating popular modes of expression, the parade and effigy, Peale and fellow radicals spoke in the compelling vernacular of folk ritual. They endeavored to sway broad segments of the voting population. Congressman Benjamin Huntington described the crowd that witnessed the second parade as "the Greatest Concourse of People I ever Saw"; William Churchill Houston estimated that "thousands of Spectatours" bore witness to the event.[55] Given Pennsylvania's liberal polling requirements—all taxpaying males over twenty-one could cast a ballot—we may reasonably conclude that a large number of parade spectators were eligible to vote in the upcoming election. In the end, however, Constitutionalists could not sustain their grip on Pennsylvania politics. Their efforts to trumpet Arnold's greed and thereby to preserve an economy founded on virtue and self-sacrifice did not sway voters. Less than two weeks after Peale re-paraded Arnold, Pennsylvanians turned Constitutionalist incumbents out of office in favor of fiscal modernizers such as Robert

Morris. In Philadelphia, an erstwhile radical stronghold, Republicans enjoyed a three-to-one margin of victory. Not for four more years would the Constitutionalists mount a significant challenge to the Republican administration.[56]

"[T]o strain every nerve of Finance"

By the time that Philadelphians carted their two Arnold effigies about town, the power and prestige of the Continental Congress had both greatly diminished. Having exhausted its credit, Congress no longer possessed the resources to finance even the modest ceremony and civic entertainment by which it had formerly acclaimed the United States. Other governments and institutions began to perform these functions: the Commonwealth of Massachusetts, for example, in its welcoming reception for the admiral Comte d'Estaing, or the Continental Army, in its grand celebration at Pluckemin for the anniversary of the Franco-American alliance. In the final years of the war, Congress managed to scrape together meager pageantry when occasion demanded, as for instance on the ratification of the Articles of Confederation in 1781. But when victory came, Congress had no choice but to leave the festivity to the triumphant army, to the well-funded French ministry, and to the jubilant people out of doors. In both the spontaneous rejoice that erupted after the British surrender at Yorktown and the ostentatious conviviality that marked the birth of the dauphin, male heir to the French throne, Congress played a conspicuously subordinate role.

For the anniversary of independence in 1780, the Continental Congress orchestrated little fanfare, but it could not permit the final ratification of the Articles of Confederation—a process that had dragged on more than three years—to pass unnoticed the following spring. To mark the occasion, Congress arranged a humble ceremony. At noon on March 1, the delegates hoisted a flag atop the state house. At that prearranged signal, Captain John Paul Jones—recently returned from distinguished naval service off the coast of England—ordered the firing of a *feu-de-joie* aboard his ship, the *Ariel*, anchored in the Delaware River. Later that day, after Congress received the congratulations of state authorities and military officers, President Samuel Huntington offered a cold buffet at his home. The firing of cannons and the pealing of bells punctuated the remainder of the afternoon; an exhibition of fireworks lit up the night. The paltriness of U.S. finance at this time is suggested by the Georgia delegate George Walton's proposal that Congress open its chambers and offer guests "a keg of biscuit in the room of cake."[57]

Bereft of funds even for the purchase of cake, the Confederation Congress assumed a diminished role in the civic festivities of the infant republic. Later that year, Cornwallis's surrender breathed new life into the war-weary capital and sparked weeks of jubilation. Congress received the captured British standards in a grand ceremony choreographed to exalt the United States. But aside from that event, Congress took little share in the city's rejoice. A much greater part of the celebration originated with the people out of doors and with the French minister, Anne César de La Luzerne.

On the morning of October 24, Lieutenant Colonel Tench Tilghman, aide-de-camp of General Washington, delivered to Congress news of Cornwallis's defeat at Yorktown. On the motion of the Virginian Edmund Randolph, Congress immediately voted to spend the afternoon in worship. At two o'clock, the delegates—together with the French minister La Luzerne, members of the Pennsylvania council, and "a number of great and respectable characters, both in the civil and military line"—proceeded to the Dutch Lutheran Church, where the congressional chaplain George Duffield returned thanks for the allies' "glorious and signal success." The following month, at La Luzerne's invitation, the delegates gathered at the Catholic chapel, to sing the Te Deum once again and to hear a sermon by Abbé Bandole, almoner to the French embassy.[58]

On November 3, ten days after Congress received word of the French and American victory, Colonel David Humphreys, a second of Washington's aides, carried into Philadelphia twenty-four standards surrendered by the British army at Yorktown. In the rich ceremony of early modern nations, the presentation and exhibition of conquered standards bespoke the glory and might of the triumphant sovereign.[59] Extremely rare in the revolutionary United States, these ceremonies carried extraordinary significance; they bore witness to the strength of continental arms and validated the republic's claim to independence. In 1775, after General Schuyler forwarded the British flags captured at Fort Chambly, the congressional president John Hancock invited local dignitaries to view them hanging in his lodgings. The failure or refusal of Horatio Gates to secure the British and German colors at Saratoga unfortunately deprived Congress of a similar opportunity in 1777.[60]

For the arrival of Cornwallis's flags, Congress and Pennsylvania state officials prepared a spectacle. The Philadelphia light horse met Colonel Humphreys at the Schuylkill River and escorted him into town in an "ever memorable procession" that consisted of music, an advanced party of light dragoons, "[t]he colours of the United States of America and the French nation, displayed . . . twenty four British and German standards, also displayed," and a detail of light horse. Parading along Market Street, "amid the acclamation of thousands," the procession at last arrived at the State House, where, as the *Maryland Gazette* reported, Col. Humphreys "laid" the standards "at Congress's feet."[61] As the *Gazette's* gallant language suggested, this presentment ceremony not only affirmed the sovereignty of Congress but also signified the subordinacy of military to civil authorities. By dispatching Humphreys to hand over the spoils of war, Washington paid symbolic deference to Congress, his master.

In a reciprocal gesture, and in the spirit of exultation that swept over the United States after word of the victory broke, Congress bestowed a variety of laurels, as lavishly as circumstances would permit, on the allied armies. Doling out the trophies that had been "laid at its feet," Congress granted "two stands of colours" to General Washington, as well as "two pieces of the field ordnance, taken from the British army" and suitably engraved for the occasion, to the Comte de Rochambeau. Congress also voted its gratitude to the artillists and engineers of the army who sustained the siege in spite of "extraordinary fatigue and danger." For settling terms of the capitulation, Congress recognized Lieutenant Colonel John Laurens and the Vicomte de Noailles. For bringing news of the surrender and for delivering the standards, Congress awarded "elegant swords" to Colonels Tilghman and Humphreys, as well as "a horse properly caparisoned" to Tilghman. To perpetuate the memory of the triumph, Congress voted that a "marble column, adorned with emblems of the alliance between the United States and his Most Christian Majesty; and inscribed with a succinct narrative of the surrender of Earl Cornwallis" be erected in Yorktown, Virginia.[62] Finally, Congress resolved to honor the generals Nathanael Greene and Francis Marion, by whose leadership continental forces had surprised the British army at Eutaw Springs, inflicting severe casualties and compelling the British to retreat to Charleston rather than reinforcing Cornwallis in Virginia.[63]

Having formally received these captured standards and heaped honors on the heroes of the Southern campaign, the Confederation Congress mostly withdrew from public festivities. Out of doors, word of the British surrender exhilarated Philadelphians, who celebrated by illuminating their city with candles and bonfires. In this moment of rejoice, unlit Quaker dwellings once again drew hostile attention. Noted one local diarist, "The city was handsomely illuminated in consequence of Lord Cornwallis's surrender, but [I] am sorry to have to add that so many doors and windows have been destroyed in houses of Friends."[64]

The Yorktown victory fixed Americans' admiration and gratitude on the allied military forces, most particularly on General Washington. In November, when the commander-in-chief returned, fresh from the field of conquest, Philadelphians treated him to a hero's welcome, particularly notable for its outpouring of art. Charles Willson Peale painted an homage to Washington and Rochambeau, as well as a "Temple of Independence," on the windows of his three-story home. James Robins, a French instructor living in Philadelphia, displayed an emblematic tableau consisting of the Gallic cock, standing on the British lion, wounded by thirteen American arrows. Still another French teacher, Alexander Quesnay de Glouvay, decorated his windows with a variety of patriotic images including a portrait of General Washington, from which radiated thirteen republican virtues. In Washington's honor, Glouvay also staged a theatrical production—consisting of short comedies, dances, and a display of thirteen illuminated pillars—at the Southwark Theatre early in the new year.[65]

The French embassy also feted the triumphant American commander. On December 11, La Luzerne treated Generals Washington and Greene, their wives, and "a very polite circle of gentlemen and ladies" to an "elegant Concert" as his home at Laurel Hill.[66] This performance—of Francis Hopkinson's libretto, the "Temple of Minerva"—had been many months in the making, apparently with the minister's patronage. As Martha Dangerfield Bland, wife of the Virginia congressman Theodorick Bland, reported to her friends, "[t]he Minister sacrifices his time to the policy of the french Court—he dislikes Music, never dances—and is a domestick Man yet he has a Ball or a Concert every week and his house full to dinner every day."[67]

Notably, Congress assumed a comparatively modest role in the celebration of Washington. Writing in late November to report the commander's arrival in the city, the congressional president John Hanson predicted, "[E]very testimony of Joy and respect will I dare Say be shewn on the Occasion." But as it happened, most of those testimonies were tendered by the citizens of Philadelphia and by the French minister. Though Congress did grant Washington an audience, it did so privately and very briefly. Far from effusing praise on the general, as it had in the wake of victory one month before, Congress acknowledged him with a single, stolid sentence: "Congress, at all times happy in seeing your Excellency, feel particular pleasure in your presence at this time, after the glorious success of the allied arms in Virginia." Congress's restraint on this occasion likely owed in large measure to its concern for the dignity and primacy of civil authority. Having already formally thanked the commander for his "eminent services," Congress did not believe it decorous to pay him further obeisance. Congress, moreover, understood that the victory at Yorktown had not yet brought a truce, let alone a peace. When Congress met with Washington in the late fall of 1781, it kept one eye on the following spring's campaign, presenting for his consideration a list of resolves aimed at strengthening the army. Such business presumably diverted Congress from excessive congratulations.[68]

Yet it was also the case that Congress's material and political circumstances had changed. Having greatly depleted its finances, Congress now possessed fewer resources to spend on elaborate ceremonies or City Tavern banquets. In consequence, the French legation had begun to assume an increasingly prominent role in the alliance's festivity and ritual. During the summer of 1781, for example, La Luzerne commemorated the birthday of King Louis XVI with notably more fanfare than Congress marked the anniversary of independence.[69] By the end of the war, La Luzerne worked a slow accommodation of the polite sociability once deemed abhorrent to Congress's republican ideals. "[T]he policy of the french Court," to borrow Martha Dangerfield Bland's suggestive phrase, comported neither with the letter nor the spirit of Congress's proscriptions against "expensive diversions and entertainments." Nevertheless, as the Articles of Association lost their moral sway, La Luzerne's balls and concerts became weekly affairs. Francis Hopkinson deflected negative attention from his "Temple of Minerva" merely by styling it an "oratorical entertainment" rather than a play. And though local authorities intervened to prevent an *encore* presentation of Quesnay de Glouvay's theatrical homage to the Franco-American alliance, his first performance at the Southwark Theatre was sufficiently well tolerated that Washington, La Luzerne, and the Pennsylvania council president William Moore felt no compunction in attending.[70]

In mid-December, Congress kept a previously appointed day of thanksgiving, but amid weeks of jubilation—illuminations, transparent paintings, Te Deums, oratorios, and theater—this pious holiday seemed sadly out of season. Congress resolved to observe this thanksgiving, its fall tradition, in mid-September, before the siege of Yorktown had even begun. But it did not draft a formal proclamation until late October, after Cornwallis surrendered. Written by the New Jersey congressman and Presbyterian minister John Witherspoon, Congress's thanksgiving proclamation briefly heralded the allied victory, by which "a General of the first Rank, with his whole army, ha[d] been captured." But the remainder of the text, which looked back over the long course of war, struck an awkward, almost self-defeating tone. To inspire his countrymen to grateful worship, Witherspoon recounted the darkest days of their despair. He measured divine benevolence by sounding the depths from which God had lifted the American people. Witherspoon reminded readers of the "most discouraging appearance" of their affairs, of the "savage devastation" of their property, and of the "difficulties" they had faced in recovering lands "overrun" by the enemy. Witherspoon even offered the mutinies of 1781 as proof of "the goodness of God," for rather than defecting to the British army, disgruntled continental soldiers had merely sought redress "tumultuously." (Before sending the proclamation to press, Congress redacted Witherspoon's bright-side remembrance of the mutiny in the Pennsylvania line.)[71] By recalling the war's most painful moments, Witherspoon very nearly echoed the lament of an embittered *loyalist*, who censured the audacity by which Congress ordered a thanksgiving "festival" after bringing the country to "the precipice of utter destruction."[72] At the height of American rejoice, Congress demanded extraordinary humility. Perhaps for that reason, the thanksgiving of 1781 passed with little public notice.[73]

By the spring of 1782, the Confederation Congress possessed little energy for patriotic ceremony or festivity. The imminent peace had rendered Congress's moral strictures and behavioral proscriptions obsolete. The individual states, the continental officer corps, and the French ministry all supplanted Congress as sponsors of postwar merriment. This process culminated in the summer of 1782, after La Luzerne requested an audience to announce the birth of the dauphin. For the patriarchal French monarchy, the long-awaited birth of a prince was a source of exultation, of far greater consequence than the birth of a princess two years before. By happy coincidence, Marie Antoinette had delivered her son only three days after Britain's decisive surrender at Yorktown. The birth of the dauphin thus provided Congress, enervated thought it was, an opportunity to express the states' gratitude for French military and financial assistance. Another, more pressing diplomatic consideration also motivated Congress to fete the dauphin. The allies expected preliminary peace talks to open in Paris any day, and in fact, but unbeknownst to Congress, they already had. Though the Treaty of Alliance of 1778 bound the United States and France from conducting separate negotiations, both parties anticipated British efforts to divide them. By celebrating the dauphin's birth, Congress could reassure the French of the United States' good faith. "It was deemed politic at this crisis," James Madison reported, "to display every proper evidence of affectionate attachment to our Ally."[74]

Accordingly, Congress granted La Luzerne an audience on May 13. To bring the United States into more perfect conformity with European diplomatic custom, Congress refined the etiquette by which it had received Conrad-Alexandre Gérard back in 1778. First, Congress obliged the minister to provide his own coach. This innovation comported with the practice of European courts, which typically reserved carriages for ambassadors. It also fortuitously spared Congress the expense of livery.[75] Second, members of Congress did not reciprocate La Luzerne's bow, undoubtedly to the dismay of Congress's foes, who had so lampooned that gesture years before. Finally, President John Hanson remained covered throughout the audience, while La Luzerne and the delegates all removed their hats. In 1782, as in 1778, Congress perceived that the sovereignty of the United States resided in these small gestures. For the sake of newspaper coverage, and in such meticulous detail as to suggest he anticipated a painting of the event, congressional secretary Charles Thomson drafted a careful report of the ceremony. Ironically, when Thomson presented this account for inclusion in the minutes, President Hanson deemed it "too minute . . . to trouble Congress for an order to insert it." Perhaps out of concern for congressional dignity or perhaps in regard for "true republican principles," Hanson believed that Congress should not appear concerned with matters that had manifestly absorbed its studious attention.[76]

That evening, after the reception was complete, Congress hosted a dinner for La Luzerne and a train of distinguished civil and military officers. Though this celebration threatened to "strain every nerve of Finance," members of Congress thought it a "duty." No "demonstration of Joy Shd. be omitted," wrote Virginia delegate Theodorick Bland. "The Reasons are too obvious to point out. It wd. affront the Understanding to mention them."[77] And so, as it had so many times before, Congress invited the minister and guests to an "elegant" meal at the City Tavern. The bill of fare, standard for Congress's public events, included toasts, cannonade, and a display of fireworks. Just for the occasion, Charles Willson Peale constructed an elaborate "triumphant arch," which featured illuminated paintings of the French king and queen.[78] As they retired to their lodgings that evening, members of Congress did not know that they had just returned from their last public entertainment at the City Tavern. For eight years now—seven since the people of Philadelphia threatened to tear it down—the tavern had stood as the center of congressional ceremony and festivity. Having served as a point of rendezvous for delegates to the First Continental Congress, having functioned ever since as their informal meeting place and banquet hall, having hosted the first anniversaries of independence and alliance as well this reception in honor of the dauphin, this, the "most genteel" tavern in America, was in many ways the birthplace of U.S. national identity. But its heyday as the site of Revolutionary festivity had come to an end.

The announcement of the dauphin's birth kicked off a long summer of revelry and catharsis. In coming months, Americans honored the House of

Bourbon with at least thirty public festivals. They likewise filled their gazettes with songs and poems in tribute to the French prince.[79] Various state governments drafted congratulatory resolves; the Delaware assembly ordered the construction of a "triumphal arch."[80] At West Point, General Washington hosted an "elegant entertainment" for French and American officers, civil authorities, and genteel citizens.[81] Congress did not call for or direct these celebrations. Nor amid the jubilation was Congress particularly acclaimed. Rather, at the conclusion of the war Americans showered accolades chiefly on their French allies and on General Washington.[82]

The grandest of these celebrations, hosted in mid-July by the minister La Luzerne himself, vastly exceeded Congress's dinner, both in grandeur and expense. Signaling that the austerity and self-sacrifice once demanded by the Association had finally fallen out of fashion, La Luzerne's exorbitant soirée marked the close of an era. Unconstrained by continental finance or republican asceticism, La Luzerne distributed more than a thousand tickets, to George Washington and the continental officers, to the governors of all the states, and to distinguished persons throughout the city. His guest list included members of every profession—lawyers, doctors, ministers, and faculty of the college—as well as artists, musicians, and philosophers. It included "the most ancient as well as modern families." It included at least one "Indian chief in his savage habits." In a spirit of reconciliation, it included Whigs and Tories alike. "For ten days before," Benjamin Rush recorded, "nothing else was talked of in our city." In preparation for the event, the minister ordered the construction of large pavilions, supported by painted pillars. He directed his gardeners to create artificial groves of cedar and pine branches and to hang glass lamps about the lawn. Tailors, milliners, and dressmakers busily embroidered silk costumes for both male and female guests. On the day of the event, the city's hair dressers began their work before dawn. So that Quaker guests, in their modest attire, might suffer no embarrassment, La Luzerne erected for them a private room concealed by a curtain of gauze.[83]

Upon entering the pavilions La Luzerne's guests discovered painted scenes representative of two empires: the rising American and the brilliantly ascendant French. They spent the evening listening to poetry composed for the occasion and dancing to the music of a French orchestra. Late in the night, they supped on a meal prepared by thirty chefs from the French army. In order that uninvited townsfolk might share in the spectacle, La Luzerne arranged for the demolition of a plank fence surrounding his property and the erection of palisades in its place. To manage traffic and to prevent any disturbance, La Luzerne hired a guard of French soldiers. As he anticipated, large crowds of Philadelphians—Rush estimated 10,000 persons—gathered to witness the event. Though dissuaded from his original plan of distributing wine and coins to these onlookers, La Luzerne donated the sums instead to the prisoners of the city's jails and the patients at the Pennsylvania hospital. For the general amusement, he orchestrated a display of fireworks.[84]

La Luzerne's extravaganza was one of the most elaborate ever hosted in Philadelphia, rivaled only perhaps by the notorious Meschianza. It far outshined Congress's humble Independence Day dinner at the City Tavern later that summer.[85] John Beatty, a colonel in the Continental Army and future member of Congress, watched the "great *Raree show*" from the streets rather than joining in the festivities. To Beatty, the gala portended a shameful renunciation of republican principles. "I am bold to say," wrote Beatty, "this city will vie with the first Courts in Europe for dissipation, luxury, & extravagance, & sorry I am so young a Country should have so ill a precedent set them."[86] In spite of Beatty's misgivings, the revival of festivity and opulence thus brought Congress's long campaign for virtue to an end.

"[C]ross accidents"

Congress's tenure in Philadelphia was also coming to an end. The following summer, in response to a perceived affront, Congress resolved to leave the city once and for all. Impoverished and ineffectual, Congress commanded little of the public's esteem. When a contingent of angry soldiers organized a protest in demand of back wages, and in the process exhibited blatant disregard for the authority of the United States government, Congress resolved that the dignity of the nation depended on its removal from Philadelphia. The events that gave rise to Congress's departure, the sense of its own inconsequentiality that Congress was made to feel, and the vain, almost farcical efforts by which Congress endeavored to reassert the glory of the United States upon arriving at its new home in Princeton, New Jersey, all bespeak the decline of Congress. They bear witness as well to the withdrawal of Congress from the making of a material and ceremonial culture for the United States.

Trouble began brewing in early June 1783, when word broke that Congress intended to furlough the Continental Army without first having made arrangements for the payment of its back wages. Many officers and enlisted men feared that if Congress disbanded the army, it would never pay the money owed them. To win redress, soldiers in the Pennsylvania, Maryland, and Lancaster lines marched on Philadelphia. These mutineers arrived in the city on

Friday, June 20; soon thereafter rumors began to circulate that they intended to seize funds deposited in the national bank. Alexander Hamilton, chairman of a congressional committee specially appointed to deal with army grievances, and Robert Morris, the superintendent of finance, both appealed to Pennsylvania's Supreme Executive Council to call out the militia, but the council refused, observing that the soldiers had not committed any outrageous or violent acts and doubting in any event whether the local militia would take arms against beleaguered veterans. With no means of putting the insurgency down, Hamilton, along with the assistant superintendent of finance Gouverneur Morris and the assistant secretary of war William Jackson, instead attempted to negotiate a settlement. Meeting with the soldiers that evening, Hamilton offered a cash payment of one month's salary to all who accepted the furlough. Insulted by this paltry concession, the soldiers resolved to protest. The following day, a Saturday, at half past noon, nearly thirty soldiers of the Pennsylvania line defiantly took arms, paraded to the state house, and began forming themselves with menacingly good order along Chestnut Street.[87]

Congress was not the object of this demonstration. It no longer regularly convened on Saturdays and was not in chambers that particular day. As the *Pennsylvania Packet* later explained, "The intended application of the men was to the executive council [of Pennsylvania, which met on the second floor of the state house], and not to Congress."[88] Alarmed by the show of force, however, the congressional president Elias Boudinot called an emergency session.[89] Despite the short notice, a handful of delegates turned out, making their way through the swelling crowd of insolent troops. Determined to vindicate the honor of the United States, this rump Congress brooked no intimidation. Though never obtaining sufficient numbers to conduct business, the delegates agreed not to rise until three o'clock, their "usual hour of adjournment."[90]

Meanwhile, out in the street, upward of three hundred additional soldiers, housed at the nearby Philadelphia barracks, joined their aggrieved comrades in a display of solidarity. Some of these soldiers apparently fortified themselves with "spirituous drink from the tipling houses adjoining." Nevertheless, the demonstration ended without violence, thanks in large part to the intervention of General Arthur St. Clair, who persuaded the troops to disperse on the condition that the Executive Council meet with a party of commissioned and noncommissioned officers. Both the council and Congress gave their blessing to this arrangement, and at the designated hour of adjournment, members of Congress began filing out of the State House. Aside from an instance or two of "mock obstruction," the troops permitted the delegates to pass unmolested.[91]

That evening, after the crowd of soldiers and citizens had dispersed, members of Congress reconvened at the state house. In the intervening hours, the delegates had grown increasingly perturbed by both the soldiers' uprising and the Pennsylvania council's refusal to suppress it. The soldiers' insubordination grossly affronted public order and lawfulness. It could not go unpunished. Convinced that swift action was necessary to break the mutiny, President Boudinot wrote to army headquarters, begging Washington for a dispatch of troops to quell the disorder. The fact that the mutiny had been directed against a state and not against the federal government added salt to Congress's wounds. Regardless to whom the soldiers turned for redress, some delegates now argued, they impugned Congress's honor, for their insurrection arose in response to the congressional furlough policy. On these grounds, Congress instructed Hamilton and his committee to secure proper assurances from the Supreme Executive Council that it would endeavor to preserve the peace and protect the federal government against threats of this nature. In short, the delegates demanded some guarantee that the council would call out the militia if necessary to defend Congress. Failing that, Congress determined that it could no longer remain in Philadelphia.[92]

On Monday, Hamilton and his committee approached the council with Congress's demands. The Sabbath having passed in relative tranquility, and the soldiers evincing no further hint of mischief to person or property, the council refused to reconsider its previous position. Pressed to submit their refusal in writing, the councilors again demurred: the state of Pennsylvania might correspond with Congress, but it would not deign to address a congressional committee. Infuriated, Hamilton decried the council's "weak and disgusting position." Back in Congress, the delegates shared his contempt. On Tuesday, Congress, true to its word, resolved to adjourn from Philadelphia. To justify this course of conduct, President Boudinot drafted a proclamation declaring that "the dignity and authority of the United States would be constantly exposed to a repetition of insult, while Congress shall continue to sit in this City." He also drafted a terse note announcing the departure of Congress, and ordered it delivered upstairs to the Pennsylvania Executive Council. Before day's end, members of Congress began to pack their bags. The following week they resumed business in Princeton, New Jersey, never to return to Philadelphia, their host city of ten years.[93]

This episode suggests just how far Congress had fallen since the close of the war. As the historian Kenneth R. Bowling has explained, the soldiers' decision to bypass Congress and plead directly with the Pennsylvania council turned on "a realistic assessment of the constitutional and financial realities of the United States in 1783: Pennsylvania was simply wealthier and more important than the federal government." A correspondent to the *Independent Gazetteer* stated the matter more pointedly, "[T]he soldiery have long considered [Congress], like their paper currency, in a state of *depreciation*, having no *solidity* or *real worth*" (italics in original). That this worthless Congress could not pay its debts was pathetic enough, but that it had fled from its own soldiers was altogether unbecoming of its sovereign character, or so detractors charged. "[I]f the king of England was to withdraw every time he conceived himself affronted," wrote an editorialist in the *Pennsylvania Packet*, "he would long before now have been in Hanover." "We know of no country where soldiers have not at times shewn such a disposition," concurred the *Independent Gazetteer*, "but we know of no sovereign power, or but a very few, who acted as our Congress did." "The late congressional proceedings exhibit neither dignity, fortitude, nor perseverance."[94]

Seeking to deflect such criticism, members of Congress heaped blame on state and local authorities who failed to quash the mutinous rebellion. The Delaware congressman Eleazer McComb condemned Pennsylvania's "scandalous neglect" of its duty. President Boudinot likewise censured city officials, who, to their "everlasting reproach," made no effort to relieve Congress from the "humiliating and dishonorable situation."[95] Writing to the *Freeman's Journal*, "A Lover of Facts" denied that Congress's flight was "the base born brat of petulant haste," as some newspapers supposedly characterized it. Rather, the dignity of the United States demanded that Congress leave the city: "What must the insulted majesty of America do in this predicament?"[96]

Members of Congress hoped that the "majesty of America" might recover from insult in the bucolic environs of Princeton. Prior to departing Philadelphia, President Boudinot, himself a native of Elizabethtown, wrote to the New Jersey governor, William Livingston, and requested official assurance that the state would give Congress its "fullest protection." Livingston promptly replied that "the Citizens of New Jersey will chearfully turn out to repel any violence that may be attempted against them."[97] Presumably on Livingston's hint, the inhabitants of Trenton and Princeton gathered that same day and pledged their "lives and fortunes" to defend Congress from "foreign invasions" and "intestine tumults." In further witness to their hospitality, these Jersey folk declared, "[W]e take the earliest opportunity to testify our zeal in support of [Congress's] dignity and privileges, and . . . we will use our utmost exertions for their comfortable accommodation."[98] Good to their word, the people of Princeton offered up their every convenience: the college's Nassau Hall and George Morgan's farmhouse, as well as several local homes, kitchens, stables, and gardens. Workmen offered to build new quarters; local innkeepers volunteered to cater to the delegates with fresh fruits and seafoods; student orators prepared "effusions of flattery & encomiums" to shower on Congress; and the poet Annis Boudinot Stockton, sister of the president and widow of the congressman Richard Stockton, entertained guests at her Morven estate.[99]

Back in Philadelphia, certain "wicked" persons, embittered by Congress's hasty departure, quipped that Princeton's air would perhaps be wholesome enough to cure that "species of *madness* called Congromania."[100] But not even the temperate climes of the New Jersey countryside could bring Congress back to health. Enfeebled, insolvent, and eclipsed both by its allies and by the army of its own creation, Congress faltered at the end. Far from remedying Congress's ills, the stay at Princeton seemed almost to mock them, particularly on the Fourth of July, 1783. In recent years, Congress had scarcely acknowledged the anniversary of independence, but now, having been so contemptibly mistreated by Pennsylvania officials, Congress eagerly wished to assert its own prestige as well as that of the union. In sudden preparation for the day, Congress sent to Philadelphia for a batch of fireworks, the College of New Jersey arranged for a student debate on the virtues of republican government, and local officials raised the stars-and-stripes, featuring the motto, "Virtue, Liberty, & Independence," atop a prominent flag pole. The celebration, however, fell short of expectations, in part because the weather refused to cooperate, but in part because Princeton, for all its obliging inhabitants, was still but "a little obscure village."[101] In a letter to his wife, Secretary Charles Thomson recorded the day's forlorn events in characteristic detail, but with uncharacteristic irony:

> Yesterday was celebrated at Princeton the eighth [i.e., seventh] anniversary of the Independence of America. . . . The Morning was ushered in, I cannot say with the ringing of Bells, but with the jingle of the College bell, which being cracked exhibits exactly such a sound as a farmer makes with a frying pan when bees are swarming & he wants to settle them. . . . A Bower was erected on the green, under which the company were to dine. I cannot indeed boast of its columns, colonades or festoons nor of its triumphal arches or commodious apartments. It was composed of stakes stuck in the ground with forked tops, on which were laid rails & across these some poles to support the heavy branches lopt from the neighbouring forrest which served for a covering. In the front of Mrs. Stockden's house, I mean the palace was erected a grand arcade for the exhibition of fire works which had been sent for in

all haste from Philadelphia. But o cruel & fickle fortune, how oft by the turn of thy wheel dost thou disappoint the designs of men, & ruin the best planned projects. About three o clock the Sky which had hitherto been serene began to be overcast, the clouds thickened, the tempest brewed and about four there fell a deluge of rain, which disconcerted all the measures taken & obliged the stewards and managers to remove the tables into Mrs. Stockden's office. . . . Dinner was to have been on the table at four, but I found I was in time enough at six. The table was well furnished with hams & rounds of beef. But unfortunately the benches on which the company sat had felt the effects of the storm. However we had this comfort, that though our heads might be heated with wine, we would be cool at bottom. In the evening the ladies collected, and crouds of people attended to see the exhibition of fire works. But, alas, cruel fortune as if she meant to sport herself with our misfortunes had by some strange interposition prevented the arrival of the fire works. Neither Lamps nor oil were provided to illuminate the cherry trees. And the grand arcade, which had braved the storm, stood naked and unadorned & seemed to say, here am I, ready to have exhibited a grand spectacle for the celebration of the day and an Amusement of the quality, people & inhabitants of Princeton, the capital of the United states had not cross accidents prevented. However that the day might not pass without some noise, A Cannon was dragged up from town. But unfortunately in the way the spunge was broken[,] the only spunge in town to clean the gun. This was thought to be irremediable, but happily there was an old bombardier present who undertook to fire without a spunge. Hereupon a rocket was played about seen set as a signal, and the cannon began to fire, but for want of a spunge they were ob[l]iged to fire so slow that it appeared to be minute guns fired on the death of some eminent commander. Afterward a few rockets were played off, the company then dispersed & thus this Memorable day was closed.[102]

Thus the refugee Congress, which on a Fourth of July not so long ago had commanded festooned ships, parading battalions, and *feu-de-joie*, now celebrated that anniversary with a clanky school bell, a rain-soaked arbor, and plaintive minute fire.

Conclusion

"[T]HE SIGN OF THE THIRTEEN STARRS"

IN THE LATE SUMMER OF 1784, the South Carolina congressman Jacob Read drafted an advertisement for the return of three runaway servants, Jonathan, Frank, and Sam. His advertisement read in part,

> Stop them! Stop them!! O, Stop them!!!
> Ten pounds old Tenor, Reward
> . . . . .
> Jonathan is tall & Straight made, much marked with the Small pox . . . has a thin Sharp Visage, is remarkable for Repeating his Words or Sentences . . .
> Frank is of Low Stature and Small limbs, Stoops and is a good deal round Shouldered . . . Has a down look and very Weak Optics . . . He is the most artful and disigning of the Two and is Supposed to have inveigled away poor Simple Jonathan of whom he intends to make a Cats paw . . .
> Jonathan generally Wears a Jean Coat & Nankeen Waistcoat & Breeches. Frank a light Blue Cloth Coat with White Under Cloaths . . .
> Sam who is very Well intentioned and of a good Character . . . tis feared has been seduced away by the persuasions of the other[s].

In its careful attention to bodies, speech, and dress, Read's advertisement closely resembled the dozens of notices for runaway slaves and indentured servants that every day lined the newspapers of the early United States.[1] Read's runaways, however, were neither slaves nor indentured servants. Rather, they were *civil* servants, congressmen absconded from "the New Temporary Shop," which is to say, from the vagabond Congress's latest meeting place, the state house in Annapolis. Whoever apprehended these runaways, Read's ad informed, could collect their reward "at the Sign of the Thirteen Starrs."[2]

The humor of Read's runaway advertisement, such as it was, arose from its absurd inversion of the social order. Read reduced propertied statesmen, the most privileged citizens of the United States, to the rank of unfree laborers. In this manner, Read mocked his fellow delegates, but simultaneously affirmed persistent distinctions of class and race in American society. The force of his lampoon may be measured in the social and economic distance that continued to separate congressmen from ordinary people in the post-Revolutionary United States.

Yet, if congressmen's place in society remained secure, their place in office did not. Read's runaway ad must be understood not only as a commentary on social order, but on political order as well, for grave anxieties about the state of the union darkened his satire. Read's reference to "the New Temporary Shop" alluded to the transience and instability of Congress. His offer of an "old Tenor" reward hinted at the worthlessness of the continental currency. The very circumstances that occasioned Read's satire—the abrupt departure of Jonathan Blanchard, Francis Dana, and Samuel Dick from the Committee of the States, a caretaking committee responsible for the management of U.S. affairs during the summer recess of 1784, and the subsequent collapse of that committee for want of a quorum—recalled the chronic absenteeism that had plagued Congress almost since its inception. The Pennsylvania delegate Edward Hand proclaimed that the committee's dissolution "exposed the Foederal government to all the danger that may result from the want of a foederal head." The Maryland congressman James McHenry lamented, "Owing to this circumstance we shall have no visible confederal sovereignty. . . . [O]ur enemies in Europe will construe this event into a proof of a spirit of disorder and disunion among the States." Read himself disparaged the Confederation Congress, powerless to compel the attendance of its members let alone to impose its will on the states, as an "Unnecessary & Useless Burden." As invoked in Read's mock runaway ad, the "Thirteen Starrs"—a constellation Francis Hopkinson invoked to emblematize the ascendance of the confederation—now signified its sad decline.[3]

Partly in consequence of that decline and partly in consequence of the war's end, the Confederation Congress produced fewer material artifacts and ceremonies of state than did its predecessor. It continued to grant audiences to foreign ministers, but its etiquette proved "more conformable to present circumstances & embarrassmts than to the Representatives of a Great Nation," as the Virginia delegation characterized Congress's reception for the Dutch plenipotentiary Johan van Berckel in 1783.[4] Congress also brought a modicum of political excitement and polite sociability to its temporary homes in Princeton, Annapolis, Trenton, and New York. By its many transplantations, Congress prompted public deliberations about the appropriate location, size, and character of a permanent U.S. capital. But Congress's migrations also provoked contempt. In another reworking of Hopkinson's constellatory motif, one critic proclaimed, "The high and mighty and most GRACIOUS SOVEREIGNS the C[ongres]s of the United and Independent States, not being stars of the FIRST magnitude, but rather partaking of the nature of INFERIOR luminaries, or WANDERING comets, again appear in their eccentric orb." Only by becoming "FIXED and STATIONARY," the author opined, would Congress ever acquire "BRILLIANCY."[5]

Importantly, too, the Confederation Congress contributed to the making of U.S. national identity by its adoption of land ordinances, particularly those of 1785 and 1787. Creating a grid of six-mile-square townships, the ordinance of 1785 mapped Enlightenment principles of rationality and order across the Ohio River Valley. Setting aside acreage for the recompense of veterans, it provided, at least in principle, a yeoman's existence for the soldiers who had risked their lives in defense of American liberties. Reserving central tracts for the establishment of public schools, it predicated the future of the republic on the education of its citizenry. Subsequently, the ordinance of 1787 instituted procedural mechanisms for the admission of the Northwest Territories, ensuring that the expansion of the United States would proceed in a democratic rather than colonial manner, at least as concerned the white inhabitants of those territories. And it prohibited chattel slavery, securing a place for freeholders in the cultivation of the Northwest. Congress's land ordinances thus laid the foundation for the very sort of society imagined in the Articles of Association of 1774: virtuous and industrious, voluntary and independent. In the process, however, these land ordinances established an ideological and constitutional justification for the violent confrontation and forcible removal of Native American peoples from the lower Great Lakes region.[6]

Even as the Confederation Congress pursued these measures, it abandoned many of the civic traditions established during the war. After 1784, Congress proclaimed no more days of fasting or thanksgiving. Likewise, the Confederation Congress adorned none of its debt instruments—the drafts, notes, and tax-redeemable indents by which it struggled to finance the United States' ongoing expenses—with the sort of didactic and patriotic ornamentation that graced Franklin's and Hopkinson's bills.[7] The Confederation Congress scarcely even celebrated Independence Day. In 1785, its first summer in New York City, Congress hosted an anniversary dinner, but was rivaled in this offering by the Society of the Cincinnati, at whose banquet "the utmost hilarity" reportedly prevailed. The following year, Congress declined to furnish an expensive meal, instead receiving state and local officials in a modest open house before ceding the remainder of the day to the Cincinnati. Finally, in 1787, a year in which New Yorkers purportedly commemorated the anniversary "more *pompously*" than usual, Congress apparently took no formal part, but rather conducted a full day of business, despite the absence of president Arthur St. Clair, a retired major general who spent the anniversary in the company of the Cincinnati.[8]

After the war, Congress found few occasions to bestow laurels on valorous officers. In April 1783, Congress ordered the sculpting of an equestrian statue of General Washington, to be erected at the future capital. Secretary of Foreign Affairs John Jay consulted the "celebrated Statuary" Jean-Antoine Houdon, who took Washington's bust while visiting New York, but Congress never provided funds for the statue's execution.[9] Congress commissioned only one new sword, in April 1784, in appreciation for Baron von Steuben's services as inspector general and in lieu of greater financial compensation, and only one new medal, in October 1787, in recognition of Chevalier John Paul Jones's triumph over the *Serapis* and in lieu of prize monies owed to him.[10] Similarly, Congress called for only two more monuments, one in honor of Nathanael Greene, who died in retirement of natural causes, the other to the memory of the soldiers who perished on the prison ship *Jersey*.[11]

Though the Confederation Congress rarely conferred new awards on the army, it did labor to bring some old ones to fruition. In 1785, at the instigation of Janet Livingston Montgomery, Congress at last tracked the monument of her late husband, General Richard Montgomery, to Edenton, North Carolina. Sculpted by Jean-Jacques Caffiéri in 1777, this monument had wasted in the possession of a deceased congressman's executors ever since shipped from France.[12] Congress ordered the monument delivered to New York, where Pierre Charles L'Enfant placed it below the east window in St. Paul's Chapel.[13]

Finally, in the late 1780s, as the Confederation began to disintegrate, U.S. diplomats endeavored to secure abroad the swords and medals that Congress had commissioned several years earlier. Because the United States had "not Artists at present for such works," as John Adams lamented in 1777, the task of soliciting engravers fell initially to Benjamin Franklin, who, as minister to France, continued to devise emblems and medals in honor of the United States, and subsequently to David Humphreys, who, as a retired continental officer and member of the diplomatic corps, took a personal interest in Congress's awards, himself having earned a sword for his service at Yorktown.[14] The swords came rather quickly; ten, including Humphrey's, arrived in May 1786.[15] But the medals took more time, each for its own reason: Washington's because Houdon, who cast the model bust, had departed from Paris; Gates's because the engraver refused to depict him wearing the eagle of the Cincinnati, anachronistically, at the surrender at Saratoga; Morgan's because the maker deemed Congress's proposed design not in the "style and manner" in which such medals were usually executed; and Greene's simply because the artist possessed no likeness of the subject.[16] Writing to David Humphreys, Washington expressed no disappointment at his medal's delay, but rather surprise that the chore had been taken up at all: "I expected it was to have remained on the journals of [Congress] as a dead letter."[17]

During this same period, as the Confederation Congress fell from prominence, Washington correspondingly rose. Their trajectories crossed at Annapolis, Maryland, in the formal ceremony of the general's resignation, in December 1783. In principle, this ritual—by which the commander in chief relinquished his commission to the sovereign Congress—should have functioned as the climatic subordination of military power to civil authority. But in a number of its details, Washington's resignation instead gave further proof of the very weaknesses of confederational governance. Before Congress could even appoint a committee to devise protocol for the event, there arose a disagreeable question of parliamentary procedure. The Articles of Confederation required the assent of nine states for Congress to act on matters of important continental business. This supermajority voting requirement, one of the Articles' more debilitating provisions, applied to a limited but critical range of public affairs: the making of war, the forging of alliances, the appropriation of funds, and, problematically for the present moment, the "appointment" of a commander in chief.[18] Did that same provision, Maryland congressman James McHenry now asked, implicitly require a nine-state majority to accept the commander's resignation? This was a legitimate question of constitutional interpretation for which Congress had no precedent.

And it was not at all academic. Since convening in Annapolis, Congress had never seated full delegations from more than seven states. The Treaty of Paris sat unratified and gathering dust on that very account. Congress thus found itself forced to choose between two undesirable courses of action: tabling Washington's resignation or receiving it in an audience of only seven fully represented states. The delegates voted overwhelmingly for the latter, but seized on their dishonorable situation as an opportunity to prod the states to action. On the morning of Washington's audience, Congress forwarded dispatches to the executives of every state, notifying them of the numerous matters "of great national concern" now pending before Congress, and shaming those states not properly represented.[19]

The toasts raised at Washington's farewell dinner likewise bespoke the decline of the Confederation Congress. On the eve of Washington's resignation, Congress hosted the general and two hundred local politicians and dignitaries to "an exceedingly plentiful" repast at George Mann's Tavern. At the conclusion of the meal, the guests drank not thirteen but rather fourteen toasts, in defiance of patriotic convention. After the hosts had raised their glasses to the United States, the army, the commander, and various friendly sovereigns, General Washington offered a final sentiment: "Competent powers to [C]ongress for general purposes."[20] Here was a call for constitutional reform, the necessity of which was so self-evident that the congressmen could scarcely have perceived it as a slight. If any needed further evidence of the confederation's shortcomings, they would have found it in the belatedness with which Congress paid the dinner bill. Not for four months did Congress remit payment, totaling nearly seven hundred dollars, to George Mann. Fittingly, it was in Mann's Tavern two years later that delegates to the Annapolis Convention gathered to remedy the defects of the federal government.[21]

The ceremony of Washington's resignation offered glimpses of Congress's wane, but also of the general's wax. After dinner, Governor William Paca invited guests to a ball at the Maryland State House. There, the women of Annapolis lavished attention on Washington, obliging the general to dance every set in hope that they might all "get a touch of him," as the delegate James Tilton reported.[22] The following morning, at the resignation ceremony, a "throng" of men and women compelled Congress to open its doors so that they might hear Washington speak. Congressman James McHenry noted every tremor: "[T]here was hardly a member of Congress who did not drop tears. The General's hand which held the address shook as he read it. . . . [W]hen he commended the interests of his dearest country to almighty God, and those who had the superintendence of them to his holy keeping, his voice faultered and sunk, and the whole house felt his agitations." After the ceremony, Washington reentered the chamber to bid his personal farewells, and at last "rode off," as Tilton reported, "intent upon eating his Christmas dinner at home."[23]

Tilton's invocation of a hearthside Christmas dinner illustrates the powerful sentimentalism that swept over the audience and indeed over much of the United States during and after the Revolution.[24] The end of the war, the hard-fought triumph of the patriot cause, and the hindsight realization of the prices that had been paid along the way all brought palpable catharsis to Washington's audience. As McHenry explained, "So many circumstances crowded into view and gave rise to so many affecting emotions. The events of the revolution just accomplished—the new situation into which it had thrown the affairs of the world—the great man who had borne so conspicuous a figure in it, in the act of relinquishing all public employments to return to private life—the past—the present—the future—the manner—the occasion—all conspired to render it a spectacle inexpressibly solemn and affecting."[25]

Retold in newspapers throughout the country, Washington's abdication of high command redounded to his reputation and lifted him to the heights of patriot esteem. In accepting the general's resignation, President Thomas Mifflin predicted that Washington's glory would "continue to animate remotest ages."[26] These words rang true throughout the confederation period. In victorious retirement, Washington emerged as the symbolic figurehead of the American people: the Cincinnati elected Washington to their first office; the delegates to the Constitutional Convention insisted that he take the chair; the Electoral College voted unanimously to elevate him to the presidency. In the person of George Washington, the people of the United States discovered their greatest emblem of independence. Not until the framing of the Constitution and the contentious fight for ratification would they begin to build new foundations for their nationhood and national allegiance.[27]

———————

Sometime in the mid-1790s, "a simple, good-natured fellow" awoke from twenty years of drunken slumber, as Diedrich Knickerbocker would have us believe, and ambled out of the Catskill Mountains back to his old Dutch village. There Rip Van Winkle beheld with astonishment the new Union Hotel and the Revolutionary emblems that adorned it:

> Instead of the great tree which used to shelter the quiet little
> Dutch inn of yore, there now was reared a tall naked pole, with

something on the top that looked like a red nightcap, and from it was fluttering a flag, on which was a singular assemblage of stars and stripes—all of this was strange and incomprehensible. He recognized on the sign, however, the ruby face of King George, under which he had smoked so many a peaceful pipe, but even this was singularly metamorphosed. The red coat was changed for one of blue and buff, a sword was stuck in the hand instead of a scepter, the head was decorated with a cocked hat, and underneath was painted in large characters, GENERAL WASHINGTON.[28]

Here in the imaginative prose of Washington Irving we see a triptych of early U.S. national identity: the liberty cap, a token of radical resistance, the memento of the people out of doors; the flag of the United States, the fancy work of Francis Hopkinson, adopted by Congress to signify a rising constellation; and George Washington, the hero of the war, now a president in the place of a king. The historian John Murrin has described the national identity of the postwar United States as an "unexpected, impromptu, artificial, and therefore extremely fragile creation of the Revolution." This fragile creation—this delicate faith that the people of the thirteen individual states somehow belonged to a larger and greater whole—depended on instant and newfangled symbols, symbols that bewildered poor sleepy-eyed Rip.[29]

The Continental and Confederation Congresses did much to bring those symbols about. Most histories of Congress have focused our attention on the inner, political and constitutional workings of that assembly: on the emergence of factions and parties, on parliamentary procedures and voting requirements, and on the balance of executive and legislative powers. But we cannot fully appreciate the Continental Congress solely by reference to those traditional political concerns. We must also comprehend the ways in which it endeavored to manipulate emblems and ceremony.

During the Revolution, members of Congress dedicated substantial creative energies to the contrivance of behavioral codes, processions and parades, holy days, currency designs, anniversary commemorations, diplomatic protocols, swords, medals, and monuments. By these productions, Congress worked to invigorate the colonial resistance, to boost public morale for an arduous war, to justify American claims to independence, and ultimately to promote a national identity for the United States. Many influential delegates attributed tremendous—almost talismanic—strength to these material objects and ceremonies of state. Samuel and John Adams, Benjamin Franklin, Thomas Jefferson, and a host of other congressmen believed that their creations bore the power to shape public opinion and behavior. These congressmen imagined that their inventions would compel spendthrift consumers to tighten purse strings, that they would motivate farmers and tradesmen to lay down tools and take up arms, and that they would inspire Americans to pray for deliverance and to forgo debauching pastimes. They further conceived that the establishment of decorous protocols and observances would enhance the dignity of the United States. They asserted the legitimacy of their nation by devising seals and bowing before ministers. They performed these deeds with sovereign purpose, because these were among the "Acts and Things"—to borrow the language of the Declaration—"which Independent States may of right do."

Never was Congress of a single mind. On the contrary, many delegates questioned whether Congress ought to engage in seemingly wasteful or superfluous pursuits. Some felt that anniversaries of independence were "poorly spent" on expensive dinners and fireworks. Others considered diplomatic etiquette a matter too minute for congressional concern. Still others denigrated "fancy work" as an activity unsuited for gentlemen and undeserving of public praise or compensation. Even congressmen who agreed that these costly and rarified pursuits rightly belonged within the purview of government often clashed over just how Congress should conduct them. Should civil authorities mourn a military officer? Ought governors and legislators to fete the nation in hours of public sorrow? Might a rising empire adorn itself in grandeur and imposing majesty? Or would simple manners better clothe a virtuous republic? These contentious questions engrossed the representatives of the Revolutionary United States.

Unable to achieve consensus within their own ranks, members of Congress could scarcely dictate the thoughts, feelings, or behaviors of the American people. Contrary to the delegates' belief that their material artifacts and ceremonies would make impressions on the mind, that they would excite the passions, or that they would keep up the spirits, Congress's creations never wholly persuaded or mobilized the public. They did not make impressions on the minds of the incensed townsfolk who stood ready to raze the City Tavern or of the Anglican clergymen who railed against congressional masculinity; they did not excite the passions of the satirist who discounted the continental currency or of the eulogist who enlisted the memory of the war dead in the cause of imperial reconciliation; they did not keep up the spirits of the Delaware chiefs who referred to the French minister as "Father" and the American president as "Brother" or of the crowd of angry patriots who twice paraded the effigy of a disgraced continental general.

Time and again, the people out of doors responded to Congress in unpredictable and uncontrollable ways. Time and again they embraced, rejected, or reconfigured Congress's offerings as it pleased them. Whether by seizing the anniversary of independence as an occasion for the violent harassment of supposed Tories, as some patriots did, or by mocking the pretended dignity of continental military and diplomatic parade, as some loyalists did, the American people turned Congress's emblems and ceremonies to their own, self-determined uses. Inadvertently, Congress helped to create a symbolic vocabulary by which the public articulated its support for, or opposition to, the American resistance. Rather than defining the Revolution in a peremptory way, Congress crafted an assortment of icons and rituals by which the people out of doors could wrangle over its meanings.

Many of Congress's material artifacts and ceremonies have been forgotten. The inhabitants of the United States no longer partake in national days of fasting and humiliation. They do not recognize the crane as a great symbol of American liberty. They do not salute the beaver on Franklin's *Perseverando* flag. But a few of Congress's traditions and emblems have endured. The bald eagle, the stars and stripes, and the Fourth of July all persist as symbols of U.S. nationalism and national identity.

More significantly, the people of the United States continue to invoke these and other symbols to contest the values of their nation. One of the enduring conceits of U.S. democracy is that individuals engage with the state through rational processes and in pursuit of studied self-interest. This may be true, but it is also the case that U.S. citizens comprehend and interact with the nation and state through affective mechanisms, according to the dictates of emotion, faith, and morality. In so doing, they depend heavily on material artifact and ritual. The American people organize Buy America campaigns and they vehemently resist them; they lobby for the placement of religious language on their currency and in their courthouses and they tender legal challenges against it; they outlaw flag burning and they burn flags; they stand for the national anthem and place their hands over their hearts and they remain sitting and leave their hands by their sides; they object when the president bows to a foreign sovereign and they defend him for so bowing. The Continental Congress helped to establish this vital tradition of American democracy; the people out of doors made it their own.

Abbreviations

AAS	American Antiquarian Society
AHR	*American Historical Review*
DAJA	Lyman H. Butterfield et al., eds., *Diary and Autobiography of John Adams*, 4 vols. (Cambridge, Mass., 1961)
EAL	*Early American Literature*
HSP	Historical Society of Pennsylvania
JAH	*Journal of American History*
JER	*Journal of the Early Republic*
Journals	Worthington C. Ford et al., eds., *Journals of the Continental Congress, 1774–1789*, 34 vols. (Washington, D.C., 1904–1937)
LCP	Library Company of Philadelphia
Letters	Paul H. Smith et al., eds., *Letters of Delegates to Congress, 1774–1789*, 26 vols. (Washington, D.C., 1976–2000)
NEQ	*New England Quarterly*
Papers	Papers of the Continental Congress, 1774–1789, Publication Number M247, Record Group 360, National Archives and Records Administration, Washington, D.C.
PBF	Leonard W. Labaree et al., eds., *The Papers of Benjamin Franklin*, 39 vols. (New Haven, 1959–)
PHL	Philip M. Hamer et al., eds., *The Papers of Henry Laurens*, 16 vols. (Columbia, 1968–2003)
PMHB	*Pennsylvania Magazine of History and Biography*
PTJ	Julian P. Boyd et al., eds., *The Papers of Thomas Jefferson*, 34 vols. (Princeton, 1950–)

RDCUS   Francis Wharton, ed., *Revolutionary Diplomatic Correspondence of the United States*, 6 vols. (Washington, D.C., 1889)

Secret Journals   U.S. Continental Congress, *Secret Journals of Acts and Proceedings*, 4 vols. (1820; reprint: New York, 1976)

WMQ   *William and Mary Quarterly*

Notes

Introduction

1. *Journals*, 5: 517–18. John Adams to Samuel Chase, Philadelphia, July 9, 1776, *Letters*, 4: 414–16.
2. For John Adams's account of the seal committee's deliberation, see Adams to Abigail Adams, Philadelphia, August 14, 1776, *Letters*, 4: 678–80. For the history of the Great Seal, see Richard S. Patterson and Richardson Dougall, *The Eagle and the Shield: A History of the Great Seal of the United States* (Washington, D.C., 1976). See also, Frank H. Sommer, "Emblem and Device: The Origin of the Great Seal of the United States," *Art Quarterly* 24 (1961): 57–76; and Bureau of Public Affairs, *The Great Seal of the United States* (Washington, D.C., 1996).
3. Patterson and Dougall, *The Eagle and the Shield*, 15, quoting Lyman H. Butterfield et al., eds., *Adams Family Correspondence*, 4 vols. (Cambridge, Mass., 1963–1973), 2: ix–x.
4. *Pennsylvania Evening Post*, December 14, 1775. On the likelihood of Franklin's forgery, see *PTJ*, 1: 677 79. See also, "Rebellion to Tyrants Is Obedience to God," *WMQ*, 1st ser., 14 (1905): 37–38.
5. On Jefferson's view of Saxon history and its relevance to American independence, see Joseph J. Ellis, *American Sphinx: The Character of Thomas Jefferson* (New York, 1997), 36–41. For a recent reassessment of the political and constitutional achievements of the founding generation, see Richard B. Bernstein, *The Founding Fathers Reconsidered* (New York, 2009).
6. "Imagined" nationhood is a concept borrowed from Benedict Anderson, *Imagined Communities: Reflections on the Origins and Spread of Nationalism* (London, 1983).
7. Lynn Hunt, *Politics, Culture, and Class in the French Revolution* (Berkeley,

Calif., 1984), esp. 52–119. In the late 1970s, a number of European historians began to pay serious attention to the cultural dimensions of politics in early modern France, demonstrating the vitality of symbol and ceremony to the exercise of monarchical authority, to the overthrow of King Louis XVI, and to the establishment of a republican state. Their scholarship inspires my own. In addition to Hunt, see Maurice Agulhon, *Marianne into Battle: Republican Imagery and Symbolism in France, 1789–1880* (New York, 1981); Robert Darnton, *The Great Cat Massacre and Other Episodes in French Cultural History* (New York, 1984); Mona Ozouf, *Festivals and the French Revolution* (Cambridge, Mass., 1988); and Michèle Fogel, *Les cérémonies de l'information dans la France du XVIe au XVIII siècle* (Paris, 1989). For other European contexts, see the essays collected in Sean Wilentz, ed., *Rites of Power: Symbolism, Politics, and Ritual since the Middle Ages* (Philadelphia, 1985), and in Paul Dukes and John Dunkley, eds., *Culture and Revolution* (London, 1990).

8. On this point, see Leora Auslander, *Cultural Revolutions: Everyday Life and Politics in Britain, North America, and France* (Berkeley, Calif., 2009).

9. On notions of popular sovereignty and consent in British North America, see Edmund S. Morgan, *Inventing the People: The Rise of Popular Sovereignty in England and America* (New York, 1988), and Gillian Brown, *The Consent of the Governed: The Lockean Legacy in Early American Culture* (Cambridge, Mass., 2001). On the origins of Jefferson's ideas about the social contract, see Garry Wills, *Inventing America: Jefferson's Declaration of Independence* (Garden City, N.Y., 1978), but see Ronald Hamowy, "Jefferson and the Scottish Enlightenment: A Critique of Garry Wills's *Inventing America: Jefferson's Declaration of Independence*," *WMQ*, 3rd ser., 36 (1979): 503–23. See also Thad W. Tate, "The Social Contract in America, 1774–1787: Revolutionary Theory as a Conservative Instrument," *WMQ*, 3rd ser., 22 (1965): 375–91.

10. Eric J. Hobsbawm defines an invented tradition as "a set of practices, normally governed by overtly or tacitly accepted rules and of a ritual or symbolic nature, which seek to inculcate certain values and norms of behavior by repetition." Hobsbawm and Terrence O. Ranger, eds., *The Invention of Tradition* (Cambridge, 1983), 1. Though Hobsbawm utilized this concept primarily to analyze European nationalism in the decades preceding World War I, it may be usefully adapted to the Age of Revolution.

11. I am grateful to Neil Longley York, of Brigham Young University, for suggesting this term.

12. Brendan McConville, *The King's Three Faces: The Rise and Fall of Royal America, 1688–1776* (Chapel Hill, N.C., 2006); see also Jerrilyn Greene Marston, *King and Congress: The Transfer of Political Legitimacy, 1774–1776* (Princeton, N.J., 1987), 25.

13. McConville, *The King's Three Faces*.

14. For a brief introduction to the literature of British and American national identities in the late colonial and Revolutionary periods, see J. M. Bumstead, "'Things in the Womb of Time': Ideas of American Independence, 1633 to 1763," *WMQ*, 3rd ser., 31 (1974): 533–64; John M. Murrin, "A Roof without Walls: The Dilemma of American National Identity," in *Beyond Confederation: Origins of the Constitution and American National Identity*, ed. Richard Beeman, Stephen Botein, and Edward C. Carter II (Chapel Hill, N.C., 1987), 333–48; Linda Colley, *Britons: Forging the Nation, 1707–1837* (New Haven, Conn., 1992); T. H. Breen, "Ideology and Nationalism on the Eve of the American Revolution: Revisions Once More in Need of Revising," *JAH* 84 (1997): 13–39; Simon P. Newman, *Parades and the Politics of the Streets: Festive Culture in the Early American Republic* (Philadelphia, 1997); Len Travers, *Celebrating the Fourth: Independence Day and the Rites of Nationalism in the Early Republic* (Amherst, Mass., 1997); David Waldstreicher, *In the Midst of Perpetual Fetes: The Making of American Nationalism, 1776–1820* (Chapel Hill, N.C., 1997); Dror Wahrman, *The Making of the Modern Self: Identity and Culture in Eighteenth-Century England* (New Haven, Conn., 2004), and Wahrman, "The English Problem of Identity in the American Revolution," *AHR* 106 (2001): 1236–62; and McConville, *The King's Three Faces*.

15. John Adams to William Tudor, Philadelphia, October 7, 1774 (postscript dated October 9); John Adams to Abigail Adams, Philadelphia, October 9, 1774; John Adams's Diary, October 9, 1774, *Letters*, 1: 156–57, 163–65.

16. Here I invoke church liturgy and iconography only to suggest the affective power that John Adams and his contemporaries ascribed to those phenomena. As will be seen, however, the Continental Congress worked purposefully to promote religion for the sake of the Revolution and the United States. Derek H. Davis, *Religion and the Continental Congress, 1774–1789* (New York, 2000). In so doing, Congress contributed to the formation of what Robert N. Bellah and others have termed "civil religion." By that phrase, borrowed from Rousseau, Bellah meant not only the solemn acknowledgment of divine authority in the public life of the United States, but also the sacralization of national history and myth. See Bellah, "Civil Religion in America," *Dædalus* 96 (1967): 1–21; and Bellah and Phillip E. Hammond, *Varieties of Civil Religion* (San Francisco, 1980), esp. chapter 1. On the functional commonalities of sacred and secular ritual, see David I. Kertzer, *Ritual, Politics, and Power* (New Haven, Conn., 1988), esp. 1–14.

17. John Adams to Abigail Adams, Philadelphia, April 27, 1777; John Adams to Abigail Adams, Philadelphia, July 3, 1776; John Adams to Abigail Adams, Philadelphia, April 28, 1777, *Letters*, 4: 375–76; 6: 661–62, 666–67. On passion as a motivating force in Revolutionary America, see Nicole Eustace, *Passion Is the Gale: Emotion, Power, and the Coming of the American Revolution* (Chapel Hill, N.C., 2008).

18. *Journals*, 12: 1001; Samuel Adams to John Scollay, Philadelphia, December 30, 1780; Samuel Adams to Elbridge Gerry, Philadelphia, November 27, 1780, *Letters*, 16: 386–88, 513–15.

19. Notably, and for reasons that chapter 7 will explore, Washington permitted his officers to produce plays in contravention of Congress's ban on theatrical entertainments.

20. On the apotheosis of George Washington, see François Furstenberg, *In the Name of the Father: Washington's Legacy, Slavery, and the Making of a Nation* (New York, 2006), esp. 25–70.

21. Peter S. Onuf, *Origins of the Federal Republic: Jurisdictional Controversies in the United States, 1775–1787* (Philadelphia, 1983).

22. McConville, *The King's Three Faces*, 300–11.

23. Hobsbawm notes that invented traditions often attempt "to establish continuity with a suitable historic past." Hobsbawm and Ranger, eds., *The Invention of Tradition*, 1.

24. Ethnographic historian Rhys Isaac explains, "A culture may be thought of as a related set of languages, or as a multichannelled system of communication. Consisting of more than just words, it also comprises gesture, demeanor, dress, architecture, and all the codes by which those who share in the culture convey meanings and significance to each other." To borrow Isaac's terminology, this book "translates" the "action-statements" both of Congress and of its "significant others," especially the inhabitants of Philadelphia. See Isaac, "A Discourse on the Method: Action, Structure, and Meaning," in Rhys Isaac, *The Transformation of Virginia, 1740–1790*, new paperback edition (Chapel Hill, N.C., 1999), 323–57, quoted at 324–25, 338.

25. Gordon S. Wood, *The Creation of the American Republic: 1776–1787* (Chapel Hill, N.C., 1969), 319–21.

26. On the origins, nature, and power of folk ritual in Anglo-America, see Alfred F. Young, "English Plebeian Culture and Eighteenth-Century American Radicalism," in *The Origins of Anglo-American Radicalism*, ed. Margaret Jacob and James Jacob (London, 1984), 185–212; Roger D. Abrahams, "Introduction: A Folklore Perspective," in *Riot and Revelry in Early America*, ed. William Pencak, Matthew Dennis, and Simon P. Newman (University Park, Pa., 2002), 21–37; and, generally, Robert Blair St. George, *Conversing by Signs: Poetics of Implication in Colonial New England Culture* (Chapel Hill, N.C., 1998).

27. For an introduction to the history and behaviors of Revolutionary crowds, see generally Edmund S. Morgan and Helen M. Morgan, *The Stamp Act Crisis: Prologue to Revolution* (1953; reprint, Chapel Hill, N.C., 1995); Arthur M. Schlesinger Jr., "Political Mobs and the American Revolution, 1765–1776," *Proceedings of the American Philosophical Society* 99 (1955): 244–50; Gordon S. Wood, "A Note on Mobs in the American Revolution," *WMQ*, 3rd ser., 23 (1966): 635–42; Pauline Maier, *From Resistance to*

Revolution: Colonial Radicals and the Development of American Opposition to Britain, 1765–1776 (New York, 1972); Richard Maxwell Brown, "Violence and the American Revolution," in *Essays on the American Revolution*, ed. Stephen G. Kurtz and James H. Hutson (Chapel Hill, N.C., 1973), 81–120; Dirk Hoerder, *Crowd Action in Revolutionary Massachusetts, 1765–1780* (New York, 1977); Paul A. Gilje, *The Road to Mobocracy: Popular Disorder in New York City, 1763–1834* (Chapel Hill, N.C., 1987) and Gilje, *Rioting in America* (Bloomington, Ind., 1996); Jesse Lemisch, *Jack Tar vs. John Bull: The Role of New York's Seamen in Precipitating the Revolution* (New York, 1997); Alfred F. Young, *The Shoemaker and the Tea Party: Memory and the American Revolution* (Boston, 1999), and Young, *Liberty Tree: Ordinary People and the American Revolution* (New York, 2006); McConville, *The King's Three Faces*, 183–90; Thomas P. Slaughter, "Crowds in Eighteenth-Century America: Reflections and Directions," *PMHB* 115 (1991): 3–34; Barbara Clark Smith, "Food Rioters and the American Revolution," *WMQ*, 3rd ser., 51 (1994): 3–38; and Benjamin H. Irvin, "Tar, Feathers, and the Enemies of American Liberties, 1768–1776," *NEQ* 74 (2003): 197–229. See also the pioneering European studies of George Rudé and E. P. Thompson. For a recent reexamination of the destruction of tea in Boston Harbor, see Benjamin L. Carp, *Defiance of the Patriots: The Boston Tea Party and the Making of America* (New Haven, 2010).

28. In its concern for the social and political agency of persons marginalized by the state and in its focus on cultural aspects of politics and governance, this book draws insight from, and aims to contribute to, the "newest" political history. On the significance of material culture, iconography, ritual, and festivity to politics and society in colonial America and the early republic, see Newman, *Parades and the Politics of the Streets*; Travers, *Celebrating the Fourth*; Waldstreicher, *In the Midst of Perpetual Fetes*; and McConville, *The King's Three Faces*. On the political influence of persons not possessed of the vote and otherwise excluded from institutions of political authority, see Woody Holton, *Forced Founders: Indians, Debtors, Slaves and the Making of the American Revolution in Virginia* (Chapel Hill, N.C., 1999); Catherine Allgor, *Parlor Politics: In Which the Ladies of Washington Help Build a City and a Government* (Charlottesville, Va., 2000); Susan Branson, *These Fiery Frenchified Dames: Women and Political Culture in Early National Philadelphia* (Philadelphia, 2001); and Jeffrey L. Pasley, *"The Tyranny of Printers": Newspaper Politics in the Early American Republic* (Charlottesville, Va., 2001). See also the essays collected in Jeffrey L. Pasley, Andrew W. Robertson, and David Waldstreicher, eds., *Beyond the Founders: New Approaches to the Political History of the Early American Republic* (Chapel Hill, N.C., 2004). On personal identity and the practice of politics, see Joanne B. Freeman, *Affairs of Honor: National Politics in the New Republic* (New Haven, Conn., 2001).

29. On the centrality of newspapers and letters to the making of the republic, see generally Waldstreicher, *In the Midst of Perpetual Fetes*; Pasley, *"The Tyranny of Printers"*; Michael Warner, *The Letters of the Republic: Publication and the Public Sphere in Eighteenth-Century America* (Cambridge, Mass., 1990); and Matthew Rainbow Hale, "On Their Tiptoes: Political Time and Newspapers during the Advent of the Radicalized French Revolution, circa 1792–1793," *JER* 29 (2009): 191–218.

30. A short list of works on the history of Revolutionary Philadelphia includes Robert Levere Brunhouse, *The Counter-Revolution in Pennsylvania, 1776–1790* (Philadelphia, 1942); Carl Bridenbaugh, *Cities in Revolt: Urban Life in America, 1743–1776* (New York, 1955); David Freeman Hawke, *In the Midst of a Revolution* (Philadelphia, 1961); Charles S. Olton, *Artisans for Independence: Philadelphia Mechanics and the American Revolution* (Syracuse, N.Y., 1975); Eric Foner, *Tom Paine and Revolutionary America* (New York, 1976); Richard Alan Ryerson, *The Revolution Is Now Begun: The Radical Committees of Philadelphia, 1765–1776* (Philadelphia, 1978); Gary B. Nash, *The Urban Crucible: Social Change, Political Consciousness, and the Origins of the American Revolution* (Cambridge, Mass., 1979), and Nash, *First City: Philadelphia and the Forging of Historical Memory* (Philadelphia, 2002); Jack D. Marietta, *The Reformation of American Quakerism, 1748–1783* (Philadelphia, 1984); Thomas M. Doerflinger, *A Vigorous Spirit of Enterprise: Merchants and Economic Development in Revolutionary Philadelphia* (Chapel Hill, N.C., 1986); Steven Rosswurm, *Arms, Country, and Class: The Philadelphia Militia and the "Lower Sort" during the American Revolution, 1775–1783* (New Brunswick, N.J., 1987); Billy G. Smith, *The "Lower Sort": Philadelphia's Laboring People, 1750–1800* (Ithaca, N.Y., 1990); Catherine E. Hutchins, ed., *Shaping a National Culture: The Philadelphia Experience, 1750–1800* (Winterthur, Del., 1994); Peter Thompson, *Rum Punch and Revolution: Taverngoing and Public Life in Eighteenth-Century Philadelphia* (Philadelphia, 1999); and Benjamin L. Carp, *Rebels Rising: Cities and the American Revolution* (New York, 2007).

Part I

1. See the Statement of Violation of Rights and the Petition to the King adopted by Congress, *Journals*, 1: 63–73, 115–21.

2. Patrick Henry's Draft Address to the King, October 21, 1774, *Letters*, 1: 222–25. Few if any expected that the inhabitants of Canada, St. John's and Nova Scotia, or the West Indies would send representatives to the "Continental" Congress. By accident of history and geography, the inhabitants of Britain's contiguous mainland colonies did not generally imagine those other provinces as part of their American community. On this fictive continental geography, see James Drake, "Appropriating the Continent: Geographical Categories, Scientific Metaphors, and the Construction of Nationalism

in British North America and Mexico," *Journal of World History* 15 (2004): 323–57; and Claudio Saunt, "Go West: Mapping Early American Historiography," *WMQ*, 3rd ser., 65 (2008): 745–78.

3. Henry's aim was less lofty than his rhetoric. He sought to strengthen Virginia's hand in the Continental Congress by urging that the individual colonies vote in proportion to their respective populations rather than in equal number. His speech is recorded in John Adams's Notes of Debate, Philadelphia, September 6, 1774, *Letters*, 1: 27–29.

4. T. H. Breen, *The Marketplace of Revolution: How Consumer Politics Shaped American Independence* (New York, 2004), esp. 244–53.

5. *Journals*, 1: 31–39, quoted at 36.

6. On the phallic symbolism of Congress's emblem, see Eric Slauter, "Being Alone in the Age of the Social Contract," *WMQ*, 3rd ser., 62 (2005): 31–66, especially the discussion of figure v.

7. For patriot appropriations of the *Journal* emblem, see Lester C. Olson, *Emblems of American Community in the Revolutionary Era: A Study in Rhetorical Iconology* (Washington, D.C., 1991), 42–45; Abraham Swan, *A Collection of Designs in Architecture* (Philadelphia, 1775), n.p.; and Edward W. Richardson, *Standards and Colors of the American Revolution* (Philadelphia, 1982), 45–47.

Chapter 1

1. See the entry for November 24, 1775, in *Extracts from the Diary of Christopher Marshall, Kept in Philadelphia and Lancaster, during the American Revolution, 1774–1781*, ed. William Duane (Albany, N.Y., 1877), 51–53.

2. William Vincent Wells, *The Life and Public Service of Samuel Adams*, 3 vols. (Boston, 1865), 2: 207–10. In support of this anecdote, Wells, the great-grandson of Samuel Adams, cited family tradition and the private correspondence of the Boston merchant John Andrews. Both of those sources emphasized the material quality of Adams's new wardrobe, including its fine fabrics and silver and gold accessories. Neither source suggested that the suit, a reward for Adams's public service, was made of homespun, as other patriots had begun to wear. On Adams's disregard for dress and appearance, see Carol Troyen's entry on John Singleton Copley's *Samuel Adams* in the catalog of Carrie Rebora et al., *John Singleton Copley in America* (New York, 1995), 275–78. For more on the relationship between fashion and politics in late-eighteenth-century British North America and the United States, see generally, Karin Calvert, "The Function of Fashion in Eighteenth-Century America" in *Of Consuming Interests: The Style of Life in the Eighteenth Century*, ed. Cary Carson, Ronald Hoffman, and Peter J. Albert (Charlottesville, Va., 1994), 252–83; Linda Baumgarten, *What Clothes Reveal: The Language of Clothing in Colonial and Federal America* (New Haven, Conn., 2002); Michael Zakim, *Ready-Made Democracy: A History of*

Men's Dress in the American Republic, 1760–1860 (Chicago, 2003); Linzy A. Brekke, "'The Scourge of Fashion': Political Economy and the Politics of Consumption in Post-Revolutionary America," *Early American Studies: An Interdisciplinary Journal* 3 (2005): 111–39, and Brekke, "'To Make a Figure': Clothing and Gender Politics in Early National America," in *Gender, Taste, and Material Culture in Britain and North America, 1700–1850*, ed. Amanda Vickery and John Styles (New Haven, Conn., 2006), 225–46; and Kate Haulman, "Fashion and the Culture Wars of Revolutionary Philadelphia," *WMQ*, 3rd ser., 62 (2005): 625–62.

3. For a detailed analysis of the First Continental Congress and its proceedings, see Edmund Cody Burnett, *The Continental Congress* (New York, 1941), 3–59; Lynn Montross, *The Reluctant Rebels: The Story of the Continental Congress: 1774–1789* (New York, 1950), 3–57; David Ammerman, *In the Common Cause: American Response to the Coercive Acts of 1774* (Charlottesville, Va., 1974); H. James Henderson, *Party Politics in the Continental Congress* (New York, 1974), 7–69; Jack N. Rakove, *The Beginnings of National Politics: An Interpretive History of the Continental Congress* (New York, 1979), 42–62; Jerrilyn Greene Marston, *King and Congress: The Transfer of Political Legitimacy, 1774–1776* (Princeton, N.J., 1987), 67–130; Calvin Jillson and Rick K. Wilson, *Congressional Dynamics: Structure, Coordination, and Choice in the First American Congress, 1774–1789* (Stanford, Calif., 1994), 41–59; and Neil Longley York, "The First Continental Congress and the Problem of American Rights," *PMHB* 122 (1998), 353–83.

4. Marston, *King and Congress*, 69–75.

5. Burnett, *The Continental Congress*, 46–49; Ammerman, *In the Common Cause*, 39–41, 46; Henderson, *Party Politics in the Continental Congress*, 24–25, 33, 39–41.

6. Ammerman, *In the Common Cause*, 38–41; Henderson, *Party Politics in the Continental Congress*, 24–25.

7. *DAJA*, 2: 106; John Adams to William Tudor, Philadelphia, September 29, 1774, *Letters*, 1: 129–31.

8. Joseph Galloway to William Franklin, Philadelphia, September 5, 1774; John Adams's Diary, August 29–September 5, *Letters*, 1: 4, 27.

9. Silas Deane to Elizabeth Deane, Philadelphia, September 6, 1774, *Letters*, 1: 29–30.

10. John Adams to Abigail Adams, Philadelphia, September 16, 1774, *Letters*, 1: 74–75.

11. John Adams's Diary, September 10, 1774, Philadelphia, *Letters*, 1: 60.

12. For the Suffolk Resolves, see *Journals*, 1: 31–39.

13. Rakove, *The Beginnings of National Politics*, 55; York, "The First Continental Congress and the Problem of American Rights," 371–72.

14. York, "The First Continental Congress and the Problem of American Rights," 360; Henderson, *Party Politics in the Continental Congress*, 41.

15. See generally T. H. Breen, *The Marketplace of Revolution: How Consumer Politics Shaped American Independence* (New York, 2004).

16. For the Articles of Association, see *Journals* 1: 75–81.

17. John J. McCusker and Russell R. Menard, *The Economy of British America, 1607–1789* (Chapel Hill, N.C., 1985), 279–80.

18. On the origins and history of the consumer revolution, see generally Richard L. Bushman, *The Refinement of America: Persons, Houses, Cities* (New York, 1992); Carson, Hoffman, and Albert, eds., *Of Consuming Interests*; T. H. Breen, *The Marketplace of Revolution*.

19. On the practice of giving gloves and scarves at funerals, see Steven C. Bullock and Sheila McIntyre, "'All had Gloves': Funeral Glove-Giving and the Imagined Communities of Early New England" (paper presented at "Faces & Places in Early America: An Interdisciplinary Conference on Art and the World of Objects," McNeil Center for Early American Studies, Philadelphia, Pa., December 2005).

20. See generally Sydney E. Ahlstrom, *A Religious History of the American People*, 2nd ed. (New Haven, Conn., 2004), 99–384. See also Dudley W. R. Bahlman, *The Moral Revolution of 1688* (New Haven, Conn., 1957).

21. On Anglo-American republicanism, see Caroline Robbins, *The Eighteenth-Century Commonwealthman: Studies in the Transmission, Development, and Circumstance of English Liberal Thought from the Restoration of Charles II until the War with the Thirteen Colonies* (Cambridge, Mass., 1959); Bernard Bailyn, *The Ideological Origins of the American Revolution* (Cambridge, Mass., 1967); Gordon Wood, *The Creation of the American Republic, 1776–1787* (Chapel Hill, N.C., 1969), and Wood, *The Radicalism of the American Revolution* (New York, 1992); J. G. A. Pocock, *The Machiavellian Moment: Florentine Political Thought and the Atlantic Republican Tradition*, 2nd ed. (Princeton, N.J., 2003), 401–61; and Jonathan Scott, *Commonwealth Principles: Republican Writing of the English Revolution* (Cambridge, 2004), 348–49. See also Robert E. Shalhope, "Toward a Republican Synthesis: The Emergence of an Understanding of Republicanism in American Historiography," *WMQ*, 3rd ser., 29 (1972): 49–80; and Daniel T. Rodgers, "Republicanism: The Career of a Concept," *JAH* 79 (1992): 11–38.

22. C. H. Firth and R. S. Rait, eds., *Acts and Ordinances of the Interregnum, 1642–1660*, 3 vols. (London, 1911), 1: 26, 1027, 1070; 2: 861, 941.

23. Joel Bernard, "Original Themes of Voluntary Moralism: The Anglo-American Reformation of Manners," in *Moral Problems in American Life: New Perspectives on Cultural History*, ed. Karen Halttunen and Lewis Perry (Ithaca, N.Y., 1998), 15–39, cited at 38 n. 37.

24. See vol. 2, p. 9 of the separately paginated appendix in *The Charters and Acts of Assembly of the Province of Pennsylvania*, 2 vols. (Philadelphia, 1762).

25. *The Book of the General Lawes and Libertyes Concerning the Inhabitants of the Massachusets* (Cambridge, Mass., 1660), 33; *The Sixth Assembly, First*

Sessions (New York, 1695), 112–13; *Acts and Laws, of His Majesties Colony in Connecticut* (Boston, 1702), 44; *All the Laws of Maryland* (Annapolis, Md., 1707), 109; *The Laws of the Province of Pennsilvania Collected into One Volume* (Philadelphia, 1714) 139; *Acts and Laws Passed by the General Court of Assembly of His Majesties Province of New-Hampshire in New England* (Boston, 1722), 162; *A Collection of All the Acts of Assembly, Now in Force, in the Colony of Virginia* (Williamsburg, Va., 1733), 398; *The Laws of the Province of South Carolina* (Charleston, S.C., 1736), 231; *Laws of the Government of New-Castle, Kent and Sussex upon Delaware* (Philadelphia, 1742), 116; *A Collection of all the Public Acts of Assembly, of the Province of North-Carolina* (New Bern, N.C., 1751), 153; Samuel Nevill, comp., *The Acts of the General Assembly of the Province of New Jersey* (Philadelphia, 1752), 407; *The Charter, Granted by His Majesty, King Charles II, to the Governor and Company of . . . Rhode-Island* (Newport, R.I., 1767), 132; *Acts Passed by the Assembly of Georgia* (Savannah, Ga., 1763), 11.

26. See Kenneth Silverman, *A Cultural History of the American Revolution: Painting, Music, Literature, and the Theatre in the Colonies and the United States from the Treaty of Paris to the Inauguration of George Washington, 1763–1789* (New York, 1976), 59–69, and the extensive body of literature cited there; Ann Fairfax Withington, *Toward a More Perfect Union: Virtue and the Formation of American Republics* (New York, 1991), 48–91. See also, Hugh F. Rankin, *The Theater in Colonial America* (Chapel Hill, N.C., 1965); Jean-Christophe Agnew, *Worlds Apart: The Market and the Theater in Anglo-American Thought, 1550–1750* (Cambridge, 1986); Jared Brown, *The Theatre in America during the Revolution* (Cambridge, 1995); and Jason Shaffer, *Performing Patriotism: National Identity in the Colonial and Revolutionary American Theater* (Philadelphia, 2007).

27. Rhys Isaac, *The Transformation of Virginia, 1740–1790*, new paperback edition (Chapel Hill, N.C., 1999), 98–104.

28. Silverman, *A Cultural History of the American Revolution*, 59–69.

29. Of the behaviors proscribed by Article 8, previous colonial boycotts enjoined only extravagant mourning. On pre-Revolutionary efforts to curtail this practice, see Withington, *Toward a More Perfect Union*, 116–17. See also Nicole Eustace, *Passion Is the Gale: Emotion, Power, and the Coming of the American Revolution* (Chapel Hill, N.C., 2008), 394–407.

30. Robert Treat Paine's Notes for a Speech in Congress, October 5, 1774, *Letters*, 1: 146–49.

31. Breen, *The Marketplace of Revolution*, esp. chapters 7 and 8.

32. One London correspondent accused the colonists of hypocrisy because they protested their inability to pay taxes and yet squandered money at "cock-fighting, fox-hunting, horse-racing, and every other expensive diversion." Quoted in the *Boston Evening-Post*, July 20, 1767.

33. Low is quoted in John Adams's Notes on Debate, Philadelphia, October 6, 1774; John Adams to James Warren, Philadelphia, October 19, 1775, *Letters*, 1: 151–53; 2: 206–7.

34. *Boston Gazette*, October 1, 1764.

35. On colonial sumptuary laws as mechanisms for the preservation of class and racial hierarchies, see Breen, *The Marketplace of Revolution*, 163–65.

36. See the *Boston Gazette*, October 1, 1764; the *Boston Evening-Post*, September 24, 1764; and the *Pennsylvania Gazette*, December 27, 1764.

37. Quoted in Isaac, *The Transformation of Virginia, 1740–1790*, 100.

38. Winslow C. Watson, ed., *Men and Times of the Revolution; or, Memoirs of Elkanah Watson* (New York, 1856), 261–62, quoted in Isaac, *The Transformation of Virginia, 1740–1790*, 102.

39. Eric Foner, *Tom Paine and Revolutionary America* (New York, 1976), 50; and Steven Rosswurm, *Arms, Country, and Class: The Philadelphia Militia and the "Lower Sort" during the American Revolution, 1775–1783* (New Brunswick, N.J., 1987), 37.

40. The former verses are in Foner, *Tom Paine and Revolutionary America*, 110–11. The latter, written by Jonathan Odell and originally published in Rivington's gazette, are anthologized in Winthrop Sargent, *The Loyalist Poetry of the Revolution* (Boston, 1977), 38–54, quoted at 41. See also, Rosswurm, *Arms, Country, and Class*, 37–38.

41. Ruth H. Bloch, "The Gendered Meanings of Virtue in Revolutionary America," *Signs: Journal of Women in Culture and Society* 13 (1987): 37–58. See also, Linda K. Kerber, *Women of the Republic: Intellect and Ideology in Revolutionary America* (Chapel Hill, N.C., 1980), 199–200.

42. Bloch, "The Gendered Meanings of Virtue in Revolutionary America." See also, Breen, *The Marketplace of Revolution*, 172–82; and Michal J. Rozbicki, *The Complete Colonial Gentleman: Cultural Legitimacy in Plantation America* (Charlottesville, Va., 1998), esp. 172–91.

43. John Adams to a Friend in London, February 10, 1775, *Letters*, 1: 308–10.

44. See generally Ellen Hartigan-O'Connor, *The Ties That Buy: Women and Commerce in Revolutionary America* (Philadelphia, 2009). See also Breen, *The Marketplace of Revolution*, 130.

45. David S. Shields, *Civil Tongues and Polite Letters in British America* (Chapel Hill, N.C., 1997), 55–140.

46. See generally, Hartigan-O'Connor, *The Ties That Buy*. See also Anne S. Lombard, *Making Manhood: Growing Up Male in Colonial New England* (Cambridge, Mass., 2003), 65–66; and Breen, *The Marketplace of Revolution*, 172–82, 281–83.

47. On classical and biblical notions of women's sensuousness, see Bloch, "The Gendered Meanings of Virtue in Revolutionary America," 41–42. See also Bloch, "Untangling the Roots of Modern Sex Roles: A Survey of Four

Centuries of Change," *Signs: Journal of Women in Culture and Society* 4 (1978): 237–52.

48. Breen, *The Marketplace of Revolution*, 231–34.

49. John Adams, *Thoughts on Government, Applicable to the Present State of the American Colonies* (Philadelphia, 1776), 14.

50. John Adams's Diary, September 17, 1774, *Letters*, 1: 75.

51. See Charles S. Olton, *Artisans for Independence: Philadelphia Mechanics and the American Revolution* (Syracuse, N.Y., 1975); Gary B. Nash, *The Urban Crucible: Social Change, Political Consciousness, and the Origins of the American Revolution* (Cambridge, Mass., 1979); Kerber, *Women of the Republic*, and Kerber, *No Constitutional Right to Be Ladies: Women and the Obligations of Citizenship* (New York, 1998), esp. chapter 1; Mary Beth Norton, *Liberty's Daughters: The Revolutionary Experience of American Women, 1750–1800* (Boston, 1980); Jesse Lemisch, *Jack Tar vs. John Bull: The Role of New York's Seamen in Precipitating the Revolution* (New York, 1997); Woody Holton, *Forced Founders: Indians, Debtors, Slaves, and the Making of the American Revolution in Virginia* (Chapel Hill, N.C., 1999); Alfred F. Young, *The Shoemaker and the Tea Party: Memory and the American Revolution* (Boston, 1999), and Young, *Liberty Tree: Ordinary People and the American Revolution* (New York, 2006); Carol Berkin, *Revolutionary Mothers: Women in the Struggle for America's Independence* (New York, 2005); Breen, *The Marketplace of Revolution*, 231–34; and Rosemarie Zagarri, *Revolutionary Backlash: Women and Politics in the Early American Republic* (Philadelphia, 2007).

52. New Hampshire Delegates to Meshech Weare, October 12, 1774, *Letters*, 1: 180–81.

53. Thomas Jefferson to Archibald Cary and Benjamin Harrison, Monticello, December 9, 1774, *PTJ*, 1: 154–56. Benjamin Franklin to Joseph Priestley, Philadelphia, July 7, 1775, *RCDUS*, 58–59. For congressmen in homespun, Congress's mourning of Peyton Randolph, and Adams's objection to popular diversions, see Richard Smith's Diary, September 15, 1775; John Adams to James Warren, Philadelphia, October 24, 1775; and Adams to Mercy Warren, Philadelphia, November 25, 1775, *Letters*, 2: 17, 232–33, 387–88.

54. *South Carolina Gazette*, November 21, 1774, and *Maryland Gazette*, April 15, 1775, both cited in Ammerman, *In the Common Cause*, 116; *New-York Journal*, December 15, 1774, and April 6, 1775; *Pennsylvania Gazette*, November 9, 1774; for similar episodes, see *Connecticut Journal*, December 2, 1774; and *Essex Gazette*, December 20–27, 1774, and January 10–17, 1775.

55. On the colonists' compliance with Article 8, see Ammerman, *In the Common Cause*, 116–24. See also Robert Patrick Reed, "Loyalists, Patriots, and Trimmers: The Committee System in the American Revolution, 1774–1776" (Ph.D. diss., Cornell University, 1988).

56. See generally, Bushman, *The Refinement of America*; Isaac, *The Transformation of Virginia, 1740–1790*; Carson, Hoffman, and Albert, eds., *Of Consuming*

Interests; Rozbicki, *The Complete Colonial Gentleman*; and Shields, *Civil Tongues and Polite Letters in British America*.

57. *DAJA*, 2: 97–98 n. 2, 99–104.

58. *New-York Gazette*, September 5, 1774.

59. *DAJA*, 2: 105–07.

60. John Adams's Diary, August 29–September 5, 1774, *Letters*, 1: 3–12, quoted at 3.

61. Thomas Cushing to Deborah Cushing, Philadelphia, October 4, 1774, *Letters*, 1: 142–43.

62. John Adams's Diary, September 8, 1774, *Letters*, 1: 45–46.

63. Rakove, *The Beginnings of National Politics*, 43–44; Jillson and Wilson, *Congressional Dynamics*, 176.

64. *Journals*, 1: 25.

65. John Adams's Diary, August 29–September 5, 1774, and September 12, 1774; Robert Treat Paine's Diary, September 12, 1774, *Letters*, 1: 5, 64–65, 66. As of 1772, fewer than 1 percent of Philadelphians owned coaches. In view of this fact, Dickinson's arrival "in his coach" appears all the more remarkable as a display of wealth and status. Robert F. Oaks, "Big Wheels in Philadelphia: Du Simitière's List of Carriage Owners," *PMHB* 95 (1971): 351–362. I am grateful to Jack Marietta for this citation.

66. John Adams's Diary, August 29–September 5, 1774, *Letters*, 1: 6.

67. John Adams's Diary, September 12, 1774, *Letters*, 1: 64–65.

68. John Adams's Diary, August 29–September 5, 1774, *Letters*, 1: 5.

69. Silas Deane to Elizabeth Deane, Philadelphia, September 23, 1774, *Letters*, 1: 91–92.

70. Thomas Cushing to Deborah Cushing, Philadelphia, October 4, 1774, *Letters*, 1: 142–43.

71. On the role of elite women in the making of an early national political culture, see Catherine Allgor, *Parlor Politics: In which the Ladies of Washington Help Build a City and a Government* (Charlottesville, Va., 2000); and Susan Branson, *These Fiery Frenchified Dames: Women and Political Culture in Early National Philadelphia* (Philadelphia, 2001).

72. Charles J. Stillé, *The Life and Times of John Dickinson, 1732–1808* (Philadelphia, 1891), 331–32.

73. Joseph J. Ellis, *American Sphinx: The Character of Thomas Jefferson* (New York, 1997), 24. Surviving letters and personal memoranda do not reveal precisely how many other slaves traveled with their congressmen-masters, or in what specific occupational capacities. Bondsmen rarely appear in the delegates' letters or diaries, and the Continental Congress worked assiduously to avoid discussing slavery as an institution. Declared Thomas Lynch on the floor of Congress, "If it is debated, whether their slaves are their property, there is an end of the confederation." Quoted in Peter M. Bergman and Jean McCarroll, comps., *The Negro in the Continental Congress* (New York, 1969), 16.

74. On mastery over servants, slaves, and dependents as a hallmark of genteel Southern masculinity, see Isaac, *The Transformation of Virginia, 1740–1790*, 132–35; Rozbicki, *The Complete Colonial Gentleman*, 118–19. See also Kenneth A. Lockridge, *On the Sources of Patriarchal Rage: The Commonplace Books of William Byrd and Thomas Jefferson and the Gendering of Power in the Eighteenth Century* (New York, 1992), 96; and Kathleen M. Brown, *Good Wives, Nasty Wenches, and Anxious Patriarchs: Gender, Race, and Power in Colonial Virginia* (Chapel Hill, N.C., 1996), 247–82, 319–66.

75. John Adams's Diary, August 29–September 5, 1774, *Letters*, 1: 9.

76. On oratory in eighteenth-century Anglo-America, see Sandra M. Gustafson, *Eloquence Is Power: Oratory and Performance in Early America* (Chapel Hill, N.C., 2000). See also Jay Fliegelman, *Declaring Independence: Jefferson, National Language, and the Culture of Performance* (Stanford, Calif., 1993), 28–39.

77. John Adams's Diary, August 29–September 5, 1774; Silas Deane to Elizabeth Deane, Philadelphia, September 10, 1774, *Letters*, 1: 7, 60–63.

78. John Armstrong Sr. to George Washington, Philadelphia, October 15, 1779; John Adams's Diary, August 29–September 5, 1774; Silas Deane to Elizabeth Deane, Philadelphia, September 6, 1774, *Letters*, 1: 6, 34–35; 14: 76–79.

79. John Adams to James Warren, Philadelphia, September 17, 1775, *Letters*, 2: 24–25.

80. "William Whipple's Notes of a Journey from Philadelphia to New Hampshire, in the Summer of 1777," *PMHB* 10 (1886–87), 374, quoted in Charles Royster, *A Revolutionary People at War: The Continental Army and American Character, 1775–1783* (Chapel Hill, N.C., 1979), 236.

81. Richard Smith's Diary, September 15, 1775, *Letters*, 2: 17.

82. Shields, *Civil Tongues and Polite Letters in British America*, 145–49; McConville, *The King's Three Faces*, 63–70.

83. Robert Treat Paine's Diary, [September 16, 1774]; Silas Deane to Elizabeth Deane, Philadelphia, September 12–18, 1774; Caesar Rodney to Thomas Rodney, Philadelphia, September 12, 1774, *Letters*, 1: 65–67, 75.

84. Harrison Gray claimed that the Massachusetts delegates introduced the Suffolk Resolves in an evening session, after an extravagant dinner in which members of Congress had imbibed "thirty two bumpers of the *best Madeira*." Gray, *The Two Congresses Cut Up* (New York, 1775), 7. See also, *Norwich Packet*, September 22–29, 1774; *Newport Mercury*, October 3, 1774; *Journals*, 1: 31–41. For the politics of Congress's endorsement of the Suffolk Resolves, see Marston, *King and Congress*, 44, 84–85.

85. John Adams's Diary, October 20, 1774, *Letters*, 1: 221.

86. See for example, *Essex Gazette*, September 20–27, 1774; *Norwich Packet*, September 29, 1774; and Purdie and Dixon's *Virginia Gazette*, October 6, 1774.

87. J. Thomas Scharf and Thompson Westcott, *A History of Philadelphia, 1609–1884*, 3 vols. (1884), 1: 293–95. On the United Company of Philadelphia, see *Pennsylvania Magazine; or, American Monthly Museum* 1 (1775): 482–85; and William R. Bagnall, *The Textile Industries of the United States* (Cambridge, Mass., 1893), 63–72. See also James A. Henretta, "The War for Independence and American Economic Development," in *The Economy of Early America: The Revolutionary Period, 1763–1790*, ed. Ronald Hoffman, John J. McCusker, and Russell Menard (Charlottesville, 1988): 45–87.

88. See Olton, *Artisans for Independence*; Richard Alan Ryerson, *The Revolution Is Now Begun: The Radical Committees of Philadelphia, 1765–1776* (Philadelphia, 1978), 32–33; Rosswurm, *Arms, Country, and Class*, 13–48.

89. Ryerson, *The Revolution Is Now Begun*, 96.

90. Rosswurm, *Arms, Country, and Class*, 49–75.

91. Richard Buel Jr., *In Irons: Britain's Naval Supremacy and the American Revolutionary Economy* (New Haven, Conn., 1998), 31.

92. Scharf and Westcott, *A History of Philadelphia*, 1: 299; Buel, *In Irons*, 39; on the Delaware pilots, see the entries for September 1775 in volume 2 of the National Park Service's nine-volume, unpaginated Bicentennial Daybook, Independence National Park.

93. Rosswurm, *Arms, Country, and Class*, 52–61.

94. Quoted in David Hawke, *In the Midst of a Revolution* (Philadelphia, 1961), 148.

95. A complete, colony-by-colony list of the congressmen's remuneration may be found in New York Delegates to the New York Provincial Convention, Philadelphia, November 3, 1775, *Letters*, 2: 294–95. These sums were occasionally reported in local newspapers. See for example, the *Pennsylvania Gazette*, August 17, 1774, reporting sums raised by the counties of Virginia for the expenses of that colony's Continental Congressmen; see also the *Pennsylvania Packet*, September 19, 1774, detailing the compensation allotted for North Carolina's delegates.

96. Harrison Gray, *A Few Remarks upon Some of the Votes and Resolutions of the Continental Congress* (Boston, 1775), 8.

97. *The Poor Man's Advice to His Poor Neighbours: A Ballad, to the Tune of Chevy-Chace* (New York, 1774).

98. *The Poor Man's Advice to His Poor Neighbours*, 4, 10–15, 17–18.

99. Isaac Wilkins, *Short Advice to the Counties of New-York* (New York, 1774), 14.

100. *The Poor Man's Advice to His Poor Neighbours*, 3.

101. *The Poor Man's Advice to His Poor Neighbours*, 9–10.

102. *The Poor Man's Advice to His Poor Neighbours*, 16.

103. Scharf and Westcott, *A History of Philadelphia*, 1: 304.

104. Duane, *Extracts from the Diary of Christopher Marshall*, 51–53.

105. Robert Blair St. George, *Conversing by Signs: Poetics of Implication in Colonial New England Culture* (Chapel Hill, N.C., 1998), 293–94.

106. On the establishment of the City Tavern, see Peter Thompson, *Rum Punch and Revolution: Taverngoing and Public Life in Eighteenth-Century Philadelphia* (Philadelphia, 1999), 149–51; John Adams's Diary, August 29–September 5, 1774, *Letters*, 1: 3.

107. Peter Force, comp., *American Archives*, ser. 4 (Washington, D.C, 1837–1853), 3: 170–76; Rosswurm, *Arms, Country, and Class*, 46–48; Ryerson, *The Revolution Is Now Begun*, 131–33.

108. Edmund S. Morgan and Helen M. Morgan, *The Stamp Act Crisis: Prologue to Revolution* (1953; reprint, Chapel Hill, N.C., 1995), 130–35.

109. Dixon and Hunter's *Virginia Gazette*, January 28, 1775; *Essex Gazette*, January 10–17, 1775; *South Carolina Gazette*, April 3, 1775. A Virginia committee did in fact prosecute the hosting of a ball in February 1776, three months after Congress's near indiscretion. See the *Maryland Gazette*, March 28, 1776, quoting Purdie's *Virginia Gazette*, February 16, 1776.

110. Duane, *Extracts from the Diary of Christopher Marshall*, 51–53.

Chapter 2

1. Thomas Bradbury Chandler, *A Friendly Address to All Reasonable Americans* (New York, 1774), 31–32.

2. "Address of a Committee of the Clergy of the Church of England in New York and New Jersey" to the colonial secretary, Lord Hillsborough, 1771. Quoted in Arthur Lyon Cross, *The Anglican Episcopate and the American Colonies* (New York, 1902), 255.

3. Thomas Bradbury Chandler to Daniel Burton, January 15, 1766, quoted in Judith Sumner Hanson, "For Church and State: Thomas Bradbury Chandler and the Coming of the American Revolution" (master's thesis, University of Utah, 1977), 34; Bruce E. Steiner, *Samuel Seabury, 1729–1796: A Study in High Church Tradition* (Oberlin, Ohio, 1971), 109, 122. On the Bishop's Controversy, see Carl Bridenbaugh, *Mitre and Sceptre: Transatlantic Faiths, Ideas, Personalities, and Politics, 1689–1775* (New York, 1962); Bernard Bailyn, *The Ideological Origins of the American Revolution* (Cambridge, Mass., 1967), 96–98; Nancy L. Rhoden, *Revolutionary Anglicanism: The Colonial Church of England Clergy during the American Revolution* (Houndmills, U.K., 1999), 37–63; Peter M. Doll, *Revolution, Religion, and National Identity: Imperial Anglicanism in British North America, 1745–1795* (Madison, N.J., 2000), 155–209; and James B. Bell, *A War of Religion: Dissenters, Anglicans, and the American Revolution* (Houndmills, U.K., 2008), 81–120. On regionalized sectarian conflict and the politics of colonial resistance, see H. James Henderson, *Party Politics in the Continental Congress* (New York, 1974), 23–25.

4. E. E. Beardsley, *Life and Correspondence of the Rt. Rev. Samuel Seabury, D.D.* (Boston, 1881), 30, quoted in William Nelson, *The American Tory* (1961; reprint, Westport, Conn., 1980), 73; Steiner, *Samuel Seabury, 1729–1796*, 128–29; Hanson, "For Church and State," 69. Charles Inglis, curate of Trinity Church, New York, was also a party to this pact. In 1776, Inglis wrote a handful of pamphlets in opposition to Paine's *Common Sense* and to the Declaration of Independence.

5. Throughout this and the following chapters, I use the term "loyalist" to refer to individuals who opposed the Continental Congress and the Articles of Association. Though somewhat anachronistic before independence, "loyalist" carries less opprobrium than "Tory." Similarly, I use "patriot" as Myles Cooper did, to describe individuals who supported radical economic resistance, Congress, or the Association.

6. Samuel Seabury wrote three tracts under the pseudonym A. W. Farmer in November and December 1774: *A View of the Controversy between Great Britain and Her Colonies* (New York, 1774), *Free Thoughts on the Proceedings of the Continental Congress* (New York, 1774), and *The Congress Canvassed; or, An Examination into the Conduct of the Delegates* (New York, 1774). Myles Cooper published *The Patriots of North-America: A Sketch* (New York, 1775) early in the new year. Thomas Bradbury Chandler authored *What Think Ye of the Congress Now?* (New York, 1775) later that spring.

7. For historians' assessments of this literature, see Philip Davidson, *Propaganda and the American Revolution, 1763–1783* (Chapel Hill, N.C., 1941), 249–311; Nelson, *The American Tory*, 75–80; Steiner, *Samuel Seabury, 1729–1796*, 127–76; Janice Potter, *The Liberty We Seek: Loyalist Ideology in Colonial New York and Massachusetts* (Cambridge, Mass., 1983), 132–52; Rhoden, *Revolutionary Anglicanism*, 64–87; and Bell, *A War of Religion*, 123–169. For the larger context of Revolutionary debate, see generally, Bernard Bailyn, ed., *Pamphlets of the American Revolution* (Cambridge, Mass., 1965). For literary analyses of these anticongressional pamphlets, see Moses Coit Tyler, *A Literary History of the American Revolution*, 2 vols. (New York, 1897), 1: 293–400; Bruce Ingham Granger, *Political Satire in the American Revolution, 1763–1783* (Ithaca, N.Y., 1960); 118–25; Lewis Leary, "Literature in New York, 1775," *EAL* 11 (1976): 4–21, Philip Gould, "Wit and Politics in Revolutionary British America: The Case of Samuel Seabury and Alexander Hamilton," *Eighteenth-Century Studies* 41 (2008): 383–403.

8. Chandler, *What Think Ye of the Congress Now?*, 5.

9. This fact suggests that Revolutionary political rhetoric reaffirmed traditional norms of masculine deportment. By smearing the manhood of their political adversaries, even in lampoon or patent jest, loyalist writers occasionally challenged, but more often validated, long-standing conventions of manly behavior in the home and in the state house. In so doing, they capitalized on the mobilizing power of gender in political debate, that

is, the power of gendered language to rally individuals in support of or in opposition to political leaders and platforms. This notion of the mobilizing power of gender takes inspiration from Kristin L. Hoganson's insightful analysis of the *coercive* power of gender in political debate. See Hoganson, *Fighting for American Manhood: How Gender Politics Provoked the Spanish-American and Philippine-American Wars* (New Haven, Conn., 1998), 88–106.

10. Chandler, *What Think Ye of the* Congress *Now?*, 36.

11. Seabury, *A View of the Controversy*, 23.

12. Seabury, *A View of the Controversy*, 37.

13. Seabury, *The Congress Canvassed*, 17.

14. See generally Michael Heyd, *"Be Sober and Reasonable": The Critique of Enthusiasm in the Seventeenth and Early Eighteenth Centuries* (Leiden, 1905).

15. For an introduction to the historiography of the Great (or not-so-Great) Awakening, see Alan Heimert, *Religion and the American Mind: From the Great Awakening to the Revolution* (Cambridge, Mass., 1966); Jon Butler, "Enthusiasm Described and Decried: The Great Awakening as Interpretive Fiction," *JAH* 69 (1982): 305–25, and Butler, *Awash in a Sea of Faith: Christianizing the American People* (Cambridge, Mass., 1990); Patricia U. Bonomi, *Under the Cope of Heaven: Religion, Society, and Politics in Colonial America* (New York, 1986); and Frank Lambert, *Inventing the "Great Awakening"* (Princeton, N.J., 1999).

16. "A Letter from Ebenezer Kinnersley to his Friend in the Country," *postscript to the Pennsylvania Gazette*, July 15, 1740, quoted in J. A. Leo Lemay, *Ebenezer Kinnersley: Franklin's Friend* (Philadelphia, 1964), 20–21. For similar critiques of New Light preaching, see generally, Charles Chauncy, *Enthusiasm Described and Caution'd Against* (Boston, 1742); Benjamin Doolittle, *An Enquiry into Enthusiasm, Being an Account of What It Is, the Original, Progress, and Effects of It* (Boston, 1743); Joseph Bellamy, *True Religion Delineated; or, Experimental Religion, as Distinguished from Formality on the One Hand, and Enthusiasm on the Other* (Boston, 1750); Chauncy Graham, *Enthusiasm Detected* (New York, 1751); and Thomas Hartley, *A Discourse on Mistakes Concerning Religion, Enthusiasm, Experiences, etc.* (Germantown, Pa., 1759).

17. "The Remainder of the Letter from a Gentleman in Boston, to His Friend in Edinburgh," *Boston Evening-Post*, November 5, 1744.

18. "To the Author of the Boston Weekly Post-Boy," *Boston Post Boy*, October 12, 1741. For the belittling characterization of Great Awakening enthusiasm as madness, see George Whitefield, *A Continuation of the Reverend Mr. Whitefield's Journal from a Few Days after His Arrival at Georgia* (Philadelphia, 1740), and Whitefield, *A Continuation of the Reverend Mr. Whitefield's Journal from His Embarking after the Embargo* (Philadelphia 1740), in which Whitefield repeatedly describes the denunciation of his New Light

followers as madmen. See also, "A Letter from a Gentleman in Boston, to His Friend in the Country," *Boston Evening-Post*, July 5, 1742.

19. William Hooper, *The Apostles Neither Imposters Nor Enthusiasts* (Boston, 1742), 45; Charles Chauncy, *Cornelius's Character* (Boston, 1745), 35; Samuel Niles, *Tristitae Ecclesiarum; or, A Brief and Sorrowful Account of the Present State of the Churches in New-England* (Boston, 1745), 8–9. For Old Lights' dismay at the influence that New Light ministers exerted on women and young persons, see John Hancock, *The Examiner; or, Gilbert against Tennent* (Philadelphia, 1743), 27–29; William Rand, *The Late Religious Commotions in New England Considered*, (Boston, 1743), preface p. 9; "The Remainder of the Letter from a Gentleman in Boston, to His Friend in Edinburgh, Begun in Our Last," *Boston Evening-Post*, November 5, 1744. See also Charles Chauncy, *Seasonable Thoughts on the State of Religion in New-England* (Boston, 1743), xvi n. On the role of women in the Great Awakening, see Cedric B. Cowing, "Sex and Preaching in the Great Awakening," *American Quarterly* 20 (1968): 624–44.

20. Hanson, "For Church and State," 32. On the theology of America's Revolutionary-era Anglican clergymen, see generally Rhoden, *Revolutionary Anglicanism*. On the relationship between the Great Awakening and the American Revolution, see William G. McLoughlin, "'Enthusiasm for Liberty': The Great Awakening as the Key to the Revolution," *Proceedings of the American Antiquarian Society* 87 (1977): 69–95; and John M. Murrin, "No Awakening, No Revolution? More Counterfactual Speculations," *Reviews in American History* 11 (1983): 161–71.

21. Jonathan Sewall, *The Americans Roused, In a Cure for the Spleen* (New York, 1775), 28, written under the pseudonym Sir Roger de Coverly.

22. Seabury, *The Congress Canvassed*, 6.

23. Seabury, *A View of the Controversy*, 17.

24. Chandler, *A Friendly Address to All Reasonable Americans*, 46.

25. Chandler, *What Think Ye of the* Congress *Now?*, 48.

26. Cooper, *The Patriots of North-America*, 20.

27. Grotius, *Pills for the Delegates; or, the Chairman Chastised* (New York, 1775), 8.

28. Isaac Wilkins, *Short Advice to the Counties of New-York* (New York, 1774), 8.

29. On Old Light uses of "freaks," see, for example, Archibald Cummings, *Faith Absolutely Necessary, but Not Sufficient to Salvation without Good Works* (Philadelphia 1740), xiv, 9; and Jonathan Dickinson, *A Display of God's Special Grace* (Boston 1742), 96.

30. Richard L. Bushman, *The Refinement of America: Persons, Houses, Cities* (New York, 1992), esp. 61–138; Kenneth A. Lockridge, *On the Sources of Patriarchal Rage: The Commonplace Books of William Byrd and Thomas Jefferson and the Gendering of Power in the Eighteenth Century* (New York, 1992), 95–100; Toby L. Ditz, "Shipwrecked; Or, Masculinity Imperiled:

Mercantile Representations of Failure and the Gendered Self in
Eighteenth-Century Philadelphia," *JAH* 81 (June 1994): 51–80; Kathleen
M. Brown, *Good Wives, Nasty Wenches, and Anxious Patriarchs: Gender, Race,
and Power in Colonial Virginia* (Chapel Hill, N.C., 1996), 324–28; Richard
Godbeer, "William Byrd's 'Flourish': The Sexual Cosmos of a Southern
Planter," in *Sex and Sexuality in Early America*, ed. Merril D. Smith (New
York, 1998), 135–62; Anne S. Lombard, *Making Manhood: Growing Up
Male in Colonial New England* (Cambridge, Mass., 2003), 10–11; and Sarah
Knott, *Sensibility and the American Revolution* (Chapel Hill, N.C., 2009),
56. It is important not to overstate Anglo-Americans' mistrust of passions.
For contrary perspectives, emphasizing the merit or utility of the passions
in the eighteenth century, see Nicole Eustace, *Passion Is the Gale: Emotion, Power and the Coming of the American Revolution* (Chapel Hill, N.C.,
2008).

31. Wilkins, *Short Advice to the Counties of New-York*, 4; *Alarm to the Legislature
of the Province of New-York* (New York, 1775), 10. On the feminization of
religious dissent in another Anglo-American context, see Brown, *Good
Wives, Nasty Wenches, and Anxious Patriarchs*, 140–44.

32. The authorship of *A Dialogue* has not been established. Earlier in life,
Myles Cooper published a book of poems including some that used a
similar dialogic format and others that explored themes of cuckoldry, but
the evidence is too slim to extrapolate his authorship of this particular
piece. Cooper, *Poems on Several Occasions* (Oxford, 1761).

33. William Bradford to James Madison, January 4, 1775, quoted in Norman
Philbrick, ed., *Trumpets Sounding: Propaganda Plays of the American Revolution* (1972; reprint, New York, 1976), 32.

34. Mary V. V., *A Dialogue between a Southern Delegate and His Spouse on His
Return from the Grand Continental Congress* (New York, 1774), 10, 11, 13. On
Anglo-American representations of despotism in the Muslim world, see
Robert J. Allison, *The Crescent Obscured: The United States and the Muslim
World, 1776–1815* (New York, 1995).

35. Mary V. V., *A Dialogue between a Southern Delegate and His Spouse*, 3, 6.

36. On a wife's murder of her husband as petit treason, see Linda K. Kerber,
Women of the Republic: Intellect and Ideology in Revolutionary America
(Chapel Hill, N.C., 1980), 119–20, and Kerber, *No Constitutional Right to Be
Ladies: Women and the Obligations of Citizenship* (New York, 1998), 13.

37. Mary V. V., *A Dialogue between a Southern Delegate and His Spouse*, 4, 6.

38. On the social and cultural significance of cuckoldry in the eighteenth-
century Atlantic world, see Sarah M. S. Pearsall, "'The late flagrant
instance of depravity in my Family': The Story of an Anglo-Jamaican
Cuckold," *WMQ*, 3rd ser., 60 (July 2003): 549–82.

39. Lockridge, *On the Sources of Patriarchal Rage*, 96; Brown, *Good Wives, Nasty
Wenches, and Anxious Patriarchs*, 247–82, 319–66; Michal J. Rozbicki, *The*

Complete Colonial Gentleman: Cultural Legitimacy in Plantation America (Charlottesville, Va., 1998), 118–19; and Rhys Isaac, *The Transformation of Virginia, 1740–1790*, new paperback edition (Chapel Hill, N.C., 1999), 132–35.

40. *The Virginia Almanack for the Year of Our Lord God 1770* (Williamsburg, Va., 1769), n.p. See also *The Virginia Almanack for the Year of Our Lord God 1772* (Williamsburg, Va., 1771), n.p.

41. Mary V. V., *A Dialogue between a Southern Delegate and His Spouse*, 7.

42. If the pseudonymous author of the *Dialogue* was in fact one of the three prolific loyalist-clerics—Chandler, Seabury, or Cooper—he or she may have chosen to portray the Southern delegate as a milksop husband so as to castigate Southern Anglicans for their refusal to back the New Yorkers' campaign for an episcopacy several years earlier. On Virginia's failure to support an American bishopric, see Rhoden, *Revolutionary Anglicanism*, 41–42.

43. Mary V. V., *A Dialogue between a Southern Delegate and His Spouse*, 5.

44. John Adams's Diary, September 17, 1774, *Letters*, 1: 75.

45. Mary V. V., *A Dialogue between a Southern Delegate and His Spouse*, 4, 6, 12. On the deleterious effects on women ascribed to romance novels in the eighteenth century, see Cathy N. Davidson, *Revolution and the Word: The Rise of the Novel in America* (New York, 1986), 101–20.

46. Mary V. V., *A Dialogue between a Southern Delegate and His Spouse*, 7, 8. For a very brief introduction to the ideology of gendered spheres, see Nancy Cott, *The Bonds of Womanhood: "Woman's Sphere" in New England, 1780–1835* (New Haven, Conn., 1977).

47. Brown, *Good Wives, Nasty Wenches, and Anxious Patriarchs*, 324–28; Lisa Wilson, *Ye Heart of a Man: The Domestic Life of Men in Colonial New England* (New Haven, Conn., 1999), 75–98; Lombard, *Making Manhood*, esp. 114–19.

48. Mary V. V., *A Dialogue between a Southern Delegate and His Spouse*, 7–8.

49. Mary V. V., *A Dialogue between a Southern Delegate and His Spouse*, 9.

50. Mary V. V., *A Dialogue between a Southern Delegate and His Spouse*, 13–14. Notwithstanding the many ways in which Mary V.V. challenged eighteenth-century assumptions about gender, it must also be recognized that the character of the Southern delegate's wife, as a champion of lawfulness and deference to British authorities, also served to reinforce traditional, patriarchal associations of women with order and harmony. I am grateful to Ruth Bloch and Sarah Knott for this insight.

51. Cooper, *Patriots of North-America*, 13–16.

52. Cooper, *Patriots of North-America*, 14–16, 32. The wife in *A Dialogue between a Southern Delegate and His Spouse* also compares congressional delegates, unfavorably, to schoolboys, at 8.

53. Richard L. Merritt, *Symbols of American Community, 1735–1775* (New Haven, Conn., 1966), 58; and Linda Colley, *Britons: Forging the Nation,*

1707–1837 (New Haven, Conn., 1992), 134–35. See also J. M. Bumstead, "'Things in the Womb of Time': Ideas of American Independence, 1633 to 1763," *WMQ*, 3rd ser., 31 (1974): 533–64; P. J. Marshall, "A Nation Defined by Empire, 1755–1776," in *Uniting the Kingdom? The Making of British History*, ed. Alexander Grant and Keith J. Stringer (London, 1995), 208–22; Stephen Conway, "From Fellow-Nationals to Foreigners: British Perceptions of the Americans, circa 1739–1783," *WMQ*, 3rd ser., 59 (2002): 65–100; Dror Wahrman, *The Making of the Modern Self: Identity and Culture in Eighteenth-Century England* (New Haven, Conn., 2004), and Wahrman, "The English Problem of Identity in the American Revolution," *AHR* 106 (2001): 1236–62.

54. Bernard Bailyn, *The Peopling of British North America: An Introduction* (New York, 1986), 113. See also T. H. Breen, "Ideology and Nationalism on the Eve of the American Revolution: Revisions Once More in Need of Revising," *JAH* 84 (1997): 13–39.

55. *Triumph of the Whigs; or, T'Other Congress Convened* (New York, 1775), 4–5, 8.

56. Cooper, *Patriots of North-America*, 12, 16, 22.

57. Seabury, *Congress Canvassed*, 12. A patoopatoo was a small, sharp-edged club used in war.

58. John Hawkesworth, *A New Voyage, Round the World*, 2 vols. (New York, 1774). See volume 1, page 187, for the first of many references to the patoopatoo.

59. In his endnotes, Cooper hinted that "Tools" carried a double entendre, referring not only to the implements and utensils of laboring-rank committeemen, but also to the committeemen themselves, signifying that those lowly patriots, rather than independent actors, were "tools" of artful politicians. Mocking his own rhyme scheme, Cooper wrote, "Such Tools are as little adapted to Poetry, as to Politics." Cooper, *Patriots of North-America*, 4, 30, 35–36.

60. Cooper, *Patriots of North-America*, 35. On the democratic composition of patriot committees, see Richard Alan Ryerson, *The Revolution Is Now Begun: The Radical Committees of Philadelphia, 1765–1776* (Philadelphia, 1978), 96.

61. David Lemmings, *Professors of the Law: Barristers and English Legal Culture in the Eighteenth Century* (New York, 2000), 26–27, 225–47.

62. Cooper, *Patriots of North-America*, 8, 36.

63. Cooper, *Patriots of North-America*, 37–38.

64. On the history of colonial and Revolutionary New York, see Carl L. Becker, "The History of Political Parties in the Province of New York, 1760–1776" (Ph.D. diss., University of Wisconsin, 1909); Virginia D. Harrington, *The New York Merchant on the Eve of the Revolution* (Gloucester, Mass, 1964); Patricia U. Bonomi, *A Factious People: Politics*

and Society in Colonial New York (New York, 1971); Milton M. Klein, *The Politics of Diversity: Essays in the History of Colonial New York* (Port Washington, N.Y., 1974); Michael G. Kammen, *Colonial New York: A History* (New York, 1975); and Judith L. Van Buskirk, *Generous Enemies: Patriots and Loyalists in Revolutionary New York* (Philadelphia, 2002).

65. Steiner, *Samuel Seabury, 1729–1796*, 154; Nelson, *The American Tory*, 83.

66. Steiner, *Samuel Seabury, 1729–1796*, 144–46.

67. Peter Force, comp., *American Archives*, 4th ser., 6 vols. (Washington, D.C., 1837–1853), 2: 35–36.

68. Steiner, *Samuel Seabury, 1729–1796*, 159–60.

69. Alexander Hamilton, *A Full Vindication of the Measures of the Congress* (New York, 1774), 3, 4.

70. Philip Livingston, *The Other Side of the Question; or, A Defense of the Liberties of North-America* (New York, 1774), 5.

71. William Hooper to James Duane, Philadelphia, November 22, 1774, *Letters*, 1: 262–63.

Part II

1. John Adams to Abigail Adams, Philadelphia, September 18, 1774; Samuel Ward to Samuel Ward Jr., Philadelphia, September 24, 1774; *Letters*, 1: 80–81, 98–99.

2. *Journals*, 2: 28–211.

3. *Journals*, 2: 128–57, 158–62.

4. On Dickinson's politics, see Milton E. Flower, *John Dickinson: Conservative Revolutionary* (Charlottesville, 1983); and Jane E. Calvert, *Quaker Constitutionalism and the Political Thought of John Dickinson* (Cambridge, 2009).

5. Benjamin Franklin to Silas Deane, Philadelphia, August 27, 1775, *Letters*, 1: 709–10.

6. *Pennsylvania Gazette*, September 20, 1775.

7. Benjamin Franklin to Jonathan Shipley, Philadelphia, July 7, 1775; Benjamin Franklin to Joseph Priestley, Philadelphia, October 3, 1775; *Letters*, 1: 604–8; 2: 104.

8. *Pennsylvania Gazette*, September 20, 1775.

Chapter 3

1. *Journals*, 2: 103. The historiography of Revolutionary finance is vast. For a brief introductory survey, see Anne Bezanson, *Prices and Inflation during the American Revolution: Pennsylvania, 1770–1790* (Philadelphia, 1951); E. James Ferguson, *The Power of the Purse: A History of American Public Finance, 1776–1790* (Chapel Hill, N.C., 1961); William Graham Sumner, *The Financier and the Finances of the American Revolution*, 2 vols. (1891; reprint, New York, 1968); Joseph Albert Ernst, *Money and Politics in America, 1755–1775: A Study in the Currency Act of 1764 and the Political*

Economy of the Revolution (Chapel Hill, N.C., 1973); William G. Anderson, *The Price of Liberty: The Public Debt of the American Revolution* (Charlottesville, Va., 1983); John J. McCusker and Russell R. Menard, *The Economy of British America, 1607–1789* (Chapel Hill, N.C., 1985); James A. Henretta, "The War for Independence and American Economic Development," in *The Economy of Early America: The Revolutionary Period, 1763–1790*, ed. Ronald Hoffman, John J. McCusker, and Russell Menard (Charlottesville, Va., 1988): 45–87; Cathy D. Matson and Peter S. Onuf, *A Union of Interests: Political and Economic Thought in Revolutionary America* (Lawrence, Kans. 1990); Robert A. Becker, "Currency, Taxation, and Finance, 1775–1787," in *The Blackwell Encyclopedia of the American Revolution*, ed. Jack P. Greene and J. R. Pole (Cambridge, Mass., 1991), 362–73; Cathy D. Matson, "The Revolution, the Constitution, and the New Nation," in *The Cambridge Economic History of the United States*, ed. Stanley L. Engerman and Robert E. Gallman (New York, 1996), 363–402; and Max M. Edling, *A Revolution in Favor of Government: Origins of the U.S. Constitution and the Making of the American State* (New York, 2003).

2. In Europe, private banks began to issue paper money in the 1660s, but no European or American state did so before Massachusetts. Eric P. Newman, *The Early Paper Money of America*, 4th ed. (Iola, Wis., 1997), 9, 180.

3. Newman, *The Early Paper Money of America*, 10–11.

4. See Margaret Ellen Newell, *From Dependency to Independence: Economic Revolution in Colonial New England* (Ithaca, N.Y., 1998), 107–236; and Jennifer Jordan Baker, *Securing the Commonwealth: Debt, Speculation, and Writing in the Making of Early America* (Baltimore, 2005).

5. For Parliament's efforts to regulate colonial paper money emissions, see Newman, *The Early Paper Money of America*, 12–13. See also Ernst, *Money and Politics in America, 1755–1775.*

6. Newman, *The Early Paper Money of America*, 14.

7. Congress appointed Franklin to serve on a committee "to get proper plates engraved" and to arrange printing of the currency. The committee also consisted of John Adams, John Rutledge, James Duane, and James Wilson. *Journals*, 2: 106. Of these men, Franklin had the most, perhaps the only, experience printing paper money. And as the numismatists Elston G. Bradfield and Eric P. Newman have convincingly demonstrated, Franklin bore primary responsibility for designing continental bills. See Bradfield, "Benjamin Franklin: A Numismatic Summary," *Numismatist* 69 (1956): 1347–53; Newman, "Poor Richard's Mottoes for Coins," *Numismatist* 69 (1956): 1363–67; Newman, "The Continental Dollar of 1776 Meets Its Maker," *Numismatist* 72 (1959): 915–26; Newman, "Continental Currency and the Fugio Cent: Sources of Emblems and Mottoes," *Numismatist* 79 (1966): 1587–98; David McBride, "Linked Rings: Early American Unity Illustrated" *Numismatist* 92 (1979): 2377–93; and Newman, "Benjamin

Franklin and the Chain Design: New Evidence Provides the Missing Link," *Numismatist* 96 (1983): 2271–84. Also, see generally the *Numismatist* 69 (1956), an issue devoted largely to numismatic creations by or about Franklin. And see J. A. Leo Lemay, "The American Aesthetic of Franklin's Visual Creations," *PMHB* 111 (October 1987): 465–99.

8. For currency as text to be read by bearers, see David Henkin, *City Reading: Written Words and Public Spaces in Antebellum New York* (New York, 1998), 137–66. See also Stephen Mihm, *A Nation of Counterfeiters: Capitalists, Con Men, and the Making of the United States* (Cambridge, Mass., 2007).

9. See, generally, Bradfield, "Benjamin Franklin," and *Numismatist* 69 (1956).

10. Franklin printed Pennsylvania's bills with the Penn family arms until 1760. About that time, he began to lose confidence in the proprietor and ultimately sought royal intervention in the colony's affairs. In 1764, when Pennsylvania authorized a new emission of bills, Franklin substituted the royal arms for those of the proprietary family. When Franklin retired from the printing business, his successors David Hall and William Sellers reverted to the proprietary arms. Newman, *The Early Paper Money of America*, 339–41. Robert Middlekauff, *Benjamin Franklin and His Enemies* (Berkeley, Calif., 1996), 55–114.

11. There were exceptions. Some colonial currencies featured vignettes of the public works they were printed to finance. Other currencies bore martial imagery illustrative of ongoing military campaigns. But few if any of these colonial currencies matched Franklin's continentals for breadth, complexity, or moralistic purpose. Compare the colonial currencies with the continental currency collected in Newman, *The Early Paper Money of America*.

12. Benjamin Franklin to Edward Bridgen, Passy, October 2, 1779, *PBF*, 30: 429–31.

13. See R. T. H. Halsey, "Benjamin Franklin: His Interest in the Arts," in *Benjamin Franklin and His Circle: A Catalogue of an Exhibition at the Metropolitan Museum of Art* (New York, 1936), esp. 4.

14. Franklin's moral philosophy recalls the tabula rasa, an Aristotelian model of human development revitalized by the seventeenth-century empiricist John Locke. As conceived by Locke, the human mind resembled a blank slate on which moral ideas might be written, or in Franklin's terms, impressed, through sensory experience. See Locke's *Essay Concerning Human Understanding* (1690). See also Franklin's *Proposals Relating to the Education of Youth in Pensilvania* (Philadelphia, 1749), in which he asserted, "Indeed, the general natural Tendency of Reading good History, must be, to fix in the minds of Youth deep Impressions of the Beauty and Usefulness of Virtue." Quoted at 20–21. For more on the philosophy and medical science of impressions, see Sarah Knott, *Sensibility and the American Revolution* (Chapel Hill, N.C., 2009), 10, 69–104.

15. Franklin had in mind the engravings contained in a "thin Folio" of Horace's poetry. Lester C. Olson has identified that folio as Marin le

Roy de Gomberville, *The Doctrine of Morality; or, A View of Human Life* (London, 1721). See Olson, *Benjamin Franklin's Vision of American Community: A Study in Rhetorical Iconology* (Columbia, 2004), 7.

16. In 1773, Franklin recounted his letter to Mitchell, written "more than twenty years since." See Benjamin Franklin to Peter P. Burdett, London, November 3, 1773, *PBF*, 20: 459–61.

17. *Journals*, 8: 565; 9: 1085, quoting Benjamin Franklin to David Hartley, Passy, February 2, 1780. Franklin harbored misgivings about this project. "Every kindness I hear of done by an Englishman to an American Prisoner," he explained, "makes me resolve not to proceed in the Work, hoping a Reconciliation may yet take place. But every fresh Instance of your Devilism weakens that resolution, and makes me abominate the Thought of a Reunion with such a People."

18. Benjamin Franklin to Edward Bridgen, Passy, October 2, 1779, *PBF*, 30: 429–31.

19. For Franklin's familiarity with and prior use of emblems and other visual art forms, see Lemay, "The American Aesthetic of Franklin's Visual Creations," 465.

20. Newman, *The Early Paper Money of America*, 75, and "Continental Currency and the Fugio Cent," 1592. See also Lemay, "The American Aesthetic of Franklin's Visual Creations," 481; and Olson, *Benjamin Franklin's Vision of American Community*, 7–8.

21. Newman, *The Early Paper Money of America*, 57–84.

22. Kenneth Silverman, *A Cultural History of the American Revolution: Painting, Music, Literature, and the Theatre in the Colonies and the United States from the Treaty of Paris to the Inauguration of George Washington, 1763–1789* (New York, 1976), 320. Frank H. Sommer, "Emblem and Device: The Origin of the Great Seal of the United States," *Art Quarterly* 24 (1961): 57–76.

23. *Pennsylvania Gazette*, September 20, 1775. Clericus's quotations below are taken from this piece.

24. Olson questions Franklin's authorship of this key, in part because Franklin never elsewhere employed the term, "emblematic device." Olson, *Benjamin Franklin's Vision of American Community*, 4, esp. n. 3. Franklin's earlier use of "Clericus" suggests an affinity of authorship. Moreover, at least one contemporary identified Franklin as Clericus. See Lemay, review of volume 22 of *The Papers of Benjamin Franklin*, in *PMHB* 107 (1983), 146.

25. See *New-England Courant*, April 9–16, May 7–14, 1722.

26. On Franklin's intended audience, particularly in light of his use of Latin mottoes, see Newman, "Poor Richard's Mottoes for Coins," 1363; Lemay, "The American Aesthetic of Franklin's Visual Creations," 473, 481, 493; and Olson, *Benjamin Franklin's Vision of American Community*, 4–5.

27. Clericus opened his letter with a brief discourse on the canons of emblem design. This prompted another pseudonymous author to submit his own

discourse, "On the Use and Abuse of Mottos," *Pennsylvania Magazine; or, American Monthly Museum*, supplement for the year 1775, 1 (1775): 587–89. Kenneth Silverman has demonstrated that Clericus's statements were technically imprecise; they conflated the distinct genres of emblem and device. But technical precision was not Franklin's primary concern. Silverman, *A Cultural History of the American Revolution*, 320–21.

28. Clericus's letter also appeared in the *New-York Gazette and Weekly Mercury*, September 25, 1775; *Rivington's New-York Gazetteer*, September 28, 1775; *Providence Gazette*, October 7, 1775; *Norwich Packet*, October 9–16, 1775; *Massachusetts Spy*, October 13, 1775; *Connecticut Journal*, November 1, 1775; *Connecticut Courant*, November 13, 1775; and *Essex Journal*, December 8, 1775.

29. For numismatic, historical, literary, and economic analyses of Franklin's currency designs, see the numismatists cited above, n. 7; Lemay, "The American Aesthetic of Franklin's Visual Creations"; Olson, *Benjamin Franklin's Vision of American Community*, and Olson, *Emblems of American Community in the Revolutionary Era* (Washington, D.C., 1991); Jennifer Jordan Baker, *Securing the Commonwealth*, and Baker, "Benjamin Franklin's Autobiography and the Credibility of Personality," *EAL* 35 (2000): 274–93, esp. 279–80. See also, "Editorial Note on the Design of Continental Paper Currency," *PBF*, 22: 357–58.

30. Franklin employed the metaphor of wind-blown waves to describe the British ministry's abuse of the colonies on at least two other occasions. See Lemay, "The American Aesthetic of Franklin's Visual Creations," 485–89.

31. Olson, *Benjamin Franklin's Vision of American Community*, 120, 124–25, 139. On the importance of mutuality and trust to the American nonimportation and nonexportation campaigns, see generally, T. H. Breen, *The Marketplace of Revolution: How Consumer Politics Shaped American Independence* (New York, 2004).

32. On Franklin's economic philosophy, see Lewis J. Carey, *Franklin's Economic Views* (Garden City, N.Y., 1929).

33. In the sweeping assessment that follows, I do not mean to overstate or oversimplify eighteenth-century British American economic development or to usher in prematurely the vast economic transformations that historians know collectively as the Market Revolution. The generalizations offered here are subject to regionally specific caveats and exceptions and they of course do not apply with equal force to enslaved or Native American communities. For a masterful survey of eighteenth-century economic history and historiography, see Cathy D. Matson, "A House of Many Mansions: Some Thoughts on the Field of Economic History," in *The Economy of Early America: Historical Perspectives and New Directions*, ed. Cathy D. Matson (University Park, Pa., 2006), 1–70.

34. On the social anxieties that attended the growth of markets and the creation and use of innovative financial instruments, see Jean-Christophe Agnew, *Worlds Apart: The Market and the Theater in Anglo-American Thought, 1550–1750* (Cambridge, 1986). For the precarious interdependence of eighteenth-century debtors and creditors, see Bruce H. Mann, *Republic of Debtors: Bankruptcy in the Age of American Independence* (Cambridge, Mass., 2002), 6–33.

35. Richard Saunders [pseud.], *Poor Richard Improved: Being an Almanack . . . for the Year of our Lord 1758* (Philadelphia, 1757), n.p.

36. Richard Saunders [pseud.], *Poor Richard, 1737: An Almanack for the Year of Christ 1737* (Philadelphia, 1736), n.p.

37. As Jennifer Jordan Baker has noted, Franklin claimed in his autobiography that the financial guidance he offered in *The Way to Wealth* did in fact contribute to Pennsylvania's growing prosperity. Little wonder, then, that he harbored such optimism for his currency emblems. See Baker, "Benjamin Franklin's Autobiography and the Credibility of Personality," 279.

38. Franklin's oft-repeated admonition, Mind Your Business, did not always mean the same thing. In 1776 Franklin coupled the Mind Your Business and *Fugio* mottoes with the image of a sundial to convey passage of time and the urgency of personal affairs. Newman intriguingly suggests that Franklin may have borrowed these mottoes from a clock that David Rittenhouse designed for Thomas Barton in 1756. Newman, "Poor Richard's Mottoes for Coins," 1363. See Lemay, too, for earlier, Christian uses of the *tempus fugit* motif to suggest that man's time on earth was uncertain. Lemay, "American Aesthetic of Franklin's Visual Creations," 490. By contrast, in his 1758 almanac, Franklin's Poor Richard proffered a cynical piece of advice: "In a corrupt Age, the putting the World in order would breed Confusion; then e'en mind your own Business," quoted in *PBF*, 326–56.

39. Here Clericus referred to Parliament's efforts to bind Americans "*in all cases whatsoever*," an allusion to the Declaratory Act of 1766. Lemay, "The American Aesthetic of Franklin's Visual Creations," 483.

40. Saunders [pseud.], *Poor Richard Improved*, n.p.

41. *Journals*, 1: 78.

42. Franklin added, chauvinistically, "How much more then may be done by the superior Frugality & Industry of the Men." Franklin to Richard Bache, Cambridge, October 19, 1775, *Letters*, 2: 209–10.

43. Franklin anticipated the continental's decline. He advocated "the most prudent Parsimony of the publick treasure" and he later claimed to have lobbied Congress, unsuccessfully, for fiscal policies that would have propped the continental. See Franklin to Richard Bache, Cambridge, October 19, 1775, *Letters*, 2: 209; Benjamin Franklin to Samuel Cooper, Passy, April 22, 1779, *PBF*, 29: 354–57.

44. It is uncertain whether Clericus's "learned friend" was a real-life acquaintance of Franklin's, or simply a literary device by which Franklin could introduce a second interpretation of the thirty-dollar bill.

45. Jack N. Rakove, *The Beginnings of National Politics: An Interpretive History of the Continental Congress* (New York, 1979), 193–94; Calvin Jillson and Rick K. Wilson, *Congressional Dynamics: Structure, Coordination, and Choice in the First American Congress, 1774–1789* (Stanford, Calif., 1994), 58–59.

46. On Congress's exercise of legislative and executive functions, see generally, Jerrilyn Greene Marston, *King and Congress: The Transfer of Political Legitimacy, 1774–1776* (Princeton, N.J., 1987).

47. Franklin to Edward Bridgen, Passy, October 2, 1779, *PBF*, 30: 429–31.

48. Edward W. Richardson, *Standards and Colors of the American Revolution* (Philadelphia, 1982), 42–49, 288–89. See also Lemay, "The American Aesthetic of Franklin's Visual Creations," 471–75, 481–84, 491.

49. For Franklin's influence on state currencies, see Newman, *The Early Paper Money of America*, 149, 282, 284, 418–19. See also, Olson, *Emblems of American Community in the Revolutionary Era*, 213.

50. Newman, *The Early Paper Money of America*, 170.

51. Newman, *The Early Paper Money of America*, 147, 431; David McBride, "Linked Rings"; Lemay, "The American Aesthetic of Franklin's Visual Creations," 490–91; Olson, *Benjamin Franklin's Vision of American Community*, 131–33.

52. William Browne to Samuel Curwen, Boston, January 8, 1776, in *Journals and Letters of the Late Samuel Curwen*, ed. George Atkinson Ward, 4th ed. (Boston, 1864), 48–50.

53. Quoted in Newman, *The Early Paper Money of America*, 15.

54. *Pennsylvania Ledger*, March 18, 1778.

55. *Pennsylvania Evening Post*, February 19, 1778. These verses appeared during the British occupation of Philadelphia, after the *Post* had fallen under British control.

56. The manuscript of Stansbury's "History of Peru" may be found in the Peter Force Collection of the Library of Congress. The poem is reprinted in Pastora SanJuan Cafferty, "Loyalist Rhapsodies: The Poetry of Stansbury and Odell" (Ph.D. diss., George Washington University, 1971), 155–63; and in Newman, "Benjamin Franklin and the Chain Design," 2282–84.

57. The *Oxford English Dictionary*, 2nd ed., finds "spoon," meaning "a shallow, simple, or foolish person," in common usage in 1799, its meaning apparently derived from "Wooden Spoon," a slang reference to the student who finished last in certain math classes at Cambridge. No spoon appeared on any contemporary currency design.

58. Stansbury alluded to these particular professions because they were those of prominent patriots: Daniel Roberdeau, rum distiller and militia officer;

Anthony Morris Jr., brewer and legislator; and James Cannon, school-teacher and signer of Pennsylvania paper money. Newman, "Benjamin Franklin and the Chain Design," 2284 n. 13–15.

59. On Stansbury's "History of Peru," see also Olson, *Benjamin Franklin's Vision of American Community*, 125–29, 240–41.

60. Diary of Captain Smythe of the Royal Army, 51, quoted in Frank Moore, *Diary of the American Revolution*, 2 vols. (New York, 1860), 1: 399–400.

Chapter 4

1. Washington is quoted in Samuel Chase to James Duane, Annapolis, February 5, 1775; Richard Henry Lee to William Lee, Philadelphia, May 10, 1775, *Letters*, 1: 304–7, 337–38. On the *rage militaire* that swept over Britain's North American colonies in 1775, see Charles Royster, *A Revolutionary People at War: The Continental Army and American Character, 1775–1783* (Chapel Hill, N.C., 1979), 25–53.

2. Richard Caswell to William Caswell, Philadelphia, May 11, 1775, *Letters*, 1: 339–41.

3. See the credentials of delegates to the Second Continental Congress, *Journals*, 2: 7, 13, 15, 17–20, 50. On the political legitimacy of Congress in the early years of the war, see generally Jerrilyn Greene Marston, *King and Congress: The Transfer of Political Legitimacy, 1774–1776* (Princeton, N.J., 1987).

4. Richard Caswell to William Caswell, Philadelphia, May 11, 1775; John Adams to James Warren, Philadelphia, May 21, 1775, *Letters*, 339–41, 364–65.

5. See generally *Journals*, vol. 2.

6. See Caroline Robbins, *The Eighteenth-Century Commonwealthman: Studies in the Transmission, Development and Circumstance of English Liberal Thought from the Restoration of Charles II until the War with the Thirteen Colonies* (Cambridge, Mass., 1959), 9, 31, 93–94, 101–5; Bernard Bailyn, *The Ideological Origins of the American Revolution* (Cambridge, Mass., 1967), 61–63, 112–15, 287; Gordon Wood, *The Creation of the American Republic, 1776–1787* (Chapel Hill, N.C., 1969), 30, 42; J. G. A. Pocock, *The Machiavellian Moment: Florentine Political Thought and the Atlantic Republican Tradition*, 2nd ed. (Princeton, N.J., 2003), 401–61; and Jonathan Scott, *Commonwealth Principles: Republican Writing of the English Revolution* (Cambridge, 2004), 348–49. See also Royster, *A Revolutionary People at War*, 35–40; Lawrence Delbert Cress, *Citizens in Arms: The Army and the Militia in American Society to the War of 1812* (Chapel Hill, N.C., 1982), 19, 23, 37; and E. Wayne Carp, *To Starve the Army at Pleasure: Continental Army Administration and American Political Culture, 1775–1783* (Chapel Hill, N.C., 1984), 10–11.

7. Samuel Adams to James Warren, Philadelphia, January 7, 1776, *Letters*, 3: 51–53.

8. Joseph Hewes to James Iredell, Philadelphia, May 23, 1775; Eliphalet Dyer to Joseph Trumbull, Philadelphia, June 8, 1775; John Adams to Abigail Adams, Philadelphia, June 10, 1775, *Letters*, 1: 396, 458–59, 464–65; Dixon and Hunter's *Virginia Gazette*, July 1, 1775. On the mobilization of Philadelphians in response to Lexington and Concord, see Steven Rosswurm, *Arms, Country, and Class: The Philadelphia Militia and the "Lower Sort" during the American Revolution, 1775–1783* (New Brunswick, N.J., 1987), 49.

9. On the Philadelphia associators, see Rosswurm, *Arms, Country and Class*, esp. 49–75.

10. *Pennsylvania Evening Post*, June 8, 1775.

11. John Adams to John Trumbull, Philadelphia, February 13, 1776; John Adams to Abigail Adams, Philadelphia, February 13, 1776; *Letters*, 3: 240–41, 242.

12. See Marston, *King and Congress*, 28–29, quoting Blackstone's *Commentaries on the Laws of England*, ed. Joseph Chitty, new ed. (London, 1826), 1: 262.

13. John Adams's Diary, Philadelphia, August 29–September 5, 1774; Thomas Lynch to Ralph Izard, Philadelphia, October 26, 1774; Richard Caswell to William Caswell, Philadelphia, May 11, 1775; John Adams to Abigail Adams, Philadelphia, May 29, 1775, *Letters*, 1: 5, 247–48, 339–41, 416–17.

14. Eliphalet Dyer to Jonathan Trumbull Sr., Philadelphia, June 16, 1775, *Letters*, 1: 495–96.

15. *Journals*, 2: 92.

16. Washington to Martha Washington, Philadelphia, June 18, 1775; Washington to Burwell Bassett, Philadelphia, June 19, 1775; Washington to the Captains of Several Independent Companies in Virginia, Philadelphia, June 29, 1775; Washington to John Washington, Philadelphia, June 20, 1775, *Letters*, 1: 509–11, 515–16, 27–29.

17. John Adams to Elbridge Gerry, Philadelphia, June 18, 1775; Thomas Cushing to James Bowdoin Sr., Philadelphia, June 21, 1775; Eliphalet Dyer to Joseph Trumbull, Philadelphia, June 17, 1775; Eliphalet Dyer to Jonathan Trumbull Sr., Philadelphia, June 16, 1775, *Letters*, 1: 495–96, 499–500, 503–4, 530.

18. John Adams to Elbridge Gerry, Philadelphia, June 18, 1775, *Letters*, 1: 503–4.

19. John Adams to James Warren, Philadelphia, June 20, 1775, *Letters*, 1: 518–19.

20. *Pennsylvania Evening Post*, June 22, 1775.

21. John Adams to Abigail Adams, Philadelphia, June 23, 1775, *Letters*, 1: 536–37.

22. John Adams's Diary, Philadelphia, August 29–September 5, 1774, *Letters*, 3–4.

23. William Smith, *The Christian Soldier's Duty: The Lawfulness and Dignity of His Office; and, The Importance of the Protestant Cause in the British Colonies, Stated and Explained* (Philadelphia, 1757), quoted at 27.

24. William Smith, *An Exercise; Containing, a Dialogue* (Philadelphia, 1775); Horace Wemyss Smith, *Life and Correspondence of the Rev. William Smith*, 2 vols. (Philadelphia, 1879), 1: 500–01.

25. For the sermon and Deane's response, see Smith, *Life and Correspondence*, 1: 504–20.

26. John Adams to Abigail Adams, Philadelphia, June 23, 1775, *Letters*, 1: 536–37.

27. John E. Ferling, "'Oh That I was a Soldier': John Adams and the Anguish of War," *American Quarterly* 36 (1984): 258–75. See also Ferling, *John Adams: A Life* (New York, 1996), 131–44. John Adams to a Friend in London, January 21, 1775; John Adams to Abigail Adams, Philadelphia, February 13, 1776, *Letters*, 1: 296–98, 3: 240–41.

28. John Adams to Abigail Adams, Philadelphia, February 13, 1776; John Adams to Abigail Adams, Philadelphia, May 29, 1775; *Letters*, 1: 416–17; 3: 240–41.

29. General Washington expressed dismay at the egalitarianism that prevailed in the Massachusetts regiments. His disappointment sparked Adams's indignation. See Jonathan Gregory Rossie, *The Politics of Command in the American Revolution* (Syracuse, N.Y., 1975), 28.

30. John Adams to Henry Knox, Philadelphia, November 11, 1775; John Adams to James Warren, Philadelphia, June 10, 1775; John Adams to William Tudor, Philadelphia, July 23, 1775; John Adams to Abigail Adams, Philadelphia, September 26, 1775; *Letters*, 1: 467, 650; 2: 58–59, 329–30.

31. John Adams to William Tudor, Philadelphia, October 1, 1775; John Adams to William Tudor, Philadelphia, July 26, 1775, *Letters*, 1: 667; 2: 89–90.

32. After Washington forced the British evacuation, the president of the Continental Congress John Hancock also commissioned a portrait of the commander, but this appears to have been a private act, not initiated by Congress. See *Letters*, 4: 9 n. 3.

33. Richard Smith's Diary, March 25, 1776; John Adams to George Washington, Philadelphia, April 1, 1776, *Letters*, 3: 440, 468–69.

34. Vladimir Clain-Stefanelli and Elvira Clain-Stefanelli, *Medals Commemorating Battles of the American Revolution* (Washington, D.C., 1973), 4–7. See also, Alan M. Stahl, "Medals of the *Comitia Americana* Series in the Collections of the American Numismatic Society and Other Public Institutions," in *Coinage of the Confederation Period*, ed. Philip L. Mossman (New York, 1996), 261–346.

35. Fast days and thanksgivings were introduced to the British Isles during the Roman period, but not until the Protestant Reformation did English monarchs commonly appoint them and not until the Civil War did they become frequent. William DeLoss Love Jr., *The Fast and Thanksgiving Days of New England* (Boston, 1895), 40–53. See also H. R. Trevor-Roper,

"The Fast Sermons of the Long Parliament," in *Essays in British History, Presented to Sir Keith Feiling*, ed. Trevor-Roper (London, 1964), 85–138.

36. Love Jr., *The Fast and Thanksgiving Days of New England*, esp. 177–91, 256–69.

37. During the imperial wars of the eighteenth century, the custom of fasting spread briefly beyond New England. The governments of South Carolina and Virginia sponsored fasts early in King George's War, while those of New York, New Jersey, and Pennsylvania organized fasts during the Seven Years' War. Love Jr., *The Fast and Thanksgiving Days of New England*, calendar, 464–514.

38. Love Jr., *The Fast and Thanksgiving Days of New England*, 333, 336–37; *Rivington's New-York Gazetteer*, January 5, 1775.

39. *PTJ*, 1: 106 n.; Derek H. Davis, *Religion and the Continental Congress, 1774–1789: Contributions to Original Intent* (New York, 2000), 84; Love Jr., *The Fast and Thanksgiving Days of New England*, 334; Pauline Maier, *American Scripture: Making the Declaration of Independence* (New York, 1997), 125.

40. *Journals*, 2: 81, 87–88.

41. Love Jr., *The Fast and Thanksgiving Days of New England*, 175, and calendar, 464–514.

42. John Adams to Abigail Adams, Philadelphia, June 17, 1775, *Letters*, 1: 497–98.

43. "On the Late Continental Fast," *Pennsylvania Magazine; or, American Monthly Museum* (July 1775): 309–10, attributed to Hopkinson in George Everett Hastings, *The Life and Work of Francis Hopkinson* (Chicago, 1926), 187.

44. On the Jeremiad and American national identity, see Sacvan Bercovitch, *The American Jeremiad* (Madison, Wis., 1978).

45. Silas Deane to Elizabeth Deane, Philadelphia, July 20, 1775, *Letters*, 1: 638–40.

46. Jacob Duché, *The American Vine: A Sermon Preached . . . before the Honourable Continental Congress, July 20th, 1775* (Philadelphia, 1775), iv, 26–27.

47. *Journals*, 2: 192.

48. *Journals*, 2: 87–88.

49. John Adams to Abigail Adams, Philadelphia, July 23, 1775, *Adams Family Correspondence*, ed. Lyman H. Butterfield et al., 9 vols. (Cambridge, Mass., 1963–) 1: 254. For similar reports of widespread compliance with the continental fast, see Connecticut Delegates to Jonathan Trumbull Sr, Philadelphia, July 22, 1775; Silas Deane to Elizabeth Deane, Philadelphia, July 20, 1775; Eliphalet Dyer to Joseph Trumbull, Philadelphia, July 21, 1775; John Adams to James Warren, Philadelphia, July 23, 1775, *Letters*, 1: 638–40, 642–43, 646–47, 650–51. See also the entry for July 20, 1775, in the diary of Christopher Marshall, Christopher Marshall Papers, 1774–1781, manuscript collections of the HSP. This entry contains passages not reproduced in any

of William Duane Jr.'s editions of Marshall's diary. With the exception of "the ill behavior" of Quakers who opened their shops, Marshall claimed that on Congress's fast day Philadelphia was "to appearance more still than a first day produced, as there was no riding abroad or visiting as is generally on first day."

50. [Broadside], "Savannah, July 17th, 1775. In Provincial Congress" (Savannah, Ga., 1775).

51. Benson J. Lossing, *Life of Washington: A Biography Personal, Military, and Political*, 3 vols. (New York, 1860), 1: 617.

52. *Extracts from the Diary of Christopher Marshall, Kept in Philadelphia and Lancaster, during the American Revolution, 1774–1781*, ed. William Duane (Albany, N.Y., 1877), 32.

53. See "A Sermon Preached at York-Town . . . By Daniel Batwell" (Philadelphia, 1775); "A Sermon, Preached at Christiana Bridge and Newcastle . . . By Joseph Montgomery" (Philadelphia, 1775); and "Defensive War in a Just Cause Sinless . . . by the Revd. David Jones" (Philadelphia, 1775).

54. Samuel Ward's List of Measures Adopted by Congress, Philadelphia, July 31, 1775, *Letters*, 1: 686–87.

55. See the entry for July 20, 1775, in the diary of Christopher Marshall, Christopher Marshall Papers, 1774–1781, HSP.

56. Bruce E. Steiner, *Samuel Seabury, 1729–1796: A Study in High Church Tradition* (Oberlin, Ohio, 1971), 159–60.

57. Ambrose Serle, *The American Journal of Ambrose Serle, Secretary to Lord Howe, 1776–1778*, ed. Edward H. Tatum Jr. (New York, 1969), 85–86; Thomas May, *An Epitomy of English History*, 3rd ed. (London, 1690), 186.

58. *(New York) Royal Gazette*, November 21, 1781.

59. Joseph Hewes to James Iredell, Philadelphia, May 17, 1776, *Letters*, 4: 26–27.

60. Joseph Plumb Martin, *A Narrative of a Revolutionary Soldier: Some of the Adventures, Dangers, and Sufferings of Joseph Plumb Martin* (New York, 2001), 87.

61. Lloyd A. Brown and Howard H. Peckham, eds., *Revolutionary War Journals of Henry Dearborn, 1775–1783* (Westminster, Md., 2007), 118.

62. John Adams to James Warren, Philadelphia, October 24, 1775; Samuel Ward to Henry Ward, Philadelphia, October 24, 1775, *Letters*, 2: 232–33, 247–48.

63. In a robust commemoration of Randolph's life, the Massachusetts congressmen John and Samuel Adams also perceived the means to right a political wrong. Shortly after the Second Continental Congress convened in May 1775, Randolph had been forced to resign his presidency and return to Williamsburg, where Lord Dunmore had called the House of Burgesses into session. To fill Randolph's chair, Congress appointed John Hancock, a newly elected delegate from Massachusetts. When Randolph returned to Philadelphia months later, Hancock made no offer to vacate the post.

Embarrassed by this "Impropriety," John Adams expressed gratification at Congress's determination to commemorate Randolph with "all possible Demonstrations of Respect." John Adams to James Warren, Philadelphia, September 19, 1775; John Adams to James Warren, Philadelphia, October 24, 1775, *Letters*, 2: 30, 232–33.

64. See Steven C. Bullock and Sheila McIntyre, "'All had Gloves': Funeral Glove-Giving and the Imagined Communities of Early New England" (paper presented at "Faces & Places in Early America: An Interdisciplinary Conference on Art and the World of Objects," McNeil Center for Early American Studies, Philadelphia, Pa., December 2005).

65. *Journals*, 3: 302–3.

66. Rhys Isaac, *The Transformation of Virginia, 1740–1790*, new paperback edition (Chapel Hill, N.C., 1999), 328–29.

67. *Providence Gazette*, July 15, 1769.

68. Newspaper and other contemporary accounts do not indicate whether women participated in Randolph's funeral procession. Female family members may have walked as mourners and other women may have followed among the city's inhabitants. Sinceritas's letter to the *Providence Gazette* reveals that women sometimes took part in these processions, particularly when the deceased was female. *Providence Gazette*, July 15, 1769.

69. Solomon Drowne to Miss Sally Drowne, November 12, 1775, quoted in *Journals*, 3: 303; Josiah Bartlett to Mary Bartlett, Philadelphia, October 25, 1775, *Letters*, 2: 252; *Pennsylvania Packet*, October 30, 1775.

70. *Journals*, 2: 103.

71. For the life of Montgomery, see Hal T. Shelton, *General Richard Montgomery and the American Revolution: From Redcoat to Rebel* (New York, 1994); and Michael P. Gabriel, *Major General Richard Montgomery: The Making of an American Hero* (Madison, N.J., 2002).

72. John Adams to Abigail Adams, Philadelphia, November 4, 1775, *Letters*, 2: 296. See also *Extracts from the Diary of Christopher Marshall*, 51.

73 Lynch is quoted in *Letters*, 3: 174 n. 2. As Sarah J. Purcell and other scholars have recently demonstrated, Montgomery emerged in death as one of the most beloved heroes of the Revolution. The anguish of his widow, Janet Livingston Montgomery, elicited professions of commiseration from the public. American poets and playwrights composed elegies to the general, transforming him into an icon of American resistance. Sarah J. Purcell, *Sealed with Blood: War, Sacrifice, and Memory in Revolutionary America* (Philadelphia, 2002), 24–37; Jason Shaffer, *Performing Patriotism: National Identity in the Colonial and Revolutionary American Theater* (Philadelphia, 2007), 138–65, and Shaffer, "Making 'An Excellent Die': Death, Mourning, and Patriotism in the Propaganda Plays of the American Revolution," *EAL* 41 (2006): 1–27; and Ginger Strand, "The Many

Deaths of Montgomery: Audiences and Pamphlet Plays of the Revolution," *American Literary History* 9 (1997): 1–20.

74. North Carolina Delegates to Samuel Johnston, Philadelphia, January 2, 1776, *Letters*, 3: 18–19. For details about the Canadian campaign, including Montgomery's failure to receive word of his promotion, Arnold's expedition through the Maine wilderness, and the necessity of attacking Quebec before the New Year, see James Kirby Martin, *Benedict Arnold: Revolutionary Hero: An American Warrior Reconsidered* (New York, 1997), 104–50, 169, 172.

75. For the history of Montgomery's monument, see Sally Webster's forthcoming book, *Liberty's Heroes: War and Commemoration in Eighteenth-Century New York*.

76. Richard Smith's Diary, Philadelphia, January 18, 1776, *Letters*, 3: 112–13.

77. *Journals*, 4: 89–90.

78. Committee of Congress Report on General Montgomery's Memorial, Philadelphia, January 25, 1776, *Letters*, 3: 149–50.

79. *Journals*, 4: 89–90.

80. *Pennsylvania Evening Post*, February 22, 1776; *Pennsylvania Packet*, February 26, 1776; Josiah Bartlett to Mary Bartlett, Philadelphia, February 19, 1776, *Letters*, 3: 277–79. Kenneth Silverman, *A Cultural History of the American Revolution: Painting, Music, Literature, and the Theatre in the Colonies and the United States from the Treaty of Paris to the Inauguration of George Washington, 1763–1789* (New York, 1976), 314–15.

81. Purcell, *Sealed with Blood*, 37–38. See also Jason Shaffer, "Making 'an Excellent Die,'" 6, 22. On the power of sensibility and sentiment in the Revolution and in the early republic, see generally Bruce Burgett, *Sentimental Bodies: Sex, Gender, and Citizenship in the Early Republic* (Princeton, N.J., 1998); Andrew Burstein, *Sentimental Democracy: The Evolution of America's Romantic Self-Image* (New York, 1999); Michael Meranze, "Major André's Exhumation," in *Mortal Remains: Death in Early America*, ed. Nancy Isenberg and Andrew Burstein (Philadelphia, 2003), 123–53; Nicole Eustace, *Passion Is the Gale: Emotion, Power, and the Coming of the American Revolution* (Chapel Hill, N.C., 2008); Sarah Knott, *Sensibility and the American Revolution* (Chapel Hill, N.C., 2009); and Richard Godbeer, *The Overflowing of Friendship: Love between Men and the Creation of the American Republic* (Baltimore, 2009). See also Michael Warner, *The Letters of the Republic: Publication and the Public Sphere in Eighteenth-Century America* (Cambridge, Mass., 1990); and Christopher Looby, *Voicing America: Language, Literary Form, and the Origins of the United States* (Chicago, 1996).

82. Samuel Adams to Elizabeth Adams, Philadelphia, February 26, 1776, *Letters*, 3: 303–4.

83. James Duane to Robert R. Livingston, Philadelphia, January 31, 1776, *Letters*, 3: 173, 174 n. 2.

84. William Smith, "An Oration in Memory of General Montgomery" (Philadelphia, 1776), 25, 32.
85. Smith, "An Oration in Memory of General Montgomery," 29. Though Smith and Congress disagreed about the proper course of the American resistance, they shared a common animosity toward the "savage" peoples the British had allegedly roused against the colonists, as Peter Silver notes. See Silver, *Our Savage Neighbors: How Indian War Transformed Early America* (New York, 2009), 233.
86. Samuel Adams to Elizabeth Adams, Philadelphia, February 26, 1776, *Letters*, 3: 303–4.
87. Richard Smith's Diary, Philadelphia, February 21, 1776, *Letters*, 3: 294.
88. Smith, "An Oration in Memory of General Montgomery," 29. Interestingly, Smith's footnote appeared in the Philadelphia and Newport editions (Evans nos. 15084 and 15086) but did not appear in the editions of his oration published in New York or Norwich (Evans nos. 15085 and 15087).
89. John Adams to Abigail Adams, Philadelphia, February 11, 1776; John Adams to William Tudor, Philadelphia, April 12, 1776, *Letters*, 3: 226–27, 513–14.
90. Thomas Paine, *Common Sense . . . and A Dialogue between the Ghost of General Montgomery . . . and an American Delegate* (Philadelphia, 1776), 8 (note that the *Dialogue* is separately paginated).
91. *Pennsylvania Packet*, September 5, 1774.
92. Samuel Ward to his Children, Philadelphia, June 8, 1775, *Letters*, 1: 461–62.
93. John Adams to James Warren, Philadelphia, July 26, 1776; John Adams to Abigail Adams, Philadelphia, March 29, 1776; Samuel Ward to Deborah Ward, Philadelphia, January 2, 1776, Richard Smith's Diary, Philadelphia, March 26, 1776; Stephen Hopkins to Henry Ward, Philadelphia, March 27, 1776, *Letters*, 3: 21–22, 448, 451–52; 4: 460–61, 546–47.
94. Michael Meranze, "Love and Death" (paper presented at the tenth annual conference of the Omohundro Institute of Early American History and Culture, Northampton, Mass., June 2004).
95. *Pennsylvania Packet*, April 8, 1776.
96. John Adams to James Warren, Philadelphia, April 22, 1776, *Letters*, 3: 569–70.

Part III

1. *Journals*, 5: 517–18.
2. For Du Simitière's artistry and the American Revolution, see Paul G. Sifton, ed., *Historiographer to the United States: The Revolutionary Letterbook of Pierre Eugène Du Simitière* (New York, 1987), and Sifton, "Pierre Eugène Du Simitière (1737–1784): Collector in Revolutionary America" (Ph.D. diss., University of Pennsylvania, 1960); Historical Records Survey Division of Professional and Service Projects, Works Projects Administration,

Descriptive Catalogue of the Du Simitière Papers in the Library Company of Philadelphia (Philadelphia, 1940); and Du Simitière Papers, LCP and HSP; Pierre Eugène Du Simitière, *Thirteen Portraits of American Legislators, Patriots, and Soldiers* (London, 1783).

3. *Journals*, 5: 689–91.
4. For heraldry's social and cultural functions on the eve of the American Revolution, as well as Jefferson's and Adams's uses and misuses of their families' coats of arms, see Karin Wulf, "Family Matters: Heraldry and the Contest of Arms in Revolutionary America" (paper presented at the annual meeting of the Organization of American Historians, Memphis, Tenn., April 2003).
5. Compare Du Simitière's draft with the blazon laid before Congress, both detailed in the *Journals*, 5: 689–91.
6. Silas Deane to the Committee of Secret Correspondence, Paris, November 28, 1776, *RDCUS*, 2: 196–200.

Chapter 5

1. *Journals*, 5: 507. John Adams to Abigail Adams, Philadelphia, July 3, 1776, *Letters*, 4: 375–76. Len Travers, *Celebrating the Fourth: Independence Day and the Rites of Nationalism in the Early Republic* (Amherst, Mass., 1997), 15–17.
2. John Adams to Abigail Adams 2d, Philadelphia, July 5, 1777, *Letters*, 7: 293–94.
3. John Adams to Abigail Adams, Philadelphia, July 3, 1776, *Letters*, 4: 375–76.
4. Ronald Hamowy, "Jefferson and the Scottish Enlightenment: A Critique of Garry Wills's *Inventing America: Jefferson's Declaration of Independence*," *WMQ*, 3rd ser., 36 (1979): 503–23. See also Thad W. Tate, "The Social Contract in America, 1774–1787: Revolutionary Theory as a Conservative Instrument," *WMQ*, 3rd ser., 22 (1965): 375–91.
5. John Adams to John Winthrop, Philadelphia, June 23, 1776, *Letters*, 4: 298–300. See also John Dickinson's Notes on Arguments Concerning Independence, [July 1, 1776?], *Letters*, 4: 357–58.
6. On the shifting doctrines of natural and positive international law that shaped the Declaration of Independence, see David Armitage, "The Declaration of Independence and International Law," *WMQ*, 3rd ser., 59 (2002): 39–64. See also Peter S. Onuf and Nicholas G. Onuf, *Federal Union, Modern World: The Law of Nations in an Age of Revolution, 1776–1814* (Madison, Wis., 1993); and David Armitage, *The Declaration of Independence: A Global History* (Cambridge, Mass., 2007).
7. Thomas Paine, *Common Sense; Addressed to the Inhabitants of America* (Philadelphia, 1776), 74.
8. Joseph Hawley to Samuel Adams, April 1, 1776, quoted in John Miller, *The Origins of the American Revolution*, 2nd ed. (Stanford, Calif., 1959), 485; John Dickinson's Notes on Arguments Concerning Independence, [July

1, 1776?], *Letters*, 4: 357–58. Dickinson protested that the popular spirit of independence was fueled by resentment, rather than sound principle.

9. *Journals*, 5: 516. John Hancock to the New Jersey Convention, Philadelphia, July 5, 1776, *Letters*, 4: 392–93. The following account of Congress's dissemination of the Declaration is much indebted to Jay Fliegelman, *Declaring Independence: Jefferson, Natural Language, and the Culture of Performance* (Stanford, Calif., 1993), 25; and Pauline Maier, *American Scripture: Making the Declaration of Independence* (New York, 1997), 154–60. See also, John H. Hazelton, *The Declaration of Independence: Its History* (1906; reprint, New York, 1970).

10. Hazelton, *The Declaration of Independence*, 273; Fliegelman, *Declaring Independence*, 25; Maier, *American Scripture*, 154–60; Travers, *Celebrating the Fourth*, 21–22.

11. Fliegelman, *Declaring Independence*, 4–15.

12. See Thomas Jefferson to Robert Skipwith, Monticello, August 3, 1771— including the works of William Congreve whose famous quotation on music was first published in the tragedy, *The Mourning Bride* (1697)—in *PTJ*, 1: 76–81.

13. John Adams to Thomas Pickering, August 6, 1822, in *The Works of John Adams, Second President of the United States: With a Life of the Author*, ed. Charles Francis Adams, 10 vols. (Boston, 1850–56), 2: 512–14.

14. See Christopher Marshall's diary entries for July 6 and 8, 1776, in *Extracts from the Diary of Christopher Marshall, Kept in Philadelphia and Lancaster, during the American Revolution*, ed. William Duane (Albany, N.Y., 1877), 82–83; John Adams to Samuel Chase, Philadelphia, July 9, 1776, *Letters*, 4: 414–16; Fliegelman, *Declaring Independence*, 25; Maier, *American Scripture*, 154–60. See also J. Thomas Scharf and Thompson Westcott, *A History of Philadelphia, 1609–1884*, 3 vols. (Philadelphia, 1884), 1: 321.

15. For various responses to the Declaration, see Hazelton, *The Declaration of Independence*, 240–41, quoted here at 244, 259. See also Fliegelman, *Declaring Independence*, 25; and Maier, *American Scripture*, 154–60.

16. On the role of newspapers in building a national community of patriotic sentiment, see David Waldstreicher, *In the Midst of Perpetual Fetes: The Making of American Nationalism, 1776–1820* (Chapel Hill, N.C., 1997), 32–35.

17. Quoted in Hazelton, *The Declaration of Independence*, 254.

18. John Walker to Thomas Jefferson, Philadelphia, July 13, 1780, *Letters*, 15: 315–16.

19. On liberty trees as a symbol of the Revolution, see Alfred F. Young, *Liberty Tree: Ordinary People and the American Revolution* (New York, 2006).

20. Congress's May 15 resolution created an urgent and radical preamble to its milder resolution of May 10, which authorized the American people to install new administrations "where no government sufficient to the

exigencies of their affairs have been hitherto established." *Journals*, 4: 342, 357–58.

21. On the political contest for independence in Pennsylvania, and in Philadelphia in particular, see generally, David Hawke, *In the Midst of a Revolution* (Philadelphia, 1961). See also Maier, *American Scripture*, 64–66.

22. On Thomson's efforts to preserve the Pennsylvania assembly, see Lewis Reifsneider Harley, *Life of Charles Thomson: Secretary of the Continental Congress* (Philadelphia, 1900), 78–81; J. Edwin Hendricks, *Charles Thomson and the Making of a New Nation, 1729–1824* (Rutherford, N.J., 1979), 122–27; and Boyd Stanley Schlenther, *Charles Thomson: A Patriot's Pursuit* (Newark, Del., 1990), 130–36.

23. Charles Thomson's account of the reading of the Declaration, recorded in the Logan Family Papers, HSP, is quoted in Brendan McConville, *The King's Three Faces: The Rise and Fall of Royal America, 1688–1776* (Chapel Hill, N.C., 2006), 308.

24. Biddle and Deborah Norris Logan are quoted in Scharf and Westcott, *History of Philadelphia*, 1: 321 n. 1.

25. Hazelton, *The Declaration of Independence*, 244–45, quoting late-nineteenth-century family history reported in *Harper's New Monthly Magazine*, July 1892.

26. See McConville, *The King's Three Faces*, 306.

27. See Christopher Marshall's diary entry for June 4, 1774, in *Extracts from the Diary of Christopher Marshall*, 6.

28. On the transmission of folk practices from England to the Americas, see Alfred F. Young, "English Plebeian Culture and Eighteenth-Century American Radicalism," in *The Origins of Anglo-American Radicalism*, ed. Margaret Jacob and James Jacob (London, 1984), 185–212. On pre-Revolutionary folk protests, see Peter Shaw, *American Patriots and the Rituals of Revolution* (Cambridge, Mass., 1981), 204–31.

29. *Connecticut Journal*, October 30, 1776.

30. See Christopher Marshall's diary entries for July 6 and 8, 1776, in *Extracts from the Diary of Christopher Marshall*, 82–83.

31. Hazelton, *The Declaration of Independence*, 253; Beverly Orlove Held, "'To instruct and improve . . . to entertain and please': American Civic Protests and Pageants, 1765–1784" (Ph.D. diss., University of Michigan, 1987), 122; McConville, *The King's Three Faces*, 309; *Pennsylvania Evening Post*, July 13, 1776.

32. *New-York Journal*, August 8, 1776.

33. For the burning of the king's arms and emblems, see Hazelton, *The Declaration of Independence*, 251, 255; Held, "'To instruct and improve . . . to entertain and please,'" 120, 122; Simon P. Newman, *Parades and the Politics of the Streets: Festive Culture in the Early American Republic* (Philadelphia,

1997), 33–34; Maier, *American Scripture*, 158; and McConville, *The King's Three Faces*, 307–9.

34. See generally McConville, *The King's Three Faces*.

35. Hazelton, *The Declaration of Independence*, 256.

36. Robert Levere Brunhouse, *The Counter-Revolution in Pennsylvania, 1776–1790* (1942; reprint, Harrisburg, Pa., 1971), 40, 49; Jack D. Marietta, *The Reformation of American Quakerism, 1748–1783* (Philadelphia, 1984), 239, 267–70.

37. On the New York and New Jersey campaigns, see David Hackett Fischer, *Washington's Crossing* (New York, 2004).

38. See Christopher Marshall's diary entries for early December 1776, as well as Appendix E, General Putnam's orders, in *Extracts from the Diary of Christopher Marshall*, 105–7, 295–97.

39. *Journals*, 6: 1023, 1027. General Washington suppressed and Congress subsequently rescinded its resolution denouncing the "scandalous report" and proclaiming its refusal to depart Philadelphia. Jared Sparks, ed., *The Writings of General Washington; Being the Correspondence, Address, Messages, and Other Papers, Official and Private, Selected and Published from the Original Manuscripts*, 12 vols. (Boston, 1855), 4: 210–12.

40. Edmund Cody Burnett, *The Continental Congress* (New York, 1941), 232–34. Some New England delegates disavowed the flight to Baltimore and claimed to have protested it. See Elbridge Gerry to James Warren?, Baltimore, December 23, 1776; William Whipple to John Langdon, Baltimore, December 24, 1776, *Letters*, 5: 640–42, 659–60.

41. John Adams's Diary, Baltimore, February 8, 1777, *Letters*, 6: 237.

42. Elbridge Gerry to James Warren?, Baltimore, December 23, 1776; Samuel Adams to John Adams, Baltimore, January 9, 1777; Robert Morris to John Jay, Philadelphia, January 12, 1777, *Letters*, 5: 640–42; 6: 63–66, 87–88.

43. Unbeknownst to Congress and the people of Philadelphia, General Howe decided in early December not to cross the Delaware, but rather to hold New Jersey through the winter. Fischer, *Washington's Crossing*, 135.

44. Executive Committee to John Hancock, Philadelphia, February 4, 1777, *Letters*, 6: 212–15.

45. John Adams to Abigail Adams, Philadelphia, March 7, 1777, *Letters*, 6: 409–10.

46. *Pennsylvania Evening Post*, March 6, 1777; Thomas Burke to Richard Caswell, Philadelphia, July 5, 1777, *Letters*, 7: 295–96.

47. Travers, *Celebrating the Fourth*, 21–22.

48. Charles Carroll of Carrollton to Charles Carroll Sr., Philadelphia, July 4, 1777; Thomas Burke to Richard Caswell, Philadelphia, July 5, 1777, *Letters*, 7: 289–90, 295–96.

49. *Pennsylvania Evening Post*, July 3, 1777.

50. The following accounts of Philadelphia's 1777 Independence Day celebration are taken from John Adams to Abigail Adams 2d, Philadelphia, July 5, 1777, *Letters*, 7: 293–94; *Pennsylvania Evening Post*, July 5, 1777; and George Bryan to His Wife, Philadelphia, July 4, 1777, quoted in *The Loyal Verses of Joseph Stansbury and Doctor Jonathan Odell*, ed. Winthrop Sargent (Albany, N.Y., 1860), 118.

51. *Journals*, 8: 464.

52. The standard history of the U.S. flag is George Henry Preble's *Origin and History of the American Flag and of the Naval and Yacht-Club Signals, Seals and Arms, and Principal National Songs of the United States, with a Chronicle of the Symbols, Standards, Banners, and Flags of Ancient and Modern Nations*, new ed., 2 vols. (Philadelphia, 1917). For more recent treatment, see Edward W. Richardson, *Standards and Colors of the American Revolution* (Philadelphia, 1982); and David Hackett Fischer, *Liberty and Freedom* (New York, 2005), 152–58. On the role and life of Betsy Ross, see Marla R. Miller, *Betsy Ross and the Making of America* (New York, 2010).

53. John Jay to Alexander McDougall, Philadelphia, March 23, 1776, *Letters*, 3: 433–34.

54. See, for example, Naval Committee to the Virginia Convention, Philadelphia, December 2, 1775; Marine Committee to Nicholas Biddle, February 15, 1777, *Letters* 2: 543–44; 6: 291–93. These instructions suggest both a concern for operational security at sea and a lack of clear standards for the use of flags in the Revolutionary United States. See also Benjamin Franklin and John Adams to the Ambassador of Naples, Passy, October 9, 1776, Papers, No. 85, folio 236.

55. Richardson, *Standards and Colors of the American Revolution*, 1–12, 17–72.

56. The patriots of Charleston, South Carolina, also celebrated the first anniversary of independence by flying "American colours." Presumably, those colors did not include the official stars-and-stripes so recently adopted by Congress. *Pennsylvania Evening Post*, July 29, 1777.

57. Samuel Huntington to Matthew Griswold, Eliphalet Dyer, and William Pitkin, Philadelphia, August 30, 1776, *Letters*, 5: 86–88.

58. John Adams to Abigail Adams 2d, Philadelphia, July 5, 1777, *Letters*, 7: 293–94.

59. John Adams to Abigail Adams 2d, Philadelphia, July 5, 1777, *Letters*, 7: 293–94.

60. See, for example, Newman, *Parades and the Politics of the Street*, 29–31; David S. Shields, *Civil Tongues and Polite Letters in British America* (Chapel Hill, N.C., 1997), xvii, 66–67; Waldstreicher, *In the Midst of Perpetual Fetes*, 129–31; and Peter Thompson, *Rum Punch and Revolution: Taverngoing and Public Life in Eighteenth-Century Philadelphia* (Philadelphia, 1999), 99, 192–93.

61. *Pennsylvania Evening Post*, July 5, 1777.

62. John Adams to Abigail Adams 2d, Philadelphia, July 5, 1777, *Letters*, 7: 293–94; and *Pennsylvania Evening Post*, July 5, 1777. See also, Thomas J. McGuire, *The Philadelphia Campaign: Brandywine and the Fall of Philadelphia*, 2 vols. (Mechanicsburg, Pa., 2006), 1: 64–65 n. 8.

63. Christopher Marshall noted that the prisoners, many of them conscripts, "made a poor, despicable appearance." Scharf and Westcott, *History of Philadelphia*, 1: 335. See also, Edward J. Lowell, *The Hessians and the Other German Auxiliaries of Great Britain in the Revolutionary War* (1884; reprint, Port Washington, N.Y., 1965), 104–5.

64. Scharf and Westcott, *History of Philadelphia*, 1: 338.

65. Thomas Burke to Richard Caswell, Philadelphia, July 5, 1777, *Letters*, 7: 295–96.

66. Kenneth Silverman, *A Cultural History of the American Revolution: Painting, Music, Literature, and the Theatre in the Colonies and the United States from the Treaty of Paris to the Inauguration of George Washington, 1763–1789* (New York, 1976), 355–59.

67. In the spring of 1778, this or another Hessian band performed at patriot balls in Lancaster, Pennsylvania, for a sum of £15. Hessian musicians also appeared for American audiences in Maryland. See the entry for March 6, 1778, in *Extracts from the Diary of Christopher Marshall*, 170; Johann Conrad Döhla, *A Hessian Diary of the American Revolution*, trans. and ed. Bruce E. Burgoyne (Norman, Okla., 1990), 220–21; and Johann Ernst Prechtel, *A Hessian Officer's Diary of the American Revolution*, trans. and ed. Bruce E. Burgoyne (Westminster, Md., 1994), 251–52. See also C. W. Heckert, ed., *Diary of Captain Wiederholdt: Defeat and Captivity at Trenton* (Buckhannon, W.Va., 1984), 4–5. I am grateful to Kenneth Miller for introducing me to these sources.

68. Adams, Burke, and the *Pennsylvania Evening Post* all characterized the Hessian musicians as "taken." John Adams to Abigail Adams 2d, Philadelphia, July 5, 1777; Thomas Burke to Richard Caswell, Philadelphia, July 5, 1777, *Letters*, 7: 293–95, 295–96; and *Pennsylvania Evening Post*, July 5, 1777.

69. Jerrilyn Greene Marston, *King and Congress: The Transfer of Political Legitimacy, 1774–1776* (Princeton, N.J., 1987), 52–55.

70. Thomas Burke to Richard Caswell, Philadelphia, July 5, 1777, *Letters*, 7: 295–96.

71. John Adams to Abigail Adams 2d, Philadelphia, July 5, 1777, *Letters*, 7: 293–94; and *Pennsylvania Evening Post*, July 5, 1777.

72. For a more detailed analysis of the political and military circumstances that made possible the Continental Army's victories at Trenton and Princeton and for the aftermath of those victories, see Fischer, *Washington's Crossing*, esp. 142–43, 346–62.

73. Howard H. Peckham, ed., *The Toll of Independence: Engagements and Battle Casualties of the American Revolution* (Chicago, 1974), 22–26.

74. John Adams to Abigail Adams 2d, Philadelphia, July 5, 1777, *Letters*, 7: 293–94.
75. Sarah Fisher, "'A Diary of Trifling Occurrences': Philadelphia, 1776–1778," ed. Nicholas B. Wainwright, *PMHB* 82 (1958): 411–65, at 437–38.
76. *Pennsylvania Evening Post*, July 5, 1777.
77. John Adams to Abigail Adams 2d, Philadelphia, July 5, 1777, *Letters*, 7: 293–94.
78. *Pennsylvania Evening Post*, July 5, 1777.
79. Quoted in Winthrop Sargent, ed., *The Loyal Verses of Joseph Stansbury and Doctor Jonathan Odell*, 118.
80. Fisher, "'Diary of Trifling Occurrences,'" 438. See also Marietta, *The Reformation of American Quakerism*, 244–45; Elaine Forman Crane, ed., *The Diary of Elizabeth Drinker* (Boston, 1991), 1: 225; Newman, *Parades and the Politics of the Streets*, 36; and Travers, *Celebrating the Fourth*, 23–24.
81. Sargent, ed., *The Loyal Verses of Joseph Stansbury and Doctor Jonathan Odell*, 119. See also Arthur J. Mekeel, *The Quakers and the American Revolution* (York, U.K., 1996), 192.
82. For Humphreys's allegations, see *Pennsylvania Evening Post*, July 5 and 10, 1777.
83. For Peters's denial see, *Pennsylvania Evening Post*, July 12, 1777.
84. *Pennsylvania Ledger*, December 10, 1777.
85. John Adams to Abigail Adams 2d, Philadelphia, July 5, 1777, *Letters*, 7: 293–94. The continental officer who deemed unlit windows a product of "Obstinacy" is quoted in Travers, *Celebrating the Fourth*, 24.
86. Henry Laurens to John Lewis Gervais, Philadelphia, August 5, 1777, *Letters*, 418–25.
87. John Adams to Abigail Adams 2d, Philadelphia, July 5, 1777, *Letters*, 7: 293–94
88. William Williams to Jonathan Trumbull Sr., Philadelphia, July 5, 1777; *Letters*, 7: 301–4. On Williams's moderate father Solomon, see Douglas L. Winiarski, "Souls Filled with Ravishing Transport: Heavenly Visions and the Radical Awakening in New England," *WMQ*, 3rd ser., 61 (2004): 3–46.
89. See generally, Stephen R. Taaffe, *The Philadelphia Campaign, 1777–1778* (Lawrence, Kans., 2003); McGuire, *The Philadelphia Campaign*.
90. *Journals*, 8: 694–95. On the arrest of Philadelphia Quakers, see Robert F. Oaks, "Philadelphians in Exile: The Problem of Loyalty during the American Revolution," *PMHB* 96 (1972): 298–325. On the Quaker experience in the Revolutionary War more generally, see Marietta, *The Reformation of American Quakerism*, 222–79; and Mekeel, *The Quakers and the American Revolution*.
91. John Hancock to Dorothy Hancock, York, October 1, 1777, *Letters*, 8: 38–40.
92. Gouverneur Morris to John Jay, Valley Forge, February 1, 1778, *Letters*, 9: 3–4. During the winter of 1777–78, the continental currency in fact fell off

as much as 50 percent. This drop resulted primarily from the exorbitant sum Congress had emitted over the past year—more than twenty million dollars—as well as from an extensive British campaign to counterfeit American money. See E. J. Ferguson, *The Power of the Purse: A History of American Public Finance, 1776–1790* (Chapel Hill, N.C., 1961), 32; and Eric P. Newman, *The Early Paper Money of America*, 4th ed. (Iola, Wis., 1997), 478.

93. Scharf and Westcott, *History of Philadelphia*, 1: 365–74. See also George Winthrop Geib, "A History of Philadelphia, 1776–1789" (Ph.D. diss., University of Wisconsin, 1969); John M. Coleman, "Joseph Galloway and the British Occupation of Philadelphia," *Pennsylvania History* 30 (1963): 272–300.

94. See generally Fisher, "'A Diary of Trifling Occurrences': Philadelphia, 1776–1778"; Darlene Emmert Fisher, "Social Life in Philadelphia during the British Occupation," *Pennsylvania History* 37 (1970): 237–60; John W. Jackson, *With the British Army in Philadelphia, 1777–1778* (San Rafael, Calif., 1979); and Judith Van Buskirk, "They Didn't Join the Band: Disaffected Women in Revolutionary Philadelphia," *Pennsylvania History* 62 (1995): 306–29.

95. Rebecca Franks, "A Letter of Miss Rebecca Franks," *PMHB* 16 (1892): 216–18. See also Jared Brown, *The Theatre in America during the Revolution* (Cambridge, 1995), and Brown, "Plays and Amusements Offered for and by the American Military during the Revolutionary War," *Theatre Research International* 4 (1978): 12–24.

96. Fisher, "Social Life in Philadelphia," 251–52. See also Geib, "A History of Philadelphia, 1776–1789"; Charles C. Norris Jr., *"The Mischianza of 1778": An Address Delivered to the Members of the Society of Colonial Wars in the Commonwealth of Pennsylvania, March 11, 1943* (Philadelphia, 1943), 1–16; Scharf and Westcott, *History of Philadelphia*, 1: 377–82; and John André, "Particulars of the Mischianza in America," *Gentleman's Magazine* 48 (1778): 353–57.

97. According to Howe's census, the city population included 10,331 males and 13,403 females. Scharf and Westcott, *History of Philadelphia*, 1: 367.

98. On the incidence of rape in the previous year's New York and New Jersey campaigns, see Fischer, *Washington's Crossing*, 178–79.

99. Crane, ed., *The Diary of Elizabeth Drinker*, 1: 258–60, 266, 273. The circumstances suggest that the servant ran away with the officer of her own accord.

100. Fisher, "Diary of Trifling Occurrences,'" 462. See also Fisher, "Social Life in Philadelphia," 239, 243–44, 246; and generally Van Buskirk, "They Didn't Join the Band"; Crane, ed., *The Diary of Elizabeth Drinker*, 1: 266.

101. Jared Brown, *The Theater in America during the Revolution*, 51–56.

102. André, "Particulars of the Mischianza in America," 353–57.

103. On the Meschianza as a commentary on race and ethnicity in British America, see Randall Fuller, "Theaters of the American Revolution: The Valley Forge *Cato* and the Meschianza in Their Transcultural Contexts," *EAL* 34 (September 1999): 126–46, esp. 139–40. On representations of Islam and the Middle East in modern European and American discourses, see generally James R. Lewis, "Savages of the Seas: Barbary Captivity Tales and Images of Muslims in the Early Republic," *Journal of American Culture* 13 (1990): 75–84; Robert J. Allison, *The Crescent Obscured: The United States and the Muslim World, 1776–1815* (New York, 1995); and Anne G. Myles, "Slaves in Algiers, Captives in Iraq: The Strange Career of the Barbary Captivity Narrative," *Common-place: The Interactive Journal of Early American Life* 5 (2004), http://www.common-place.org.

104. On the social power of women in Philadelphia during and after the occupation, see Susan E. Klepp, "Rough Music on Independence Day: Philadelphia, 1778," in *Riot and Revelry in Early America*, ed. William Pencak, Matthew Dennis, and Simon P. Newman (University Park, Pa., 2002), 156–76.

105. For the outcry against Philadelphia women who socialized with British officers, including Wayne's, see Scharf and Westcott, *History of Philadelphia*, 2: 899–901. For the entertainment at the City Tavern, see the *Pennsylvania Evening Post*, July 25, 1778.

106. Cornelius Harnett to William Wilkinson, York, December 28, 1777, *Letters*, 8: 489–90.

107. Gouverneur Morris to Robert R. Livingston, Valley Forge, February 5, 1778; James Lovell to Abigail Adams, York, June 13, 1778; *Letters*, 9: 35–36; 10: 89–90.

108. John Durand, trans., *New Materials for the History of the American Revolution* (New York, 1889), 166–67.

109. *North Carolina Gazette*, September 4, 1778.

110. Crane, ed., *The Diary of Elizabeth Drinker*, 1: 314.

111. *Journals*, 11: 641.

112. Josiah Bartlett to Mary Bartlett, Philadelphia, July 20, 1778; Henry Laurens to Rawlins Lowndes, Philadelphia, July 15, 1778; Henry Laurens to Rawlins Lowndes, York, May 17, 1778; Josiah Bartlett to Mary Bartlett, Philadelphia, July 14, 1778, *Letters*, 9: 696–704; 10: 275–76, 283–87, 319–20.

113. Richard Henry Lee to Francis Lightfoot Lee, Philadelphia, July 5, 1778, *Letters*, 10: 223–24.

114. On the Cadwalader-Conway duel, see Alexander Graydon, *Memoirs of a Life, Chiefly Passed in Philadelphia, Within the Last Sixty Years* (1811; reprint, Bedford, Mass., 2009), 278–79. On the so-called Conway Cabal, see James Lovell to Horatio Gates, York, November 27, 1777, *Letters*, 8: 329–31, esp. n. 1 and the literature cited there. See also, Don Higginbotham, *The War of*

American Independence: Military Attitudes, Policies, and Practice, 1763–1789 (New York, 1971), 216–20.

115. Supplement to the *Pennsylvania Packet*, July 4, 1778.

116. Henrietta C. Ellery, ed., "Diary of the Hon. William Ellery, of Rhode Island, June 28–July 23, 1778," *PMHB* 11 (1887): 477–78, quoted in *Letters*, 10: 221–22 n. 1.

117. Supplement to the *Pennsylvania Packet*, July 4, 1778.

118. Ellery, ed., "Diary of the Hon. William Ellery, of Rhode Island, June 28–July 23, 1778," quoted in *Letters*, 10: 221–22 n. 1. A *fête champêtre* is a country or garden party, in this case the Meschianza.

119. In the *Pennsylvania Packet*, July 4, 1778, appeared the admonition dated July 3, "Notice is given to the inhabitants of Philadelphia that the Honorable the Congress does not expect they will illuminate their houses to-morrow evening." See also Travers, *Celebrating the Fourth*, 25.

120. The details of the episode come from Ellery, ed., "Diary of the Hon. William Ellery, of Rhode Island, June 28–July 23, 1778," quoted in *Letters*, 10: 221–22 n. 1; Richard Henry Lee to Francis Lightfoot Lee, Philadelphia, July 5, 1778; Josiah Bartlett to Mary Bartlett, Philadelphia, August 24, 1778, *Letters*, 10: 223–24, 495–97; Crane, ed., *The Diary of Elizabeth Drinker*, 1: 314; and the *New-Jersey Gazette*, July 8, 1778. See also Theodore G. Tappert and John W. Doberstein, eds. and trans., *The Journals of Henry Melchior Muhlenberg* (Philadelphia, 1942–58), 3: 171–72. No surviving evidence directly links members of Congress with this Philadelphia crowd. Recounting the event more than a month later, Josiah Bartlett wrote that "Gentlemen" dressed the woman in the wig and the "mob" paraded her about town. As Susan E. Klepp has argued, the drummer in the crowd may indicate militia participation, while the complexity of the paraded woman's headdress suggests that the event was staged, rather than spontaneous. Klepp, "Rough Music on Independence Day: Philadelphia, 1778," 160–61. In any case, such raucous street theater was not beneath congressional delegates. In 1765, Richard Henry Lee led a procession of slaves, brandishing effigies in protest over the Stamp Act, to the county courthouse in Montross, Virginia. See J. Kent McGaughy, *Richard Henry Lee: A Portrait of an American Revolutionary* (Lanham, Md., 2004), 78.

121. In a vivid and insightful analysis of this episode and its implications for gender, fashion, and politics in postoccupation Philadelphia, Klepp identifies "respectable love" and companionate marriage as elements of the crowd's latent agenda. Klepp, "Rough Music on Independence Day: Philadelphia, 1778," 156–76. See also, Mary Beth Norton, *Liberty's Daughters: The Revolutionary Experience of American Women, 1750–1800* (Boston, 1980), 352 n. 48; Linda K. Kerber, *Women of the Republic: Intellect and Ideology in Revolutionary America* (Chapel Hill, N.C., 1980), 44; Steven Rosswurm, *Arms, Country, and Class: The Philadelphia Militia and the "Lower Sort" during*

the American Revolution, 1775–1783 (New Brunswick, N.J., 1987), 154; and Newman, *Parades and the Politics of the Streets*, 36.

122. For more on saturnalia, see Natalie Zemon Davis, "The Reasons of Misrule: Youth Groups and Charivaris in Sixteenth-Century France," *Past and Present* 50 (1971): 41–75; Peter Shaw, "Fathers, Sons, and the Ambiguities of Revolution in 'My Kinsman, Major Molineux,'" *NEQ* 49 (1976): 559–76, and generally Shaw, *American Patriots and the Rituals of Revolution*.

123. John F. Watson, *Annals of Philadelphia and Pennsylvania*, 2 vols. (Philadelphia, 1870), 1: 184.

124. Susan E. Klepp suggests that the paraded woman may not have been black, but merely portrayed as black by elites who wished to diffuse the power of the episode by sexually and racially degrading its central figure. Klepp, "Rough Music on Independence Day," 169.

125. Crane, ed., *The Diary of Elizabeth Drinker*, 1: 314.

126. Franks is quoted in Scharf and Westcott, *History of Philadelphia*, 2: 900. Smith's participation is recorded in Richard Henry Lee to Francis Lightfoot Lee, Philadelphia, July 5, 1778, *Letters*, 10: 223–24.

127. Richard Henry Lee to Francis Lightfoot Lee, Philadelphia, July 5, 1778; Henry Laurens to the *Pennsylvania Packet*, Philadelphia, October 3, 1778, *Letters*, 10: 223–24; 11: 15–17.

128. *New-Jersey Gazette*, July 8, 1778.

129. Patriot efforts to rebuke such women bear witness to the extraordinary mobilizing power of fashion in eighteenth-century America. Kate Haulman has discussed this episode and its implications for the "high roll" hairstyle in "A Short History of the High Roll," *Common-place: The Interactive Journal of Early American Life* 2 (2001), http://www.commonplace.org. On the relationship between fashion and politics in late-colonial British North America and the early republic, see generally Karin Calvert, "The Function of Fashion in Eighteenth-Century America" in *Of Consuming Interests: The Style of Life in the Eighteenth Century*, ed. Cary Carson, Ronald Hoffman, and Peter J. Albert (Charlottesville, Va., 1994), 252–83; Linda Baumgarten, *What Clothes Reveal: The Language of Clothing in Colonial and Federal America* (New Haven, Conn., 2002); Michael Zakim, *Ready-Made Democracy: A History of Men's Dress in the American Republic, 1760–1860* (Chicago, 2003); Linzy A. Brekke, "'The Scourge of Fashion': Political Economy and the Politics of Consumption in Post-Revolutionary America," *Early American Studies: An Interdisciplinary Journal* 3 (2005): 111–39, and Brekke, "'To Make a Figure': Clothing and Gender Politics in Early National America," in *Gender, Taste, and Material Culture in Britain and North America, 1700–1850*, ed. Amanda Vickery and John Styles (New Haven, Conn., 2006), 225–46; and Kate Haulman, "Fashion and the Culture Wars of Revolutionary Philadelphia," *WMQ*, 3rd ser., 62 (2005): 625–62.

130. For the development of Independence Day rituals in the early republic, see generally Newman, *Parades and the Politics of the Streets*, 83–119; Travers, *Celebrating the Fourth*; and Waldstreicher, *In the Midst of Perpetual Fetes*.

131. Henry Laurens's Notes of Debates, Philadelphia, July 2, 1779, *Letters*, 13: 135–36; *Pennsylvania Packet*, July 8, 1779; Travers, *Celebrating the Fourth*, 25; Charles Warren, "Fourth of July Myths," *WMQ*, 3rd ser., 2 (1945): 238–72, at 257.

132. *Pennsylvania Packet*, July 8, 1779.

Chapter 6

1. *Pennsylvania Packet*, August 1, 1778. The conventional term for the Roman soothsayer is *haruspex*.

2. Henry Marchant to John Carter, Philadelphia, July 14, 1778; Henry Laurens to Certain States, [Philadelphia], July 12, 1778, *Letters*, 10: 264–65, 278–80.

3. Thomas Burke's Notes of Debates, Baltimore, February 21, 1777, *Letters*, 6: 336–37.

4. *Secret Journals*, 2: 30.

5. Emmerich de Vattel, *The Law of Nations; or, Principles of the Law of Nature, Applied to the Conduct and Affairs of Nations and Sovereigns* (Dublin, 1787), 16.

6. Jerrilyn Greene Marston, *King and Congress: The Transfer of Political Legitimacy, 1774–1776* (Princeton, N.J., 1987), 8–9.

7. William Emmett O'Donnell, *The Chevalier de La Luzerne, French Minister to the United States, 1779–84* (Bruges, 1938), 54–55.

8. Thomas Jefferson's Notes of Proceedings in Congress, Philadelphia, June 7–28, 1776, *Letters*, 158–65.

9. See generally O'Donnell, *The Chevalier de La Luzerne*; Ralph L. Ketcham, "France and American Politics, 1763–1793," *Political Science Quarterly* 78 (June 1963): 198–223; William C. Stinchcombe, *The American Revolution and the French Alliance* (Syracuse, N.Y., 1969); Neil Thomas Storch, "Congressional Politics and Diplomacy, 1775–1783" (Ph.D. diss., University of Wisconsin, 1969); Jonathan R. Dull, *A Diplomatic History of the American Revolution* (New Haven, Conn., 1985); the introductions and notes to the following edited collections: *RDCUS*; John J. Meng, ed., *Despatches and Instructions of Conrad Alexandre Gérard, 1778–1780* (Baltimore, 1939); and Mary A. Giunta et al., eds., *The Emerging Nation: A Documentary History of the Foreign Relations of the United States under the Articles of Confederation, 1780–1789*, 3 vols. (Washington, D.C., 1996); and the essays collected in Ronald Hoffman and Peter J. Albert, eds., *Diplomacy and Revolution: The Franco-American Alliance of 1778* (Charlottesville, Va., 1981). See also Martha Elena Rojas, "Diplomatic Letters: The Conduct and Culture of

Foreign Affairs in the Early Republic," (Ph.D. diss., Stanford University, 2003), esp. chapter 1.

10. Henry Laurens to Rawlins Lowndes, [York?], May 17, 1778, *Letters*, 9: 696–704.

11. Elias Boudinot to Hannah Boudinot, Philadelphia, July 14, 1778, *Letters*, 10: 276–77; Conrad-Alexandre Gérard to Charles Gravier, Comte de Vergennes, Philadelphia, July 15, 1778, *Despatches and Instructions*, 147–50. Raymond C. Werner, "Diary of Grace Growden Galloway," *PMHB* 55 (1933): 32–94, at 39.

12. *(New York) Royal Gazette*, July 29, 1778.

13. Werner, "Diary of Grace Growden Galloway," 38, 39, 46, 48. See also Charles Coleman Sellers, *Charles Willson Peale* (New York, 1969), 163–64; Edward Lawler Jr., "The President's House in Philadelphia: The Rediscovery of a Lost Landmark," *PMHB* 196 (2002): 5–95, at 22.

14. Henry Marchant to the Rhode Island Assembly, Philadelphia, August 11, 1778, *Letters*, 10: 431.

15. See generally Garrett Mattingly, *Renaissance Diplomacy* (Boston, 1955); David Ogg, *Europe in the Seventeenth Century*, 8th ed., rev. (New York, 1962); John R. Wood and Jean Serres, *Diplomatic Ceremonial and Protocol: Principles, Procedures and Practices* (New York, 1970); William James Roosen, *The Age of Louis XIV: The Rise of Modern Diplomacy* (Cambridge, Mass., 1976); and M. S. Anderson, *The Rise of Modern Diplomacy, 1450–1919* (London, 1993). See also Norbert Elias, *The Court Society*, trans. Edmund Jephcott (New York, 1983).

16. Conrad-Alexandre Gérard to Charles Gravier, Comte de Vergennes, Philadelphia, August 7, 1778, *Despatches and Instructions*, 201–5.

17. For some sense of the books available to Congress, see and compare *The Charter, Laws, and Catalogue of Books, of the Library Company of Philadelphia* (Philadelphia, 1770) with *A Catalogue of the Books Belonging to the Library Company of Philadelphia* (Philadelphia, 1789). See also Jack P. Greene, *The Intellectual Heritage of the Constitutional Era: The Delegates' Library* (Philadelphia, 1986).

18. Benjamin Franklin to Charles William Frederic Dumas, Philadelphia, December 9, 1775, *Letters*, 2: 465–68.

19. Maximilien Robespierre, "Rapport sur les principes du gouvernement révolutionnaire," December 25, 1793, in *Oeuvres de Maximilien Robespierre* 10 (Discours: 27 juillet 1793–27 juillet 1794) (Paris, 1967), 274, quoted in Lynn Hunt, *Politics, Culture, and Class in the French Revolution* (Berkeley, Calif., 1984), 54–55.

20. Joining Adams on the committee were his political ally, Richard Henry Lee, and the New Yorker Gouverneur Morris. *Journals*, 11: 688.

21. Samuel Adams to James Warren, Philadelphia, July 15, 1778, *Letters*, 10: 280–81.

22. *Journals*, 12: 1001.
23. Samuel Adams to Elbridge Gerry, Philadelphia, November 27, 1780, *Letters*, 16: 386–88.
24. Samuel Adams to James Warren, Philadelphia, July 15, 1778, *Letters*, 10: 280–81. Adams might also have wished to dampen Gérard's prestige and influence. In the months that followed, Adams aligned himself firmly against the "Gallican" interest, largely as a result of the highly partisan Deane-Lee quarrel. See O'Donnell, *The Chevalier de La Luzerne*, 54–55. But it is difficult to know whether Adams foresaw this political tension as early as the summer of 1778.
25. Conrad-Alexandre Gérard to Charles Gravier, Comte de Vergennes, Philadelphia, August 7, 1778, *Despatches and Instructions*, 201–2.
26. *Secret Journals*, 2: 92–93.
27. Drayton's demand for grander diplomatic ceremonials, if in fact such were his demand, would have been consonant with his insistence, the following summer, on a robust celebration of the anniversary of American independence. It would also have comported with Drayton's jury instructions of October 15, 1776, in which he, as chief justice of the South Carolina court of general sessions, charged a grand jury, "And thus has suddenly arisen in the World, a new empire, styled The United States of America. An empire that as soon as started into Existence, attracts the attention of the Rest of the Universe, and bids fair, by the Blessing of God, to be the most glorious of any upon record." Quoted in Neil Longley York, *Turning the World Upside Down: The War of American Independence and the Problem of Empire* (Westport, Conn., 2003), 77.
28. Benjamin Rush to Ebenezer Hazard, London, October 22, 1768, quoted in Scott J. Hammond, Kevin R. Hardwick, Howard Leslie Lubert, eds., *Classics of American Political and Constitutional Thought: Origins through the Civil War*, 2 vols. (Indianapolis, 2007), 1: 199.
29. Vattel, *The Law of Nations*, 48, 677.
30. Perhaps owing to the youth and frailty of the United States, Gérard appeared only in the character of a minister plenipotentiary, not as ambassador in the representative character of Louis XVI. Gérard's appointment as minister was contingent on Congress bestowing the same rank on Benjamin Franklin. See Henry Laurens to Rawlins Lowndes, Philadelphia, July 15, 1778, *Letters*, 10: 283–87.
31. *Journals*, 11: 696–701, 703.
32. Richard Henry Lee to Thomas Jefferson, Philadelphia, July 20, 1778, *Letters*, 10: 322–23; Conrad-Alexandre Gérard to Charles Gravier, Comte de Vergennes, Philadelphia, August 7, 1778, *Despatches and Instructions*, 201–2.
33. The following account is drawn from the *Journals* of Congress, from a private letter written by the congressman Elias Boudinot, and from the

proceedings published in the *Pennsylvania Packet*. Those sources differ on a few minor details; in such instances, I have relied on the *Journals* and the *Packet*, both more comprehensive than Boudinot's letter. *Journals*, 11: 707–08; Elias Boudinot to Hannah Boudinot, Princeton, August 8, 1778, *Letters*, 10: 405–06; *Pennsylvania Packet*, August 11, 1778.

34. Committee of Congress to the Pennsylvania Council, August 6, 1778, *Letters*, 10: 395.

35. In keeping with European practice, Congress devised a tiered program of ceremonials in which ambassadors received greater honors than ministers and envoys. See François de Callières, *On the Manner of Negotiating with Princes*, trans. by A. F. Whyte (Notre Dame, Ind., 1963), 70–79. Congress did not finalize ceremonials for ambassadors until after its reception of Gérard, but it presumably intended to reserve for ambassadors the military honors customarily paid to general officers of the first rank.

36. Calvin Jillson and Rick K. Wilson, *Congressional Dynamics: Structure, Coordination, and Choice in the First American Congress, 1774–1789* (Stanford, Calif., 1994), 70–95. See also Jennings B. Sanders, *The Presidency of the Continental Congress 1774–1789: A Study in American Institutional History*, 2nd ed. (Gloucester, Mass., 1971).

37. Conrad-Alexandre Gérard to Charles Gravier, Comte de Vergennes, Philadelphia, August 7, 1778, *Despatches and Instructions*, 201–2; *Secret Journals*, 2: 93.

38. Conrad-Alexandre Gérard to Charles Gravier, Comte de Vergennes, Philadelphia, August 7, 1778, *Despatches and Instructions*, 201–02.

39. On the audience, see John J. Meng, "Philadelphia Welcomes America's First Foreign Representative," *Records of the American Catholic Historical Society of Philadelphia* 45 (March 1934): 51–67.

40. Compare Congress's proceedings, for example, with those described in Callières, *On the Manner of Negotiating with Princes*, 70–79. See also John Finet, *Finetti Philoxenis: Som Choice Observations of Sr. John Finett Knight, and Master of the Ceremonies to the Two Last Kings, Touching the Reception, and Precedence, the Treatment and Audience, The Punctillios and Contests of Forren Ambassadors in England* (London, 1656); and "Ceremonial de esta embaxada: Añadese al fin lo perteneciente al despacho de correos (1750–1785)," Fernán Núñez Collection, Bancroft Library, University of California, Berkeley.

41. Conrad-Alexandre Gérard to Charles Gravier, Comte de Vergennes, Philadelphia, August 7, 1778, *Despatches and Instructions*, 201–2.

42. Elias Boudinot to Hannah Boudinot, Princeton, August 8, 1778, *Letters*, 10: 405–6.

43. Conrad-Alexandre Gérard to Charles Gravier, Comte de Vergennes, Philadelphia, August 7, 1778, *Despatches and Instructions*, 201–2.

44. *Pennsylvania Packet*, August 11, 1778.

45. David Armitage, "The Declaration of Independence and International Law," *WMQ*, 3rd ser., 59 (2002): 39–64.

46. William Whipple to Josiah Bartlett, Philadelphia, May 21, 1779; John Mathews to Nathanael Greene, Philadelphia, August 23, 1781; James Duane to George Washington, Philadelphia, October 12, 1782; David Howell to Thomas G. Hazard, Princeton, August 26, 1783, *Letters*, 2: 50–53; 17: 554–56; 19: 248–51; 20: 590–97.

47. The Articles of Confederation prohibited the individual states from dispatching embassies and entering into alliances or treaties (Article VI) and instead vested those powers in the United States in Congress assembled (Article IX).

48. Vattel wrote ambiguously about the sovereignty and legal rights of Native Americans. On the one hand, he decried "ambitious Europeans who attacked the American nations, and subjected them to their insatiable avidity of dominion," and he declared the Spanish conquests of the Mexican and Peruvian Empires to be "notorious usurpations." On the other, Vattel asserted that Europeans were legally justified in colonizing the lands of those "erratic nations" who, by nomadically hunting rather than cultivating the earth, occupied more territory than was lawful: "the Indians of North America had no right to appropriate all that vast continent to themselves." Vattel, *The Law of Nations*, 67, 165, 217, 265.

49. For a brief introduction to Euro-Indian diplomatic ceremony in the late colonial and revolutionary periods, particularly in the northern department, see Francis Jennings, ed., *The History and Culture of Iroquois Diplomacy: An Interdisciplinary Guide to the Treaties of the Six Nations and Their League* (Syracuse, N.Y., 1985); Eric Hinderaker, *Elusive Empires: Constructing Colonialism in the Ohio Valley, 1673–1800* (Cambridge, 1997); James H. Merrell, *Into the American Woods: Negotiators on the Pennsylvania Frontier* (New York, 1999); Alan Taylor, *The Divided Ground: Indians, Settlers, and the Northern Borderland of the American Revolution* (New York, 2006); and Timothy J. Shannon, *Iroquois Diplomacy on the Early American Frontier* (New York, 2008).

50. *Journals*, 2: 177–84.

51. See generally Walter H. Mohr, *Federal Indian Relations, 1774–1788* (Philadelphia, 1933); Barbara Graymont, *The Iroquois in the American Revolution* (Syracuse, N.Y., 1972); Gregory Evans Dowd, *A Spirited Resistance: The North American Indian Struggle for Unity, 1745–1815* (Baltimore, 1992); and Colin G. Calloway, *The American Revolution in Indian Country: Crisis and Diversity in Native American Communities* (Cambridge, 1995).

52. Richard White, *The Middle Ground: Indians, Empires, and Republics in the Great Lakes Region, 1650–1815* (Cambridge, 1991).

53. John J. Zimmerman, "Charles Thomson: 'The Sam Adams of Philadelphia,'" *Mississippi Valley Historical Review* 45 (1958): 466; J. Edwin

Hendricks, *Charles Thomson and the Making of a New Nation, 1729–1824*
(Rutherford, N.J., 1979), 15–24; and Boyd Stanley Schlenther, *Charles
Thomson: A Patriot's Pursuit* (Newark, Del., 1990), 32–42. See also Anthony
F. C. Wallace, *King of the Delawares: Teedyuscung, 1700–1763* (1949; reprint,
Syracuse, N.Y., 1990), 155–60.

54. James Wilson to Jasper Yeates, Philadelphia, July 10, 1776, *Letters*, 4: 434.
55. On the centrality of gift-giving to Euro-Indian diplomacy, see White,
The Middle Ground, 36, 179–85. See also Gregory Evans Dowd, "'Insidious
Friends': Gift Giving and the Cherokee-British Alliance in the Seven
Years' War," in *Contact Points: American Frontiers from the Mohawk Valley to
the Mississippi, 1750–1830*, ed. Andrew R. L. Cayton and Fredrika J. Teute
(Chapel Hill, N.C., 1998), 114–50.
56. David Dixon, *Never Come to Peace Again: Pontiac's Uprising and the Fate of
the British Empire in North America* (Norman, Okla., 2005), 76–82. See also
Fred Anderson, *Crucible of War: The Seven Years' War and the Fate of Empire
in British North America, 1754–1766* (New York, 2000), 469–70; William R.
Nester, *"Haughty Conquerors": Amherst and the Great Indian Uprising of 1763*
(Westport, Conn., 2000), 9–14; Gregory Evans Dowd, *War under Heaven:
Pontiac, the Indian Nations, and the British Empire* (Baltimore, 2002), 73–76;
Colin G. Calloway, *The Scratch of a Pen: 1763 and the Transformation of
North America* (New York, 2006), 69.
57. Samuel Ward's List of Measures Adopted by Congress, Philadelphia, July
31, 1775, *Letters*, 1: 686–87.
58. *Journals*, 3: 401; 4: 268; 11: 537. George Morgan to Henry Laurens, York
Town, May 10, 1778, Papers, No. 163, folio 337. It does not appear that Congress presented the medal before Quequedegatha's murder in November of
that year.
59. See Silas Deane to Committee of Secret Correspondence, Paris, November 28, 1776; Silas Deane to John Jay, Paris, December 3, 1776, *RDCUS*, 2:
196–200, 212–16.
60. John Adams to Abigail Adams, Philadelphia, May 10, 1777, *Letters*, 7:
57–59. It does not appear that Congress ever followed through on this
plan to ingratiate itself with Marie Antoinette, but in this failure the
United States' diplomatic relationship with France again resembled the
relationship it sustained with various Native groups. Because the United
States possessed limited manufacturing capabilities and because its trade
was severely hindered by the war, the Continental Congress could not
supply its Native allies with many gifts and was repeatedly obliged to
apologize for that fact. See for example Speech to the Delaware Indians,
Papers, No. 166, folio. 427.
61. Henry Laurens to Rawlins Lowndes, Philadelphia, July 15, 1778; Samuel
Adams to James Warren, Philadelphia, October 11, 1778, *Letters*, 10: 283–87;
11: 47–49.

62. *Journals*, 9: 994–99; Henry Laurens to James Duane, York, December 24, 1777, *Letters*, 8: 469–71. Eagle feathers and rattles, elemental to Creek ceremonial music and dance, served Creek diplomatic purposes as well. In 1765, a delegation of Creeks presented eagle feathers and a rattle box to the governor of East Florida at the Congress of Picolata. Kathryn E. Holland Braund, *Deerskins and Duffels: The Creek Indian Trade with Anglo-America, 1685–1815* (Lincoln, Neb., 1993), 228 n. 71. See also *PHL*, 12: 117 n. 15, and the secondary literature cited there.

63. Henry Laurens to Rawlins Lowndes, Philadelphia, August 7, 1778, *Letters*, 10: 400–04.

64. See Shannon, *Iroquois Diplomacy on the Early American Frontier*, 78–102.

65. Proceedings of a Treaty Held at Easton, January 30–February 6, 1777; Richard Smith's Diary, December 16, 1775, *Letters*, 2: 492–93; 25: 601–11. Benjamin Rush, *The Autobiography of Benjamin Rush*, ed. George W. Corner (Princeton, N.J., 1948), 121–22, quoted in *Letters*, 5: 578 n. 2. See also Executive Committee to John Hancock, Philadelphia, January 17, 1777, *Letters*, 6: 118 n. 3.

66. Giovanni Della Casa, *The Refin'd Courtier; or, A Correction of Several Indecencies Crept into Civil Conversation*, trans. by Nathaniel Waker (London, 1663), 161–62; see also Anna Bryson, *From Courtesy to Civility: Changing Codes of Conduct in Early Modern England* (New York, 1998), 80; and C. Dallett Hemphill, *Bowing to Necessities: A History of Manners in America, 1620–1860* (New York, 1999), tracing the customs of handshaking and bowing in British North America and the United States.

67. Mary A. Druke, "Linking Arms: The Structure of Iroquois Intertribal Diplomacy," *Beyond the Covenant Chain: The Iroquois and Their Neighbors in Indian North America, 1600–1800*, ed. Daniel K. Richter and James H. Merrell (Syracuse, N.Y., 1987), 29–40. The word for "chain" in Iroquoian language translates literally as "arms linked together." Francis Jennings, ed., *The History and Culture of Iroquois Diplomacy: An Interdisciplinary Guide to the Treaties of the Six Nations and Their League* (Syracuse, N.Y., 1985), 116–17, 135–36. See also Robert A. Williams, *Linking Arms Together: American Indian Treaty Visions of Law and Peace, 1600–1800* (New York, 1997), 98–123.

68. James Hart Merrell, *The Indians' New World: Catawbas and Their Neighbors from European Contact through the Era of Removal* (Chapel Hill, N.C., 1989), 147.

69. In addition to the citations above, for examples see John Lawson, *A New Voyage to Carolina: Containing the Exact Description and Natural History of that Country* (London, 1709), 201; William Johnson, *An Account of Conferences Held, and Treaties Made, between Major-General Sir William Johnson, Bart. and the Chief Sachems and Warriours of the . . . Indian nations in North America* (London, 1756), 29, 31; Elijah Middlebrook Haines, *The American Indian* (Chicago, 1888), 524. Michael N. McConnell, *A Country*

Between: The Upper Ohio Valley and Its Peoples, 1724–1774 (Lincoln, Neb., 1992), 75; Wallace, *King of the Delawares,* 109, 143; Susan Kalter, ed., *Benjamin Franklin, Pennsylvania, and the First Nations: The Treaties of 1736–62* (Urbana, Ill., 2006), 228, 301, 335. See also the wampum belt presented by the Delawares to William Penn, fig. 11 in Jane T. Merritt, *At the Crossroads: Indians and Empires on a Mid-Atlantic Frontier, 1700–1763* (Chapel Hill, N.C., 2003), 205.

70. Della Casa, *The Refin'd Courtier,* 161.

71. Hemphill, *Bowing to Necessities,* 27.

72. Linda Frey and Marsha Frey, "The Reign of Charlatans is Over: The French Revolutionary Attack on Diplomatic Practice," *Journal of Modern History* 65 (1993): 706–44, quoting the French diplomat Jean Debry at 729–30. On the United States' wish to comply with European court practice, see Robert Ralph Davis Jr., "Diplomatic Plumage: American Court Dress in the Early National Period," *American Quarterly* 20 (1968): 164–79.

73. Johnstone's slur against Congress and Drayton's rebuttal both appeared in the *Pennsylvania Packet,* September 12, 1778. On Gérard's participation in the crafting of Drayton's response, see William Henry Drayton to the Carlisle Commissioners, Philadelphia, September 4, 1778, *Letters,* 10: 570 n. 1.

74. *(New York) Royal Gazette,* October 3, 1778.

75. *(New York) Royal Gazette,* October 21, 1778. See also "Mary Cay, or Miss in Her Teens," a ballad that mocked France, as represented in the character of "Puff, the Barber," for the way he *"chatter'd, grinn'd,* and *bow'd," (New York) Royal Gazette,* January 22, 1780.

76. *Journals,* 11: 468–69.

77. Henry Laurens to the Chevalier de Mauduit Du Plessis, Philadelphia, May 11, 1778, *Letters,* 9: 640.

78. United States Continental Congress, *The Articles, Published by Congress, of a Treaty of Amity and Commerce, and of a Treaty of Alliance between the Crown of France and these United States* (Lancaster, Pa., 1778), 12.

79. Henry Laurens to Louis Le Begue de Presle Duportail, Philadelphia, May 20, 1778; Elbridge Gerry to James Warren, York, May 26, 1778, *Letters,* 9: 640, 722–23, 750–52.

80. *Connecticut Courant,* July 21, 1778.

81. Conrad-Alexandre Gérard to Charles Gravier, Comte de Vergennes, Philadelphia, July 15, 1778, *Despatches and Instructions,* 147–150.

82. Proceedings of a Treaty Held at Easton, January 30–February 6, 1777, *Letters,* 25: 601–11.

83. *Journals,* 5: 430–31. Jennings, ed., *The History and Culture of Iroquois Diplomacy,* 122. See also Samuel Alexander Harrison, ed., *Memoir of Lieut. Col. Tench Tilghman* (Albany, N.Y., 1876), 92–93.

84. The translations here are from Robert Treat Paine's Diary, December 8, 1775, *Letters*, 2: 461–62.

85. Conrad-Alexandre Gérard to Charles Gravier, Comte de Vergennes, Philadelphia, August 7, 1778, *Despatches and Instructions*, 707–12.

86. On the bestowal of ceremonial names by the Iroquois, see Shannon, *Iroquois Diplomacy on the Early American Frontier*, 86–87. The United States and its agents at times referred to their Native allies by English names, as in the case of the Delaware Gelelemend, who had apparently inherited the English moniker, John Kilbuck, from his father. It is difficult to compare this naming practice with that of Native peoples, but the former seems more assimilative than adoptive or honorific.

87. White, *The Middle Ground*, 306.

88. Various Native American and European peoples understood these masculine familial titles quite differently. On the uses and misuses of such titles in early Euro-Indian diplomacy, see White, *The Middle Ground*, 84–85; Nancy Shoemaker, "An Alliance between Men: Gender Metaphors in Eighteenth-Century American Indian Diplomacy East of the Mississippi," *Ethnohistory* 46 (1999): 239–63, and Shoemaker, *A Strange Likeness: Becoming Red and White in Eighteenth-Century North America* (New York, 2004), 105–24; Richard White, "The Fictions of Patriarchy: Indians and Whites in the Early Republic," in *Native Americans and the Early Republic*, ed. Frederick E. Hoxie, Ronald Hoffman, and Peter J. Albert, (Charlottesville, Va., 1999), 62–84; Jane T. Merritt, "Metaphor, Meaning, and Misunderstanding: Language and Power on the Pennsylvania Frontier," 60–87; Patricia Galloway, "The Chief Who Is Your Father: Choctaw and French Views of the Diplomatic Relation," in *Powhatan's Mantle: Indians in the Colonial Southeast*, ed. Gregory A. Waselkov, Peter H. Wood, and Tom Hatley, revised and expanded edition (Lincoln, Neb., 2006), 345–70; and generally Cynthia J. Van Zandt, *Brothers among Nations: The Pursuit of Intercultural Alliances in Early America, 1580–1660* (New York, 2008).

89. For more background on the Delawares' meeting with Congress, see Max Savelle, *George Morgan: Colony Builder* (New York, 1932), esp. 153–64. See also Milo M. Quaife, ed., *Collections of the State Historical Society of Wisconsin*, Draper Series (Madison, Wis., 1914), 23: 315–60.

90. As reported by Gérard, "Ils m'apelloient leur pere, en m'appliquant selon leur usage le titre qu'ils donnent au Roi, et le Roi d'Espagne leur second pere, ne donnant que le titre de freres aux Etats-Unis et aux présidents." See Conrad-Alexandre Gérard to Charles Gravier, Comte de Vergennes, Philadelphia, June 5, 1779, *Despatches and Instructions*, 707–10.

91. For brotherhood as a diplomatic metaphor, and age-gradations among diplomatic brothers, see Jennings, ed., *The History and Culture of Iroquois Diplomacy*, 119–20; Williams, *Linking Arms Together*, 71; and Shoemaker, "An Alliance between Men," 249–63. For the use of "brother" by Native

Americans in a suggestive albeit more remote diplomatic context, see generally Juliana Barr, *Peace Came in the Form of a Woman: Indians and Spaniards in the Texas Borderlands* (Chapel Hill, N.C., 2007).

92. See Conrad-Alexandre Gérard to Charles Gravier, Comte de Vergennes, Philadelphia, May 30, 1779, June 1, 1779, and June 5, 1779, *Despatches and Instructions*, 694–710.

93. *Journals*, 15: 1250–51.

94. *Journals*, 25: 590.

95. On this point, European diplomacy must again be distinguished from Native American diplomacy, in which the term "father" bore different connotations.

96. Vattel, *The Law of Nations*, 36, 140.

97. *Journals*, 22: 261–62.

98. David Ramsay, *The History of the American Revolution*, 2 vols. (Dublin, 1793), 1: 187.

99. *Journals*, 2: 177–83; 3: 433; 9: 994–99.

100. Samuel Adams to John Adams, Philadelphia, December 20, 1780, *Letters*, 16: 470–71. This exchange, secondhand to Adams, was relayed by the Georgia planter Jonathan Bryan. Native agents also employed metaphors of the body and of ritual cleansing to suggest the intimacy of the diplomatic relationship and to oblige their treating partners to reciprocal acts of kindness: "Brothers," declared a deputation of Six Nation, Delaware, and Shawnee Indians in its appearance before Congress, "[W]e received the commissioners you sent us at the little council fire at Pittsburgh. We wiped the sweat from their bodies. We cleaned the dust from their legs. We pulled the thorns from their feet." Rush, *The Autobiography of Benjamin Rush*, 121–22, quoted in *Letters*, 5: 578 n. 2. On such metaphors in Native diplomacy, see Merritt, "Metaphor, Meaning, and Misunderstanding," 75.

101. *Journals*, 9: 994–99. Congress delivered this address in December 1777, two months after Burgoyne's surrender. As this quotation demonstrates, the United States had formally begun to demand the active involvement of Iroquois peoples in the war against Britain.

102. Treaty with the Delawares 1778, in Charles J. Kappler, comp. and ed., *Indian Affairs: Laws and Treaties*, 5 vols. (Washington, D.C., 1904) 2: 3–5.

103. *Journals*, 9: 994–99.

104. The Treaty of Amity and Commerce was predicated on John Adams's Plan of Treaties, 1776, which in turn drew language from European diplomatic precedent. Compare, for example, an opening line from Adams's Plan of Treaties, "There shall be a firm inviolable and universal peace and a true and sincere friendship between the most serene and mighty Prince Lewis sixteenth the most Christian King his heirs and successors and the United States of America," with the first article of the Treaty of Utrecht,

1713, "That there be an universal perpetual peace, and a true and sincere friendship, between the most Serene and most Potent Princess *Anne,* Queen of *Great Britain,* and the most Serene and most Potent Prince *Lewis* XIV."

105. *Journals,* 11: 432; 15: 1283; 22: 262. On friendship as a foundation for the Franco-American alliance see Rojas, "Diplomatic Letters," esp. chapter 1.

106. *Journals,* 11: 753–57; 15: 1278–84.

107. Sarah Knott, *Sensibility and the American Revolution* (Chapel Hill, N.C., 2009), esp. 1–22, 69–104, 153–95.

108. James Duane to Robert Livingston, Philadelphia, June 7, 1775; John Adams to Horatio Gates, Philadelphia, April 27, 1776; James Monroe to Joseph Brant, New York, February 5, 1786, *Letters,* 1: 453–55; 3: 586–87; 22: 166–68. United States Continental Congress, *Observations on the American Revolution* (Philadelphia, 1779), 49.

109. White, *The Middle Ground,* 384.

110. John Adams to James Warren, Philadelphia, April 16, 1776; Henry Laurens to William Livingston, York, January 27, 1778; Henry Laurens to John Lewis Gervais, September 5, 1777; Samuel Osgood to John Adams, Annapolis, December 7, 1783; *Letters,* 3: 535–37; 7: 606–19; 8: 663–66; 21: 184–96.

111. James Wilson to John Montgomery and Jasper Yeates, Philadelphia, July 20, 1776; Joseph Hewes to Samuel Johnston, Philadelphia, May 26, 1776, *Letters,* 4: 77–78; 503–4. George Washington also reportedly attempted to awe Native American diplomats with demonstrations of military capability. Ordering a review of troops for a delegation of Delaware Indians in 1779, Washington supposedly harangued them: "You see these warriors. They are well armed, well clothed, well disciplined, full of courage and valor. And well these warriors will defend you if you remain peacefully in your hearths, but if you dare to take up the hatchet, they will burn your dwellings and massacre you, your wives and your children." This story was reported by Gérard to the French ministry. Conrad-Alexandre Gérard to Charles Gravier, Comte de Vergennes, Philadelphia, August 30, 1779, *Despatches and Instructions,* 703.

112. Elbridge Gerry to John Adams, Philadelphia, November 23, 1783, *Letters,* 21: 157–62.

113. Josiah Bartlett to Mary Bartlett, Philadelphia, August 24, 1778, *Letters,* 10: 495–97.

114. *Pennsylvania Packet,* September 1, 1778.

115. *Pennsylvania Packet,* February 9, 1779.

116. *Journals,* 14: 736–37; Rhode Island Delegates to William Greene, Philadelphia, May 8, 1779; John Fell's Diary, Philadelphia, May 4, 1779, *Letters,* 12: 425, 441–42; *Secret Journals,* 3: 462–63.

346 NOTES TO PAGES 193–198

117. *Despatches and Instructions*, 120; Conrad-Alexandre Gérard to Charles
Gravier, Comte de Vergennes, Philadelphia, September 8, 1779, *Despatches and Instructions*, 878–83.

118. For La Luzerne's audience, see *New-Jersey Gazette*, November 24, 1779.
On La Luzerne's service as minister, see O'Donnell, *The Chevalier de La Luzerne*; Stinchcombe, *The American Revolution and the French Alliance*, and William C. Stinchcombe, "Americans Celebrate the Birth of the Dauphin," in *Diplomacy and Revolution*, 39–71.

119. Samuel Holten's Diary, [Philadelphia], September 12, 1778, *Letters*, 10: 624.

120. Oliver Ellsworth to Abigail Ellsworth, Philadelphia, January 9, 1779, *Letters*, 11: 438–39.

121. On anti-Catholicism and British nationalism in the seventeenth and eighteenth centuries, see generally Brendan McConville, *The King's Three Faces: The Rise and Fall of Royal America, 1688–1776* (Chapel Hill, N.C., 2006).

122. See *Letters*, 3: 256–57 n. 1. For the Carrolls's mission to Canada, see Ronald Hoffman, *Princes of Ireland, Planters of Maryland: A Carroll Saga, 1500–1782*, collab. Sally D. Mason (Chapel Hill, N.C., 2000), 358–60.

123. Kenneth J. Banks, *Chasing Empire across the Sea: Communications and the State in the French Atlantic, 1713–1763* (Montreal, 2003), 107–8, 120–22. See also Michèle Fogel, *Les cérémonies de l'information dans la France du XVIe au XVIII siècle* (Paris, 1989).

124. Conrad-Alexandre Gérard to Charles Gravier, Comte de Vergennes, Philadelphia, September 8, 1779, *Despatches and Instructions*, 748–53. See also *Pennsylvania Packet*, July 10, 1779.

125. *(New York) Royal Gazette*, October 17, 1778; John Gill's *Continental (Boston) Journal*, November 5, 1778. See also *Exeter Journal*, November 10, 1778, and *New-Hampshire Gazette*, November 10, 1778.

126. *(New York) Royal Gazette*, December 5, 1781.

127. Ketcham, "France and American Politics, 1763–1793," 206.

128. Samuel Adams to James Warren, Philadelphia, October 20, 1778, *Letters*, 11: 80–81.

129. Don Juan de Miralles to Diego José Navarro, Edenton, May 13, 1778, quoted in *Letters*, 10: 82–84, at n. 1.

130. Conrad-Alexandre Gérard to Charles Gravier, Comte de Vergennes, Philadelphia, August 7, 1778, *Despatches and Instructions*, 201–2.

131. John Jay to Conrad-Alexandre Gérard, Philadelphia, May 4, 1779, *Letters*, 12: 426 n. 2.

132. Callières, *On the Manner of Negotiating with Princes*, 118.

133. Gouverneur Morris to Robert R. Livingston, Philadelphia, August 28, 1778, *Letters*, 10: 518–19.

134. Cyrus Griffin to Benjamin Franklin, Philadelphia, September 1779, *Letters*, 13: 605–6.

135. John Durand, trans., *New Materials for the History of the American Revolution* (New York, 1889), 168.

136. Thomas Burke to the North Carolina Assembly, Philadelphia, October 25, 1779; *Letters*, 14: 108–20.

137. H. James Henderson, *Party Politics in the Continental Congress* (New York, 1974), 187–206.

138. O'Donnell, *The Chevalier de La Luzerne*, 54–55; Ketcham, "France and American Politics, 1763–1793," 203–5.

139. Charles Thomson to Robert R. Livingston, Philadelphia, May 10, 1782, *Letters*, 18: 501–3, esp. n. 1.

140. O'Donnell, *The Chevalier de La Luzerne*, 63; Ketcham, "France and American Politics, 1763–1793," 207; Henderson, *Party Politics in the Continental Congress*, 302.

141. Charles Thomson to Robert R. Livingston, Philadelphia, May 10, 1782, *Letters*, 18: 501–3, esp. n. 1.

142. Charles Thomson's Notes of Debate, Philadelphia, August 28, 1782, *Letters*, 19: 104–7.

143. At Lee's urging, Congress appointed a committee to propose alterations and additions to its ceremonials regarding foreign ministers. Several months later, that committee brought a number of recommendations, including a provision that required foreign ministers to pay the first visit to individual members of Congress, but that provision was not adopted by Congress. See Charles Thomson's Notes of Debate, Philadelphia, August 28, 1782, *Letters*, 19: 104–7, esp. n. 5. See also *Journals*, 24: 390–91, and Papers, No. 25, 2, folio 221.

144. John Adams to James Warren, Philadelphia, October 19, 1775, *Letters*, 2: 206–7. Jan Willem Schulte Nordholt, *The Dutch Republic and American Independence*, trans. by Herbert H. Rowen (Chapel Hill, N.C., 1982), 161. See also Mary Briant Foley, "The Triumph of Militia Diplomacy: John Adams in the Netherlands, 1780–82" (Ph.D. diss., Loyola University, 1968), 125–27.

145. John Adams to Vergennes, Paris, April 18, 1781, *RDCUS*, 4: 589–90.

Part IV

1. Richard S. Patterson and Richardson Dougall, *The Eagle and the Shield: A History of the Great Seal of the United States* (Washington, D.C., 1976), 32–70.

2. Benjamin Franklin to Sarah Bache, Passy, January 26, 1784, *The Writings of Benjamin Franklin*, ed. Albert Henry Smyth, 10 vols. (1907; reprint, New York, 1970), 9: 161–68.

3. Patterson and Dougall, *The Eagle and the Shield*, 86–87.

4. *Journals*, 15: 1051–62.

5. On the theme of empire in the Revolution and in the early republic,

see Neil Longley York, *Turning the World Upside Down: The War for American Independence and the Problem of Empire* (Westport, Conn., 2003).

6. Quoted in Patterson and Dougall, *The Eagle and the Shield*, 88.

7. On the infirmities of Congress, see H. James Henderson, *Party Politics in the Continental Congress* (New York, 1974), 130–349; Jack N. Rakove, *The Beginnings of National Politics: An Interpretive History of the Continental Congress* (New York, 1979), 192–329; Eugene R. Sheridan and John M. Murrin, introduction to *Congress at Princeton: Being the Letters of Charles Thomson to Hannah Thomson, June–October, 1783* (Princeton, N.J., 1985); Jerrilyn Greene Marston, *King and Congress: The Transfer of Political Legitimacy, 1774–1776* (Princeton, 1987), esp. 304–9; and generally Calvin Jillson and Rick K. Wilson, *Congressional Dynamics: Structure, Coordination, and Choice in the First American Congress, 1774–1789* (Stanford, Calif., 1994). See also Merrill Jensen, *The Articles of Confederation: An Interpretation of the Social-Constitutional History of the American Revolution, 1774–1781* (Madison, Wis., 1940), and Jensen, *The New Nation: A History of the United States during the Confederation, 1781–1789* (New York, 1950); Edmund Cody Burnett, *The Continental Congress* (New York, 1941); Lynn Montross, *The Reluctant Rebels: The Story of the Continental Congress: 1774–1789* (New York, 1950).

8. For Congress's struggle to provision the army, see generally, E. Wayne Carp, *To Starve the Army at Pleasure: Continental Army Administration and American Political Culture, 1775–1783* (Chapel Hill, N.C., 1984). For Congress's reluctance to fund a pension for continental officers and for the consequent disgruntlement of the officer corps, see Minor Myers Jr., *Liberty without Anarchy: A History of the Society of the Cincinnati* (Charlottesville, Va., 1983), 1–22.

9. On the army's disillusionment with Congress and the American people, see Charles Royster, *A Revolutionary People at War: The Continental Army and American Character, 1775–1783* (Chapel Hill, N.C., 1979), esp. 295–330.

Chapter 7

1. Ezra L'Hommedieu to George Clinton, Philadelphia, September 8, 1781, *Letters*, 18: 23–26.

2. *Pennsylvania Packet*, September 1, 1781; J. Thomas Scharf and Thompson Westcott, *A History of Philadelphia, 1609–1884*, 3 vols. (1884) 1: 414–15 n. 1.

3. *Pennsylvania Packet*, September 8, 1781. Samuel Livermore to Meshech Weare, Philadelphia, September 4, 1781, *Letters*, 18: 7.

4. Ezra L'Hommedieu to George Clinton, Philadelphia, September 8, 1781, *Letters*, 18: 23–26. *Journals*, 21: 932 n. 2. See also *Pennsylvania Packet*, September 8, 1781.

5. On the Continental Army and its relationship with Congress, see generally, Louis Clinton Hatch, *The Administration of the American Revolutionary Army* (New York, 1904); Carl Van Doren, *Mutiny in January* (New York, 1943); Lynn Montross, *Rag, Tag, and Bobtail: The Story of the Continental Army, 1775–1783* (New York, 1952); Allen Bowman, *The Morale of the American Revolutionary Army* (1943; reprint, Port Washington, N.Y., 1964); Jonathan Gregory Rossie, *The Politics of Command in the American Revolution* (Syracuse, N.Y., 1975); John Womack Wright, *Some Notes on the Continental Army* (Vails Gate, N.Y., 1975); Charles Royster, *A Revolutionary People at War: The Continental Army and American Character, 1775–1783* (Chapel Hill, N.C., 1979); Lawrence Delbert Cress, *Citizens in Arms: The Army and the Militia in American Society to the War of 1812* (Chapel Hill, N.C., 1982); James Kirby Martin and Mark Edward Lender, *A Respectable Army: The Military Origins of the Republic, 1763–1789* (Arlington Heights, Ill., 1982); Minor Myers Jr., *Liberty without Anarchy: A History of the Society of the Cincinnati* (Charlottesville, Va., 1983); Robert K. Wright Jr., *The Continental Army* (Washington, D.C., 1983); E. Wayne Carp, *To Starve the Army at Pleasure: Continental Army Administration and American Political Culture, 1775–1783* (Chapel Hill, N.C., 1984); Ronald Hoffman and Peter J. Albert, eds., *Arms and Independence: The Military Character of the American Revolution* (Charlottesville, Va., 1984); James A. Huston, *Logistics of Liberty: American Services of Supply in the Revolutionary War and After* (Newark, Del., 1991); Charles Patrick Neimeyer, *America Goes to War: A Social History of the Continental Army* (New York, 1996); Lucille E. Horgan, *Forged in War: The Continental Congress and the Origin of Military Supply and Acquisition Policy* (Westport, Conn., 2002); Caroline Cox, *A Proper Sense of Honor: Service and Sacrifice in George Washington's Army* (Chapel Hill, N.C., 2004); David Hackett Fischer, *Washington's Crossing* (New York, 2004); Gregory T. Knouff, *The Soldiers' Revolution: Pennsylvanians in Arms and the Forging of Early American Identity* (University Park, Pa., 2004); and Michael A. McDonnell, *The Politics of War: Race, Class, and Conflict in Revolutionary Virginia* (Chapel Hill, N.C., 2007).

6. John Austin Stevens, "Route of the Allies, King's Ferry to Head of Elk," *Magazine of American History* 5 (1880): 1–21, quoted at 14–15. The duke diminished Congress's numbers but not by much. Accounting for an absentee rate of 10–15 percent, at least twenty-three or twenty-four delegates should have been present at this event. For congressional attendance rates, see Calvin Jillson and Rick K. Wilson, *Congressional Dynamics: Structure, Coordination, and Choice in the First American Congress, 1774–1789* (Stanford, Calif., 1994), 158.

7. For more detailed analysis of Congress's administration of military affairs, see Hatch, *The Administration of the American Revolutionary Army*, 18–46, 86–123; Rossie, *The Politics of Command in the American Revolution*, 17–30,

174–202; Royster, *A Revolutionary People at War*, 179–89, 199–204, 302–3, 308–21, 332–51; Carp, *To Starve the Army at Pleasure*, 17–73, 169–217; and Cox, *A Proper Sense of Honor*, 46–49, 94–96, 135–37, 157–58.

8. Schuyler's praise of Livingston may be found in Papers, No. 153, 1, folio 294. *Journals*, 3: 424–25.

9. Henry Beekman Livingston to John Hancock, n.p., n.d., Papers, No. 78, 14, folio 51.

10. On the politics of officer promotions in 1775, see Rossie, *The Politics of Command in the American Revolution*, 1–30, 61–77.

11. John Brewer Brown, *Swords Voted to Officers of the Revolution by the Continental Congress, 1775–1784* (Washington, D.C., 1965).

12. *Journals*, 4: 89–90; 7: 242–43, 258.

13. *Journals*, 7: 258.

14. Nathanael Greene to John Adams, May 2, 1777, in George Washington Greene, *The Life of Nathanael Greene*, 3 vols. (Boston, 1900) 1: 405–6.

15. John Adams to Nathanael Greene, Philadelphia, May 9, 1777, *Letters*, 7: 48–50. For the history of passions and Revolutionary mobilization, see Nicole Eustace, *Passion Is the Gale: Emotion, Power, and the Coming of the American Revolution* (Chapel Hill, N.C., 2008).

16. See, for example, *(Providence) American Journal and General Advertiser*, August 12, 1779.

17. Henry Knox to Samuel Hodgdon, New Windsor, December 4, 1780, Papers, No. 147, 6, folio 25.

18. *Journals*, 19: 8–9.

19. Henry Laurens to Horatio Gates, Philadelphia, June 29, 1779, *Letters*, 13: 122–23.

20. On Congress's practice of awarding brevet promotions, see *Letters*, 13: 297–98 n. 2.

21. See generally Rossie, *The Politics of Command in the American Revolution*. See also Samuel Tenny to Elihue Greene, Valley Forge, June 15, 1778, in the papers of Nathanael Greene, AAS.

22. John Adams to Nathanael Greene, Philadelphia, March 9, 1777, *Letters*, 6: 416–20.

23. *Journals*, 10: 226.

24. *Journals*, 18: 109.

25. *Journals*, 28: 320–21. Congress's order passed unfulfilled. Not until 1908 was a monument built for the *Jersey* dead. See Robert E. Cray Jr., "Commemorating the Prison Ship Dead: Revolutionary Memory and the Politics of Sepulture in the Early Republic, 1776–1808," *WMQ*, 3rd ser., 56 (1999): 565–90.

26. *Journals*, 15: 1101–2.

27. Royster, *A Revolutionary People at War*, 152–368. See also Myers Jr., *Liberty without Anarchy*, 1–22; Sarah Knott, *Sensibility and the American*

Revolution (Chapel Hill, N.C., 2009), 153–93, for the importance of sensibility to continental officer camaraderie.

28. Bowman, *The Morale of the American Revolutionary Army*, 94.

29. For a revision of this old narrative, see Wayne K. Bodle, *The Valley Forge Winter: Civilians and Soldiers in War* (University Park, Pa., 2002). Bodle concludes that the provisions crisis, though real, was not utterly desperate; rather, Washington and his staff shrewdly accentuated the army's distress to spur Congress to action.

30. On the celebration of St. Tammany's Day, see Edwin P. Kilroe, *Saint Tammany and the Origin of the Tammany Society* (New York, 1913).

31. See the entry for May 1, 1778, in George Ewing, *The Military Journal of George Ewing (1754–1824): A Soldier of Valley Forge*, transcribed by Thomas Ewing (Yonkers, N.Y., 1928).

32. This account is drawn from Royster, *A Revolutionary People at War*, 250–54.

33. Col. William Bradford to his sister, Rachel, May 14, 1778, quoted in Paul Leicester Ford, *Washington and the Theatre* (New York, 1899), 26.

34. Randall Fuller, "Theaters of the American Revolution: The Valley Forge *Cato* and the Meschianza in Their Transcultural Contexts," *EAL* 34 (Sept. 1999): 126–46, quoted at 128. See also Jared Brown, *The Theatre in America during the Revolution* (Cambridge, 1995), 58–59; Jason Shaffer, *Performing Patriotism: National Identity in the Colonial and Revolutionary American Theater* (Philadelphia, 2007), and Shaffer, "Making 'An Excellent Die': Death, Mourning, and Patriotism in the Propaganda Plays of the American Revolution," *EAL* 41 (2006): 1–27.

35. For that comparison, see Fuller, "Theaters of the American Revolution."

36. See the entry for April 15, 1778, in George Ewing, *The Military Journal of George Ewing*; Ford, *Washington and the Theatre*, quoting Colonel William Bradford, 26; and Kenneth Silverman, *A Cultural History of the American Revolution: Painting, Music, Literature, and the Theatre in the Colonies and the United States from the Treaty of Paris to the Inauguration of George Washington, 1763–1789* (New York, 1976), 350. See also Mark Evans Bryan, "'Slideing into Monarchical extravagance': *Cato* at Valley Forge and the Testimony of William Bradford Jr.," *WMQ*, 3rd ser., 67 (January 2010): 123–44, particularly for his doubts about the prospective staging of *The Fair Penitent*, *The Padlock*, and *The Recruiting Officer*.

37. Samuel Adams to Samuel P. Savage, Philadelphia, October 17, 1778, *Letters*, 11: 65–66.

38. *Journals*, 12: 1001–2. See also *Pennsylvania Packet*, October 13, 1778.

39. John Durand, trans., *New Materials for the History of the American Revolution* (New York, 1889), 167–68.

40. Samuel Adams to Samuel P. Savage, Philadelphia, October 17, 1778, *Letters*, 11: 65–66.

41. *Pennsylvania Packet*, October 17, 1778.

42. Samuel Adams to Samuel P. Savage, Philadelphia, October 17, 1778, *Letters*, 11: 65–66.

43. *Journals*, 12: 1018–19. See also *Pennsylvania Packet*, October 17, 1778.

44. Fred Anderson Berg, *Encyclopedia of Continental Army Units: Battalions, Regiments, and Independent Corps* (Harrisburg, Pa., 1972), 22–24.

45. Richard Francis Veit, *Digging New Jersey's Past: Historical Archaeology in the Garden State* (New Brunswick, N.J., 2002), 65; George Washington to Brigadier General William Maxwell, February 16, 1779, in *The Writings of George Washington from the Original Manuscript Sources, 1745–1799*, ed. John C. Fitzpatrick, 34 vols. (Washington, D.C., 1931–44); 14: 122–23.

46. The description of guests appears in William S. Baker, "Itinerary of General Washington from June 15, 1775, to December 23, 1783," *PMHB* 15 (1891): 41–87, at 44.

47. *New-Jersey Gazette*, March 3, 1779. Knox is quoted in Baker, "Itinerary of George Washington from June 15, 1775, to December 23, 1783," 44. Knox's celebration became a matter of pride in New Jerseyans' local history of the Revolution. In 1913, the inhabitants of Pluckemin gathered near the site of the artillery encampment to commemorate the Grand Alliance Ball. See "An Anniversary Celebration at Pluckemin," *Somerset County Historical Quarterly* 2 (1913): 155–56.

48. John Jay to Catharine Livingston, Philadelphia, February 29, 1779, *Letters*, 12: 112–13.

49. Bowman, *The Morale of the American Revolutionary Army*, 94; Baker, "Itinerary of General Washington, from June 15, 1775, to December 23, 1783," 63.

50. Cox, *A Proper Sense of Honor*, 21–22.

51. Royster, *A Revolutionary People at War*, 46–47, 86–87.

52. John Adams to Nathanael Greene, Philadelphia, August 4, 1776, *Letters*, 4: 620–21. Congress quickly discovered that the appointments and promotions of continental officers, such as those of which Greene complained, were fraught with political discord. See generally Rossie, *The Politics of Command in the American Revolution*.

53. John Adams to William Tudor, Philadelphia, August 24, 1776, *Letters*, 5: 54–56.

54. Cox, *A Proper Sense of Honor*, 46–47.

55. *Journals*, 14: 978.

56. Papers, No. 41, 7, folio 259. Samuel Huntington to Alexander McDougall, Philadelphia, August 13, 1780, *Letters*, 15: 572–73 n. 1. See also Roger J. Champagne, *Alexander McDougall and the American Revolution in New York* (Schenectady, N.Y., 1975), 157–64.

57. Papers, No. 43, folio 259.

58. Henry Laurens to Richard Henry Lee, Philadelphia, August 1, 1780, *Letters*, 15: 530–33.

59. James Lovell to Samuel Holten, Philadelphia, September 5, 1780, *Letters*, 16: 21–22; *Journals*, 17: 725–27.

60. For the history of the Society of the Cincinnati, see Myers Jr., *Liberty without Anarchy*. See also Markus Hünemörder, *The Society of the Cincinnati: Conspiracy and Distrust in Early America* (New York, 2006); and Sarah J. Purcell, *Sealed with Blood: War, Sacrifice, and Memory in Revolutionary America* (Philadelphia, 2002), 86–91.

61. William Ellery to Francis Dana, Philadelphia, December 4, 1783, *Letters*, 21: 173–81; *Connecticut Journal*, June 5, 1783; David Howell to William Greene, Princeton, September 9, 1783, *Letters*, 20: 646–48, esp. n. 3; *Journals*, 25: 528 n. 3, 26: 7.

62. Myers Jr., *Liberty without Anarchy*, 14–15.

63. Myers Jr., *Liberty without Anarchy*, 24–32.

64. The Institution of the Society of the Cincinnati, printed in the appendix of Myers Jr., *Liberty without Anarchy*, 258–65.

65. Myers Jr., *Liberty without Anarchy*, 48–69; Hünemörder, *The Society of the Cincinnati*, 143–46.

66. Cassius [Aedanus Burke], *Considerations on the Society or Order of Cincinnati . . . Proving that It Creates a Race of Hereditary Patricians, or Nobility* (Hartford, Conn., 1783), 5, 6, 11.

67. James Tilton to George Washington, Annapolis, January 10, 1784; Elias Boudinot to Elias Dayton, Princeton, September 16, 1783; Elias Boudinot to Elias Dayton, Princeton, November 6, 1783; Thomas Rodney to Caesar Rodney, Philadelphia, July 10, 1781, *Letters*, 17: 394–96 n. 3; 20: 675 n. 6; 21: 147–48, 297–98.

68. Elbridge Gerry to John Adams, Philadelphia, November 23, 1783; Samuel Osgood to John Adams, Annapolis, January 14, 1784; Thomas Jefferson to George Washington, Annapolis, April 16, 1784, *Letters*, 21: 157–62, 276–79, 521–24. Benjamin Franklin to Sarah Bache, Passy, January 26, 1784, *The Writings of Benjamin Franklin*, ed. Albert Henry Smyth, 10 vols. (1907; reprint, New York, 1970), 9: 161–68.

69. Elbridge Gerry to Stephen Higginson, Annapolis, March 4, 1784; Samuel Osgood to Stephen Higginson, Annapolis, February 2, 1784; Samuel Osgood to John Adams, Annapolis, January 14, 1784; Elbridge Gerry to Stephen Higginson, Annapolis, May 13, 1784, *Letters*, 21: 276–79, 323–33, 407–12, 609–11.

70. Myers Jr., *Liberty without Anarchy*, 26. See also Forrest MacDonald, *E Pluribus Unum* (Boston, 1965), 33.

71. The Institution of the Society of the Cincinnati, printed in the appendix of Myers Jr., *Liberty without Anarchy*, 258; Elbridge Gerry to Samuel Adams, New York, September 30, 1785, *Letters*, 22: 651–52.

72. Jay is quoted in Elbridge Gerry to Stephen Higginson, Annapolis, May 13, 1784; David Howell to Jabez Bowen, Annapolis, May 31, 1784, *Letters*, 21: 609–11, 651–56.

73. Samuel Osgood to Stephen Higginson, Annapolis, February 2, 1784; Elbridge Gerry to Stephen Higginson, Annapolis, March 4, 1784; Samuel Osgood to John Adams, Annapolis, January 14, 1784, *Letters*, 21: 276–79, 323–33, 407–12.

74. Myers Jr., *Liberty without Anarchy*, 24, 48.

75. Adams shared this story with Thomas Jefferson, who recorded it in his diary. *PTJ*, 14: 11.

76. William Heath, *Heath's Memoirs of the American War* (New York, 1904), 397–99, quoted in Myers Jr., *Liberty without Anarchy*, 19, 27–28.

77. Burke, *Considerations on the Society or Order of Cincinnati*, 17.

78. Benjamin Franklin to Sarah Bache, Passy, January 26, 1784.

79. John Adams, *Defence of the Constitutions of the Government of the United States of America*, 3rd ed., 3 vols. (Philadelphia, 1797) 3: 207–8.

80. William Ellery to Francis Dana, Philadelphia, December 3, 1783, *Letters*, 21: 173–81.

81. *Journals*, 29: 700–01.

82. William Ellery to Francis Dana, Philadelphia, December 3, 1783; Elbridge Gerry to Samuel Adams, Annapolis, May 14, 1784, *Letters*, 21: 173–81, 615–16 n. 2.

83. Myers Jr., *Liberty without Anarchy*, 48–69.

84. Myers Jr., *Liberty without Anarchy*, 63–64.

85. Henry Lee to George Washington, New York, July 3, 1786, *Letters*, 23: 381–83.

86. Myers Jr., *Liberty without Anarchy*, 74–75. Rufus King to Elbridge Gerry, New York, July 4, 1786, *Letters*, 23: 386–87.

Chapter 8

1. Nathaniel Scudder to Richard Henry Lee, Philadelphia, November 16, 1779, *Letters*, 14: 205–7.

2. Some of these new emissions were necessary to replace currency counterfeited by British agents, but most of them represented entirely new financial obligations. See Eric P. Newman, *The Early Paper Money of America*, 4th ed. (Iola, Wis., 1997), 65–69.

3. On Hopkinson's harpsichord, see Thomas Nelson to Thomas Jefferson, Baltimore, January 2, 1777, *Letters*, 6: 24–25. For Hopkinson's life and literary career, see George Everett Hastings, *The Life and Works of Francis Hopkinson* (Chicago, 1926); see also Paul M. Zall, ed., *The Comical Spirit of Seventy-Six: The Humor of Francis Hopkinson* (San Marino, Calif., 1976). Nicole Eustace's biographical treatment of Hopkinson also deserves

careful attention. See Eustace, *Passion Is the Gale: Emotion, Power and the Coming of the American Revolution* (Chapel Hill, 2008), esp. 61–105.

4. Hastings, *The Life and Works of Francis Hopkinson*, 238–57; Francis Hopkinson to Richard Smith, Philadelphia, September 10, 1776, *Letters*, 5: 130–31; Richard S. Patterson and Richardson Dougall, *The Eagle and the Shield: A History of the Great Seal of the United States* (Washington, D.C., 1976), 34–39.

5. Though Hopkinson claimed to have first proposed the stars and stripes, Betsy Ross is often credited or miscredited with having arranged the stars in a circle, thus giving the constellation its best remembered form. Historians have not been able to trace the precise lineage of this constellatory pattern, but Hopkinson's forty-dollar bill featured a circle of stars before that arrangement commonly appeared on revolutionary flags. See Edward W. Richardson, *Standards and Colors of the American Revolution* (Philadelphia, 1982), 22, 268–73. See also Marla R. Miller, *Betsy Ross and the Making of America* (New York, 2010).

6. *Pennsylvania Packet*, February 9, 1779; July 8, 1779.

7. Hopkinson's pyramid has often been interpreted as a Masonic symbol and Hopkinson is believed to have been a Mason, but Patterson and Dougall have found no evidence that Hopkinson intended his pyramid to suggest Masonic themes. The more compelling argument is that Hopkinson, the various contributors to the Great Seal design, and the Masons all drew on a shared iconographic heritage. See Patterson and Dougall, *The Eagle and the Shield*, 530–31.

8. Hastings, *The Life and Works of Francis Hopkinson*, 207–9.

9. Newman, *The Early Paper Money of America*, 65–69, 75.

10. Hopkinson knew the deleterious effects of Congress's excessive money-making all too well. In July 1779, after rapid depreciation so devalued his salary that Hopkinson considered it no longer equal to his "base support," he petitioned Congress for a raise. Francis Hopkinson to Benjamin Franklin, Philadelphia, October 22, 1778, in *PBF*, 27: 605–7; Memorial of Francis Hopkinson, Treasurer of Loans, to the Continental Congress, Philadelphia, July 12, 1779, Papers, No. 41, 4, folio 79.

11. This rough computation is based on mid-1779 depreciation rates. See Newman, *The Early Paper Money of America*, 478.

12. Francis Hopkinson to Benjamin Franklin, Philadelphia, October 22, 1778, *PBF*, 27: 605–7.

13. Francis Hopkinson to the Board of Admiralty, Philadelphia, May 25, 1780, Papers, No. 136, 4, folio 685. Hopkinson's efforts to obtain payment for his "fancy work," are detailed in Hastings, *The Life and Works of Francis Hopkinson*, 240–57. See also *Journals*, 18: 983–85, 1091–92.

14. Were it a commodity he was after, Hopkinson might well have pled for candles, stationery, postage, or firewood, items of which, as treasurer, he was always in short supply. See *Journals*, 13: 441; 14: 550, 862; 16: 154.

15. Hastings, *The Life and Works of Francis Hopkinson*, 240–57. See also, Reports of the Board of Treasury, 1776–81, in Papers, No. 136, 4, folio 671.
16. Hastings, *The Life and Works of Francis Hopkinson*, 240–57. *Journals*, 18: 983–85.
17. Hastings, *The Life and Works of Francis Hopkinson*, 247–49. *Journals*, 18: 983–85.
18. Treasury Inquiry Committee Minutes, October 21, 1780, *Letters*, 16: 226–33.
19. *Pennsylvania Packet*, February 25, 1783.
20. John Adams to Abigail Adams, Philadelphia, August 21, 1776, *Letters*, 5: 39–40. William Nelson and A. Van Doren Honeyman, eds., *Documents Relating to the Colonial History of the State of New Jersey*, 1st ser. (Paterson, N.J., 1917), 29: 337–38; Hastings, *The Life and Works of Francis Hopkinson*, 451–53.
21. Newman, *The Early Paper Money of America*, 478. See also Anne Bezanson, *Prices and Inflation during the American Revolution: Pennsylvania, 1770–1790* (Philadelphia, 1951), 65; and E. James Ferguson, *The Power of the Purse: A History of American Public Finance, 1776–1790* (Chapel Hill, N.C., 1961), 32.
22. *Journals*, 14: 1013–14; 16: 262–67.
23. Anne Rawle to Rebecca Shoemaker, May 18, 1781, HSP, quoted in Judith Van Buskirk, "They Didn't Join the Band: Disaffected Women in Revolutionary Philadelphia," *Pennsylvania History* 62 (1995): 306–29, at 313; Oliver Wolcott to Jonathan Trumbull Sr., Philadelphia, December 18, 1780, *Letters*, 16: 461–64; "The Representation and Remonstrance of Hard Money," *United States Magazine* (January 1779): 28–31.
24. J. Thomas Scharf and Thompson Westcott, *A History of Philadelphia, 1609–1884*, 3 vols. (1884), 1: 417 n. 2.
25. *Journals*, 15: 1316–18, 17: 613.
26. Paul G. Sifton, "Pierre Eugène Du Simitière (1737–1784): Collector in Revolutionary America," (Ph.D. diss., University of Pennsylvania, 1960), 414–17. See also Du Simitière's copy of Pierre Bizot's *Medalische Historie Der Republyk van Holland* (Amsterdam, 1690), LCP.
27. Quoted in Paul G. Sifton, ed., *Historiographer to the United States: The Revolutionary Letterbook of Pierre Eugène Du Simitière* (New York, 1987), 20.
28. Committee on Publishing a Bible to Sundry Philadelphia Printers, Philadelphia, ca. July 7, 1777, *Letters*, 7: 311–12, esp. n. 1; *Journals*, 8: 733–35. See also Thomas C. Pears, "The Story of the Aitken Bible," *Journal of the Presbyterian Historical Society* 18 (June 1939): 225–41; Margaret T. Hills, "The First American Bible, as Published by Robert Aitken," *Bible Society Record* 113 (Jan. 1968): 2–5; William H. Gaines Jr., "The Continental Congress Considers the Publication of a Bible, 1777," *Studies in Bibliography* 3 (1950–51): 274–81.
29. Committee of Congress to George Duffield and William White, Philadelphia, September 1, 1782, *Letters*, 19: 118, esp. n. 1; *Journals*, 23: 572–74. See

also Pears, "The Story of the Aitken Bible," 233; Hills, "The First American
Bible, as Published by Robert Aitken"; Gaines Jr., "The Continental Congress Considers the Publication of a Bible 1777."

30. H. James Henderson, *Party Politics in the Continental Congress* (New
York, 1974), 187–96; Jack N. Rakove, *The Beginnings of National Politics: An
Interpretive History of the Continental Congress* (New York, 1979), 198–205,
270–72; Calvin Jillson and Rick K. Wilson, *Congressional Dynamics:
Structure, Coordination, and Choice in the First American Congress, 1774–1789*
(Stanford, Calif., 1994), 132–63. On Congress's failures during the Valley
Forge and Morristown encampments and resulting popular dismay, see
Charles Royster, *A Revolutionary People at War: The Continental Army and
American Character, 1775–1783* (Chapel Hill, N.C., 1979), 194–204; 308–20;
and E. Wayne Carp, *To Starve the Army at Pleasure: Continental Army
Administration and American Political Culture, 1775–1783* (Chapel Hill, N.C.,
1984), 42–45, 171–76.

31. Scharf and Westcott, *History of Philadelphia*, 1: 392; Lillian B. Miller et al.,
eds., *The Selected Papers of Charles Willson Peale and His Family*, 5 vols. (New
Haven, Conn., 1983–2000), 1: 352–55; *Pennsylvania Packet*, October 3, 1780;
Anna Wharton Morris, contrib., "Journal of Samuel Rowland Fisher, of
Philadelphia, 1779–1781," *PMHB* 41 (1917): 274–333, quoted at 314; Martha
Bland to St. George Tucker, October 8, 1780, Tucker-Coleman Papers,
Swem Library, College of William and Mary. For the parading of Arnold
as a cautionary tale of human depravity, see Michael Meranze, *Laboratories
of Virtue: Punishment, Revolution, and Authority in Philadelphia, 1760–1835*
(Chapel Hill, N.C., 1996), 72–78. For another instance of Peale using his
art to moralize against worldly desire and greed, see David Steinberg,
"Acquisition, Interrupted: Charles Willson Peale's *Stewart Children* and
the Labor of Conscience," *Common-place: The Interactive Journal of Early
American Life* 4 (2004), http://www.common-place.org. See also David C.
Ward, *Charles Willson Peale: Art and Selfhood in the Early Republic* (Berkeley,
Calif., 2004).

32. James Duane to Philip Schuyler, Philadelphia, January 3, 1779, *Letters*, 11:
404–5

33. James Thomas Flexner, *The Traitor and the Spy: Benedict Arnold and John
André* (New York, 1953), 222–25. See also Ray Thompson, *Benedict Arnold in
Philadelphia* (Fort Washington, Pa., 1975).

34. John Jay to Joseph Reed, Philadelphia, January 27, 1779; Committee on
Appeals Decree, December 15, 1778, *Letters*, 11: 341–43 n. 1; 522–23 n. 2;
Scharf and Westcott, *History of Philadelphia*, 1: 389; Flexner, *Traitor and the
Spy*, 238.

35. Supreme Executive Council of Pennsylvania, "In Council, Philadelphia,
February 3rd, 1779" (Philadelphia, 1779).

36. Flexner, *Traitor and the Spy*, 230.

37. Flexner, *Traitor and the Spy*, 228–39; Reed quoted at 233. Margaret Shippen was widely associated with the Meschianza, her name having appeared on the program as Lady of the Blended Rose. But her actual presence at the event was disputed by a family tradition that her father, upon seeing the Turkish dresses designed for the occasion, forbade her attendance. See Scharf and Westcott, *History of Philadelphia*, 1: 379.

38. Supreme Executive Council of Pennsylvania, "In Council, Philadelphia, February 3rd, 1779"; Daniel Roberdeau to Timothy Matlack, February 6, 1779, *Letters*, 12: 26.

39. *Journals*, 12: 1018–20.

40. For a catalog of these grievances, see Henry Laurens's Notes of Debate, March 26, 1779, *Letters*, 12: 249–53, esp. n. 1.

41. Francis Lewis to George Clinton, Philadelphia, March 8, 1779, *Letters*, 12: 163–64. H. James Henderson has demonstrated that Arnold's case divided Congress into camps very similar to those created by the Deane-Lee controversy. Henderson, *Party Politics in the Continental Congress*, 165–66, 188, 234.

42. Eric Foner, *Tom Paine and Revolutionary America* (New York, 1976), 161. Also, see generally Thomas M. Doerflinger, *A Vigorous Spirit of Enterprise: Merchants and Economic Development in Revolutionary Philadelphia* (Chapel Hill, N.C., 1986); and Billy G. Smith, *The "Lower Sort": Philadelphia's Laboring People, 1750–1800* (Ithaca, N.Y., 1990).

43. George Winthrop Geib, "A History of Philadelphia, 1776–1789" (Ph.D. diss., University of Wisconsin, 1969), 96–97.

44. For radical republicans' distrust of men whose fortunes were based on highly fungible liquid assets and credit, see Toby L. Ditz, "Shipwrecked; or, Masculinity Imperiled: Mercantile Representations of Failure and the Gendered Self in Eighteenth-Century Philadelphia," *JAH* 81 (June 1994): 51–80, esp. 57–58.

45. Geib, "A History of Philadelphia, 1776–1789," 97–98, 116; John K. Alexander, "The Fort Wilson Incident of 1779: A Case Study of the Revolutionary Crowd," *WMQ*, 3rd ser., 31 (1974): 589–62, at 596–97.

46. On the continuities between nonimportation campaigns and the price-control movement, see Richard Buel Jr., "The Committee Movement of 1779 and the Formation of Public Authority in Revolutionary America," in *The Transformation of Early American History: Society, Authority, and Ideology*, ed. James A. Henretta, Michael Kammen, and Stanley N. Katz (New York, 1991), 151–69.

47. Quoted in Alexander, "Fort Wilson Incident," 589.

48. Samuel Huntington to Benedict Arnold, Philadelphia, October 6, 1779, *Letters*, 14: 35 n. 1.

49. Steven Rosswurm, *Arms, Country, and Class: The Philadelphia Militia and the "Lower Sort" during the American Revolution, 1775–1783* (New

Brunswick, N.J., 1987), 172–99; Geib, "A History of Philadelphia, 1776–1789," 128, 146–47; Foner, *Tom Paine and Revolutionary America*, 178–80; Robert Levere Brunhouse, *The Counter-Revolution in Pennsylvania, 1776–1790* (Philadelphia, 1942), 89–90.

50. *Proceedings of a General Court Martial, Held at Raritan* (Philadelphia, 1780), 55.

51. *Journals*, 18: 899, 950, 1009–10.

52. Morris, contrib., "Journal of Samuel Rowland Fisher, of Philadelphia, 1779–1781," 311–14. Fisher's descriptions of the two Arnold parades is ironic in its detail because Fisher was imprisoned at the time. Fisher was able to hear the crowd in the streets; presumably, he could either see the parade or it was described to him by visitors. See also the entry for September 30, 1780, in George Nelson, Diary, 1780–1792, HSP.

53. *Pennsylvania Packet*, October 3, 1780; William Churchill Houston to William Livingston, Philadelphia, September 27, 1780, *Letters*, 16: 114–16.

54. Morris, contrib., "Journal of Samuel Rowland Fisher," 314.

55. Benjamin Huntington to Oliver Ellsworth, Philadelphia, October 2, 1780; William Churchill Houston to William Livingston, Philadelphia, October 2, 1780, *Letters*, 16: 128, 129–30.

56. Brunhouse, *The Counter-Revolution in Pennsylvania*, 89–90, 164.

57. Scharf and Westcott, *History of Philadelphia*, 1: 418; see also the entry for March 1, 1781, in George Nelson, Diary, 1780–1792, HSP. *Journals*, 19: 191–92.

58. *Journals*, 21: 1071–72; *New-Hampshire Gazette*, December 15, 1781.

59. See, for example, the description of King George II's display of the eleven French standards captured at Louisbourg in September 1758, as reprinted in the *Gentleman's Magazine* 28 (1758): 447.

60. On the fate of the Saratoga standards and Congress's seeming disappointment at having not received them, see Burnet Landreth, "Notes and Queries," *PMHB* 31 (1907): 495–98; Charles Deane, *Lieutenant-General John Burgoyne and the Convention of Saratoga One Hundred Years Ago* (Worcester, Mass., 1878), 37–39; and Horatio Gates to Henry Laurens, Albany, December 3, 1777, in *PHI.*, 12: 126–28.

61. *Maryland Gazette*, November 15, 1781. See also Jacob Cox Parsons, ed., *Extracts from the Diary of Jacob Hiltzheimer of Philadelphia, 1765–1798* (Philadelphia, 1893), 46.

62. *Journals*, 21: 1079–85, 1108.

63. *Journals*, 21: 1059, 1079–85. Christine R. Swager, *The Valiant Died: The Battle of Eutaw Springs September 8, 1781* (Westminster, Md., 2006).

64. Parsons, ed., *Extracts from the Diary of Jacob Hiltzheimer of Philadelphia, 1765–98*, 46.

65. *Pennsylvania Packet*, November 1, 1781; *Freeman's Journal* (Philadelphia), December 5 and 12, 1781; William S. Baker, "Itinerary of General

Washington from June 15, 1775, to December 23, 1783," *PMHB* 15 (1891): 291–92. See also, Jared Brown, *The Theatre in America during the Revolution* (Cambridge, 1995), 139–140.

66. *Freeman's Journal* (Philadelphia), December 19, 1781.

67. Quoted in Gillian B. Anderson, "The Temple of Minerva and Francis Hopkinson," *Proceedings of the American Philosophical Society*, 120 (June 1976): 166–77, at 171.

68. John Hanson to Thomas Sim Lee, Philadelphia, November 27, 1781; Committee of Congress to George Washington, Philadelphia, December 5, 1781, *Letters*, 18: 214–15, 232.

69. Compare Congress's celebration of Independence Day, as described in the *Newport Mercury*, July 21, 1781, with La Luzerne's commemoration of the king's birthday, in the *Freeman's Journal* (Philadelphia), August 29, 1781. See also Scharf and Thompson Westcott, *History of Philadelphia*, 1: 418.

70. Mary Elizabeth Doherty, "Francis Hopkinson (1737–1791): Creative Aspects of an American Statesman" (master's thesis, University of Washington, 1964), 76; Brown, *The Theatre during the American Revolution*, 139–140.

71. *Journals*, 21: 1074–76; *Pennsylvania Packet*, November 6, 1781. During the January 1781 mutiny of the Pennsylvania Line, British General Sir Henry Clinton dispatched a messenger bearing offers of pardon and back pay to mutineers who defected. Patriot leaders made much of the mutineers' rejection of these offers, much as Witherspoon did in his draft fast-day proclamation. See generally Carl Van Doren, *Mutiny in January* (New York, 1943).

72. *Freeman's Journal* (Philadelphia), December 12, 1781, reprinted from Rivington's *(New York) Royal Gazette*.

73. The Pennsylvania delegate George Clymer wrote a patriotic hymn, said to have been sung in "several churches" that thanksgiving day. See *Letters*, 18: 247–48 n. 1, and in the *New-Jersey Gazette*, December 26, 1781.

74. William C. Stinchcombe, "Americans Celebrate the Birth of the Dauphin," in *Diplomacy and Revolution: The Franco-American Alliance of 1778*, ed. Ronald Hoffman and Peter J. Albert (Charlottesville, Va., 1981), 58–60; James Madison to Edmund Randolph, Philadelphia, May 14, 1782, *Letters*, 18: 509–11.

75. See François de Callières, *On the Manner of Negotiating with Princes*, trans. by A. F. Whyte (Notre Dame, Ind., 1963), 71–72.

76. Charles Thomson's Report on the Audience with La Luzerne, May 13, 1782, *Letters*, 18: 506–8. See also William T. Hutchinson et al., eds., *Papers of James Madison*, 17 vols. (Chicago, 1962–1991) 4: 211–14; and Papers, No. 79, folio 217; No. 79, folio 221; No. 119, folio 104; No 119, folio 120.

77. Theodorick Bland to St. George Tucker, May 13, 1782, *Letters*, 18: 505–6.

78. *New-Jersey Gazette*, May 29, 1782.

79. Stinchcombe, "Americans Celebrate the Birth of the Dauphin," 56–57, esp. n. 40, which offers a list of the newspapers that carried such songs and poems, collected by Gillian B. Anderson.

80. For a description of the arch of Delaware's celebration, see the *Pennsylvania Packet*, July 4, 1782. See also the resolves of the Pennsylvania council, *Freeman's Journal* (Philadelphia), May 22, 1782, and of the New Jersey legislature, *Pennsylvania Packet*, June 25, 1782.

81. *Pennsylvania Packet*, June 11, 1782.

82. Stinchcombe, "Americans Celebrate the Birth of the Dauphin," 43, 66.

83. The fullest account of La Luzerne's party appears in Benjamin Rush, "The French Fête in Philadelphia in Honor of the Dauphin's Birthday, 1792," *PMHB* 21 (1897): 257–62. See also Parsons, ed., *Extracts from the Diary of Jacob Hiltzheimer of Philadelphia, 1765–1798*, 50. The best scholarly treatment of the event may be found in the prologue to David S. Shields, *Civil Tongues and Polite Letters in British America* (Chapel Hill, N.C., 1997), 1–10. For the political and diplomatic context in which this celebration unfolded, see generally Stinchcombe, "Americans Celebrate the Birth of the Dauphin."

84. Stinchcombe, "Americans Celebrate the Birth of the Dauphin," 61–64.

85. See the *Pennsylvania Packet*, July 6, 1782.

86. Joseph Beatty, ed., "Letters of the Four Beatty Brothers of the Continental Army, 1774–1794," *PMHB* 44 (1920): 193–263, quoted at 228–29.

87. The following account draws on Kenneth R. Bowling, "New Light on the Philadelphia Mutiny of 1783: Federal-State Confrontation at the Close of the War for Independence," *PMHB* 101 (1977): 419–50, and Bowling, *The Creation of Washington, D.C.: The Idea and Location of the American Capital* (Fairfax, Va., 1991); as well as Varnum Lansing Collins, *The Continental Congress at Princeton* (Princeton, N.J., 1908). See also James Madison's Notes of Debates, Philadelphia, June 21, 1783; Elias Boudinot to William Livingston, Philadelphia, June 23, 1783, *Letters*, 20: 351–53, 357–59. See also *New-Jersey Gazette*, July 9, 1783.

88. *Pennsylvania Packet*, June 28, 1783; *(Philadelphia) Independent Gazetteer*, June 28, 1783; Bowling, "New Light on the Philadelphia Mutiny of 1783," 420–21.

89. Bowling suggests that centralists in Congress, especially Elias Boudinot and Alexander Hamilton, favored the calling of an emergency session because they hoped to draw attention to the weakness of Congress and thus to rouse public support for a stronger federal government. Bowling, "New Light on the Philadelphia Mutiny of 1783," 432, 440–42.

90. James Madison's Notes of Debates, Philadelphia, June 21, 1783, *Letters*, 20: 351–53.

91. James Madison's Notes of Debates, Philadelphia, June 21, 1783, *Letters*, 20: 351–53.

92. Elias Boudinot to George Washington, Philadelphia, June 21, 1783, *Letters*, 20: 349–50. See also *Journals*, 24: 410.

93. Alexander Hamilton to George Clinton, June 29, 1783, in *The Papers of Alexander Hamilton*, ed. Harold C. Syrett et al., 27 vols. (New York, 1961–87), 3: 408, quoted at 436 of Bowling, "New Light on the Philadelphia Mutiny of 1783." Elias Boudinot's Proclamation, June 24, 1783, *Letters*, 20: 360–61.

94. Bowling, "New Light on the Philadelphia Mutiny of 1783," 430–31; *Pennsylvania Packet*, June 28, 1783; *(Philadelphia) Independent Gazetteer*, June 28, 1783.

95. Eleazer McComb to Nicholas Van Dyke, Princeton, June 27, 1783; Elias Boudinot to William Livingston, Philadelphia, June 23, 1783, *Letters*, 20: 357–59, 371–73.

96. *Freeman's Journal* (Philadelphia), July 16, 1783.

97. Elias Boudinot to William Livingston, Philadelphia, June 23, 1783, *Letters*, 20: 357–59.

98. *Pennsylvania Packet*, July 17, 1783.

99. On Congress at Princeton, see Collins, *The Continental Congress at Princeton*; Gary B. Nash, ". . . and Distinguished Guests": The Continental Congress at Princeton, 1783* (Princeton, N.J., 1962); Eugene R. Sheridan and John M. Murrin, eds., *Congress at Princeton: Being the Letters of Charles Thomson to Hannah Thomson, June–October 1783* (Princeton, N.J., 1985); and Carla Mulford, ed., *Only for the Eye of a Friend: The Poems of Annis Boudinot Stockton* (Charlottesville, Va., 1995), esp. 25–28.

100. Nash, ". . . and Distinguished Guests,"* 13, quoting Benjamin Rush.

101. Nash, ". . . and Distinguished Guests,"* 5, quoting College of New Jersey student Ashbel Green.

102. Charles Thomson to Hannah Thomson, Princeton, July 5, 1783, *Letters*, 25: 748–50.

Conclusion

1. See Daniel E. Meaders, "South Carolina Fugitives as Viewed through Local Colonial Newspapers with Emphasis on Runaway Notices, 1732–1801," *Journal of Negro History* 60 (April 1975): 288–319; Billy G. Smith and Richard Wojtowicz, comps., *Blacks Who Stole Themselves: Advertisements for Runaways in the Pennsylvania Gazette, 1728–1790* (Philadelphia, 1989); Jonathan Prude, "To Look upon the 'Lower Sort': Runaway Ads and the Appearance of Unfree Laborers in America, 1750–1800," *JAH* 78 (June 1991): 124–59; David Waldstreicher, "Reading the Runaways: Self-Fashioning, Print Culture, and Confidence in Slavery in the Eighteenth-Century Mid-Atlantic," *WMQ*, 3rd ser., 56 (April 1999): 243–72; and Gwenda Morgan and Peter Rushton, "Visible Bodies: Power, Subordination and Identity in the Eighteenth-Century Atlantic World," *Journal of Social History* 39 (2005): 39–65. As a slaveowner who had published and would continue to

publish advertisements for runaway bondsmen, Jacob Read knew the genre well. See for example his advertisements in the *South-Carolina Gazette and General Advertiser*, May 24, 1783, and in the *(Philadelphia) Gazette of the United States*, June 25, 1800.

2. Read enclosed this advertisement in a letter to Secretary Charles Thomson. See Jacob Read to Charles Thomson, Annapolis, August 13, 1784, *Letters*, 21: 764–67. During and after the Revolution, a number of taverns and shops—in Portsmouth, New York, Princeton, Trenton, and Baltimore—opened business under the Sign of the Thirteen Stars.

3. *Journals*, 27: 630–35. Jacob Read to Charles Thomson, Annapolis, August 13, 1784; Jacob Read to George Washington, Annapolis, August 13, 1784, *Letters*, 21: 764–67; 768–69.

4. Virginia Delegates to Benjamin Harrison, Princeton, November 1, 1783, *Letters*, 21: 128–29.

5. *(Philadelphia) Independent Gazetteer*, November 1, 1783.

6. Peter S. Onuf, *Statehood and Union: A History of the Northwest Ordinance* (Bloomington, Ind., 1987).

7. Many of these notes were drawn on the credit of Robert Morris. See Eric P. Newman, *The Early Paper Money of America*, 4th ed. (Iola, Wis., 1997), 70–73. Though the Confederation Congress did authorize the establishment of a mint, it never appropriated funds for that purpose. The various coins and tokens that circulated during the 1780s—many bearing Franklin's and Hopkinson's iconography—most commonly originated in state or private manufacture. For more on the currency and coinage of the Revolutionary and Confederation period, see Philip L. Mossman, ed., *Coinage of the Confederation Period* (New York, 1996). See also the websites *Colonial Currency* and *Colonial Coins*, a project of the Robert H. Gore Jr. Numismatic Endowment of the University of Notre Dame, http://www.coins.nd.edu/ColCurrency/ and http://www.coins.nd.edu/ColCoin/.

8. See the *(New York) Independent Journal*, July 6, 1785; *New-York Journal*, July 6, 1786; and *(New York) Independent Journal*, July 7, 1787; *Journals*, 32: 297–303. See also Charles Warren, "Fourth of July Myths," *WMQ*, 3rd ser., 2 (1945): 238–72, at 257 58.

9. *Journals*, 29: 869. Not long thereafter, and perhaps in consequence of Congress's failure, the legislature of Virginia commissioned Houdon to sculpt a statue of Washington.

10. *Journals*, 26: 216–18, 227–34; 33: 687–88. See also Phillips Russell, *John Paul Jones: Man of Action* (1927; reprint, Whitefish, Mont., 2004), 219–22.

11. *Journals*, 28: 320–21.

12. *Journals*, 27: 504–5; 28: 321; 29: 895 n.; Richard Dobbs Spaight to James Iredell, New York, March 10, 1785, *Letters*, 22: 264–66.

13. See Michael P. Gabriel, *Major General Richard Montgomery: The Making of an American Hero* (Madison, N.J., 2002), 188; Charles Royster, *A*

Revolutionary People at War: The Continental Army and American Character, *1775–1783* (Chapel Hill, N.C., 1979), 122–26; Michael Meranze, "Major André's Exhumation," in *Mortal Remains: Death in Early America,* ed. Nancy Isenberg and Andrew Burstein (Philadelphia, 2003), 123–53. I am grateful to the art historian Sally Webster for sharing her expertise on Montgomery and the fate of his monument.

14. John Adams to Nathanael Greene, Philadelphia, May 9, 1777, *Letters,* 7: 48–50. Vladimir Clain-Stefanelli and Elvira Clain-Stefanelli, *Medals Commemorating Battles of the American Revolution* (Washington, D.C., 1973), 36–39; Joseph Florimond Loubat, *The Medallic History of the United States,* *1776–1876* (1848; reprint, New Milford, Conn., 1967); Lester C. Olson, *Benjamin Franklin's Vision of American Community: A Study in Rhetorical Iconology* (Columbia, S.C., 2004), 141–94.

15. *Journals,* 30: 311; John Brewer Brown, *Swords Voted to Officers of the Revolution by the Continental Congress, 1775–1784* (Washington D.C., 1965).

16. Clain-Stefanelli and Clain-Stefanelli, *Medals Commemorating Battles of the American Revolution,* 7, 10, 27, 34. *Journals,* 28: 411–12. Minor Myers Jr., *Liberty without Anarchy: A History of the Society of the Cincinnati* (Charlottesville, Va., 1983), 73.

17. Not until 1790 did Franklin's successor, Thomas Jefferson, then serving as secretary of state, at last deliver a complete set of medals to the president of the United States. Washington is quoted in Clain-Stefanelli and Clain-Stefanelli, *Medals Commemorating Battles of the American Revolution,* 7. Greatly pleased with the earliest completed medals, Jefferson recommended that Congress procure copies for placement in American colleges and universities. He further proposed that silver editions be presented to the "crowned heads" of Europe. Secretary of Foreign Affairs John Jay justifiably presumed that Jefferson meant neither to include King George III nor to exclude the "free states" of Europe. *Journals,* 33: 421–23.

18. On supermajority voting requirements under the Articles of Confederation, see Calvin Jillson and Rick K. Wilson, *Congressional Dynamics: Structure, Coordination, and Choice in the First American Congress, 1774–1789* (Stanford, Calif., 1994), 139–42, 193–94.

19. *Journals,* 25: 818–20, 836–37.

20. *Journals,* 26: 309–10; James Tilton to Gunning Bedford Jr., Annapolis, December 25, 1783, *Letters,* 21: 232–33. *Providence Gazette and Country Journal,* January 17, 1784.

21. *Journals,* 26: 309–10.

22. James Tilton to Gunning Bedford Jr., Annapolis, December 25, 1783, *Letters,* 21: 232–33.

23. *Secret Journals,* 1: 260–61. James Tilton to Gunning Bedford Jr., Annapolis, December 25, 1783; James McHenry to Margaret Caldwell, Annapolis, December 23, 1783, *Letters,* 21: 221–22, 232–33.

24. Sarah Knott, *Sensibility and the American Revolution* (Chapel Hill, N.C., 2009). See also, Andrew Burstein, *Sentimental Democracy: The Evolution of America's Romantic Self Image* (New York, 1999); and Nicole Eustace, *Passion Is the Gale: Emotion, Power, and the Coming of the American Revolution* (Chapel Hill, N.C., 2008).

25. James McHenry to Margaret Caldwell, Annapolis, December 23, 1783, *Letters*, 21: 221–22.

26. *Journals*, 25: 837–39.

27. François Furstenberg, *In the Name of the Father: Washington's Legacy, Slavery, and the Making of a Nation* (New York, 2006), esp. 25–70.

28. Washington Irving, *The Complete Works of Washington Irving in One Volume* (Paris, 1843), 237.

29. John M. Murrin, "A Roof without Walls: The Dilemma of American National Identity," in *Beyond Confederation: Origins of the Constitution and American National Identity*, ed. Richard Beeman, Stephen Botein, and Edward C. Carter II (Chapel Hill, N.C., 1987), 344. For a very brief introduction to the literature of nationalism and national identity in the early United States, see Russel B. Nye, *The Cultural Life of the New Nation, 1776–1830* (New York, 1960); Simon P. Newman, *Parades and the Politics of the Streets: Festive Culture in the Early American Republic* (Philadelphia, 1997); Len Travers, *Celebrating the Fourth: Independence Day and the Rites of Nationalism* (Amherst, Mass., 1997); David Waldstreicher, *In the Midst of Perpetual Fetes: The Making of American Nationalism, 1776–1820* (Chapel Hill, N.C., 1997); Rogan Kersh, *Dreams of a More Perfect Union* (Ithaca, N.Y., 2001); Andrew W. Robertson, "'Look on This Picture . . . And This!' Nationalism, Localism, and Partisan Images of Otherness in the United States, 1787–1820," *AHR* 106 (2001): 1263–80; Kariann Yokota, "Postcolonialism and Material Culture in the Early United States," *WMQ*, 3rd ser., 64 (2007): 263–70, and Yokota, "Post-Colonial America: Transatlantic Networks of Exchange in the Early National Period" (Ph.D. diss., University of California, Los Angeles, 2002).

Index

Act of Settlement of 1701, 5

Adams, John: on the anniversary of independence, 133–37, 145–46, 149, 151–52; on the Articles of Association, 33–34; on the City Tavern in Philadelphia, 49; on the Coercive Acts, 25–28; on Congress's adjournment to Baltimore in 1776, 143; and the continental fast of 1775, 111, 113–14; *Defence of the Constitutions of the United States of America*, 235; as foreign minister to the Netherlands, 200–201; on Francis Hopkinson, 248; on General Washington and celebrations in his honor, 104–5, 106; and the Great Seal of the United States, 1–2; on the legitimization of political authority during the American Revolution, 126; longings for soldierly life, 107–8; on the military, 102, 107, 318n29; on military honors, 213–14, 217, 226–27, 278; Plan of Treaties, 344n104; on refinement and ceremony, 39–43; on Reverend William Smith, 105, 124; on rumors of the bombardment of Boston in 1774, 71; on the Society of the Cincinnati, 233–35; on the Suffolk Resolves, 61; on symbols and rituals, 6–7; *Thoughts on Government*, 37; on women and luxury, 36–37

Adams, Samuel, *26*; on civic virtue, 7, 32, 171–72, 222–23; on the Coercive Acts of 1774, 25–28; on the Continental Army, 100–101; on Creek and Chictaw diplomatic language, 189; and the Deane-Lee affair, 168, 181, 198; and diplomatic ceremony, 171–75, 184, 196–97, 336n20, 337n24; on the funeral of Richard Montgomery, 123; as a Massachusetts delegate, 25, 43, 293n2; on the public character of civil officers, 7, 171; and threats thrown out against the City Tavern, 23–24, 49–50

Addison, Joseph, 221

African Americans, 15, 35–36, 65–66, 131, 141; and racial prejudice toward, 5, 275

Aitken, Robert, 250–51

Alsop, John, 26

American Revolution: end of the war, 18, 229, 240–41, 260–67, 276–77, 281; outbreak of the war, 71–73, 75–78, 97, 117; progress of the war, 121, 142–3, 147–49, 153, 156–60, 168, 207, 213–14. *See also* revolutions

The American Vine (Duché), 113–14

The Americans Roused (Sewall), 58

Amherst, Jeffrey, 180

André, John, 9; arrest of, 218, 258; and the Meschianza, 154–56, *157*

Anglicans, 21, 52–53, 56–57, 69; Church of England, 28, 53

Annapolis, Md., 38, 275, 278–79

Arnold, Benedict: and General Washington, 253–55; as military governor of Philadelphia, 253–55; treason of, 14, 218, 241, 251–59, *252*; war heroics of, 121, 213–14

art: crafting of congressional medals and swords after the war, 277–78; "Credulity, Superstition, and Fanaticism. A Medley," (Hogarth), *57*; displayed in Philadelphia upon General Washington's return from Yorktown, 263; at the Grand Alliance Ball of 1779, 224–25; "The Hen Peck'd Grocer," *62*; paintings by Charles Willson Peale, 193, 263, 266; *Samuel Adams* (Copley), *26*; "A View in America in 1778" (Darly), *210*

Association, the Articles of, 4, 8, 52–53; American identity and solidarity fostered by, 20–21, 23–24, 28–38; Committees of Inspection and Observation, 23, 44–46, 50–51, 60; congressional delegates' compliance and noncompliance with,

37–38, 44–51, 118–19, 299n65, 300n84; eighth article of, 30–35, 38, 47–51; extravagant mourning and, 30, 34, 118–19, 121–23, 296n29; fast days and, 111, 114; Franklin promotes economic imperatives of, 85–86; loyalist opposition to, 55–56, 58, 60, 65, 68–69; public support for, 70

Baltimore, 143
Bartlett, Josiah, 120, 159, 163, 333n120
Barton, William, *203*, 203–4
Beatty, John, 268
behavioral proscriptions, 30
Bibles, 250–51
Biddle, Charles, 139
Bingham, William, 193
Blackstone, Sir William, 102
Blanchard, Jonathan, 274–75
Bland, Martha Dangerfield, 263
Bland, Theodorick, 266
Board of Admiralty, 243, 245–47
Board of Treasury, 243, 245–49
Board of War, 210, 214, 258
Boston, 14, 97, 212; Declaration of Independence prompts destruction in, 141; false rumors of the bombardment of, 1774, 27, 71; General Washington and the liberation of, 99, 105, 108–9, 213; and New England radicals, 55–56; Samuel Adams in, 25; sympathy for blockaded city of, 7–8, 27, 33, 55
Boston Gazette, 34
Boston Post Boy, 56
Boudinot, Elias, 176, 231, 269–71, 337–38n33, 361n89
boycotts: popular support for, 26–28. *See also* Association, the Articles of
brevet commissions, 217–18
Britain: Act of Settlement of 1701, 5; Church of England, 28, 53; Coercive Acts of 1774, 20, 25–28, 81, 110–11; Declaratory Act of 1766, 314n39; English Civil War, 31, 110–11; House of Lords, 172; Magna Carta, 19, 91; and Native Americans, 179–80, 323n85; New England Trade and Fisheries Act of 1775, 111; occupation of Philadelphia in 1777, 17, 135, 151–59, 253–55, 331n97; perception of Americans in, 65–69, 115–16, 156; provisional peace with United States in 1782, 229; relations with American colonies, 5–6, 10–14, 26–28, 52–53, 94, 112–13, 124–27; relations with United States, 130–131, 135–40; social and political authority in, 69; and the supposed "peopling" of North America, 130, 145–46; trade with, 29, 45, 75–76, 118, 179; Treaty of Paris (1783), 279; use of symbols and ritual by monarchs of, 5, 10–11, 138, 141, 318n35. *See also* Parliament
British army, 26–27, 102, 153, 154–56; Cornwallis's surrender, 260–62; deserters of, 147–48, 360n71

Browne, William, 92
Bryan, George, 149–50
Bunker Hill, Battle of, 73, 114, 211
Burgoyne, John, 168, 214, 217–18
Burke, Aedanus, 230, 235–36; *Considerations on the Society or Order of Cincinnati*, 230–32, 236
Burke, Thomas, 144, 147–48

Cadwalader, John, 159–60
Caffiéri, Jean-Jacques, 277
Calvinist Church, German, 122, 126
Camerarius, Joachim: *Symbolorum ac Emblematum Ethico-Politicorum*, 79
Canada, 100, 124, 194, 292n2; assault on Quebec, 72, 118, 120–21, 194–95
Cannon, James, 256, 315–16n58
Carleton, Guy, 124, 141
Carlos III, king of Spain, 196
Carpenters' Hall in Philadelphia, 16, 27
Carroll, Charles, 144, 194
Caswell, Richard, 97–98
Catawbas, 182. *See also* Native Americans
Catholicism, 164, 192–96, 232, 261; and anti-Catholic sentiment, 185
Cato (Addison), 221
celebrations, 6, 8–11, 14, 265, 302n109; of the anniversary of independence, 131, 133–34, 137, 277; of the birth of the dauphin, in 1782, 188, 199–200, 266–68; of the birthday of Louis XVI in 1781, 264; of the British surrender at Yorktown, 260–64; in commemoration of the Battle of Sullivan's Island, 143; in conjunction with General Washington's resignation, 278–80; in the Continental Army, 205, 208–9, 220–21, 224–25; Grand Alliance Ball of 1779, 224–25, 352n47; in honor of the Continental Congress, 39–41, 43–44; in honor of the Franco-American alliance, 192–93, 224–25, 244, 352n47; in honor of Martha Washington in 1775, 23–24, 48–51; hosted by the Society of the Cincinnati, 234, 237; of the inauguration of the Pennsylvania Supreme Executive Council in 1776, 143; the Meschianza, 154–58; on the presentment to Congress of captured British standards, 261–62; of ratification of the Articles of Confederation, 260
ceremonies. *See* celebrations; rituals
Chandler, Reverend Thomas Bradbury, 52–53, 55, 58, 70; *A Friendly Address to All Reasonable Americans*, 70; *What Think Ye of the Congress Now?* 54
Charleston, S.C., 38, 144, 262, 328n56
Charlestown, Mass., 27, 91
Chase, Samuel, 118
Christ Church in Philadelphia, 105, 113–14, 118, 126, 164
The Christian Soldier's Duty, 105–6
Church of England, 28, 53
Cincinnati, Society of the. *See* Society of the Cincinnati

City Tavern, 24, 44, 50, 154, 193, 266; anniversary of independence celebrated at, 146–48, 160; threatened razing of, 14, 48–51

civic virtue, 7, 9, 221–22; and diplomacy, 171–72, 191–92; and the eighth article of the Association, 32–33, 36. *See also* republicanism

class and social rank, 21, 24, 37, 184, 275; and the Articles of Association, 34–35, 46–51; divisiveness of, in Independence Day celebrations, 140, 152, 162–63, 283, 324–25n8; loyalist pamphlets appeal to prejudices of, 54, 55, 65, 67–68; as manifest in funeral processions, 119–20; in the military, 45–46, 218–19, 222–32, 238, 352n52. *See also* poor and laboring ranks; social elites

Clericus (pseud.). *See* Franklin, Benjamin

Clinton, Sir Henry, 253, 360n71

Clymer, George, 360n73

coat of arms, United States, *129*, 129–30, 203

Coercive Acts of 1774, 20, 25–28, 81, 110–11

College of Philadelphia, 106

The Columbian Magazine, 204

Committee of the States, 275

Common Sense (Paine), 121, 124, 136

confederation, 91, 228–29; incomplete, 131, 240, 243–44

Confederation, Articles of, 160, 260, 278, 339n47

Confederation Congress: absenteeism, 274–76; and audience with General Washington after Yorktown, 263–64; diminishing efforts to create symbols and ceremonies, 240, 242, 261–68, 272–73, 276–77, 282; factionalism in, 231–32; and the Great Seal, 203; La Luzerne announces birth of the dauphin to, 265–67; military honors awarded by, 262–63, 276–78; and the mutiny of 1783, 269, 361n89; presentment of British standards to, 261–62; remove from Philadelphia, 268, 270, 272, 275–76; and the Society of the Cincinnati, 231–38; and the Treaty of Paris (1783), 279; weaknesses of, 204, 238, 264–72, 275, 278–79

The Congress Canvassed (Seabury), 58, 66–67

Connecticut, 39, 46, 90, 110

Connecticut Journal, 229

Constitutionalist faction (Pennsylvania), 251, 255–60

constitutions, state, 15, 127, 136; of Pennsylvania, 142–43, 256–57

consumer revolution, 29–30, 36–37

Continental Army: assault on Quebec, 72, 118, 120–21, 194–95; and the Confederation Congress, 207–8, 260, 262–63, 268–71, 278; and the Continental Congress, 9, 71–73, 98–110, 205, 207–29, *210*; crossing of the Delaware River in 1776, 148; disbandment of, 229–30; failure of Continental and Confederation Congresses to provision, 205, 210, 225, 240, 251, 351n29;

fast days and thanksgivings kept in, 114–15, 117; flags of, 90; and the funeral of Richard Montgomery, 120–23; and the Grand Alliance Ball of 1779, 224–25, 352n47; material and ceremonial culture of, 205, 208–9, 220–21, 224–25, 281–83; New York and New Jersey campaigns of, 1776–1777, 142–43; Newburgh conspiracy of 1783 and formation of the Society of the Cincinnati, 229–30; officer corps, 208, 214, 218–19, 222–38, 265–66, 352n52; pay and pensions owed, 209, 227–30, 268–70, 276, 360n71; reaction to the Meschianza in, 156–59; readings of the Declaration of Independence in, 136, 148. *See also* Society of the Cincinnati; Washington, George

Continental Congress: Articles of Confederation, 160, 260, 278, 339n47; and Benedict Arnold, 255, 257–58; Board of Admiralty, 243, 245–47; Board of Treasury, 243, 245–49; Board of War, 210, 214, 258; civil authority of, versus military authority, 8, 100–101, 107–8, 262–63, 268–71, 278; commemorations of deceased civil and military officers, 117–27; and the Continental Army, 9, 101–10, 205, 207–29, *210*; and the Deane-Lee affair, 198–99, 255; Declaration on Taking Arms, 4, 72, 81, 100, 135; delegates as white Englishmen, 5, 13, 54–55, 66, 111; diplomatic protocol of, 166–74, 187; diplomatic relations with Native Americans, 167–68, 178–80, 182–83, 185–91, 340n60, 344nn100–101; exercise of executive authority by, 9, 72, 88, 98–110, 129, 207–29; factionalism in, 54–55, 64–65, 198–99, 222–23, 226; and fast days and thanksgivings, 111–17; First or Grand Continental Congress, *19*, 19–21, 24–28, 52–55, 71, 88; flight to Baltimore in 1776, 142–43, 327nn39–40; flight to York, Pa., in 1777, 153, 158–59; Franco-American alliance influences the celebrations of, 193–96, 199–200, 265; and the Great Seal, 1–3, 132, 133, 203–4, 242; inefficiencies of, 246, 250–51, 255–61; investigation of Francis Hopkinson dispute, 249; issuance of currency, 75–77, 87–88, 98, 129, 205, 241; opposition to, 20–21, 46–47, 52–70, 92–96, 99 (*see also* loyalists and people out of doors, 13–15, 24); presidency of, 8, 174–75; reception of Conrad-Alexandre Gérard, 131–32, 158–59, 169–76, 183–84, 337–38n33; relationship with Pennsylvania government, 253–55, 257–58; Second Continental Congress, 23–24, 38, 70–73, 75–77, 88, 97–99, 103, 106–18, 320–21n63; social authority of its members, 24, 38–44, 49, 54, 61, 65; Treaties of Alliance and of Amity and Commerce (1778), 187, 189, 192, 265, 344n104; Treaty of Paris (1783), 279; use of symbols and rituals diminishes late in the war, 18, 241, 246, 249–50, 260; use of symbols and rituals to invent a national identity, 3–12, 71–74, 106–7, 110–27, 133–34, 281–83, 287–88n7, 288n10; use of

symbols and rituals to justify revolution, 129–52, 163; use of symbols and rituals to legitimize authority, 10–13, 39, 44, 98–99, 108, 118–20; vision of the United States, 177–78, 191–92, 204. *See also* Association, Articles of; Confederation Congress; Declaration of Independence
Continental Navy, 144–46, 148, 260
Conway, Thomas, 159–60
Cooper, Myles, 52–53, 59, 66–70, 308n59; *Patriots of North-America: A Sketch*, 55, 65–70
Copley, John Singleton: *Samuel Adams*, 26
Cornwallis, Lord Charles, 142; surrender of, 261–62
Creeks, 181, 189, 341n62; *See also* Native Americans
continental currency, 75–96, 310n2, 311n11; collapse of, late in the war, 225, 227, 240–42, 249–50; depreciation of, 197, 205, 241, 245, 255–59, 314n43, 330n92, 355n10; design of, in 1775, *71*, 72–73, *75–97, 80, 81, 82, 85, 86, 88, 89, 93*, 204; design of, in 1778 and 1779, 241–45, *243, 244*, 354n2, 355n5; economic instruction on the faces of continental bills, 83–87, 90, 95; political assertions on the faces of continental bills, 83
Cromwell, Oliver, 31
Cushing, Deborah Fletcher, 41
Cushing, Thomas, 28, 40, 41, 104

Dana, Francis, 274–75
Darly, M.: "A View in America in 1778," *210*
Dayton, Elias, 231
Deane, Silas, 27, 41, 42, 106, 131–32, 169, 180–81; Deane-Lee affair, 168, 181, 192, 198–99
Dearborn, Henry, 117
Declaration of Independence, 4, 11, 129–32, 136–41, 177
Declaration on Taking Arms, 4, 72, 81, 100, 135
Declaratory Act of 1766, 314n39
Defence of the Constitutions of the United States of America (Adams), 235
Delaware, 69, 115, 160, 165, 220, 267
Delaware (frigate), 144, 146, 148
Delaware River, 45, 134, 144–46, 154–55, 207, 260
Delawares, 180, 186–87, 189, 344n100; Treaty of Easton (1757), 179, 182. *See also* Gelelemend; Native Americans; Quequedegatha; Teedyuscung
d'Estaing, Charles-Henri, comte, 196
destructive acts, 48–51, 131, 135, 149–51, 256–57; iconoclasm, 10, 140–41, *142*
A Dialogue between the Ghost of General Montgomery . . . and an American Delegate (Paine), 124–25
A Dialogue between a Southern Delegate and His Spouse on His Return from the Grand Continental Congress (pseud. Mary V. V.), 55, 59–64, 306n32, 307n42

Dick, Samuel, 274–75
Dickinson, John, 26–27, 40–41, 72, 102; on independence, 136, 324–24n8; *Letters from a Farmer in Pennsylvania*, 40–41, 72; Olive Branch Petition, 72–73, 123–24
Dickinson, Mary Norris, 41
diplomacy, 339n47; comparative ethnographic analysis of, 178–81, 183–86, 188–92, 340n60, 344n95; between the Continental Congress and Native Americans, 167–68, 178–80, 182–83, 185–91, 340n60, 344nn100–101, 345n111, 339n48; and the Deane-Lee affair, 168, 181, 198–99; and diplomatic ceremonies, 131–32, 166–71, 192–93, 199–200; expense of, 197, 199–200; French embassy to the Continental Congress, 131–32, 158–59, 169–76, 183–84, 337–38n33; French influence on America, 188, 193–95; and international law, 170, 177–78, 187–88, 339n48; New England versus Southern congressmen's expectations of, 167–68; political maneuvering and, 166–68, 198–200, 337n24; satirized by loyalists, 195–96
diplomatic protocol: and alleged delivery of seizin to France in, 169–70; gift exchange, 178, 180–82, 340n60, 341n62; idioms and language of alliance, 178, 188–92, 344nn100–101, 345n111; rituals of salutation, 178, 182, 184–88, 343n86. *See also* gestures, in diplomatic protocol; honorific titles in diplomatic protocol
Dover, Del., 141
Drayton, William Henry, 70, 164, 172, 183, 337n27
Drinker, Elizabeth Sandwith, 156, 162
Droit des Gens (Vattel), 167, 170–71, 173
Du Simitière, Pierre Eugène, 9, *129*, 129–31, 203, 250
Duane, James, 26–27, 177, 253
Duché, Reverend Jacob, 9, 28, 113–14, 118; *The American Vine*, 113–14
duel fought in Philadelphia on the anniversary of independence in 1778, 159–60
Duer, William, 223–24
Dumas, Charles-Guillaume-Frédéric, 170
Dunmore, John Murray, fourth earl of, 111, 121, 141
Duvivier, Benjamin, 109
Dyer, Eliphalet, 103, 104

Easton, Pa., 182
economic development: British American, 83–84, 313n33; and the consumer revolution, 29–30, 36–37; wartime debt and inflation, 225–32, 240–42, 249–51, 255–60, 314n43, 330n92, 355n10. *See also* currency; taxation; trade
economic resistance. *See* Association, Articles of; boycotts
effigies, 14, 333n120; of Benedict Arnold, 251–53, *252*, 258–59; of British commanders, 7; of George III, 140–41

Ellery, William, 161, 229, 235–36
Ellsworth, Oliver, 193–94
emblems, 213; beaver gnawing a tree, 84, *85*, 86, 89, 314n39; buckskinned rifleman, 130; chain, 91–92, *93*, 95, 130; on continental currency, 78–79, 94, 311n11, 312–13n27; crane and eagle, *71*, 72–73, *89*; eye of Providence, 130, *243*; Goddess Liberty, 3–4, 91, 130, 155; hand threshing wheat, 87, *88*, 91, 93, 95; hive of bees, 243; of military valor, 213–14; North wind, 80–82, *81*, 313n30; plough, 243; pyramid, *244*, 244, 355n7; royal insignia, 77–78, 311n10; seal of the First Continental Congress, *19*, 21; of the six countries said to have "peopled" the United States, 130; sundial, 84, *85*, 86, 314n38; thirteen-string harp, 82, *83*, 95; thorny bush, *80*, 80; tree, 138, 244; on the "Washington before Boston" medal, 108–9, *109*; wild boar, 81, *82*, 91; wreath on altar, 87–88, *89*, 90, 94; wreath of olive branches, 181. *See also* symbols
"Essay upon Enthusiasm," 56
Europe: diplomatic traditions of, 170–76, 183–84, 191–94, 200, 265–66, 338n35, 344n95; European and Native American diplomatic relations, 179–80; and the supposed "peopling" of the United States, 130, 145–46; and United States' independence, 131–32, 166–67
Eutaw Springs, S.C., 262
Ewing, George, 220

Fajardo, Diego de Saavedra: *Idea Principis Christiano-Politici Symbolis*, 79
fast days, 7–8, 110–16, *112*, 277, 318n35, 319n37
fireworks, 164, 224, 260, 268, 272–73
Fisher, Samuel Rowland, 258–59, 359n52
Fisher, Sarah Logan, 150, 156
flags, 90–91, 145–46, 281, 328n54, 328n56; presentment of captured British standards to Congress, 261–62; stars and stripes on, 145–46, 242–43, 272
Fleury, François-Louis Teissèdre de, 214
Foote, Samuel: *The Mayor of Garratt*, 60–61, 63
foreign affairs. *See* diplomacy
Forman, Ezekiel, 246
Fort Chambly (Quebec), 120, 261
Fort Liberty (Rhode Island), 137
Fourth of July. *See* Independence Day
France: birth of the dauphin, 188, 199–200, 266–68; French army in the United States, 207–9, 214, 221, 227–28, 233, 267; French diplomatic relations with Britain, 168; French diplomatic relations with Native Americans, 102, 180, 186–87; French diplomatic relations with the United Colonies and United States, 131–32, 165–69, 178–200, 220–21, 241, 264–68, 340n60; French navy, 165, 168–69, 256; French Revolution, compared to American Revolution, 3–4, 11, 171, 183, 200–201; and New France, 180, 194; reputation for vice, 167–68, 195; and the

Society of the Cincinnati, 232, 235, 236; and the supposed "peopling" of the United States, 130, 145–46; Treaties of Alliance and of Amity and Commerce (1778), 187, 189, 192, 265, 344n104. *See also* French embassy
Franklin, Benjamin: and the Articles of Association, 38, 85–86; and Charles-Guillaume-Frédéric Dumas, 170; as Clericus, on the continental currency, 79–89, 312n24, 312–13n27, 315n44; and currency design in 1775, *71*, 72–73, 76–97, 80, *81*, 82, *83*, *85*, 86, 88, 89, *93*, 204, 310n7, 311n10–11, 311n14, 314n37; on engravings of British war atrocities, 78, 312n17; and Francis Hopkinson, 245; and the Great Seal, 2, 129; as minister to France, 187, 193, 197, 198, 278, 337n30; *A Modest Enquiry into the Nature and Necessity of a Paper Currency*, 77; and the monument for Richard Montgomery, 122; and the motto Rebellion to Tyrants Is Obedience to God, 2, 9; Poor Richard's almanac, 2, 7, 83–85, 90, 314n38; Silence Dogood, 2, 79; and the Society of the Cincinnati, 232, 235; on the use of symbols to make impressions upon the mind, 6–8, 76–79, 281–82; *The Way to Wealth*, 314n37
Franks, Rebecca, 154–55, 162
Fredericksburg, Va., 212
French embassy, in the United States: celebration of British surrender at Yorktown, 260, 261, 263–64, 267–68; celebration of Louis XVI's birthday in 1781, 264; festivities yielded to, 18, 240–41, 265; La Luzerne's celebration of the birth of the dauphin in 1782, 188, 199–200, 260, 265–68. *See also* Gérard, Conrad-Alexandre; La Luzerne, Anne César, chevalier de
A Full Vindication of the Measures of the Congress (Hamilton), 70
funerals and commemorations, 117–18, 126–27; mock, 140; for Peyton Randolph, 117–25; for Richard Montgomery, 118, *120*, 120–22; for Samuel Ward, 125–26. *See also* mourning

Gadsden, Christopher, 25–26
Galloway, Grace Growden, 169–70, 254
Galloway, Joseph, 26–27, 28, 154
gaming, ban on, 30–31, 33–35, 154, 222–23
Gates, Horatio, 146, 214, *217*, 231, 261, 278
Gelelemend, 179, 186, 343n86
gender: and the Articles of Association, 21, 24, 34, 37; and the British occupation of Philadelphia in 1777, 156, 159, 162–63; and the Francis Hopkinson controversy, 246; and loyalist satire, 54–56, 63–64. *See also* masculinity; women
George III, 4, 91, 185; colonial attitudes toward, 2, 19, 25–26, 46; effigies of, and iconoclasm, 10, 140–41, *142*; enlistment of German soldiers, 6, 147–48; and Olive Branch Petition, 72–73; treatment of colonists, 4, 6

Georgia, 91, 114, 146, 233

Gérard, Conrad-Alexandre, 158–59, 165–70, 186, 192–99, 222–23, 337n30; audience with Continental Congress in 1778, 169–76, 181, 183–85

German soldiers, 6, 147–48, 329n63; Hessian musicians, 147–48, 329n67–68

Germany, 130, 145–46

Gerry, Elbridge, 185, 187, 192, 231–33, 236–37

gestures, in diplomatic protocol, 196; bowing, 174, 175, 183–84, 208, 266; lowering of swords, 208; *The Refin'd Courtier*, 182–83; removing of hats, 208–9, 266; salutations, 208; shaking hands/linking arms, 182–84, 341n67. *See also* toasts

government: civil authority versus military authority, 262–63, 268–71, 278; and the consent of the governed, 4–5; monarchical versus republican, 172–73, 176, 183; of states, 196, 270, 339n47

Grand Alliance Ball of 1779, 224–25, 352n47

Gray, Harrison, 46, 53, 300n84

Great Seal of the United States, 1–3, 8–9, 129–32, 133, 203, 203–4

Green, Frederick, 91, 92

Green Mountains, 55, 92, 96

Greene, Nathanael, 213, 217, 226, 262–63; commemoration of, 219, 277, 278

Griffin, Cyrus, 197–98

Grotius (pseud.), 59

Hamilton, Alexander, 269–70, 361n89; *A Full Vindication of the Measures of the Congress*, 70

Hancock, Dorothy Quincy, 121, 158

Hancock, John, 67; and the ball in honor of Martha Washington, 48, 50; and the British standards captured at Fort Chambly, 120–21, 261; and the Declaration of Independence, 136; at the funeral of Peyton Randolph, 119; and General Washington, 153, 318n32; as president of the Continental Congress, 23–24, 110, 138, 146, 320–21n63

Hand, Edward, 275

Hanson, John, 263, 266

Harnett, Cornelius, 158

Harrison, Benjamin, 26–27, 50–51

Hawley, Joseph, 136

Head of Elk, Md., 153

Heath, William, 234–35

"The Hen Peck'd Grocer," 62

Hengist and Horsa, 2–3, 10, 129

Henry, Patrick, 20, 25–26, 42, 102, 111, 293n3

Hercules, 2–3, 4, 9, 129

Hewes, Joseph, 117, 191

Hillegas, Michael, 247

"The History of Peru" (Stansbury), 94–96, 315–16n58

Hodgdon, Samuel, 214

Hogarth, William: "Credulity, Superstition, and Fanaticism. A Medley," 57

holidays, national, 160, 164, 192–93, 220, 234. *See also* Independence Day

Holland, 130, 145–46, 200–201

honorific titles in diplomatic protocol, 176, 178, 184–88, 343n86

Hooper, William (Boston minister), 56

Hooper, William (North Carolina congressman), 70, 111, 121

Hopkinson, Francis, 8, 113, 249, 355n10; controversial bid for public recognition, 245–48, 355n14; design of continental currency in 1778, 1779, 240, 242–46, 243, 244, 250; popular motifs created by, 275–76, 281, 355n5, 355n7; "A Prophecy," 244; "Temple of Minerva," 263–64

Hopkinson, Stephen, 118

Horace, 78, 88, 89, 311–12n15

Houdon, Jean-Antoine, 277–78, 363n9

Houston, William Churchill, 259

Howe, William, 7, 9, 167; expected to invade Philadelphia in 1776, 143, 327n43; occupies Philadelphia in 1777, 152–56

Howell, David, 177, 233

Humphreys, Daniel, 150–51

Humphreys, David, 261–62, 278

Huntington, Benjamin, 259

Huntington, N.Y., 141

Huntington, Samuel, 187, 197, 246, 260

Hutchinson, Thomas, 49, 110

iconoclasm, 10, 140–41, 142

Idea Principis Christiano-Politici Symbolis (Fajardo), 79

illumination of windows and streets, 5–11, 137, 149–51, 161, 262, 333n119

imitation of traditions: civic, by Congress and people out of doors, 11–12, 137–38, 290n23; diplomatic, by Congress, 171, 176, 191, 200, 338n35, 344n104

Independence Day, 133–37, 234, 277, 282–83; 1777 anniversary, 134, 142, 144–52; 1778 anniversary, 152, 159–60, 244, 333n119; 1779 and 1780 anniversaries, 163–64, 194, 260; 1783 anniversary, 272–73; anniversary date, 133, 144; socially and politically divisive, 131, 135, 140, 152, 163, 283, 324–25n8

independence, politics of, and reconciliation, 55, 72–73, 112–13, 121–27, 325n20. *See also* Declaration of Independence

Independent Gazetteer, 271

Inglis, Charles, 303n4

Ireland, 130, 145–46

Iroquois Confederacy and peoples, 15, 178–82, 186, 186, 191, 341n67, 344nn100–101. *See also* Native Americans; Onondagas; Senecas

Irving, Washington: "Rip Van Winkle," 280–81

Italy, 170

Jackson, William, 269

Jay, John, 26–27, 145, 225, 233; as president of the Continental Congress, 112, 186, 197, 204

Jefferson, Thomas: and the Articles of Association, 37–38; and the Declaration of Independence, 137, 177; fast day proclamation in Virginia, 111; and the Great Seal, 2, 129; and slavery, 42; on the Society of the Cincinnati, 232–33, 236; *Summary View of the Rights of British America*, 2; on symbols and rituals, 6, 7–8; and "Washington before Boston" medal, 109, 364n17

Jeremiad, 111, 113–14

Jersey (British prison ship), 218, 277, 350n25

Johnstone, George, 183–84

Jones, John Paul, 260

King, Rufus, 237

Knox, Henry, 107, 214, 224–25, 352n47; and the Society of the Cincinnati, 229–30, 233–34

La Luzerne, Anne César, chevalier de, 187, 193; celebrates the birth of the dauphin in 1782, 188, 198–200, 265–68; celebrates the British surrender at Yorktown in 1781, 261, 263

Lafayette, Gilbert du Motier, marquis de, 211, 223

land ordinances of 1785 and 1787, 276

Latin, 79–80, 89, 94

Laurens, Henry, 151, 164, 166, 228, 256; and the Deane-Lee affair, 198; and the French minister's audience before Congress in 1778, 169, 174–76, 181, 184–85

Laurens, John, 262

law, international, 170, 177–78, 187–88, 339n48

law of nations. *See* law, international

Lee, Arthur, 199–200, 347n143; and the Deane-Lee affair, 168, 181, 192, 198–99

Lee, Henry, 218, 237

Lee, Richard Henry, 25–26, 42, 97, 111, 198; and diplomatic ceremony, 174–75, 336n20; and street theater, 163, 333n120

L'Enfant, Pierre Charles, 236, 277

Letters from a Farmer in Pennsylvania (Dickinson), 40–41, 72

Lewis, Francis, 255

Lexington and Concord, Battles of, 21, 112, 160; militant volunteerism inspired by, 17, 45, 71, 97, 101

L'Hommedieu, Ezra, 208

Liberty, Goddess, 3–4, 91, 130, 155

Livingston, Henry B., 210–11

Livingston, Philip: *The Other Side of the Question*, 70

Livingston, Robert R., 186, 199

Livingston, William, 42, 53, 124, 271

Logan, Deborah Norris, 139

London, 72, 92, 172

Louis XVI, 181, 191, 196; and the birth of the dauphin, 188, 199–200, 265–66; birthday celebrations of, 192–93, 264; and the Continental Congress, 167, 168, 178, 181, 187, 191, 208; and the Deane-Lee affair, 198; dispatches Conrad-Alexandre Gérard as minister plenipotentiary to the United States, 131, 165, 169–70; honorific appellations of, 184–87; tribute to at the Grand Alliance Ball of 1779, 225

Lovell, James, 158, 197, 228

Low, Isaac, 26–27, 33

loyalists, 15, 20–21, 210, 303n5; and diplomatic protocol, 169–70, 183–84, 192; driven out of Philadelphia, 153, 253–54; on Independence Day, 135, 140, 144, 149–51; opposition to the Articles of Association, 55–56, 58, 60, 65, 68–69; opposition to congressional thanksgivings, 115; opposition to the Continental Congress, 52–64, 62, 64–70; opposition to continental currency, 92–96, 315n55; and treason of Benedict Arnold, 251; women, 156–59, 161–62

Lynch, Hannah Motte, 41

Lynch, Thomas, 25–27, 41, 42–43, 121

Madison, James, 265

Magna Carta, 19, 91

Marblehead, Mass., 51

Marchant, Henry, 166, 170

Marie Antoinette, 180, 193, 265, 340n60

Marion, Francis, 262

Marshall, Christopher, 23–24, 49–50, 115, 140, 329n63

Martin, Joseph Plumb, 117

Martinique, 193, 194

Maryland, 153; and confederation, 160; and currency design, 91, 93; and General Washington's resignation, 278–79; military preparations in, 97–98, 100

Maryland Gazette, 262

Mary V. V. (pseud.): *A Dialogue between a Southern Delegate and His Spouse on His Return from the Grand Continental Congress*, 55, 59–64, 306n32, 307n42

masculinity: of congressional delegates challenged, 21, 54–65, 69, 303–4n9; in controversy over Francis Hopkinson's art and public service, 245–49; eighth article of the Association and notions of masculine virtue, 36–37, 40; and familial titles in diplomacy, 185–88, 343n88, 344n95; women as arbiters of, 157–59, 163

Masonic symbols, 355n7

Massachusetts, 25–26, 136, 260; fast days and thanksgivings in, 110–12; outbreak of war in, 71–72, 100, 107–8, 318n29; radical delegates of, 26–28, 54, 55, 58, 65, 82

Massachusetts Bay Council, 75

Massachusetts Spy, 91

Mathews, John, 172, 177
Matlack, Timothy, 35–36, 254, 255, 256
Maxwell, William, 224
The Mayor of Garratt (Foote), 60–61, 63
McComb, Eleazer, 271
McDougall, Alexander, 27, 227
McHenry, James, 275, 278, 279–80
McKean, Thomas, 207–9
Mease, James, 150–51
medals, 6–9, 213–14, 215–16, 218, 278, 364n17;
    the badge of the Society of the Cincinnati, 230,
    234–36; for Conrad-Alexandre Gérard, 193; for
    the Delaware alliance chief Quequedegatha,
    180–81, 340n58; for Daniel Morgan, 278; for
    Horatio Gates, *217*, 278; for John Paul Jones,
    277; for Nathanael Greene, 278; "Washington
    before Boston," 108–9, *109*, 278
Meigs, Jonathan, 214
Mercer, Hugh, 211
Meschianza, 154–58, *157*, 254, 358n37
Middleton, Henry, 118
Mifflin, Thomas, 280
military: ceremonies of, 101, 114–15, 148–49, 174,
    191, 261–62; Continental Navy, 144–46, 148, 260;
    honors, 211–18, 226–27, 338n35 (*see also* medals;
    swords; monuments); military versus civil
    authority, 8, 100–101, 107–8, 262–63, 268–71,
    278; militias, 114–15, 218; Pennsylvania military
    associators, 45–46, 101, 105, 191, 269–70;
    promotions in, 226–27, 217–18; volunteerism and,
    71–72, 97–98. *See also* Continental Army; parades
    and military drills; war
Miralles, Juan de, 186, 196
Mitchell, John, 78
*A Modest Enquiry into the Nature and Necessity of a
    Paper Currency* (Franklin), 77
Monmouth, Battle of, 156, 160
Montgomery, Richard, 117–18, 120–26, 211–13, 277,
    321n73
Montreal, 210
monuments, 3–5, 10–12, 70, 208, 218; in
    celebration of Cornwallis's surrender, 262;
    commissioned by the Continental and
    Confederation Congresses, 219; destruction of
    George III's, 140–41, *142*; in honor of General
    Washington, 277, 363n9; in honor of Hugh
    Mercer, 211; in honor of the *Jersey* dead, 277,
    350n25; in honor of Joseph Warren, 211; in
    honor of Nathanael Greene, 277; in honor of
    Richard Montgomery, 121–22, 211–13, 277
Moore, William, 264
Morgan, Daniel, 115, 216, 278
Morris, Gouverneur, 153, 158, 197, 269, 336n20
Morris Jr., Anthony, 315–16n58
Morris, Robert, 91, 207, 256, 269, 363n7; and the
    Deane-Lee affair, 168, 198
Morristown, N.J., 225, 251
Morton, John, 26–27

Moses, 2–3, 129
mottoes, 79, 89; *Deus Regnat Exultet Terra*, 243; *E
    Pluribus Unum*, 130–31; *Et In Secula Seculorum
    Florescebit*, 244; on Franklin's three-dollar
    bill, 73; *Fugio*, 84, 314n38; *Majora Minoribus
    Consonant*, 82; Mercy and Justice, 94; Mind
    Your Business, 84, *85*, 86, 89, 91, 95, 314n38; *Nil
    Desperandum Reipublicae*, 224; *Pax Triumphis
    Potior*, 91; *Perennis*, 244; *Perseverando*, 84–85;
    Poor Richard's, 90; Rebellion to Tyrants Is
    Obedience to God (Franklin), 2, 9; *Si Recte
    Facies*, 87–88; *Sustine Vel Abstine*, 80; *Tribulatio
    Ditat*, 87; Vermont calls for justice, 92; *Vim
    Procellarum Quadrennium Sustinuit*, 244; Virtue,
    Liberty, & Independence, 272
mourning, ban on extravagant, 30, 34, 118–19,
    121–23, 296n29
music: in ceremonies and observances, 122, 176,
    261, 360n73; Hessian musicians, 147–48; *The
    Poor Man's Advice to His Poor Neighbours*, 46–48;
    Te Deum, 194–95; "Temple of
    Minerva" (Hopkinson), 263–64

Native Americans: and Britain, 141, 179–80,
    323n85; Catawbas, 182; Creeks, 181, 189, 341n62;
    Delawares, 180, 186–87, 189, 344n100; and diplo-
    matic relations with Europeans, 179–80, 339n48;
    and France, 102, 180, 186–87, 267; Iroquois
    Confederacy and peoples, 15, 178–82, 186, 188,
    191, 341n67, 344nn100–101; Onondagas, 185–86;
    Pontiac's Rebellion, 180; prejudice against, 5,
    131–32, 141, 188–91, 323n85; satire of congres-
    sional delegates as, 54, 65–67, *67*; Senecas, 182;
    Shawnees, 179, 182, 344n100; Treaty of Easton
    (1757), 179, 182; United States' diplomatic
    relations with, 167–68, 178–80, 182–83, 185–91,
    276, 340n60, 344nn100–101, 345n111
Naval and Marine Committees, 144–46, 328n54
Navarro, Diego José, 196
necropolitics of the Revolutionary Era, 126
New Brunswick, N.J., 139–40
New-England Courant, 79
New England radicals, 54–59, 64–65, 103–5, 110,
    198, 226, 230–31
New England Trade and Fisheries Act of 1775, 111
New France, 180, 194
New Hampshire, 110
New Jersey, 69, 139–40; Anglicans in, 21, 52, 160;
    Grand Alliance Ball of 1779 in, 224–25, 352n47;
    home of the Confederation Congress, 271–72;
    progress of war in, *142*, 148, 156–160
New Jersey, College of, 271–72, 234
New Jersey Gazette, 225
New Light ministers, 56
New York, 26, 91, 218; Anglicans in, 21, 52, 67, 115;
    and the Articles of Association, 38, 69; fast days
    in, 114, 115, 319n37; Independence Day celebrations
    in, 140–41, 277; progress of war in, *142*, 148, 168;

New York (*continued*)
　regional prejudice in, 55, 58; response to Suffolk
　　Resolves in, 28, 37, 59, 61, 300n84; treatment of
　　congressional delegates in, 39–40, 69
New York City, 31, 38, 66, 148, 276–77;
　British occupation of, 254–55; home of the
　Confederation Congress, 276–77
New York Gazette and Weekly Mercury, 92
New-York Gazetteer, 110
New-York Journal, 120
Newburgh conspiracy of 1783, 229–30
newspapers, 16; *Boston Gazette*, 34; *Boston Post
　Boy*, 56; boycott of, 69–70; Clericus's key to the
　continental currency printed in, 72, 80, 88–89;
　congressional accolades of army officers printed
　in, 214; *Connecticut Journal*, 229; continental
　fast days proclamations printed in, 111; and the
　Deane-Lee affair, 198; Declaration of Independ-
　ence printed in, 136; *Independent Gazetteer*, 271;
　Maryland Gazette, 262; *Massachusetts Spy*, 91;
　New-England Courant, 79; *New Jersey Gazette*,
　225; *New York Gazette and Weekly Mercury*, 92;
　New-York Gazetteer, 110; *New-York Journal*,
　120; *Pennsylvania Gazette*, 7, 72, 79–80, 88–89;
　Providence Gazette, 119, 321n68; *Royal Gazette*,
　116, 169, 195; *Virginia Gazette*, 50–51. See also
　Pennsylvania Evening Post; *Pennsylvania Packet*
Noailles, Louis, vicomte de, 262
Norfolk, Va., 121
North Carolina, 51, 61, 196
North, Lord Frederick, 67, 72, 81

Ohio River Valley, 102, 178, 276
Old Light ministers, 56–59
Olive Branch Petition, 72–73, 123–24
Onondagas, 185–86. *See also* Native Americans
"An Oration in Memory of General
　Montgomery" (Smith), 123–24, 323n88
oratory, 42, 63, 122–24, 137–40
Osgood, Samuel, 232–33, 236
The Other Side of the Question (Livingston), 70

Paca, William, 279
pacifists, 76, 131, 144, 151. *See also* Quakers
Paine, Robert Treat, 32, 41, 43, 111, 186
Paine, Thomas, 196, 256, 257; *Common Sense*, 121,
　124, 136; *A Dialogue between the Ghost of General
　Montgomery . . . and an American Delegate*, 124–25
parades and military drills, 7–8, 143; Benedict
　Arnold paraded in effigy, 251, 255, 258–59,
　359n52; and military ceremony, 101, 114–15,
　148–49, 174, 191, 261–62; street theater, 14, 140,
　161–63, 333nn120–21, 334n124
Paris, 122; American commissioners in, 169,
　180–81, 192, 198; peace talks in, 1782, 204, 265;
　Treaty of Paris (1783), 279
Parliament: Coercive Acts of 1774, 20, 25–28, 81,
　110–11; Declaratory Act of 1766, 314n39; New

England Trade and Fisheries Act of 1775, 111;
　and taxation, 5–6, 14, 28, 31, 110
The Patriots of North-America: A Sketch (Cooper),
　55, 65–70
Peale, Charles Willson, 9, 256; paintings of, 193,
　263, 266; and treason of Benedict Arnold,
　251–55, 258
Penn, William, 138, 220
Pennsylvania, 26; boycott of loyalist newspapers
　organized in, 69–70; Charter of Liberties
　(1682), 31, 138; constitution of, 142, 143;
　Constitutionalist Society of, 251, 255–60; cur-
　rency of, 77, 94, 311n10; financial state of, 255–57,
　314n37; military preparations in, 45–46, 100–102,
　105, 107, 191, 269–70; mutiny in, 1783, 268–70;
　regimental standards of, 90; relationship with
　Continental Congress, 43–44, 253–55, 257–58;
　St. Tammany's Day celebrated in, 220; Treaty
　of Easton (1757), 179; University of the State of
　Pennsylvania, 164
Pennsylvania assembly, 44, 77, 120, 122, 143, 255–57
Pennsylvania Evening Post, 2, 93, 101, 105, 315n55;
　independence Day celebrations reported in,
　144–45, 152
Pennsylvania Gazette, 7, 72, 79–80, 88–89
Pennsylvania Magazine, 113
Pennsylvania Packet, 126, 165–66, 208, 223, 269–70;
　French minister's audience before the Conti-
　nental Congress reported in, 176–77, 337–38n33;
　parade of Benedict Arnold in effigy reported
　in, 252–53, 255, 259
Pennsylvania State House, 27, 159, *174*, 262; Dec-
　laration of Independence read on lawn of, 137,
　139; monuments ordered to be placed in, 125,
　212; mutiny at, in 1783, 238, 269
Pennsylvania Supreme Executive Council, 143,
　149–50, 153, 253–59, 269–71
people out of doors, 8–9; and the Articles of As-
　sociation, 37, 44, 48–51; Continental Congress
　creates symbols and ceremonies for, 13–15, 18, 24,
　282–83; Declaration of Independence and, 131–
　32, 133–35, 139, 140–41; defined, 13–15; festivities
　of, at the end of the war, 240–41, 260, 261–62;
　at General Washington's resignation, 279; and
　loyalist writings, 69–70; and political protest,
　13–14, 66, 251–53, 255–57, 267–72; response of
　Continental Congress to, 72; and street theater,
　14, 140, 161–63, 333nn120–21, 334n124. *See also*
　African Americans; Native Americans; poor
　and laboring ranks; Whigs; women
Peters, Richard, 150–51
Philadelphia, *16–17*; Articles of Association
　enforced in, 14, 23–24, 26, 35, 39–41, 44–46,
　48–51l; ball in honor of Martha Washington
　in, 23–24, 48–51; British occupation of, 17, 135,
　151–59, 253–55, 331n97; Carpenters' Hall, 16, 27;
　Christ Church, 105, 113–14, 118, 126, 164; City
　Tavern, 24, 44, 48–51, *50*, 146–48, 154, 160, 193,

266; College of Philadelphia, 106; Confederation Congress in, 261–70, 272; continental fast day kept in, 113–15; delegations of Indians visit, 179–80, 182, 185–86; effigies of Benedict Arnold paraded in, 251–59, 252; evangelical revivals in, 56; financial state of, 240, 249–50, 255–57; First Continental Congress in, 19, 19–21, 24–28, 43–44, 52–55, 71, 88; First Presbyterian Church, 114; Fort Wilson Riot of 1779, 256–57; French minister Anne César de La Luzerne announces birth of dauphin in, 266–68; French minister Conrad Alexandre Gérard received in, 165–70, 181, 183–85, 192–95; funerals of Richard Montgomery, Peyton Randolph, and Samuel Ward in, 117–26, 320–21n63, 321n68; German Calvinist Church, 122–23, 126; Independence Day celebrations in, 134–35, 139–40, 144–52, 159–63; Library Company of Philadelphia, 16, 170; military associators in, 101; mutiny in, 1783, 268–72; parades and military drills in, 98; parading of standards captured at Yorktown in, 261–62; people out of doors in, 8–9, 14–18, 24, 48–51, 161–63, 240–41, 251–59, 261–62, 267–72; sailors' riot for higher pay in, 256; Second Continental Congress in, 23–24, 38, 70–73, 75–77, 88, 97–99, 103, 106–18, 320–21n63; as setting of congressional rituals, 8–9; smallpox in, 125; Southwark Theatre, 154, 263–64; street theater in, 161–63, 240–41, 251–59; theater in, 222–23; United Company of Philadelphia for Promoting American Manufactures, 44; Washington's first appearance as commander in, 102–5; Washington's passage through en route to Yorktown, 207–9; Washington's triumphant return from Yorktown, 263
Pills for the Delegates (pseud. Grotius), 59
Platt, Zephaniah, 39
Pluckemin, N.J., 224–25
political authority: of the Confederation Congress versus the Society of the Cincinnati, 229, 231–38; reinforced by symbols and ceremonies, 208–9, 212–13; and social authority, 12, 24, 38, 40, 43–44, 69, 205
political protest, 13–14, 66, 251–53, 255–59, 267–72; street theater, 14, 140, 333nn120–21, 334n124
politics: and diplomacy, 198–200, 337n24; and economics, 255–57, 314n37; and the military, 229–230, 352n52; and religion, 176, 192–94, 222, 243, 261
Pontiac's Rebellion, 180
poor and laboring ranks, 15, 256–57; and the Articles of Association, 34, 46–49; economic instruction for the, 83–85, 90; and the military, 45–46, 47
The Poor Man's Advice to His Poor Neighbours, 46–48
Poor Richard. *See* Franklin, Benjamin
prejudices, 24; gender, 37; imperial, 21, 65–66; racial and ethnic, in diplomacy, 167–68,

178, 190; regional, 54, 55–56, 126; religious, 54, 56, 195–96. *See also* class; gender; racial prejudice
Pre-Revolutionary political resistance in British North America, 14, 45
Presbyterians, 53, 114
Princeton, Battle of, 143, 147–48, 211
Princeton, N.J., 137; Confederation Congress arrives in, 267, 270–72
Protestantism and Protestant tradition, 30, 36, 89
Providence Gazette, 119, 321n68
public service, fine arts, and masculinity, 246–49
Puritans, 110–11
Putnam, Israel, 142

Quakers, 17–18, 45, 153, 162; and behavioral proscriptions, 33–35; opposition to continental currency, 76, 82, 250; opposition to fast days, 74, 115; refusal to illuminate windows, 149–51, 262
Quebec, 72, 118, 120–21, 194–95, 211
Quequedegatha, 180–82, 340n58
Quesnay de Glouvay, Alexander, 263–64

racial and ethnic prejudice, 34–35; and African Americans, 5, 275; invoked to besmirch congressional delegates and Whigs, 54–55, 65–66, 67; and Muslims, 156; and Native Americans, 5, 131–32, 141, 188–91, 323n85
Ramsey, David, 188
Randolph, Edmund, 261
Randolph, Peyton, death and funeral of, 38, 117–25, 120, 126, 320–21n63, 321n68
Read, Jacob, 274–76, 362–63n1
Reed, Esther DeBerdt, 41
Reed, Joseph, 254
The Refin'd Courtier, 182–83
religion: Anglicans, 21, 52–53, 56–57, 69; and the Articles of Association 8, 32; Catholicism, 164, 185, 192–96, 232, 261; Christianity and republicanism, 7, 28, 53, 105–6, 110–17, 289n16; Church of England, 28, 53; diversity of, in the United Colonies, 126; enthusiasm versus reason, 56–59; evangelical revivals, 56; low-church pietism, 30–31; Old Light versus New Light ministers, 56–59; and politics, 176, 192–94, 222, 243, 261; prejudices of, 54, 56, 195–96; Presbyterians, 53, 114; Protestantism and Protestant tradition, 30, 36, 89; Puritans, 110–11; use of symbols and rituals in, 6. *See also* Quakers
republicanism, 30–32, 55; and the appointment of General Washington, 102–4; and Christianity, 7, 28, 53, 105–6, 110–17, 289n16; and the Continental Army, 221–23; and diplomacy, 131–32, 162, 167, 173, 191, 200
revolutions: French, compared to American, 3–4, 11, 200; national identity created anew in symbols and ceremonies, 3, 5, 12, 129–138, 281. *See also* American Revolution; Continental Army; military; war

Rhode Island, 46, 137
Ridgefield, Battle of (1777), 213–15
"Rip Van Winkle" (Irving), 280–81
rituals: audiences before Congress, 169–76, 181, 183–85, 187, 196, 263–66; commemoration of the dead, 99, 117–27, 219, 277, 278; and destructive acts, 10, 48–51, 131, 135, 140–41, 149–51, 256–57; fast days and thanksgivings, 7–8, 110–17, 220–21, 264–65, 277, 318n35, 319n37; fireworks, 164, 224, 260, 268, 272–73; illumination of windows and streets, 5–11, 137, 149–51, 161, 262, 333n119; of mourning, 30, 34, 117–27, 296n29; and music, 14, 46–48, 147–48, 176, 194–95, 261, 263–64, 360n73; political authority reinforced by, 208–9; power to shape public opinion, 237; public readings of the Declaration of Independence, 136–40, 148; street theater, 14, 133, 140–41, 240, 251–53, 258–59, 333n120; theater and, 31, 221–24, 255, 263–64, 290n19; toasts, 146–47, 160, 185, 193, 196, 244, 279. See also celebrations; diplomatic protocol; parades and military drills
Rivington, James, 67, 69–70, 110, 184, 195; "Intelligence Extraordinary," 184; New-York Gazetteer, 110; and The Poor Man's Advice to His Poor Neighbours, 46–48
Roberdeau, Daniel, 48, 315–16n58
Robespierre, Maximilien, 171
Robins, James, 263
Rochambeau, Jean-Baptiste Donatien de Vimeur, comte de, 207–8, 262–63
Rodney, Caesar, 43–44
Rodney, Thomas, 231
Ross, George, 26–27
Royal Gazette, 116, 169, 195
Rush, Benjamin, 105, 172–73, 256, 267–68
Rutledge, Edward, 26–27, 42
Rutledge, John, 26–27

Sag Harbor, N.Y., raid on, 214
Saratoga, N.Y., Burgoyne's surrender at, 214, 217–18, 261; commemoration of, 115, 160, 278
saturnalia. See street theater
Savannah, Ga., 137, 140
Schuyler, Philip, 120, 210, 261
Schuylkill River, 48, 220, 261
Scotland, 130, 145–46
Scott, John Morin, 39, 53
Scudder, Nathaniel, 239–41
Seabury, Samuel, 52–53, 55–56, 58, 66, 69–70, 115; The Congress Canvassed, 58, 66–67; A View of the Controversy, 58
Senecas, 182. See also Native Americans
Serle Ambrose, 115–16
Sewall, Jonathan, 53; The Americans Roused, 58
Shawnees, 179, 182, 344n100. See also Native Americans

Shippen, Margaret, 254, 358n37
Silence Dogood. See Franklin, Benjamin
Simitière, Pierre Eugène Du. See Du Simitière, Pierre Eugène
Sinceritas (pseud.), 119, 321n68
Six Nations. See Iroquois Confederacy and peoples
slavery, 29, 91, 164, 276; Southerners and, 42, 61, 102, 299n73
smallpox, 125
Smith, Rebecca Moore, 162
Smith, Reverend William, 9, 105–6, 323n85; The Christian Soldier's Duty, 105–6; "An Oration in Memory of General Montgomery," 123–24, 323n88
Smith, Richard, 43, 121
Smith, Thomas, 199–200
social authority: of Congress, 24, 38–44, 49, 54, 61, 65, 275; of officer corps, 226–27; political authority enhanced by, 12, 24, 38–40, 43–44, 69, 205; and refinement, 39–44; of women, 157–59, 161–63
social elites: and aspirations of the continental officer corps, 208, 214, 218–19, 222–38, 265, 352n52; and aspirations of members of Congress, 13, 24, 38–50, 197–201, 228; class resentment toward, 46–61, 132, 149–53, 161–63, 254, 257; high living and aspirations of Benedict Arnold, 254–55; luxurious pastimes and customs relinquished by, 30, 31–32, 34, 35; reaction to reading of Declaration of Independence, 139; women, 152, 154–56, 162–63. See also Society of the Cincinnati
Society of the Cincinnati, 18, 205, 209, 229–38, 277–78; and the Confederation Congress, 229–30, 231–38; constitution, or Institution, of, 230–31, 234, 236; Newburgh conspiracy, 229–30; symbols and ceremonies of, 229–30, 233, 237, 277–78
Sons of Liberty, 25, 37, 115, 141
South Carolina, 25–27, 46, 91
southerners, 54–55, 59–64, 62, 226, 307n42
Southwark Theatre, 154, 263–64
Spain, 186, 196
Sparrow, Thomas, 91, 92
St. Clair, Arthur, 269, 277
St. Tammany's Day, 220
Stamp Act of 1775, 28, 49, 52–53, 140, 141, 333n120
Stansbury, Joseph, 93–96; "The History of Peru," 94–96, 315–16n58
Steuben, Baron Friedrich Wilhelm von, 211, 220–21, 237
Stewart, John, 214
Stillman, Reverend Samuel, 125
Stockton, Annis Boudinot, 272–73
Stony Point, storming of, 214
street theater, 14, 140, 161–63, 333nn120–21, 334n124
Suffolk Resolves, 28, 37, 59, 61, 300n84
Sullivan's Island, Battle of, 143, 147, 160

swords, 205, 211, *212*, 214–16, 277, 278
symbols, 6; aloe tree in Philadelphia, 165–66; constellation, 145, *243*, 243–44, 275–76, 281, 355n5, 363n2; eagle, 203–5, 235–36, *237*, 278, 283; and the Great Seal of the United States, 1–3, 8–9, 129–32, 133, *203*, 203–4; Hengist and Horsa, 2–3, 10, 129; Hercules, 2–3, 4, 9, 129; and impressions upon the mind, 78–79, 89–90, 96, 311n14; liberty cap, 25, 281; Moses, 2–3, 129; stars and stripes, 145, 203, 242–44, 283, 355n5; throne, 172, 175, 237. *See also* coat of arms; emblems; thirteen, number

taxes: Congress's lack of power to levy, 75–76, 209, 218; levied without representation, 5–6, 14, 28, 31, 110, 296n32
Tea Act, 17, 81
Teedyuscung, 179
"Temple of Minerva" (Hopkinson), 263–64
thanksgivings, 7–8, 73, 110–11, 113, 115–17, 264–65, 277, 318n35; congressional, 116; at Valley Forge, 220–21
theater and theatrical performances: *The Americans Roused* (Sewall), 58; *Cato* (Addison), 221; in honor of General Washington, 263–64; *The Mayor of Garratt* (Foote), 60–61, 63; and the military, 221–24, 226, 290n19; street theater, 14, 140–41, 161–63, 333nn120–21, 334n124; suppression of, 31, 38, 154, 221–24, 255, 264
thirteen, number, 165–66; in celebrations, 137–38, 146–47, 149, 184, 193, 224; in emblems, 145–46, 203, 244
Thomson, Charles, 8, 27, 139, 179, 272; and birth of the French dauphin, 199–200, 266; and design of the Great Seal of the United States, *203*, 203–4
Thoughts on Government (Adams), 37
Ticonderoga, N.Y., 138
Tilghman, Tench, 261–62
Tilton, James, 231, 279–80
toasts, 146–47, 196, 279; to the Franco-American alliance, 193, 244; on Independence Day, 1778, 160, 185
Tories, 132, 149–53, 161–63, 254, 257. *See also,* loyalists; pacifists; Quakers
Townshend Revenue Act, 17, 28, 45, 140
trade: boycotts, 26–27, 45; consumer revolution, 29–30, 36–37; intercolonial markets, 83–84; New England Trade and Fisheries Act of 1775, 111; transatlantic, 29, 45, 75–76, 118–19, 168, 179. *See also* Association, the Articles of
Treaties of Alliance and of Amity and Commerce (1778), 187, 189, 192, 265, 344n104
Treaty of Easton (1757), 179, 182
Treaty of Paris (1783), 279
Trenton, Battle of, 143, 147–48, 160
Trenton, N.J., 271, 276
The Triumph of the Whigs, 66

Tudor, William, 107–8

United Company of Philadelphia for Promoting American Manufactures, 44
United States: appellation, 138; the Continental Congress's vision of, 177–78, 191–92, 204; diplomatic relations with Britain, 130–131, 135–40; diplomatic relations with France, 131–32, 165–69, 178–200, 220–21, 241, 264–68, 340n60; diplomatic relations with Native Americans, 167–68, 178–80, 182–83, 185–91, 276, 340n60, 344nn100–101, 345n111; national identity invented through symbols and ceremonies, 3–5, 9–10, 12–13, 129–138, 192, 281
University of the State of Pennsylvania, 164

Valley Forge, Pa., 117; encampment of 1777–1778, 220–22, 251, 253
Vattel, Emmerich de, 188, 339n48; *Droit des Gens*, 167, 170–71, 173
Vermont, 91–92
"A View in America in 1778" (Darly), *210*
A View of the Controversy (Seabury), 58
violence. *See* destructive acts
Virginia: the Articles of Association in, 34–35, 37–38, 50–51, 223, 302n109; bombardment of Norfolk, 121; claims to Indiana and Illinois countries, 198; and Congress, 69, 293n3; and the Declaration of Independence, 136; fast day in, 7–8, 111, 319n37; General Washington and 102–4, 363n9; House of Burgesses, 7–8, 111; military preparations in, 97–98, 100, 102; radical delegates from, 25–27, 54, 61, 65, 82, 231–32
Virginia Almanack, 61
Virginia Gazette, 50–51

Walton, George, 260
war: Board of War, 120, 214, 258; considered good for country, 77, 87, 90, 93; expenses of, 75–77, 86, 205. *See also* Continental Army; military; American Revolution
Ward, Samuel, 115, 121–22, 180; death of, 118, 125–26
Warren, James, 107
Warren, Joseph, 211–13
"Washington before Boston" medal, 108–9, *109*, 278
Washington, George: appointed commander of the Continental Army, 97–100, 102–9; and Benedict Arnold, 253–55; celebrations attended by, 220–21, 224–26, 267; and the continental fast, 114; duel fought in vindication of, 159–60; honored at the end of the war, 213, 262–64, 267, 277, 278, 363n9; and the liberation of Boston, 99, 105, 108–9, 213; and Native Americans, 345n111; as president, 281; and the reading of the Declaration of Independence, 136; resignation ceremony of, 278–80; and Revolutionary War, 142–43,

Washington, George (*continued*)
147–49, 153, 207, 318n29, 351n29; and the
Society of the Cincinnati, 230, 236–37; as
symbol, 8, 108–9, *109*, 138, 280, 281, 318n32;
and theater, 264, 290n19; on the use of
ceremony, 8
Washington, Martha, 24, 48, 50, 103–5
Wayne, Anthony, 46, 156–58, 214
West Point, N.Y., 251, 259, 267
Wharton, Joseph, estate of, 155–56
Wharton, Thomas Jr., 147, 150
Whigs: and the Articles of Association,
28, 32, 34, 36–37, 44; boycott of loyalist
newspapers, 69; and the British occupation
of Philadelphia, 158, 162–63, 253–54; celebrate
Independence Day, 147, 150–52, 161–63; commemorate battles in Philadelphia, 143, 147; and
the controversy over an American bishopric,
53; and the Declaration of Independence,
139; and masculinity, 36–37; racial diversity
of disparaged, 66; on the supremacy of civil
authority over the military, 100–101, 107;
The Triumph of the Whigs, 66; writings in
support of Congress, 68–70
Whipple, William, 177

Whitefield, George, 56–58
Wilkins, Isaac, 53, 59
Wilkinson, James, 217–18
Willett, Marinus, 211, *212*
William III, king of England, 31
Williams, William, 152
Wilson, James, 70, 191, 256
Winchester, Va., 153
Witherspoon, John, 264–65, 360n71
Wolcott, Oliver, 250
women: Benjamin Franklin on, 86, 314n42;
during the British occupation of
Philadelphia, 135, 152, 154–59, 331n99, 334n129;
elite and Tory, 41, 152, 154–59, 161–63; and
employment, 44; and the feminization of
luxury, 36–37, 54; at funeral services, 123, 321n68;
loyalist, 156–59, 161–62; at Meschianza, 161–63;
and notions of womanly work, 247; as people
out of doors, 8, 15; portrayed as henpecking
wives, 59–64, *62*, 307n50; and sexual assault, 156

York, Pa., 153, 158–60
Yorktown, Va., 207; Congress and Philadelphians
celebrate British surrender at, 240–41, 260–65;
Cornwallis's surrender at, 116, 260, 261, 264